THE WINNING WEAPON

THE WINNING WEAPON

THE ATOMIC BOMB IN THE COLD WAR
1945-1950

GREGG HERKEN

Vintage Books
A Division of Random House
New York

First Vintage Books Edition, February 1982

Library of Congress Cataloging in Publication Data
Herken, Gregg, 1947–
The winning weapon.
Bibliography: p.
Includes index.
1. World politics—1945–1955. 2. Atomic bomb.
3. World War, 1939–1945—Diplomatic history.
4. United States—Foreign relations—1933–1945.
5. United States—Foreign relations—1945–1953.
I. Title.
D843.H438   1982   327'.09044   81-52265
ISBN 0-394-75160-4   AACR2

For Caspar, Bernard, Marguerite, and Dottie

Before a country is ready to relinquish any winning weapons, it must have more than words to reassure it.

—*Bernard M. Baruch, June 1946*

I like Mr. Baruch's idea of calling the bomb our "winning weapon"—a weapon which we give up only when we are sure the world will remain safe. . . . If we cannot be sure, we must arm to the teeth with the winning weapon.

—*Major General Thomas Farrell, August 1946*

CONTENTS

Contents

ACKNOWLEDGMENTS

I have become grateful to many people during the nearly seven years it has taken to write this book. Support for research or writing has come from Princeton University, the Harry S Truman Library Institute, and the Griswold Fellowship at Yale. The faculty and staff of Merrill College at my undergraduate alma mater, the University of California at Santa Cruz, were always generous in giving me a place to write during my frequent visits. I feel a special gratitude to Bunny O'Meara, John Marcum, and David Sweet at Merrill, as well as to Lil Ozuna and Pam Fusari of the Board of Studies in History at Santa Cruz. I owe an intellectual debt to two teachers, friends, and subsequent colleagues there: George Baer and Bruce Larkin. Jim Price has been a long-term friend and mentor.

My thanks also to the members of the Historiska Institutionen at Lund University, Sweden—particularly its director, Göran Rystad, and a colleague, Joseph Zitomersky—for the opportunity to complete the manuscript while a visitor in 1978. For ensuring that my stay in Sweden was as enjoyable as it was productive, I am grateful to Karin Linton and her staff at the Fulbright Commission in Sweden.

I am equally appreciative toward those who read the manuscript in its various stages. These include my dissertation adviser at Princeton, Richard Challener, and Barton Bernstein and Gaddis Smith. Edward Reese at the National Archives was of great help in bringing documents to my attention. Jim Gormly, David Rosenberg, and Robert Messer were most helpful in providing additional research material or drafts of their own work. Professor Martin Sherwin was a friend and counselor concerning both the manuscript and the rites of publishing, as was my editor, Ashbel Green. Mary Whitney and Betty Paine of the Yale History Department showed infinite patience in typing the manuscript. For the book's flaws, needless to say, none of those I have mentioned here is to blame; that responsibility is mine alone.

Finally, I would like to acknowledge my gratitude to close friends—including many of the above—who provided succor, bed and breakfast, and welcome encouragement.

Gregg Herken

Ezra Stiles College
New Haven, Connecticut

Рис. КУКРЫНИКСЫ

АТОМЩИКИ
ЗА РАБОТОЙ,
или
опасная игра с огнём.

"ATOM-MEN AT WORK, or, A dangerous playing with fire."
Krokodil (Moscow, 1950)

from *The Herblock Book* (Beacon Press, 1952)

'Now Meet My Younger Brother!'

Hutton, Philadelphia *Inquirer*

IN THE LABORATORY OF HUMAN AFFAIRS

Fitzpatrick, St. Louis
Post-Dispatch

"Don't Mind Me—Just Go Right On Talking"

from *The Herblock Book* (Beacon Press, 1952)

THE WINNING WEAPON

PROLOGUE

Some on the ground cheered when they saw the parachutes—certainly the sign of a bomber in trouble. At an altitude of just under two thousand feet the bomb detonated, obeying the simultaneous command of a multitude of fusing devices meant to guarantee success. Hiroshima, the director of the Manhattan Project later explained, had been purposely chosen as a target for its flatness, so that "the effects of the bomb would run out," thereby affording the most convincing demonstration possible of the weapon's power. At a range of up to five hundred yards from ground zero, objects engulfed by the fireball became incandescent in the million-degree heat. Total destruction stretched out in a half-mile radius from the point of the explosion, leaving the rubble of one building indistinguishable from that of the next. Up to two miles from ground zero, fires familiar to the survivors of incendiary raids upon other Japanese cities began to spring up, with the difference that the fires this time were everywhere at once. By nightfall, victims of poisoning by what was thought to be a mysterious "gas"—actually, radiation sickness—began to appear at aid stations around the destroyed city.

Altogether, a minimum of 78,000 Japanese were killed outright or died in succeeding weeks from the effects of blast, fire, and radiation. Still uncounted among the casualties of the bomb were twenty American airmen, prisoners of war at Hiroshima.*

Reaction in the United States to the atomic bombing of Hiroshima on August 6, 1945, and to the destruction of Nagasaki three days later could be characterized, at least initially, as unambivalent. "This is the greatest thing in history," President Harry S Truman enthused when he

---

*The remains of the airmen were later returned to the United States by the Japanese government, along with their names and the simple listing "atomic bomb" under "cause of death." A few of the victims had been prisoners of war since 1942. The Pentagon has never acknowledged these deaths and has listed the airmen as "missing in action." I am indebted to Professor Martin Sherwin for finally resolving the mystery of American victims at Hiroshima.[1]

received word on board the cruiser *Augusta,* returning from his first and last meeting with Soviet Premier Stalin. Later, Truman said he had never been happier to make an announcement.

A sense of relief if not celebration overcame the one million American servicemen who might have taken part in Operation Olympic, the first invasion of the Japanese home islands, scheduled for the following November. The surrender of Japan little more than a week later made that invasion unnecessary.

In the thirty-five years since the destruction of Hiroshima, the consensus that existed to use the atomic bomb has disappeared. Within three years after the war the charge would be made that the bomb had been dropped not so much to force a Japanese surrender—already assured in any event, it is argued—but to keep the Russians out of Manchuria and to impress them with the power of the new weapon. The subsequent claim that the Truman administration practiced "atomic diplomacy"—using the U.S. monopoly of the bomb to gain political advantage—has perhaps become the centerpiece of the controversy over reinterpretation of cold war origins that continues today.[2] Begun among historians, this debate over the means and motives of American foreign policy since 1945 now extends, in this era of renewed cold war, to the way we see ourselves in the world.

Previous studies on the atomic bomb have focused upon President Truman's wartime decision to use that weapon against Japan. This emphasis upon events during the opening year of the atomic age has come about because of the dramatic and tragic manner of the bomb's first use, the prior unavailability of sources beyond that date, and the continuing furor over atomic diplomacy. But Hiroshima is—properly—only the beginning of the story of the atomic bomb in the cold war.

Responsible traditional as well as revisionist accounts of the decision to drop the bomb now recognize that the act had behind it *both* an immediate military rationale regarding Japan and a possible diplomatic advantage concerning Russia. Apart, these two considerations reinforced the already existing inclination of Truman and most of his advisers to use the weapon. Together, their effect was compelling to that decision.[3]

The true test of intention concerning America's future plans for the atomic bomb, therefore, comes after the weapon has been demonstrated to the world at Hiroshima. Unlike the decision to use the bomb, there was no compelling direction for U.S. atomic-energy policy following the surrender of Japan. Rather, the fact that America alone possessed atomic bombs gave her a perhaps unique position of power and responsibility in history, as well as the opportunity to attempt to use that monopoly as a bargaining card of some worth in the approaching peace settlement, and possibly beyond.

The role of the atomic bomb in the cold war after Hiroshima—from the surrender of Japan in 1945 to the end of the U.S. nuclear monopoly in 1949 and the subsequent decision to proceed with development of the hydrogen bomb—is the subject of this book. Some of its conclusions collide with the assumptions and tenets held by those on both sides of the atomic-diplomacy debate. But new evidence made available by the declassification of government documents, the opening of previously restricted personal papers, and the passage of time warrant a reassessment of earlier wisdom.

The findings of this study confirm, for example, that some in the Truman administration believed the bomb might make a decisive difference in America's postwar dealings with Russia. But the evidence beyond Hiroshima makes it equally clear that miscalculation, illusion, and classic irony accompanied and transformed this expectation on its way to becoming policy. Thus Secretary of State James F. Byrnes, who initially hoped to use the atomic bomb as a lever to move the Russians closer to the American vision of a postwar world, himself became the victim of atomic diplomacy turned around at the first meeting of the victorious powers. There a humbled Byrnes observed that the Russians were, after all, "stubborn, obstinate, and they don't scare."[4]

At the same time, the previous definition of atomic diplomacy merely as a threat—implicit or explicit—is seen here as too restrictive to describe U.S. policy on the bomb after the war. A view so limited overlooks the important role played by the *promise* of atomic energy's cooperative control after the war, held out to the Russians first by Byrnes, and then by Bernard Baruch at the United Nations. This promise of cooperation was potentially as powerful an instrument of persuasion as the bomb's threat, and was another means by which America's atomic monopoly could be the country's "winning weapon."

The connection between foreign policy and domestic politics as they both concerned the bomb is, in addition to the evidence of atomic diplomacy, a concern of this study that might provoke controversy. Here it will be argued that the rejection by Truman of a plan to approach the Russians openly on the bomb after the war unavoidably meant adoption of a policy of monopoly—a policy doomed by its futile effort to continue wartime secrecy, and one which eventually excluded not only the Russians but even our allies, the British, from America's knowledge of atomic energy.

Contrary to popular belief, President Truman's initial response to the problems and opportunities posed by the bomb after Hiroshima was not decisive, but hesitant and even vacillating. The emphasis of the policy of monopoly upon secrecy, moreover, not only undermined the administration's announced goal of international control of the bomb, but also virtually guaranteed the victory of conservative forces in the congressional struggle over the domestic control of atomic energy. Even as the United States accused Russia of raising an "iron curtain" against the West, America erected an "atomic curtain" shutting out the rest of the world.

A third and final focus of this book is upon the place that the atomic bomb came to have in American strategic thinking and planning to 1950. Here again, previous assumptions are often found to be misleading, if not wholly untrue. The duration of the U.S. nuclear monopoly, Defense Secretary Forrestal wrote in late 1947, would be America's "years of opportunity." Yet an "air-atomic" strategy—integrating air power with atomic weapons—was surprisingly slow to gain acceptance by U.S. military planners, even after hopes for the cooperative control of the bomb had been abandoned. The modern doctrine of nuclear deterrence which developed from this strategy also actually followed by some time the practice of deterrence, as represented by Truman's decision to base long-range bombers overseas during the 1948 crisis in Berlin. It is only with that crisis, in fact, that the bomb and America's atomic monopoly became integral to U.S. war plans and to the administration's strategy for containing Russian expansion. But even then the shockingly small number of bombs in the U.S. arsenal and the continuing lag in adapting military doctrine to the atomic age meant that America's nuclear deterrent remained a hollow threat during the years that the United States alone had the bomb. And it is likely that the Russians, through espionage, knew well the emptiness of that threat.

America's policy of monopoly concerning the bomb had been based upon the belief that the United States could retain such weapons exclusively and in "trust" for as long as a generation. The error of this expectation, and of a policy founded upon American nuclear hegemony, was demonstrated barely a year after the Berlin crisis when the Russians tested their first atomic bomb. That event ended the U.S. monopoly years before it was expected in Washington—and showed the much-heralded atomic secret to have been a myth rooted in misconceptions and wishful thinking. Other myths, however, were not exploded with the Russian bomb. From the surprise and disappointment which followed the premature collapse of the atomic monopoly there grew an illusion which has proved as pervasive as that of the atomic secret in our time —that America's nuclear monopoly was not lost to time and miscalculation, but stolen by spies.

President Truman's decision in early 1950 to proceed with a comprehensive rearmament plan, including development of the hydrogen bomb, rather than reassess earlier thinking toward both the bomb and Russia, marked a continuation of the policies of monopoly, secrecy, and exclusion. Here too the administration was caught in a dilemma that was to a significant degree of its own making. For the atomic monopoly's premature end had already shown those policies to have been founded upon illusion—the recurrent illusion that the bomb would be America's decisive advantage in war or peace; and the "most deadly illusion," as one scientist wrote, that America could retain a unilateral advantage until her objectives in diplomacy were met.[5]

Neither as threat nor as promise did the U.S. nuclear monopoly create the secure Pax Atomica that some sought. It was not in increased security or prestige, but in contributing to the subsequent militarization of the cold war, to heightened Soviet-American tensions, and to a portentous furor over domestic "atom spies" that American postwar policy on the atomic bomb found its ironic fulfillment.

Irony, indeed, characterizes the atomic bomb's history. Deemed the "winning weapon" in 1946, the bomb seemed to promise victory for the United States in the cold war. It could be either a unique bargaining card in negotiations, or an ultimate weapon should diplomacy fail. In its dual role as a winning weapon, the bomb thus made difficult decisions seem easier, and some choices appear unnecessary altogether.

The consequence of treating the bomb as a winning weapon was not victory, but a climate of fear and suspicion, beginning even before the Russians surprised the Truman administration and ended the U.S.

nuclear monopoly. That fear and suspicion continue today as a peculiar product of the atomic age, when nearly a dozen nations have or may soon have nuclear weapons. In a world fundamentally altered by atomic energy since 1945, the political, diplomatic, and military role of the atomic bomb in the cold war is today not only history—but legacy.

BOOK ONE

Hiroshima and After
The Atomic Bomb
in Diplomacy,
1945-1946

1

Hiroshima and Potsdam:
The Prelude

G. Slam would be about 10,000 lbs of TNT, smaller than Tarzon

> "It is certainly a good thing for the world that Hitler's crowd or
> Stalin's did not discover this atomic bomb. It seems to be the most
> terrible thing ever discovered, but it can be made the most useful."
> *President Harry Truman, journal, July 1945*

> "Truman said he had given orders to stop the atomic bombing. He said
> the thought of wiping out another 100,000 people was too horrible.
> He didn't like the idea of killing, as he said, 'all those kids.' "
> *Commerce Secretary Henry A. Wallace, diary entry, August 1945*

"It's a Hell of a Story"

Eben Ayers, President Truman's assistant press secretary, started off his
press briefing that Monday morning, August 6, with what he thought
was "a darned good story." "It's a statement by the President," Ayers
announced, "which starts off this way:

> Sixteen hours ago an American airplane dropped one bomb on
> Hiroshima, an important Japanese Army base. That bomb had
> more power than 20,000 tons of T.N.T. It had more than two
> thousand times the blast power of the British "Grand Slam"
> which is the largest bomb ever yet used in the history of
> warfare. . . .

For a moment "the reporters seemed unable to grasp what it was
about," Ayers noted in his diary. "They did not break for the door on
a run or run to their phones. . . . Some of them had difficulty in getting
their news desks to grasp the import of it." As comprehension dawned,
Ayers chided the reporters to wait for the full story "so you won't ball
it all up." "It's a big story," he promised. "It's a hell of a story!" one
journalist corrected.*

---

*Returning from the Potsdam conference on board the cruiser *Augusta*, Truman almost missed
the news of the Hiroshima bombing. According to Potsdam aide Walter Brown, the President and

Like the reporters at the White House that day and most other Americans, Ayers first learned of the existence of the atomic bomb from Truman's announcement. Though surprised by the news itself, he later wrote in his diary that he was not surprised the United States would use the new weapon against the enemy. Citing Secretary of War Henry L. Stimson, Ayers noted that "at no time from 1941 to 1945 did he [Stimson] ever hear it suggested by the President or any other responsible member of the government that atomic energy should not be used in the war." Stimson had "emphasized that it was the common objective throughout the war 'to be the first to develop an atomic weapon and to use it.' "[2]

Having given approval to the start of the Manhattan Project—first as the "Uranium Committee" in 1940 and then as the "Manhattan Engineer District" when the army assumed command of the project early in 1942—President Roosevelt maintained a detailed interest in the bomb, and in its postwar implications, up to his death in the spring of 1945. Indeed, the bomb's nascent role as a force in American diplomacy had been recognized as early as 1943, when FDR committed the United States to a policy of cooperating with Great Britain in the development of atomic energy under the Quebec Agreement. The move in that agreement toward "restricted interchange" with the British on the bomb actually put a greater emphasis upon guaranteeing postwar Anglo-American control of the bomb than on steady wartime progress toward creation of the weapon itself. The Hyde Park aide-mémoire signed by FDR and Churchill late in 1944, the "Agreement and Declaration of Trust," further cemented the tacit Anglo-American alliance on both the use and the postwar control of the bomb, and marked the weapon's emergence, one historian of the agreement notes, as "a powerful diplomatic bargaining counter."[3]

Yet, even as there was virtual unanimity concerning the bomb's use when Stimson saw the President for the last time, on March 15, the question of its postwar control remained undecided. At that meeting, Stimson had stressed the importance of choosing between a continued Anglo-American monopoly of the bomb or a policy of wider cooperation,

---

his top advisers were huddled in the ship's ward room that Monday, listening to a radio for the White House announcement. The only signal they could pick up, however, was from a small station in Maine. Truman was furious and berated Brown—a former journalist—when the station interrupted its program, a murder whodunit, for a terse announcement of the bombing and then returned to the mystery show.[1]

eventually involving Russia, before the weapon was actually used. Though FDR had certainly tended toward the former arrangement in his secret negotiations of 1943 and 1944 with Churchill, the resulting agreements fell short of a firm and declared policy of excluding Russia in either statement or intent. This ambiguity concerning Russia and the bomb was likely a conscious part of Roosevelt's strategy, designed (as were his domestic policies) to give him the greatest flexibility and maximum bargaining strength when the decision finally had to be made. If so, the flaw in this strategy of delay became dramatically evident with Roosevelt's sudden and unexpected passing.

Because he was never informed of Roosevelt's intentions in the matter of atomic policy, Truman inherited neither the flexibility nor the diplomatic subtlety of his predecessor's planning. He did, however, fall heir to the assumption that the bomb would be used.* New to the job and unconfident of his ability, Truman was disinclined to challenge that assumption.

"Like People from Across the Tracks"

The neophyte President's first real information on the bomb came from Stimson, in a briefing on the afternoon of April 25, 1945. Accompanying Stimson on this mission was Brigadier General Leslie R. Groves, who had been chosen in 1942 to head the Manhattan Project. So carefully was the secret of that project guarded by spring 1945 that Groves entered Truman's office through a side door, unobserved even by the President's appointment secretary, Matthew Connelly. It was Groves rather than Stimson who was the real repository of knowledge concerning the bomb. Two days previous to his meeting with the President, at Stimson's urging, Groves had prepared a twenty-four-page memoran-

---

*A recently declassified document sheds light upon the longstanding controversy over whether the United States government would have dropped the atomic bomb upon occidentals. At a meeting on August 24, 1945, General Groves told a committee considering "foreseeable new developments" in warfare that he and the scientists of the Manhattan Project had always known the bomb "would probably be completed too late for use against Germany." There were other reasons as well militating against the choice of Germany as the target for the first atomic bomb—the fact that German atomic scientists would be able to analyze a dud "accurately," the initial absence of B-29 bombers in Europe to carry the weapon, and the greater attraction of the Japanese fleet as a target. But racism was not one of these reasons. "President Roosevelt asked if we were prepared to drop bombs on Germany if it was necessary to do so and we replied that we would be prepared to do so if necessary," Groves reported.[4]

dum summarizing the progress of the Manhattan Project scientists. The
general summarized that memo for the President in their meeting,
stressing its two most important points. First, a deliverable atomic bomb
seemed assured, and would be ready for its first test sometime that
summer. Second, the United States and Britain together had virtually
cornered the world's known market of fissionable materials, uranium and
thorium, thereby ensuring a plentiful—even preclusive—supply of
atomic bombs for the war's duration and for an indefinite period beyond.
Truman was also told by Groves of Russian spying upon the Manhattan
Project.[5]

Stimson's own concern at this meeting differed from Groves'. The
secretary of war was already thinking beyond the military application of
the bomb. In December of the previous year, he had met with President
Roosevelt to argue that the United States should not offer to share the
production secrets of the atomic bomb with Russia "until we were sure to
get a real *quid pro quo* for our frankness." On that occasion Stimson did
not specify what he expected from Russia in exchange for such cooperation. In a later meeting with Roosevelt shortly after the President's return from the Yalta Conference, however, Stimson spelled out the kind of
trade he wanted. He suggested that the United States might want to demand the liberalization of Soviet internal rule in exchange for information
on the bomb. But Roosevelt must first choose between the "secret, close-
in attempted control of the object by those who control it now," or "international control based upon freedom both of science and of access."[6]

With Roosevelt's death, the problem of what to do with the atomic
bomb after the war had to be raised again, and Stimson could not be
sure this time how his advice might be received. Moreover, his own
thinking on the subject had changed in the interim. For one thing, the
problem of the bomb's possible effect upon international affairs was
made more important in his briefing to Truman by the fact that the first
meeting of the United Nations was scheduled to begin in San Francisco
in a few days. For another, the President just two days earlier had had
a stormy session about Poland with Soviet Foreign Minister V. M.
Molotov. The Russian probably—and properly—interpreted that incident as a signal that American policy on eastern Europe was now taking
a firmer stand.

The bitter exchange between Truman and Molotov had been just one
indication of the marked deterioration in the spirit, at least, of Soviet-

American relations since the high point of wartime cooperation under Roosevelt. Even on the day of the German surrender—at a time when American newspapers showed U.S. and Soviet troops embracing along the Elbe River—one participant in a White House meeting lamented that the "relationship with Russia was never worse." Later that same month the President commented to FDR's daughter that the advisers he had inherited from her father were urging him "to be hard with the Russians"—a trend that alarmed the administration's liberal secretary of commerce, Henry A. Wallace.

Truman professed no doubts as to the root cause of the problem. After a Cabinet meeting of mid-May he told Wallace that the Russians "were like people from across the tracks whose manners were very bad." His own messages to Stalin "had been couched in the most friendly language," the President complained, but the Russians had been thus far unresponsive. Truman also revealed another motive for these continued overtures to the Soviets. The President's "one objective," Wallace noted, "was to be sure to get the Russians into the Japanese war so as to save the lives of 100,000 American boys." As long as the possibility of Soviet aid in the planned invasion of Japan existed, Wallace concluded, the Big Three alliance would not be allowed to break up.[7]

Perhaps fearful of exacerbating the growing tension in Soviet-American relations by introducing a confrontation over the atomic bomb, Stimson sidestepped the issue of a *quid pro quo* in his presentation on the 25th. Instead, he simply tried to apprise Truman of the perils and the opportunities presented by atomic energy. The memo Stimson had prepared for the occasion warned the President that a small and unscrupulous nation with the atomic bomb might be able to conquer or at least blackmail larger, democratic countries. No present system of control seemed adequate to harness the bomb's capacity for evil. "On the other hand," Stimson brightened, "if the problem of the proper use of the weapon can be solved, we would have the opportunity to bring the world into a pattern in which the peace of the world and our civilization can be saved."

Significantly, unlike his advice in previous meetings with Roosevelt, Stimson's presentation for Truman contained no direct suggestions other than to urge that the President appoint a temporary panel of experts to advise him on atomic policy. The meeting was only fifteen minutes in length, remarkably brief considering the complexity and

importance of the subject. "I don't like to read long papers," Truman
explained to Groves. Because of this brevity, however, at least one vital
issue originally on the agenda—the probable duration of the United
States atomic monopoly—was never discussed.

Truman's own recollection of this briefing records that he listened
to Stimson's presentation "with absorbed interest," but neither in his
memoirs nor by his actions at the time is there an indication that the
President was moved to make any decisions there concerning the future
of the bomb other than to appoint the recommended Interim Committee of advisers. In deference to Stimson's senior status, Truman appointed him head of the committee.[8]

Truman, it is true, was under no direct pressure at that time to
make a decision on the bomb beyond ordering its use against Japan. But
the bomb was subtly, inextricably, becoming a dominant issue in postwar
planning nonetheless. On June 6, Stimson gave Truman the Interim
Committee's recommendation that the atomic bomb be used against a
Japanese city, without warning, as soon as preparations could be made.
The committee had also advised that the Russians not be told about the
weapon prior to its use. Finally, Stimson added his own thinking to the
committee's recommendation in a memo he handed to the President in
which he returned to the theme of a *quid pro quo*. Here he suggested
that as a condition of sharing the secrets of the bomb, Truman demand
of the Soviets either participation in an international control commission
on atomic energy after the war, or the "solution of our present troubles"
over the political complexion of postwar governments in eastern
Europe.[9] The President, Stimson noted, seemed especially receptive to
the latter approach. Truman's response was hardly surprising. Beginning
with Yalta, and particularly since the confrontation between the President and Molotov, eastern Europe had become a focus of the increasing
strain in Soviet-American relations.

"We . . . Might Have to Have It Out with the Russians"

By the summer of 1945, Stimson realized that the question of whether
and what to tell the Russians about the atomic bomb was becoming
acute. The Big Three had scheduled what was to be their final wartime

meeting at Potsdam in July. The stakes at that meeting were already well defined—eastern Europe, the disposition of the liberated territories in Asia, and Russian entry into the war against Japan. But Stimson predicted that these would become "burning" issues at the conference table. "We . . . might have to have it out with the Russians" after the war on the question of Soviet influence in Asia, he wrote in his diary. Surely this would fall short of an actual physical confrontation, but the bomb would play no small part in the diplomacy of the meeting. "Over any such tangled weave of problems, the . . . secret would be dominant."

Yet America's bargaining position at the negotiating table, Stimson realized, was still less than assured. It seemed "a terrible thing," he mused in this same entry, "to gamble with such big stakes in diplomacy without having your master card in your hand."[10]

Upon Stimson's urging, Truman already had postponed the meeting once with Stalin "to give us more time" to resolve the question of how to approach the Russians on the bomb. Specifically, both Truman and Stimson were hoping that the first bomb would be tested by mid-July as scheduled, before the end of the summit meeting with Stalin. Then the Americans would know, Stimson admitted, "whether this is a weapon in our hands or not."

The approaching meeting with the Russians began to assume the argot—if not the spirit—of a poker showdown. Stimson had written in May that the combination of postwar economic strength and the atomic bomb would give the United States "a royal straight flush and we mustn't be a fool about the way we play it."[11] The President seemed to share Stimson's view, claiming that the "cards" were "in American hands" and that he meant "to play them as American cards." Truman assured his aides that Stalin would not beat him in the upcoming poker game.[12]

To complicate matters at Potsdam, the advice Truman received in the weeks prior to his meeting with Stalin was neither uniform nor consistent concerning the atomic bomb. By late June the Interim Committee had reversed itself and now recommended that the President not wait until the bomb was used in the war before informing the Soviets of its existence. Stimson himself, in one last meeting with Truman before Potsdam, suggested a compromise approach: Truman would inform Stalin of the bomb's existence and of America's peaceful intentions concerning it after the war, but the President would turn aside any inquiries or suggestions by the Russians of an atomic partnership. By this method Stimson hoped to achieve, if not the *quid pro quo,* some sign of Russia's willingness to cooperate with the West. The advice of Truman's other advisers and confidants on the subject was mixed. British Prime Minister Churchill—already concerned about what England was "going to have between the white snows of Russia and the white cliffs of Dover"—favored telling Stalin outright in order to gain a diplomatic advantage at the conference, but he urged that Truman wait until the bomb was successfully tested. James F. Byrnes, a member of the Interim Committee and Truman's secretary of state, looked to the bomb as a way of ending the war before the Russians could enter it against Japan and thereby establish a Soviet base in Manchuria. Byrnes had already advised the President not to accept a conditional surrender from Japan, since the bomb and Russian entry into the war would make this compromise unnecessary.[13]

The successful test of an atomic weapon in New Mexico on July 16, at the start of the summit conference, both encouraged the American delegation at Potsdam and underscored the need for a decision on what to do about the Russians and the bomb. "The bomb as a merely probable weapon had seemed a weak reed on which to rely, but the bomb as a colossal reality was very different," Stimson wrote of his own reaction to the test. He added that the United States now had "a badly needed 'equalizer' " of Russian power. The fact that the bomb worked, however, did not resolve the problem of approaching the Russians. Instead, the differences between the United States and her difficult ally were, Stimson thought, being brought to a focus by the atomic bomb. The question remained to what purpose the master card would be used. Until Russia was dealt with, Stimson lamented, he and the Interim Committee were "thinking in a vacuum."[14]

A tangible result of the successful test was Truman's order to his military aides that they reconsider their plans for the invasion of Japan. Those preparations called for Russian participation in the final campaign. But the bomb suddenly made Russian entry into the war potentially more a liability than an asset. Ironically, one of Truman's earliest concerns had been that Stalin could not be coaxed into entering the war against the Japanese, with whom the Russians had signed a nonaggression treaty before the German invasion. Stalin apparently suspected that the United States wanted to prevent Russia's entry into the Pacific war. He complained, therefore, that the U.S. attitude toward Soviet participation had "cooled" since Germany's surrender, "as though the Americans were now saying that the Russians were no longer needed."

Truman's concern was without foundation. Stalin had assured the President on the first day of the Potsdam Conference that Russia would enter the war against Japan in mid-August. Surprised and relieved, Truman told an aide that he felt he "could go home now." But the advent of the bomb had since changed his mind. The bomb, not Russia's entry into the war, became the single most important issue at Potsdam.[15]

Other changes had come about in the wake of the atomic test. By July 20, Stimson's further thoughts on the bomb and of what he considered to be evidence of Soviet authoritarianism at the summit caused him to reconsider his views in another memorandum to the President. Entitled "Reflections on the Basic Problems Which Confront Us," the document revealed his response to the fearsome realities of the atomic age.[16] The secretary of war had abandoned his earlier hopes for international control of the bomb, and now believed that "*no* world organization containing as one of its dominant members a nation whose people are not possessed of free speech . . . can give effective control of this agency with its devastating possibilities." Instead, Stimson revived his earlier notion of forcing a change in Russia and extended it to demand the liberalization of Soviet society as a precondition for cooperation on the bomb.

Ultimately, Truman proved to be more cautious—or more devious—than any of his advisers. On July 24, the President casually approached Stalin after one conference session and told him only that the United States had developed a "new weapon of unusual destructive force."[17] He did not indicate that the bomb could become a force for peace after the war, or that America might be willing, under some circumstances, to share it; he did not even mention that it was an *atomic* bomb. Thus Truman technically fulfilled his responsibility to inform an ally without at the same time incurring the obligation of sharing the bomb's discovery. By this polite subterfuge, the President had in fact dodged the issue of approaching Russia about the bomb—leaving that task for a later day. As events developed, it would not come up again until after the war.

Accounts of this episode note how disappointed the American delegation was that Stalin had no response to the President's announcement, other than to express hope that the United States would make "good use" of the weapon against the Japanese. Indeed, the dour reaction of the Russian leader led Byrnes to believe that "Stalin did not grasp the importance" of Truman's message. This seems incredible in light of the fact that the Russians were spying on the Manhattan Project as early as 1942. It is more likely, therefore, that Stalin's laconic reply at Potsdam— and his later public disparagement of the bomb as "a weapon to frighten the weak"—was sheer bravado. The memoirs of Soviet Marshal Georgei Zhukov, published in the West in 1971, indicate that Stalin knew precisely what Truman had alluded to. Soviet Premier Nikita Khrushchev, in the second volume of his memoirs, claimed that "Stalin was frightened to the point of cowardice" by news of the American bomb.[18]

Stalin's poker face may also have been the first example of atomic diplomacy in reverse, with the Russians upsetting American expectations by being—or appearing to be—unimpressed with the U.S. monopoly of nuclear weapons.

"On Plots and Errors, Happen"

On the same day that Truman decided not to tell Stalin about the dawn of the atomic age, he gave final authorization for the order to drop atomic bombs upon Japan.[19] The order simply directed that they be released as soon as they were ready upon a preselected list of Japanese cities until that government surrendered. The first bomb was dropped upon Hiroshima two weeks later. Three days after Hiroshima a second city, Nagasaki, was bombed.

Neither at the time nor on any subsequent occasion did Truman publicly express doubts about his decision to use the bomb.* The Presi-

---

*Contrary to his popular image, Truman was acutely sensitive to postwar criticism of his decision to use the bomb. He wrote in his memoirs that he "never had any doubt that [the bomb] should be used." A later, personal letter from the President to an actor who had played the part of Truman in a Hollywood film on the bomb was equally as blunt and as assured: "I have no qualms about [the decision] whatever for the simple reason that it was believed the dropping of not more than two of these bombs would bring the war to a close. The Japanese in their conduct of the war had been vicious and cruel savages and I came to the conclusion that if two hundred and fifty thousand young Americans could be saved from slaughter the bomb should be dropped, and it was."

This evident detachment concerning the decision, however, was belied by Truman's comment in the Cabinet meeting of August 10 (see below), and by the evidence of the private journal he kept at Potsdam. Truman wrote on July 25: "Even if the Japs are savages, ruthless, merciless and fanatic, we as the leader of the world for the common welfare cannot drop this terrible bomb on the old Capitol [Kyoto] or the new [Tokyo]. . . . It is certainly a good thing for the world that Hitler's crowd or Stalin's did not discover this atomic bomb. It seems to be the most terrible thing ever

dent was, however, obviously concerned with reaction to the decision, especially as to how it might affect events after the war. Two days after the bombing of Hiroshima, Ayers noted that "the President expressed concern about the attitude of the Pope concerning the bomb development. [Truman] pointed out that the cooperation of the Vatican is needed in days to come, particularly in dealing with the Catholic countries of Europe, and admitted he was troubled as to how to reach the Pope to reassure him."[21]

The third target in Japan, meant to be either Kokura or Niigata, was spared destruction first by an accident of the weather—Nagasaki had been an alternate target on the 9th—and then by the Japanese surrender overture on the 10th. A third atomic bomb, still unassembled by that date, would not have been ready until nearly the end of August. There is some reason to believe that the third bomb would not have been used in any case. At a Cabinet meeting on the 10th, Truman had ordered the further atomic bombing of Japan suspended. The "thought of wiping out another 100,000 people was too horrible," he admitted. Wallace recalled of the President's remarks on that occasion: "He didn't like the idea of killing, as he said, 'all those kids.' "[22]

Truman's humanitarian motive may, in fact, have outweighed a political consideration which he expressed at the same meeting. It was, he told the Cabinet, "to our interest that the Russians not push too far into Manchuria."* The Japanese surrender meant that the two conflict-

---

discovered, but it can be made the most useful." Perhaps the most telling indication of Truman's secret doubts about the bomb was his underlining of Horatio's speech in the last scene of *Hamlet*, cited in a book on the decision contained in the President's personal library. Truman had twice underscored the last line of the passage:

> Of accidental judgements, casual slaughters,
> Of deaths put on by cunning and forced cause,
> And, in this upshot, purposes mistook
> Fall'n on the inventors' heads . . .
> But let this same be presently perform'd,
> Even while men's minds are wild; lest more mischance,
> On plots and errors, happen.[20]

*The Hiroshima bombing evidently accelerated Russian plans to enter the war against Japan, which Stalin at Potsdam had told Truman he would do on August 15. Soviet troops invaded Manchuria on August 8 and achieved their objectives there before the war ended. Japanese records suggest that it was the unexpected Russian invasion—more than the atomic bombings—which compelled the government's surrender. Hence the destruction of Nagasaki neither hastened the war's end nor kept the Russians out of Manchuria. The dropping of the second bomb was not a case of cold war *realpolitik*, however, so much as of wartime bureaucratic inertia. Thus Truman, in his order of July 24, had simply instructed that "atomic bomb*s*" [emphasis added] be dropped on Japan as soon as they were made ready.[23]

ing motives would not be put to a test. Truman's decision to stop the atomic bombing was perhaps an early and tacit recognition of the peculiarly horrific nature of atomic warfare. But the conventional and incendiary bombing of Tokyo and other Japanese cities was not stopped by the President after Hiroshima, and it continued until the formal Japanese surrender was accepted on August 14.

It was not until August 9, the day Nagasaki was bombed, that Truman gave any public indication of what his attitude toward postwar control of the atomic bomb might be. Arguing that the "atomic bomb is too dangerous to be loose in a lawless world," he announced that those nations possessing the secrets of its production, the United States and Great Britain, must constitute themselves "trustees of this new force—to prevent its misuse, and to turn it into channels of service to mankind." Truman emphasized the tentative nature of this decision at the end of his radio address when he promised that the formulation of atomic-energy policy would await the recommendations of his committee of advisers. He meant it to be only an interim decision. Yet, if not a definite statement of policy, the President's choice of the word "trustees" seemed to presage an approach that implicitly rejected the sort of "international control based upon freedom both of science and of access" which Stimson had written of six months earlier.[24]

In the spring and summer months of 1945 the bomb had moved from laboratory to war and then to the negotiating table, but its future in American planning was still uncertain. Contrary to the hope and advice of Stimson and his aides, the weapon had been used before the questions surrounding its postwar control had been properly considered. The death of Roosevelt had been the cause of the first unexpected delay, followed by Truman's preoccupation with mastering his new role and with keeping the Grand Alliance together until victory. The bomb had inexorably entered international politics at Potsdam, but it was not until the destruction of Hiroshima that it became the "colossal reality" of war and diplomacy that Stimson earlier predicted. In the shadow of that event, the focus of the Truman administration upon America's wartime enemies faded and was replaced by a dominant new concern: Russia and the bomb.

2
Washington:
A Direct Approach to Russia

". . . I consider the problem of our satisfactory relations with Russia as not merely connected with but as virtually dominated by the problem of the atomic bomb."

Secretary of War Henry L. Stimson to President Truman,
September 1945

"The possession in our hands of this new power of destruction we regard as a sacred trust."

President Truman, speech, September 1945

"The World Is Changed"

In March 1945—when the atomic bomb was not yet the "colossal reality" he predicted—Stimson wrote that his decisions concerning the bomb were "by far the most searching and important thing that I had to do since I have been here in the office of Secretary of War because [they touch] matters which are deeper even than the principles of present government." According to War Department aide Gordon Arneson, as early as the end of 1944 Stimson had asked George Marshall to run the department while he worked on atomic energy. On the occasion of his April 1945 meeting with Truman, Stimson had written of America's "moral responsibility" concerning the bomb. Planning for the use of the weapon and problems with Russia had distracted him from that theme in subsequent days, but Stimson returned to it in his diary on the day that Nagasaki was bombed: "Great events have happened. The world is changed and it is time for sober thought."[1]

On that same day, Stimson spoke of the bomb to a nationwide radio audience. The pride of discovery that Americans felt with regard to the weapon, he cautioned in that message, "must be overshadowed by deeper emotion. The result of the bomb is so terrific that the responsibility of its possession and its use must weigh heavier on our minds and on our hearts."[2]

That responsibility seemed to weigh especially heavily upon Stimson.* Nearly seventy-eight, he looked forward to retirement once the war was over. His tenure in that office, first under Roosevelt and then Truman, had been an ironic vindication of Stimson's own judgment. In the early 1930s, as secretary of state, he had vainly urged the Hoover administration to abandon its policy of isolationism by condemning Japanese aggression in Manchuria. It had been, in fact, the early and futile stand of the "Stimson doctrine" against fascist aggression that prompted FDR to choose Stimson to run the War Department a year before Pearl Harbor.[3]

Leaving for a three-week vacation at war's end, Stimson began drafting a last memorandum for the President on the bomb and the future of Soviet-American relations. The counsel that Stimson now prepared to offer represented more than the final reflections of a trusted adviser; it was as well the culmination of his uniquely long and distinguished career in government service.

"The crux of the problem is Russia," Stimson intended to inform the President. The "problem of our satisfactory relations with Russia," he wrote, was "not merely connected with but [was] virtually dominated by the problem of the atomic bomb."

The destruction of two cities by atomic bombs—and a conversation at Potsdam with American Ambassador to Russia Averell Harriman—had altered Stimson's earlier thinking on the problem of Russia and the bomb. Convinced that the international control of atomic energy was well into the future, and might still require as a precondition the transformation of Soviet society, Stimson no longer believed that America's possession of the bomb could be used to bring that transformation about. Any such "demand by us as a condition of sharing in the atomic weapon would be so resented that it would make the objective we have in view less probable." With this passage—appended in a note to the President in which Stimson explained the reason for his change of heart—the idea of a *quid pro quo* with Russia involving the bomb was finally abandoned.

---

*One of his biographers, Elting Morison, has noted that Stimson's references to the bomb in his diary were a sort of litany of apprehension. There the bomb becomes "the most secret," "the dreadful," "the terrible," "the dire," "the awful," and "the diabolical." By contrast, Oppenheimer and other scientists in the Manhattan Project often used the term "the gadget" for the bomb before Hiroshima. David Lilienthal's later code name for the hydrogen or "Super" bomb was a pun— "Campbell."

Instead, what Stimson envisioned in his last advisory to Truman was not a legal arrangement between antagonists or an international treaty, but a "covenant" between the United States, Great Britain, and Russia. Under the terms of this agreement the Soviets would refrain from efforts to develop an atomic bomb while the West would freely make available information on atomic energy's peaceful application, and would also "undertake not to employ the atomic bomb or any development of it as an instrument of warfare."

In touch with aides at the Pentagon from his retreat in the Adirondacks, Stimson sensed a positive response to his ideas within the War Department.* He learned at the same time, however, of opposition from an unexpected quarter—the State Department.

"A Secret Armaments Race of a Rather Desperate Character"

Stimson's return to Washington in early September further dampened the optimism that he had felt in the mountains. Meeting at the State Department with Byrnes, who was about to leave for the first postwar meeting with the Russians in London, Stimson learned that the thinking of the new secretary of state concerning Russia and the bomb differed dramatically from his own: "I found that Byrnes was very much against any attempt to cooperate with Russia." Byrnes seemed preoccupied with the upcoming conference of foreign ministers, Stimson recalled, "and he looks to having the presence of the bomb in his pocket so to speak as a great weapon to get through the thing."[5]

Later that same day, Stimson indicated to Truman his dissatisfaction with Byrnes' attitude, arguing that the secretary of state's approach meant a return to "power politics." Stimson did not deem the time right, however, to discuss the content of his still-unfinished memorandum with the President.

Returning once again to his mountain retreat, Stimson set about

---

*Stimson had chosen the Adirondacks rather than Highhold, his resort home on Long Island, in order to get farther away from Washington. The name of the Long Island estate had become intertwined in the atomic-bomb drama. A telegram sent to Stimson at Potsdam announcing the successful bomb test had employed a simple metaphor to give an indication of the weapon's power. Noting that the "baby had been born," the message declared that "the light in his eyes [was] discernible from here to Highhold."[4]

revising his proposals in light of the distressing encounter with Byrnes. Added was a new note of urgency. The alternative to an agreement with the Russians on the bomb would be "a secret armament race of a rather desperate character," Stimson decided to warn the President. The nature of the dilemma facing the United States, he suggested in a further change, was not technical but political. Mention of the question of how long it might take the Soviets to develop a bomb—a topic of heated and unresolved debate in the last meetings of the Interim Committee—was deleted from the revised draft by Stimson as "not nearly so important" a matter as assuring Russian cooperation in the postwar world.

Stimson's revisions reflected more than a new earnestness on his part, or another change of mind. What was vital to the future of Soviet-American relations, he now intended to argue, was the *timing* and *method* of approaching the Russians rather than any specific proposal. "Those relations may be perhaps irretrievably embittered by the way in which we approach the solution of the bomb with Russia." In what was plainly an allusion to Byrnes and his methods, Stimson concluded the memo to Truman with the caveat that if the United States failed to approach the Russians immediately and merely continued to negotiate with them—"having this weapon rather ostentatiously on our hip"— then "their suspicions and their distrust of our purposes and motives will increase."

The emphasis that Stimson put upon the manner of approaching the Russians caused him to omit from the revised memo the specifics of what that approach should offer. Those details—such as a prohibition on the manufacture of future bombs—could be worked out, Stimson now seemed to be saying, once the approach was made and the Russians had responded. While decrying the "power politics" approach of Byrnes, Stimson was careful to demonstrate to Truman that there was no element of naivete in his proposal. "We may be gambling on their good faith and risk their getting into production of bombs a little sooner than they would otherwise," he conceded, but the proposed direct approach to the Soviets was both the best and "the most realistic means" of settling the still-unresolved problem of Russia and the bomb.[6]

Of greatest importance to Stimson was a passage that he added urging Truman to undertake this initiative on the bomb as "peculiarly the proposal of the United States." Backing from Britain would eventually be necessary, but the approach should not be made "part of a general international scheme." "The loose debates which would surround such a proposal, if put before a conference of nations, would provoke but scant favor from the Soviet," Stimson cautioned.

It would be, as events developed, a prophetic warning.

"It Has Been Found Necessary to Employ a Sheriff"

Stimson presented his proposal to Truman on September 12, in what he hoped would be his "wind-up" conference with the President. Reading the memo, Truman initialed each paragraph of the six-page document and, Stimson noted brightly, agreed with him that "we must take Russia into our confidence."[7]

That the President was actually converted to Stimson's proposal at this meeting is, however, doubtful. Truman had with equal facility agreed to Stimson's assessment some six weeks earlier that the Russians were not to be trusted. It is likely, instead, that the President—like others in Washington—saw no point in challenging the advice of an elder statesman approaching retirement. On September 18, Truman asked Stimson to delay his departure from the government for a few more days so that he might present his views personally at a Cabinet meeting to be devoted entirely to discussion of the atomic bomb. It was Truman's evident hope that general discussion in the Cabinet might clarify the issues Stimson had raised in his memo.

The President too was now forced to give more attention to the subject of the atomic bomb than he had since Hiroshima. On the same day that Stimson had handed his memorandum to Truman an editorial appeared in the *New York Times* by military correspondent Hanson Baldwin entitled "Atomic Bomb Responsibilities." Ironically, Baldwin's argument—that the bomb represented a supreme scientific achievement but the apparent end of America's moral leadership—echoed that of Stimson's memo. Five weeks had passed since the destruction of Hiroshima, Baldwin lamented, "but nothing has been done about the atomic bomb."[8]

Despite the growing pressure for action, Truman appeared genuinely undecided in the fall of 1945 on the subject of approaching Russia on the bomb. On at least one occasion that September, the President seemed to be considering Stimson's advice. When pressed on the subject of the bomb by former U.S. ambassador to Russia Joseph E. Davies—who urged Truman to pledge that the bomb would be used only on directions of the UN and not to go "ganging up" on the Soviets—Truman admitted that he had been thinking about just such a pledge and "a letter to Stalin with that assurance." But this line of thought had stopped short of an actual decision to that effect. "It was a most serious situation," Davies quoted Truman as saying, "and he had to go slow."[9]

What might have been a clue to Truman's thinking had come the week before Stimson handed his memo to the President. Discussion then in the Cabinet had revolved around Truman's proposal for a peacetime army to be established by universal military training. Here Leo Crowley, FDR's close adviser who became director of the lend-lease program under Truman, had disputed both the wisdom of "policing the world" and the need for a large citizen army in light of America's preeminent position in the world economy. Truman had answered Crowley's objections with a simple analogy. "In order to carry out a just decision the courts must have a marshal," and "in order to collect monies for county governments it has been found necessary to employ a sheriff," the President pointed out.[10] Truman's implication was clear. America—at least on occasion—would have to be both marshal and sheriff.

There was not much time left if the spirit and purpose of Stimson's direct approach to Russia were to be achieved. Truman himself seemed to acknowledge the need for further consultation—if not haste—the day after Davies' visit when he invited a powerful collection of senators to the White House. Senators Arthur Vandenberg of Michigan, Tom Connally of Texas, and Scott Lucas of Illinois—all members of the newly formed Joint Committee on Atomic Energy—had asked for such a meeting after hearing rumors that Truman intended to "share" the bomb with the Russians. The senators were also disturbed that the President had as yet announced no plans for a domestic atomic energy commission.

Truman's reply to the senators' worries was genial but noncommittal, informing them that his administration's policy on domestic control of atomic energy would be set forth in a speech of early October. Privately, however, he was apparently unimpressed with his visitors and their arguments that the United States should retain indefinitely the secret of the bomb—as well as resentful of the pressure upon him. After the senators had left, Ayers records, Truman remarked that they "were all publicity seekers and wanted to get publicity out of it—that they had their eyes more on that than on the subject itself."[11]

One other pressure upon Truman to resolve the problems created by the atomic bomb came from overseas, though not from Russia. Since the bombing of Hiroshima, British Prime Minister Clement Attlee had been importuning the President for a meeting and a joint "declaration of intentions" concerning the bomb's future use.[12] Attlee noted gently that Roosevelt had established the foundation for close Anglo-American co-operation on the atomic bomb, but Truman had thus far given no sign that such cooperation would be continued. By a declaration of intention, Attlee was really looking for some assurance from Truman that the British were not going to be excluded from a voice in the postwar handling of the bomb. The prime minister's requests for a meeting, at first casual, took on an insistent tone as Truman delayed. For the British —as for Stimson, Davies, Vandenberg, and others—the President's silence on the subject of the bomb became the more unnerving the more it was prolonged.

"The Secret Will Give Itself Away"

The issue of the bomb had begun to cause dissension within the Cabinet even before it was brought up there for discussion. In the regular Cabinet meeting on September 18, Wallace recalled, Truman "took the stand that while we should keep the secret of the atomic bomb we should inform the UN about atomic energy." Secretary of Agriculture Clinton Anderson offered the strongest dissent to sharing information on atomic energy, citing a recent Gallup poll which showed overwhelming popular support for strict secrecy on the bomb. Wallace had countered with the claim that by such a policy of secrecy the United States risked blame for "a dog-in-the-manger attitude" and "a Maginot Line psychology."[13]

After introducing the subject of the bomb at the special Cabinet meeting on September 21, Truman passed the initiative to Stimson. It was the secretary of war's last official act in the government—and the occasion of his seventy-eighth birthday. Speaking extemporaneously on the memo that only he and the President had seen, Stimson summarized his argument for a direct approach to Russia, stressing that a distinction could be made between disclosures of basic scientific information concerning atomic energy and of the technological secrets of the bomb. The former would be the basis of America's initiative; the latter couldn't last long in any event. "We do not have a secret to give away—the secret will give itself away," Stimson claimed.[14]

This was an opinion that Stimson already shared with a majority of the atomic scientists, but that he held almost alone in the government. The mention by Stimson of atomic "secrets" was a tactical mistake at the outset, moreover, and may have been fatal to his argument before the Cabinet. The discussion that ensued was not, therefore, concerned with Stimson's direct approach but with a totally spurious issue—whether or not the United States should "give" the bomb to the Russians. Truman twice tried to get the meeting back on track. Interrupting Cabinet members, he reminded them that the subject under discussion was only an interchange of scientific knowledge and not sharing the bomb with the Russians. The President even seemed to support Stimson at these junctures, arguing that "relationships are improving between Russia, Great Britain and ourselves," and that "we must maintain mutual trust." Truman and Stimson, however, labored in vain to steer the discussion away from its mistaken emphasis upon "secrets" and "giving away" the bomb.

The strongest opposition to approaching Russia came from Treasury Secretary Fred M. Vinson and Secretary of the Navy James V. Forrestal. Forrestal contended that the Russians could not be trusted and were "Oriental" in their thinking—clearly an invidious comparison after Pearl Harbor. He preferred "a trusteeship over the atomic bomb on behalf of the United Nations."[15] Opposed to the "trusteeship" idea were Under Secretary of State Dean Acheson, sitting in while Byrnes was at the London Council of Foreign Ministers, and Henry Wallace.

Stimson may have had cause to regret Wallace as his ally. The eccentric Iowan apparently championed the false cause of sharing the bomb with Russia and then, according to Acheson's later account, "soared into abstractions, trailing clouds of aphorisms as he went."*

The Cabinet meeting ended as it had begun—in confusion, and with both sides divided on the entirely false issue of whether to give

---

*Wallace's detailed diary entry on the meeting compares his role as a "moderator" of the heated discussion there to that of the neutron-absorbing moderators in a nuclear reactor. This role—and Wallace's logic—became ever more diffuse at the meeting, however, when, in countering Forrestal's charge that the Russians had ambitions in Manchuria, Wallace reminisced fondly and at length about his visit to a Mongolian animal-disease laboratory.[16]

atomic secrets to the Russians. "The discussion was unworthy of the subject," Acheson recollected of the session. "No one had had a chance to prepare for its complexities."[17]

Surprisingly, Stimson departed from the gathering—and the government—with the impression that Forrestal and the others had "ultimately rather yielded" to his views on approaching Russia.[18] He had taken no active part in the debate—perhaps because of an old-fashioned belief that advocacy of his own cause would be ill-mannered.

There is another explanation for his puzzling behavior at the meeting, however. Stimson had actually hoped to focus attention upon the spirit of his initiative, biographer McGeorge Bundy later wrote, and did not expect to become bogged down in a technical discussion of secrets. It was an appeal that another advocate of direct diplomacy, Franklin Roosevelt, might have understood.[19] But in a new and different administration Stimson's indirection merely confused the issue, with the result that he ultimately misinterpreted deference from the Cabinet as agreement.

Truman did not seem disappointed by the Cabinet's inability to focus on the issue. The meeting on Stimson's proposal had probably even further confused the question of approaching Russia, but he professed to find the discussion "exhilarating." At the end of the Cabinet meeting the participants were asked by the President to submit their opinions in writing. The actual "decisions," Truman reminded them, "had to be mine to make."[20]

"Can We Work with Russia and Trust Russia?"

"Plea to Give Soviet Atom Secret Stirs Debate in Cabinet; Wallace Plan to Share Bomb Data as Peace Insurance" was the *New York Times* headline the day after the frustrating session at the White House. The paper's account of the Cabinet meeting, including quotations from the principals and a garbled account of Stimson's proposal—which was mislabeled the "Wallace plan"—clearly came from one who had been there. Acheson and Wallace suspected that the *Times'* source was someone in Forrestal's camp—possibly even the navy secretary himself—who intended to stir up opposition in the country to cooperating with Russia on the bomb. If so, the leak served its purpose well. Truman's immediate assurance that he alone would decide policy on the bomb was not sufficient, therefore, to prevent a prompt national debate on the false and emotional issue of giving the bomb to the Russians.

From the start, there could be no question about the final resolution of that particular debate in the popular mind. Since the bombing of Hiroshima the "atomic secret" had become an article of public as well as official faith. Stoutly defended but never understood, the idea of the secret was sacrosanct to Americans. Public-opinion surveys at the end of September 1945 revealed that some 70 percent of the citizens and over 90 percent of the congressmen questioned objected to "sharing the atomic-bomb secret" with other nations.

Curiously, this consensus existed despite the fact that more than 80 percent of the same respondents believed the United States would not "be able to keep for just its own use the secret of how to make atomic bombs." Additionally, of those believing the secret could not be kept, more than half thought it would be only one to five years "before some other countries find out as much about atomic bombs as we know now." The majority also thought Russia would be the next country to have a bomb.[21] The message, it would seem, was that Americans were anxious to hold on to the atomic monopoly even while they acknowledged it to be a wasting asset.[22]

The pressure upon Truman mounted even as discord within the administration over the bomb increased. Concerned that Vandenberg, Connally, and Lucas had not made their message sufficiently clear to Truman, a delegation of congressmen called upon the President at the beginning of October to urge that the secret be kept. Other voices were added to the chorus opposing the feared giveaway to Russia. Speaking to an assembly of IBM executives on the same day that the "Wallace plan" story appeared in newspapers, Manhattan Project director General Leslie Groves advocated continuing secrecy on the bomb.

Surely the approach that the congressmen and Groves urged was a far cry from Stimson's proposal, and was much more nearly in line with what Acheson—concerned with the drift of policy in the administration —warned Truman in a letter might become a "futile" and "dangerous" policy of exclusion.[23] Acheson's letter and a similar endorsement of the direct approach from Truman adviser Vannevar Bush arrived at the White House on September 25. The director of the President's Office of Scientific Research and Development and a former consultant to

FDR on the bomb, Bush favored Stimson's proposal as a test case of Russia's intentions. "Can we work with Russia and trust Russia?" was the rhetorical question Bush posed in his letter to the President. "To some extent this move would enable us to find out." Stimson's approach would as well, Bush believed, "announce to the world that we wish to proceed down the path of international good will and understanding."[24]

Reaction to the "Wallace plan" and its presumed giveaway of atomic secrets had made traveling the path that Bush outlined more difficult, however. The day before he received the letters from Acheson and Bush, Truman had complained once more about the constraints and pressures developing around his decision on what to do with the bomb. There was, he claimed to Cabinet members, a "general misunderstanding of the situation" which now made the proposed exchange of scientific information between nations impossible. That information, Truman asserted, was "developed largely from what some German scientists already had done," but other countries would still be unable to develop the atomic bomb unless the United States were to "turn over the plants and equipment to do it." And this Truman said he would not do. Yet the opposite tack—to keep the bomb alone—was equally no solution, for that would mean the end of the United Nations.[25] Another Cabinet meeting broke up without any clear idea of what to do about the Russians and the bomb.

"The Russians Are Direct Action Fellows"

The dilemma facing Truman had been put into sharp relief just two days after Stimson's presentation to the Cabinet when Byrnes reported discouraging news from London about the Council of Foreign Ministers there. The conference, Truman told the Cabinet, seemed "in a fair way to breaking up without success, due largely to the position of the Russians." The President, however, was philosophical about this development. "The Russians are direct action fellows and know what they want," he remarked to Eben Ayers. "[Truman] added that if we do also, he thought we could get along all right with them."[26]

Objectively, the basis for any optimism about the future of Soviet-American relations seemed to be diminishing. Thus the problem of how to deal with the Russians on the bomb—first postponed at Potsdam and since aggravated by difficulties over eastern Europe, lend-lease, and Soviet requests for a postwar loan—was only becoming more acute as September ended. Since the middle of that month Acheson had been working on a speech which would give the administration's position on the domestic control of atomic energy. Truman had promised to announce his program for the peaceful application of atomic energy soon after the war's end. In the meantime, Congress had grown increasingly anxious. Also waiting with growing impatience, of course, was Prime Minister Attlee, who reminded Truman in a letter of September 28 that the British government was still eager to know of his plans concerning the bomb.[27]

Already the issue of domestic control too had become a focus of conflicting pressures. Fearing that Truman might jeopardize further the already faltering talks at London—or even inadvertently compromise the atomic secret—Byrnes and Robert P. Patterson, Stimson's successor at the War Department, had urged the President to avoid any reference in his speech to foreign policy or the bomb. Byrnes was especially concerned that mention of international control might cause the Russians to act even tougher at London.

In fact, the two issues of domestic and international control were inevitably joined. Domestic legislation on atomic energy that took too literally the notion of atomic secrets would make the exchange of basic scientific information with other countries—and particularly Russia—impossible. Equally, an ambitious proposal for sharing atomic information with Russia might alienate the congressional support necessary for passage of a bill on domestic control. As a consequence, the question of domestic control, like that of approaching Russia on the bomb, was beginning to split the Truman administration by the fall of 1945.

His personal sympathy for the cooperative approach already known in the administration, Acheson adamantly opposed deleting from his draft of the President's speech an endorsement of the principle of international control.

The question of future international cooperation in the speech was finally resolved by Truman himself in a roundabout way—a way reminiscent, indeed, of his manner of dealing with the subject of the bomb's postwar control at Potsdam. Instructing Groves, therefore, to forward the vital details on the bomb to Samuel I. Rosenman—his close friend and personal speechwriter—Truman had Rosenman reconcile the divergent purposes of the speech. The final product, given Congress on

October 3, 1945, was stretched too thin over too many contending points to bear any real weight, but contained some significant changes from the original draft. It marked, moreover, Truman's first real step toward a decision concerning the bomb and postwar policy since he had taken office—for these deletions and additions to Acheson's version almost certainly reflected the President's own thinking.[28]

Truman chose to delete from the speech a section containing Acheson's caveat that secrecy could not prevent foreign research from coming abreast of the United States "in a comparatively short time." The President thereby tacitly upheld the notion of an atomic secret that could be kept.[29]

The speech showed other signs that Truman was quietly—but decisively—moving away from Stimson's advice. The text as delivered agreed with Stimson that discussion of international control could not be "safely delayed" until the meeting of the United Nations, but dodged the critical issue of the timing of the talks by specifying that they would begin with Great Britain and Canada first, and only then with "other nations." But most important—as newspapers of the following day pointed out—was the fact that Truman did not mention Russia once in the entire course of his remarks.

By his speech, therefore, the President had not ruled out the possibility of a direct approach to Russia on the bomb, but that approach could no longer take first precedence and would involve nothing more than the exchange of basic scientific information. Just such an exchange, significantly, had been characterized by Truman himself as "impossible" in the climate of opinion weeks earlier. Conclusive evidence that the President had considered Stimson's proposal—and rejected it—would be forthcoming less than a week later.

"A Policy of Exclusion"

An irony of the atomic age—as well as a characteristic of the informal Truman presidency—is that Truman's first declaration of policy concerning Russia and the atomic bomb came not at the modern Cecilienhof Palace in Potsdam or in the hushed chambers of Congress, but on the porch of Linda Lodge at Reelfoot Lake near Tiptonville, Tennessee.

The President's visit to the lake was part of a trip that began in Caruthersville, Missouri, and featured an appearance at the Pemiscot Country Fair, a campaign tradition for Truman since his early days in the Senate. Truman had made reference to the atomic bomb in a speech at Caruthersville on October 7, and he returned to that subject the following day in a press conference at the lodge. Despite the rustic surroundings and the impromptu nature of the press conference, Truman underscored its importance by reiterating that his remarks were "on the record." It was in this setting that he announced his decision not to share America's atomic discovery with the rest of the world.

That announcement came in response to a question on the bomb and was couched in a prepared definition of what Truman understood the atomic secret to be. Here the President made a distinction between three types of secret. First was the "scientific knowledge that resulted in the atomic bomb," and that was virtually "worldwide knowledge already." Second was the "know-how," or engineering secrets, which only the United States presently possessed, but which America's partner in the bomb project—Great Britain—might develop in a few years on her own. Third was the "combination of industrial capacity and re-sources necessary to produce the bomb," which the United States alone enjoyed and without which, Truman claimed, the first two secrets were useless. It was that combination which had enabled the United States to mass-produce automobiles and to build "the greatest long-distance bomber in the world."

Truman's definition of the atomic secret, in fact, was not unlike the distinction that Stimson had made between scientific and industrial information on the bomb. But whereas Stimson had pointed out this distinction in order to propose sharing scientific information on the bomb with the Russians, Truman now used it to justify *excluding* both the Soviets and the British from such an exchange. If no other country could build a bomb without the necessary combination of industry and resources which only the United States possessed, this argument went, there would be no point in divulging either basic scientific information *or* secret "know-how."

As though to underscore this point and to resolve any ambiguity in his statement, Truman told the assembled reporters that if other nations were to "catch up" to the United States, "they will have to do it on their own hook, just as we did."[30]

Truman's reasoning in his statement on the bomb is, at best, curious. When asked for the source of information in making his decision, the President had unhesitatingly said, "Vannevar Bush." Bush had indeed differentiated between types of secrets in the stormy Cabinet meeting's aftermath, and in his letter to Truman some days later. But the distinction he drew had been with the purpose of urging the President along the path toward international control of the weapon, and away from "a secret arms race on atomic energy." A policy of secrecy could not guarantee security, Bush reminded Truman, and might actually be to the benefit of the Russians, who were more accustomed to it.

Bush had also countered what he knew to be the most likely argument against cooperating with Russia, alluding to Stimson's characterization of Byrnes as having the bomb on his "hip." A policy of cooperation, beginning with scientific interchange and perhaps culminating in shared control of the bomb, might, he admitted, involve "giving away the gun on our hips as we carry on difficult negotiations." But "it is doubtful if [this] move . . . involves giving away anything at all." For the bomb—perhaps an ultimate weapon in war—was too large and destructive to be a useful instrument of diplomacy; a fact that was known to the Russians as well, Bush intimated: "There is no powder in the gun, for it could not be drawn, and this is certainly known."[31]

The President's argument at the lake accepted only part of Bush's logic—the distinction between types of secrets. Truman was not yet ready to concede Bush's main premise that the bomb was unusable in diplomacy, at least until the results were in from its first test in that role in London. Moreover, he had turned around the point that Bush had been trying to make. There was a promise of cooperation with the United Nations in Truman's statement, but the Russians themselves were not to be approached first—directly or indirectly—on the subject of the bomb.

The policy that Truman outlined at Linda Lodge ultimately ignored also the vital warning in Stimson's September memo that the atomic monopoly could not be kept, and that the question of when the Russians might get the bomb was "not nearly so important" as gaining their cooperation first.

In brief, the rationale for Truman's decision in favor of a policy of exclusion was partly from Bush and partly from Stimson. But its conclusion was from Groves. The President's discourse on the atomic secret accepted, therefore, the general's assurance that the monopoly would endure. Even the language of Truman's statement closely followed that of Groves' speech less than two weeks before, suggesting that the Manhattan Project director had by now become an unofficial adviser to the

President on the international as well as the domestic aspects of atomic energy.*

The significance of what Truman had said in the casual atmosphere of the Tennessee resort was not lost upon the journalists attending his press conference. The following day, for example, the *New York Times* headlined: "U.S. Will Not Share Atom Bomb Secret, President Asserts; Calls Industrial 'Know-How' the Most Important Factor, Not Scientific Knowledge: Our Resources the Key."[33]

Nor—according to one observer—did the Russians miss the importance of Truman's announcement, although they as usual had no direct comment on the President's statement at the lodge. Returning from a trip to Moscow where he had met and talked with high Soviet officials, Hugh Carter, an American pacifist and friend of Henry Wallace, related to the latter his impression of how, "after the President made his Reelfoot Lake statement, the whole attitude in Russia changed." "Carter seemed to think that the change in attitude between the time the President sent his atomic bomb statement to Congress and the time he made his offhand newspaper statement had a pronounced effect on international affairs and especially on Russia."[34]

Certainly Truman had reason to hope that his Tennessee statement would finally resolve the twin questions of Russia and the bomb, while still leaving the possibility of international control for the future. His unusual press conference at the lake, therefore, had seemingly been with the purpose of putting that controversy behind him.

The President had already taken other steps as well to disentangle himself personally, if not his administration, from the debate over the bomb. Before leaving on his trip to Missouri, Truman finally bowed to pressure from Prime Minister Attlee and Canadian Prime Minister Mackenzie King and agreed to a mid-November meeting at Washington to discuss the atomic bomb. The summit was at best a qualified concession, however, since the President's statement a few days later at Linda

---

*Groves' own notes for his October 1945 briefing of Samuel Rosenman reveal the message that he wished to convey to the President. Groves advised against any cooperation with the British in the matter of the bomb, and urged that any "Russian affair must have advantages to us other than [their] alleged word. . . . We have no reason to fear," he told Rosenman. "We can always be ahead." Significantly, on this occasion Groves also repeated his earlier prediction that, by "normal effort," the Russians would take from ten to twenty years to build a bomb. His reason was revealed in the last point he meant to bring up with Rosenman—"raw materials."[32] Concerning the supposed raw-materials monopoly and its importance to the atomic secret, see Chapter 5.

Lodge made it plain that this meeting would not include any disclosure of atomic information, even to America's allies.

In his letters to Attlee and King, and by a statement at the lodge as well, Truman indicated that Secretary of State Byrnes and not he would henceforth be responsible for carrying out the administration's policy on the bomb. Truman himself undoubtedly felt that a personal role was no longer necessary. The policy he had set dictated that a test of Russian intentions would not be made by a direct approach on the bomb. Instead—at least for the interim—the United States would follow the course of monopoly and exclusion that Stimson, Bush, and Acheson had urged against.

"Tending Toward Power Politics"

Neither at the time nor later in his recollections did Truman feel it necessary to explain his reasons for deciding against even a symbolic show of cooperation on the bomb. Concerning the source of that decision, however, there can be little doubt. Some time after the press conference at the lodge, Truman was asked how he had decided to "keep the secret." "I was relying on my own judgment," he replied.[35]

That Truman himself was aware of the importance of his remarks at Linda Lodge was indicated by a candid exchange some days after the press conference—a conversation at the White House with his longtime Missouri friend Fyke Farmer.* Citing the headline of the day about maintaining secrecy, Farmer's first inquiry at this interview was blunt. "Then, Mister President, what it amounts to is this. That the armaments race is on, is that right?" The President's guest records that Truman answered affirmatively, "but added that we would stay ahead." According to Farmer's account, the President "said that maybe we could get world government in a thousand years or something like that, but that it was nothing more than a theory at the present time."

Truman's fellow Missourian also thought that Truman's frame of mind concerning the decision was significant. "He was alert, smiling, and gracious. . . . His attitude appeared to me to be that of a man who had made up his mind and was supremely confident of the correctness of the decision which he had made."[36]

---

*A successful Washington attorney, Farmer would later achieve notoriety in a case connected with the bomb—as one of the lawyers who, in 1953, attempted to gain a last-minute stay of execution for Ethel and Julius Rosenberg, the convicted "atom spies."

Truman's candor in this private meeting is revealing, in fact, not only of the thinking behind his decision, but of his own pessimistic assessment concerning the future of international control of atomic energy. The President's words thus indicated his personal belief that the policy of monopoly and exclusion was more than the temporary expedient he was representing it to be, and that it might become a lasting feature of American diplomacy in the atomic age.

What, then, was the impetus behind Truman's decision to reject the direct approach to Russia? The collapse in early October of the Council of Foreign Ministers meeting in London was plainly a blow to Stimson's proposal. Byrnes publicly blamed the failure there on Russian intransigence. "The outlook is very dark," he confided to an aide. But the evidence, including Truman's earlier comment about the Russians being "direct action fellows" and the prospects for getting along with them, suggests that the President was neither as shocked nor as disappointed as Byrnes by the Russians' behavior; and that Truman, in any event, did not necessarily consider the fiasco in London a serious blow to Soviet-American relations. His advice to the troubled secretary of state had been blunt: "Give 'em hell and stand your guns," he wired Byrnes on September 17.[37]

Nor was public pressure alone the reason for the choice of a policy of exclusion. Unlike the decision to drop the bomb upon Hiroshima, the decision of what to do with the bomb after the war was caught up in the course of an emotional public debate. Consequently, sentiment against disclosure of atomic secrets was enormous by fall 1945. The careful line that the President purposefully drew in his Linda Lodge statement between three types of atomic secrets would nonetheless have made it possible for him to propose an international interchange on scientific information concerning atomic energy had he wished—as, indeed, was Bush's intention. For such information was, Truman admitted, "worldwide knowledge already." Yet not even this symbolic gesture of cooperation with former allies was to be attempted.

A significant clue to Truman's reason for rejecting the direct approach was forthcoming three weeks after the Tennessee statement, in the course of his first major address on foreign policy. There the President seemed to accept the inevitability of confrontation with Russia. In a clear allusion to the continuing Soviet-American imbroglio over eastern Europe, Truman announced that his administration "would refuse to recognize any government imposed upon any nation by the force of any foreign power." The atomic bomb, which he had already announced would not be shared with any other country, did not alter but rather "accelerated" the "development and application" of American foreign policy. "The possession in our hands of this new power of destruction we regard as a sacred trust," Truman assured.[38]

The President's decision to shift the responsibility for administering this trust from himself to Byrnes seemed, as well, a purposeful step away from cooperation and toward confrontation with the Russians. Byrnes was one of the earliest and most avid proponents in the administration of the aggressive use of the bomb in diplomacy. In this light, Truman's earlier comment about getting along with the Russians takes on a different—and more complex—meaning. Was the President consciously adopting a hard line toward the Russians on the bomb in the belief that confrontation, and not cooperation, would show that the members of his administration were "direct action fellows" too?

Byrnes, Stimson had warned in early September, meant to use the bomb as a bargaining counter in London. "In my plan [there are] less dangers than in his and we would be on the right path toward . . . establishment of an international world," Stimson told Truman on that occasion. He added that Byrnes' approach meant "we would . . . be tending to revert to power politics."[39] The choice of Byrnes thus suggests that a reversion to power politics—at least in the matter of the atomic bomb—was what the President desired.

This move also freed Truman to deal with other current national problems. One of these was the reconversion of the domestic economy to peacetime without the economic "letdown" that had followed previous wars. The Potsdam Conference had interrupted work on the President's program for economic reconversion, and so his message on the subject—which Truman later wrote was "my assumption of the office of President in my own right"—did not go before Congress until the fall. Initial reaction to Truman's "Economic Bill of Rights" in this program had been favorable; but the subsequent charge by conservatives that the President was actually "out-New Dealing the New Deal" by his proposed economic reforms, together with union strikes toward the end of September, signaled an approaching end to Truman's honeymoon with the people and Congress. Indeed, by early October the extent to which postwar economic problems were becoming an issue as important as the atomic bomb was dramatically shown when news of presidential action against strikers took precedence over coverage of Truman's speech on the domestic control of atomic energy in the morning papers.[40]

Contrary to Truman's evident expectation, his announcement at Linda Lodge, his declaration of the "sacred trust," and his delegation of responsibility to Byrnes did not finally settle the question of American diplomacy and the atomic bomb. In fact, discord at the London Council of Foreign Ministers had shown how policy concerning Russia and policy on the bomb were still unavoidably intertwined.

As Stimson had predicted, Byrnes meant to confront the Russians at London "having the bomb in his pocket." The unanticipated reaction of the Soviets to this effort at atomic diplomacy, however, would reopen the whole question of Russia and the bomb. For a time, at least, it would also take it out of the President's hands.

3

London:
The Dog That Didn't Bark

"I know how to deal with the Russians. It's just like the U.S. Senate. You build a post office in their state, and they'll build a post office in our state."

James F. Byrnes, September 1945

"The Russians are stubborn, obstinate, and they don't scare."

James F. Byrnes, October 1945

"The New Mexico Situation Has Given Us Great Power"

It was only fitting that Truman should assign the stewardship of diplomacy on the bomb to James F. (Jimmy) Byrnes, for the latter had been among the first to recognize how the bomb might affect the balance of world power.[1] When Stimson and Groves briefed the President in late April their news had not come as a complete surprise to Truman, since he had been told of the bomb by Byrnes upon returning from FDR's funeral. "Byrnes had already told me," Truman wrote in his memoirs, "that the weapon might be so powerful as to be potentially capable of wiping out entire cities and killing people on an unprecedented scale. And he had added that in his belief the bomb might well put us in a position to dictate our own terms at the end of the war."[2]

Byrnes' reference at that time had undoubtedly concerned only the surrender terms of America's still-undefeated enemies in the war, Germany and Japan. But his concept of the bomb's utility went beyond the war as well. The bomb, he thought, might also provide the lever by which the Russians could be moved closer to the American position on the postwar diplomatic settlement. Mere U.S. possession of the weapon, he told a scientist in May 1945, might make the Russians "more manageable" on the question of eastern Europe.[3]

Byrnes had been visibly buoyed at Potsdam by reports of the successful atomic test, and he correspondingly extended his expectations of what the bomb could accomplish. "The New Mexico situation has given us great power," he reflected. "In the last analysis it would control."[4]

Byrnes' plans for the bomb at Potsdam, indeed, went beyond mere hope and expectation. Initially opposed to telling the Russians about the bomb, he changed his mind upon hearing the dramatic results of the test explosion at Alamogordo. Along with Truman, Byrnes realized that use of the bomb might make Soviet entry into the war against Japan unnecessary. Moreover, he believed that mention of the bomb at Potsdam bolstered America's bargaining position in Asia, hence justifying more favorable terms for America's client in China, Chiang Kai-shek. Before the news from Alamogordo, Byrnes had privately conceded that Truman might have to back away from Roosevelt's Yalta pledge on self-determination by granting a stake in China to the Russians in exchange for their promised attack upon Japan. But on July 23—a week after the explosion in New Mexico—Russian intervention no longer seemed necessary. On that day Byrnes advised the Chinese foreign minister, T. V. Soong, that he should hold out against Russian demands for territory or influence.

In what was the first true practice of atomic diplomacy—using the bomb to gain a diplomatic advantage—Byrnes hoped that the U.S. atomic monopoly might be used to support Chiang against Stalin. As Byrnes' longtime aide and confidant, Walter Brown, noted in his journal at Potsdam: "JFB determined to outmaneuver Stalin on China. Hopes Soong will stand firm. Then he feels Japan will surrender before Russia goes to war and this will save China."[5]

Behind Byrnes' strategy at Potsdam there was another consideration to the bomb's effect than enabling Soong and Chiang to "stand firm," Brown observed in a late-July entry: "JFB still hoping for time, believing after atomic bomb Japan will surrender and Russia will not get in so much on the kill, thereby being in a position to press for claims against China."[6]

Even if Russia could not be prevented from entering the war, use of the bomb might still compel Japan's surrender before Soviet armies had advanced very far in Manchuria. Together, the military requirement of forcing the Japanese surrender and the political requirement of keeping Russia out of Asia resolved whatever doubts Byrnes might have had about using the bomb. "It was important to bring about an end to the

war, and if possible to do that before Russia came into the war," he
would recollect some years after Potsdam.[7]

Byrnes' interest in the bomb at Potsdam was also noted by two
members of the American delegation there—Henry Stimson and Joseph
E. Davies. Davies, in particular, was concerned with the secretary of
state's evident enthusiasm for the weapon's effect upon diplomacy:
"Byrnes' attitude that the atomic bomb assured ultimate success in
negotiations disturbed me more than his description of its success
amazed me."[8]

The first experiment in atomic diplomacy failed dismally. Even with the
use of the bomb the war did not come to an abrupt end, and the Chinese
were powerless to prevent the Soviet occupation of Manchuria. But,
significantly, this failure did not alter Byrnes' belief that the bomb might
make a difference in diplomacy—after, if not during, the war.

Less than two weeks after the destruction of Hiroshima and
Nagasaki, therefore, Byrnes told an American atomic scientist "that he
and the rest of the gang should pursue their work full force . . . to keep
ahead of the race." Byrnes was already looking forward to the possibility
of what the scientists termed a "super-bomb"—the hydrogen bomb—
many times more powerful than the weapon that had been used against
the two Japanese cities. As long as Byrnes continued to believe that the
bomb might become the "master card" of which Stimson had spoken,
he would resist any attempt to restrict development of the bomb, to
achieve its international control, or to approach the Russians directly on
the subject.[9]

The arena where the postwar value of the bomb in diplomacy would
be tested was the Council of Foreign Ministers. There Byrnes clearly
intended to play a central role. Inevitably, the bomb too would have a
not insubstantial part in such meetings. It was while Byrnes was preparing for the first council in London that Stimson—then in Washington
to put the finishing touches on his proposal for a direct approach to
Russia—discovered the extent to which the secretary of state intended
to rely on the bomb at London.

Approaching the first postwar meeting with the Russians on his
own and with, as Stimson worried, "the presence of the bomb in his
pocket," Byrnes was, however, to encounter a completely unexpected
Russian response to his further effort at atomic diplomacy. Indeed, the
importance of the London conference to Byrnes would be what did *not*

happen—specifically, the unanticipated failure of the Russians to grant concessions or to be "more manageable" because of the bomb. Like the Sherlock Holmes mystery in which the signal clue was the expected event that failed to occur—the dog not heard in the night— the significance of the bomb was its apparent insignificance at the conference.

"You Know We Have the Atomic Bomb"

That Byrnes expected to play the central role in London is especially ironic since he had come very close to playing no role at all in diplomacy by the end of the Roosevelt administration. As a former senator from South Carolina and onetime associate justice of the Supreme Court, Byrnes had self-importantly adopted the title given him by the press of FDR's "Assistant President" when Roosevelt appointed him wartime director of economic stabilization and, later, director of war mobilization. But Byrnes had already begun his slide from presidential grace by the Democratic convention of 1944, which, in a surprise move, gave the vice-presidential nomination not to him but to Truman.

Among the reasons put forward for disaffection with Byrnes were his political liabilities as a southerner, a Catholic-turned-Protestant, and —not least important—an ambitious and accomplished politician.

Resentful of the turn of fate which had kept him from being FDR's designated successor, Byrnes resigned from the administration on April 8—a move that Roosevelt characterized as "primadonnaish"—and returned to his home in South Carolina.[10]

Roosevelt's death four days later dramatically reversed Byrnes' political fortunes, bringing him out of retirement and into the new administration. Senator Truman had earlier worked with Byrnes in the latter's capacity as war mobilization director and, after a decent interval, replaced Secretary of State Edward Stettinius with the South Carolinian. Byrnes was Stimson's choice for the President's personal representative on the Interim Committee, and it was while in that role that he first came to appreciate the diplomatic as well as the military potential of the bomb.

Despite the outward ease of their relationship, from the outset Byrnes quietly resented Truman's new and unsought preeminence. For Byrnes, this attitude was more than just unhappiness over the turn of events in 1944. While in Congress he had a reputation as a "troubleshooter," and later earned the sobriquet at Yalta of the "Great Compromiser." His talent for personal diplomacy demonstrated qualities which Byrnes felt were particularly useful in foreign affairs, and which Truman obviously seemed to lack.

The new President, to be sure, had allowed his secretary of state sufficient freedom at Potsdam, even to the extent of alienating other members of the American delegation. "I'm backing up Jim Byrnes to the limits," Truman wrote from the conference.[11]

But, as Byrnes was aware, with the exception of the Council of Foreign Ministers idea—in which Truman had shown little interest—the policies followed and the decisions made at Potsdam had been Truman's.

At London, all this would be changed. Criticized at Potsdam by Stimson for "hugging matters in this conference pretty close to his bosom," Byrnes intended to have his way at the council simply by excluding rival points of view from the American delegation, and by keeping the State Department uninformed of his plans and activities. His policy of silence was a purposeful one, having its origins not only in his desire to dominate the negotiations at London but in a distrust of those in Washington who might resent his independence.

Byrnes confessed his reason for secrecy to an aide at the end of the first day's meeting: "God Almighty, I might tell the President sometime what happened, but I'm never going to tell those little bastards at the State Department anything about it."[12]

There was another reason as well for Byrnes' discretion. As it had at Potsdam, the bomb presented a tricky problem at London. Indeed, Stimson's characterization of Byrnes approaching the Russians with the bomb figuratively "in his pocket" was, as events developed, particularly apt. Nothing was likely to be gained at London by brandishing the weapon openly before the Russians, for there could be no serious threat of using the bomb against even an intractable Soviet Union. Hiroshima and Nagasaki, moreover, had surely been a sufficiently convincing demonstration of the bomb's power, and any further effort to draw attention to the weapon might well result in Russian demands that they be allowed to share in its control—Byrnes' initial concern at Potsdam. Worse, the Russians at London might use just such a heavy-handed American effort to exploit the atomic advantage as a pretext for breaking off the talks altogether.

The value of the atomic bomb as a bargaining counter, therefore, lay in its understated presence at the negotiating table—and in whatever ambiguity of American intentions Byrnes could create concerning its use. Doubtless to preserve that ambiguity, he instructed members of his delegation that they should avoid any mention of the bomb or of atomic energy while in London.[13]

Exactly how the unseen presence of the bomb might affect the Russians at the conference was evidently vague even in Byrnes' mind. But where he expected that it might have an influence had already been made clear. Among the first items upon his agenda at the conference was liberalization of the communist regimes of eastern Europe—an area where he still hoped the bomb would make the Russians "more manageable."

The opening day of the conference, September 11, was to dash this hope, however. As the council got under way it immediately became clear that substance rather than ambiguity counted for more with the Russians. Byrnes had actually intended to open the meeting with a presumedly safe subject on which the two sides would agree—the signing of a peace treaty with Italy and the disposition of former Italian colonies. Instead, Russian Foreign Minister Vyacheslav Molotov had sidetracked the conference onto the issue of ratifying the legitimacy of the governments of Romania, Bulgaria, and Hungary.[14] This block at the outset was taken as a bad omen by Byrnes, who had hoped to have all the peace treaties signed within two weeks. He was likely even more disturbed by the prospect it offered that the Russians were prepared to be less than manageable on eastern Europe.

Most ominous, however, was the fact that it was Molotov himself who broached the subject of the atomic bomb at the conference. The weapon came up in the course of a reception for the two men on September 13, following a day of deadlock, when Byrnes expressed impatience at the council's lack of progress. Molotov, in an observation disconcertingly akin to Stimson's the week before, asked Byrnes if he had "an atomic bomb in his side pocket." "You don't know southerners," Byrnes rejoined, "we carry our artillery in our pocket. If you don't cut out all this stalling and let us get down to work, I'm going to pull an atomic bomb out of my hip pocket and let you have it."[15]

This apparently good-natured repartee and the laughter of Molotov and his interpreter which followed—not shared by Byrnes—masked what was unquestionably a tense moment for the secretary of state, and probably for Molotov as well. Specifically, Molotov's outwardly casual remark served notice that the Russians were clearly aware of America's atomic advantage but were unwilling to be intimidated by the bomb.

In case this message had been unclear on the first occasion, it was conveyed to Byrnes again by Molotov later that same evening. At a cocktail party with Byrnes and British Foreign Minister Ernest Bevin, a seemingly tipsy Molotov—according to the subsequent U.S. intelligence report—stepped out of the room for a minute and then suddenly reappeared. Embracing Byrnes awkwardly, the normally dour Molotov whispered to the unsettled secretary of state: "You know we have the atomic bomb." "With nothing further being said," the report noted, "Mr. Gousev [of the Russian delegation] put his hand on Molotov's shoulder and escorted him out of the room, leaving the impression at the time upon those present that Mr. Molotov had probably said something he shouldn't."[16]

Transparent as this charade was, Byrnes took it earnestly enough to cite it when he returned to Washington as an indication of the Russians' interest in developing their own bomb. He had been confirmed in this opinion at the conference when Molotov quipped that Byrnes was not only more gifted than he, but that the American had the added advantage of an atomic bomb.

Such incidents, in fact, belied the seriousness of the stakes involved. Molotov's persistent efforts to draw unwanted attention to the atomic bomb as an issue between the two men represented not only an embarrassment for Byrnes, but a surprise turnabout in atomic diplomacy.

Since the start of the council, therefore, it had become increasingly apparent to Byrnes that the bomb was a bust as a hoped-for master card in diplomacy. As the conference continued, moreover, it began to dawn on him that America's atomic monopoly, far from being an asset at London, might be instead a diplomatic liability there.

"The Cause of All His Troubles"

In an apparent effort to get the council off dead center, Byrnes revived in overtures to Molotov the sort of diplomatic horse trading that had characterized diplomacy in the pre-atomic age. The Russian yielded to Byrnes by agreeing to discuss the disposition of Italian colonies, where Russia sought a trusteeship of the former colony of Tripolitania (part of present-day Libya). Significantly, however, even this concession from Molotov seemed to raise for Byrnes the unwelcome specter of the bomb.

The Russian claim to Tripolitania had been made as early as Potsdam, and had been given justification months before Potsdam, when

Byrnes' predecessor, Stettinius, declared that the Soviet Union would be "eligible" for trusteeship of an Italian colony after the war. At London, Molotov explained Russia's interest in the North African country "so as to have bases in the Mediterranean for her merchant fleet."[17]

Yet Byrnes professed to discover a more sinister motive in the Soviet demand. "He saw where Molotov was going," Walter Brown noted of Byrnes' comment to a member of the American delegation. Molotov would, "through the Yugoslavs and others, dominate Tripolitania and thus have a base. What he is after is the uranium in the Belgian Congo." The American contract for that uranium, Byrnes had said, was "no stronger than the battleship that guards it. If the Soviets could get Tripolitania they would be in a position to head us off from this uranium," he concluded.[18]

Byrnes' reasoning that the Russians—"through the Yugoslavs and others"—wanted an African colony so as to capture the Congo's uranium seems byzantine at best. But it was a paranoia that he at least shared at London with Bevin—and that Molotov would exploit in still another subtle jest. The Russian minister told Bevin at the council that "if you won't give us one of the Italian colonies, we should be quite content to have the Belgian Congo." Unamused, Bevin concluded from this incident "that the Russians were more interested in obtaining uranium than anything else."[19]

Although the dispute over eastern Europe was certainly a more substantive issue of diplomacy at London than the fate of Tripolitania, the latter was no less important to Byrnes for demonstrating the role that the bomb seemed to play in contributing to the rancor and distrust that had characterized the Council of Foreign Ministers.[20] Once back in Washington after the breakup of the conference, he would brand the trusteeship question "the cause of all his troubles" at London.[21]

"We Were Going to Have Troubles with the Soviets"

Unwilling even to consider the Russian demand for Tripolitania, Byrnes was desperately searching for some common ground with the Russians by the second week of the deadlocked conference. Accordingly, he proposed to Molotov that Russia and the United States join with France and Italy in a twenty-five year guarantee of cooperation against German military recrudescence. The suggested pact, which offered a symbolic revival of the wartime alliance against the Axis—and had been reserved for just that purpose—was clearly Byrnes' effort to accentuate the positive in the increasingly contentious relationship with Russia.*

This initiative, however, proved unavailing. Two days later Molotov advised Byrnes that Russia would no longer participate in the conference while France and China had representation equal to the Big Three on substantive issues such as the European peace treaties. The Soviets had, in fact, reluctantly agreed to this arrangement at Potsdam, only to be consistently outvoted, four to one, by the Western powers on procedural issues at London. Yet Molotov's sudden turnaround on this point was probably not aimed solely at rectification of what he termed an earlier "mistake."

The Russians may well have concluded, therefore, that the present pro-Soviet governments in the Balkans were a better guarantee of Russian security than the proffered pact. Also, this threat to break up the conference over the rights of the smaller powers might have been intended to restrict discussion at London to the interests of the Big Three, where Molotov was eager to add the question of Russian influence in Japan and Greece to the council's agenda.

Concerning the conference's collapse, Byrnes was in a particularly vulnerable position. Neither the administration nor the public at home —nor Byrnes himself—had expected or prepared for a debacle at the first postwar meeting of the Big Three. The secretary of state had breezily assured a member of the American delegation before they left for London that he knew "how to deal with the Russians. It's just like the U.S. Senate. You build a post office in their state, and they'll build a post office in our state."[23] Unlike his former Senate colleagues, however, the Russians had not shown themselves willing to bargain at London.

No longer complacent, Byrnes wired Truman on September 24 of a more modest goal. It was now his intention "to make every effort to hold it [the Council] together"—at least until a more cosmetic ending could be arranged for the break-off of negotiations and the formal end of Soviet-American cooperation.

---

*While the idea for such a pact had been put forward by Republican Senator Arthur Vandenberg only some weeks before the council met, the agreements reached at Potsdam made it superfluous. In a meeting with Joseph E. Davies nearly a year after the London conference, Truman indicated that he had meant the treaty to be a test case of Soviet-American relations. According to Davies' recollection, Truman said: "It was calling their bluff. [He] feared it would be of no use. It was more than fair. It would have appealed to Stalin, [but] Molotov was not that kind."[22]

Molotov proved also unresponsive to compromises on side issues, however. He even turned the treaty on German militarism against Byrnes by demanding that such an arrangement pertain equally to Japan, where the Soviets had been denied a seat on the postwar control commission.

This last demand by Molotov increased the suspicion that Byrnes had had since the start of the conference that the Russian foreign minister was himself one of the main obstacles to progress at London. Byrnes complained to Walter Brown that Molotov, "in his slick dip way," intended to dominate the smaller countries as Hitler had done, circumventing what was really Stalin's sincere desire for peace. The only hope for avoiding a collapse of the conference, he believed, lay in personal intervention by Stalin. To that end, Byrnes goaded Truman into appealing to the Soviet leader that he remove this latest stumbling block to progress in the negotiations.

Truman, who had earlier had his own run-in with Molotov, may still have shared Byrnes' favorable view of the Soviet leader. "Stalin," the President told Henry Wallace in October 1945, "was a fine man who wanted to do the right thing." Truman concluded, "Stalin is an honest man who is easy to get along with—who arrives at sound decisions." After Potsdam, the President's assessment of Stalin had been more critical—if still understanding: "I thought he was a son-of-a-bitch," Truman told a sailor on the *Augusta.* "But I guess he thought I was one too." Byrnes' respect for Stalin was evidently reciprocated. While at Potsdam the Soviet leader had called him "the most honest horse thief he had ever met."[24] Stalin, however, ultimately proved no more tractable at Potsdam than Molotov, and refused to yield on any substantive issue.

Even this did not entirely discourage the irrepressible Byrnes. Already planning a second meeting of foreign ministers for Moscow the following November—where he expected to deal with Stalin personally —Byrnes had not yet given up on the first.[25] In order to keep the conference alive—and perhaps also to salvage his own reputation—he was willing, in fact, to go a surprisingly long way toward accommodating the Soviets.

On September 30, Byrnes met privately with John Foster Dulles, the senior Republican member of the American delegation, to suggest dropping France and China from the conference in a concession to the Russians. Dulles later claimed that Byrnes was only prevented from yielding to Molotov on this sticking point by the Republican's strong assurance that he would not have bipartisan support for such a move. Reluctantly, and without discussing the matter with his staff, Byrnes decided to abandon the conference.

Stalemated virtually from its start, the Council of Foreign Ministers adjourned on October 2, 1945, without agreeing on when—or whether —to meet again. Despite this failure, Byrnes had decided not to abandon diplomacy altogether. Fearful, therefore, that any formal acknowledgment of his disagreement with Molotov might make a second conference less likely, he did not issue the press release he had drafted blaming the failure of the conference on the Russians.

Throughout the frustrating sessions with Molotov, Byrnes knew he had Truman's backing. Nonetheless, he returned to Washington dispirited. Flying home from London, the secretary of state confided to the delegation's interpreter, Charles (Chip) Bohlen, his concern about public reaction to the collapse of the council. As the architect of the conference, Byrnes considered himself to be one of the principal victims of its failure.[26]

In Washington, Byrnes also unburdened himself to Dulles. He had realized at Potsdam, he told the Republican, that "we were going to have troubles with the Soviets." But it was not until London that he fully realized the Russians were "stubborn, obstinate, and they don't scare."[27]

"Tell Them to Go to Hell"

Once back at the State Department, Byrnes reflected on the lessons that had been learned at London. It was a task necessary not only for understanding what had gone wrong at the conference but, just as important, for explaining that failure to the President and the nation.

No justification, however, was necessary for Truman. His last advice to Byrnes at London had been unconcerned with the prospects for failure there. "Do everything you can to continue, but in the final analysis do whatever you think is right and tell them to go to hell if you have to," Truman wired the secretary of state. Indeed, the President would tell Edward Stettinius at the end of October that the collapse of the council did not upset him because this "was almost bound to happen at the end of the war. It was perhaps better to [have it] happen out in the open at this stage," Truman reasoned. He had also never shared Byrnes' high expectations for what the conference might accomplish. In a meeting with Joseph E. Davies the previous month, for example, Truman had alluded defensively to "the atomic bomb situation" being "far more dangerous to the unity necessary to preserve peace than any of Jim Byrnes' conferences."[28]

Byrnes displayed no such equanimity toward the failure of his diplomacy. Nor could he afford to. His political enemies in the administration—particularly Admiral William Leahy, a Roosevelt holdover and one of many Truman advisers hostile to Byrnes—had disparaged Byrnes' idea of personal diplomacy before the conference, and now betrayed no disappointment at its frustration. It was clear to Byrnes, therefore, that he himself would take the blame for the fiasco in London, just as he had initially hoped to take credit for its success—unless the responsibility for the conference's failure could be squarely put upon the Russians.

Byrnes began the process of what one historian has aptly termed "onus-shifting" shortly after he returned from London.[29] In a nationwide radio address on the conference he attributed its collapse to the dispute over eastern Europe, and specifically to the "Soviet delegation's disappointment with the failure of Great Britain and the United States to recognize the Bulgarian Government." Bohlen professed to see a subtle change in Byrnes' mood with this speech. Before London the secretary's speeches had stressed "patience and firmness." The emphasis now, Bohlen claimed, was upon "firmness and patience."

But while Byrnes was "rather anxious to have the Russians shown up in a bad light" about London, Henry Wallace noted, he was still careful in his public utterances not to make the Soviet-American disagreements there appear irremediable. He was also visibly relieved when American newspaper editorials put the blame for the failure of the conference upon the Russians. Overall, Wallace remembered, Byrnes took "a rather judicial attitude" toward the Soviets at Cabinet meetings.

Ever conscious of both his public image and of the prospect for a second Council of Foreign Ministers, Byrnes perhaps consciously put a better face on the disappointing meeting with Molotov than he personally believed events deserved. Privately, he was bitter, if not pessimistic. He "had never been so sorely tried," Byrnes told Wallace in late October, although he agreed with Truman that "we were going to find some way to get along with the Russians." Earlier, he had told Davies "that the London conference in general and Molotov in particular were much worse" than he or the public knew. "Molotov was insufferable." "If he ever told the Senate what Molotov told him," Byrnes added, "the situation would have been very much worse."[30]

In private, Byrnes doubted that eastern Europe had been the real cause of the conference's breakdown or should be a serious obstacle to improved Soviet-American relations. At London he had ultimately been conciliatory on the question of American recognition for pro-Soviet regimes in the Balkans. The insurmountable barrier to such recognition, he had patiently explained to Molotov, was the Senate, which would refuse to ratify any peace treaty with a government that was not "sufficiently representative." Some weeks after his return to Washington, Byrnes seemed to move even closer to a compromise with Molotov. At the end of October, therefore, he delivered a public speech in which he argued that Russia had legitimate security interests in eastern Europe— a view in marked contrast to Truman's statement just days earlier that the United States would refuse to recognize governments that had been installed by the Soviet Union. Byrnes, in fact, then had or would soon develop a certain sympathy for the Russian position on eastern Europe. In a conversation of early December 1945 with Joseph E. Davies, he said that "the fact that the Soviets did not take their case to the public [concerning eastern Europe] didn't mean they didn't have a case." Byrnes, Davies records, believed that there were instances in which the Russians "might have had a good case," but they had failed to bring it up before the public.[31]

Writing for his memoirs more than a year after the breakdown of the conference, Byrnes revised his earlier explanation that the Balkans had been the cause of Soviet intransigence at London. A meeting at Moscow in November 1945 between Stalin and United States Ambassador to Russia Averell Harriman revealed, Byrnes wrote, that the Soviets at London had been upset not because of American policy on eastern Europe, but because of Russia's exclusion from the postwar control commission on Japan. "The remarkable performance that had led to the breakdown of the London Conference had been stimulated by the Russians' belief that they were not being consulted adequately by our officials in Japan," Byrnes concluded in this account.[32]

The amended view that the London debacle had been brought about because of Japan is significant in light of the subsequent Byrnes-Truman rift, since Byrnes had been willing to add the question of Russian membership on the control commission to the agenda at the conference. "I thought it not unwise," he wrote, "to make a concession on what seems to me an unimportant point." Truman, however, had not considered it such an unimportant point in his declaration of American policy toward postwar Japan on September 24. After the President's speech—which mentioned no role for Russia on the control commission —Byrnes did not allow the question of Japan to come up again at London. The dispute concerning Japan, moreover, only masked a larger disagreement between Truman and his secretary of state.[33]

In the wake of the London conference—if not at the conference itself —a rift developed between Truman and Byrnes on the way to deal with the Soviet Union. Though their differences were yet to come into the open, there was disagreement between the two men not only over the importance of the council itself, but over two potentially vital subjects affecting Russia—eastern Europe and Japan. Either undecided about what had been the fundamental cause of the Russian rejection at London or—more likely—unwilling to oppose Truman directly on a major issue of foreign policy, Byrnes set about searching in late fall of 1945 for an issue apart from eastern Europe or Japan that might serve as the basis for a successful second meeting of foreign ministers. Such an issue was U.S. policy on the atomic bomb—over which Truman had now given Byrnes personal control.

But what to do about Russia and the bomb was more a puzzle after London for Byrnes than it had been before, since Molotov's reversal of atomic diplomacy. He also remained acutely sensitive to the bomb as an issue between the United States and Russia. As he had done before leaving for London, Byrnes instructed the members of his delegation upon their return home not to speak of the bomb in public. Certainly the conspicuous failure of the London council, as well as Molotov's repeated and pointed references to the bomb there, had been evidence enough for Byrnes that the bomb did not work as a threat with the Russians. But he had never conceived of the bomb in any other role, and there could be no question of yielding to Russian demands affecting America's monopoly of the weapon. "We had compromised on Poland, Hungary, and Finland," Byrnes told Davies, and "would try to do the same on Bulgaria and Romania." But Molotov had made it plain that "there would be no settlement concerning the peace unless and until other matters were settled," including that of Tripolitania. And the African colony was too vital to American interests to surrender, Byrnes reiterated. Indeed, the importance which he attached to Russian interest in the atomic bomb now could hardly be overrated. Mistaking Byrnes' stand on Africa as founded in a concern for British holdings there, Davies recalled the "heated" response to his allegation. Byrnes declared "that the uranium deposits in the Congo was what [the Russians] were after, and he went over to the map on the wall to point them out."[34]

At a meeting of the secretaries of state, war, and the navy and their advisers a week after this exchange, Byrnes once again made the connection between the bomb and the troubles he had had at London. He thus "replied emphatically in the affirmative" when asked by one participant if the Russians were really serious about an African colony.*

Confident that the atomic bomb had been in some ways the key to his failure at London, there was as yet for Byrnes no clue on removing the weapon as a source of contention in future meetings with the Russians. Furthermore, he felt that his freedom in making policy on the bomb had been seriously curtailed by the discussions that had taken place in Washington during his absence. Though he had expressed no objections to Stimson's proposal for a direct approach to Russia before leaving for London, Byrnes—with the bitter memory of the fiasco there sharp in his mind—objected to any initiative to the Soviets upon his return. "[B]efore any international discussion of the future of the bomb could take place we must first see whether we can work out a decent peace," he warned. The question of dealing with the Russians on the bomb, Byrnes believed, had been particularly complicated by Truman's statements on atomic energy. He could "foresee," Byrnes said, "that at future meetings Molotov would refer to the President's statement and ask to discuss the whole question of the control of the atomic bomb."[36]

Byrnes' reluctance to discuss the future control of the bomb with the Russians after London is understandable, insofar as that question probably remained unresolved in his own mind. Truman believed that he had set the guidelines of American policy on the bomb in keeping with the views of his secretary of state, since that policy was against cooperating in any way with the Soviets on the bomb. Initially, the two men had shared the same attitude toward the bomb. But, like the bomb itself, the London debacle had changed Soviet-American relations—and, with them, Byrnes' view of the bomb's worth in diplomacy. Indeed, the bomb's obvious failure to make the Russians "more manageable" in negotiations had perhaps also imparted a new sense of its limitations to

---

*A concern for the Congo's uranium was also the reason why Byrnes urged at this meeting that the War Department assist in the repatriation of one thousand Belgian nationals stranded in the Congo since the outbreak of the world war: "[S]ince the world's greatest known supply of uranium lies in the Belgian Congo, special attention should be devoted to our relations with that area."[35]

the President. Reminded by a Cabinet member after the council's failure that at least he still had "an atomic bomb up your sleeve," Truman
responded: "Yes, but I am not sure it can ever be used."[37]

The reassessment of American policy on the bomb which Byrnes
secretly began under his own aegis in early November 1945 suggests that
his thinking was no longer in accord with that of the President. But this
reassessment had barely gotten under way before Byrnes was interrupted
by an urgent and unwelcome interlude with the British.

Throughout the London conference the British had maintained a dis-
creet silence on the subject of the bomb, although they had been both
aware of and disturbed by its role there. "It is our view," Prime Minister
Attlee wrote Truman in mid-October, " . . . that the meeting of Foreign
Ministers was overshadowed by the problem [of the atomic bomb], and
that the prospective conference of the United Nations will be jeopar-
dised unless we have some clearness on our attitude to the problem." By
the phrase "our attitude" Attlee clearly implied an Anglo-American
mutuality of view. The "pressure of immediate problems" at Potsdam,
he suggested genially, had been "too heavy to give us the opportunity
of discussing the implications of success." In actual fact Truman had
shown no interest in discussing the bomb with the prime minister, as
Attlee was well aware.

This was not the first time that Attlee had interceded with the
President for a decision on the bomb. Disturbed by the erroneous press
reports of the "Wallace plan" during the previous month, he had written
Truman for an assurance that Britain would not be excluded from U.S.
policy on the bomb. "Am I to plan for a peaceful or a warlike world?"
Attlee asked. By late October, neither that assurance nor an answer to
the prime minister's entreaty had been received from the President.[38]

Plainly, Truman meant to ignore the importunings of his British
allies, at least until he had made some decision on what was to be done
with the bomb. His statement at Linda Lodge had announced that
decision, and it was one which specifically excluded the kind of direct
and personal cooperation on atomic energy that had characterized the
relationship between Roosevelt and Churchill. A meeting with Attlee,
was, nonetheless, inevitable, Truman realized, if only to acquaint him
with the change in Anglo-American relations and to make that change
official by renegotiating the 1943 Quebec Agreement, which had expired
at war's end. Having postponed it as long as practicable, Truman had
announced in his Navy Day speech of late October that he would meet

in Washington with the British and Canadian prime ministers to discuss the bomb. The President himself intended to play only a minor role in this task, since he had already given notice that Byrnes would preside over policy involving the bomb.

Byrnes, however, was preoccupied at this time with the bomb as it had affected relations with the Russians, not the British. He too had hoped to put off the British until the Russians had been dealt with, but he could hardly ignore Truman's decision. Caught by this conflict, the subsequent Washington conference would inevitably be dominated by concern with an item not even on the agenda—Russia.

"We Hope Genuinely to Open Up Russia"

By late October 1945, the focus of Byrnes' efforts was still upon salvaging the Council of Foreign Ministers and getting on better terms with the Russians. To achieve those ends, he gave a public speech at month's end which he later admitted was "a message directed largely toward the Kremlin." Though the speech concerned a variety of subjects, including eastern Europe, its message was contained in the title: "International Cooperation Must Depend Upon Intelligent Compromise."[39]

Byrnes was also sounding more conciliatory to his peers, now that his anger at Molotov had cooled. In a meeting with the navy and war secretaries on November 6, he echoed the sentiment earlier expressed by Davies when he "emphasized that [the] Soviets believe [the] rest of the world is ganging up on them." According to Forrestal, Byrnes "considered it most important for the future peace of the world to try to work in cooperation with them," and was "very anxious" to get Truman's approval for at least symbolic Soviet participation in the postwar governance of Japan.[40]

On the question of preparing for the upcoming Anglo-American-Canadian summit, however, War Secretary Patterson found Byrnes "non-committal." Concerned by this indifference, Patterson instructed the War Department to prepare a tentative set of American proposals for discussion at the conference.

Patterson was not the only individual in the government concerned with the drift of American policy on the bomb since London. As the President's scientific adviser, Vannevar Bush had been without a sponsor for his views favoring international cooperation on atomic energy since Stimson's retirement. Perhaps in a bid to regain some of that lost influence, Bush had sent Byrnes a seven-page memorandum on the bomb at the beginning of November. Insofar as that memo began by affirming what Byrnes himself believed—that "the great question" at the Washington conference would be Russia—it was to Bush's advice that he now turned.

The memo was a subtle—and timely—recasting of what Bush had told Truman six weeks before. In it Bush revived the notion of three "secrets" to the development of the atomic bomb and used it to propose a three-step plan which had as its ultimate goal the abolition of nuclear weapons. Universal disarmament, however, was hardly the first or the only selling point to Bush's plan: "We hope genuinely to open up Russia, and it will take time."[41]

The first step of the plan was simply the establishment of an international clearinghouse for information on atomic energy which the United States and Britain would ask the Russians to join. "The primary objective of this step is to start Russia down the path of collaboration with us. This step "probably costs us nothing," but would test Russia's desire for cooperation with the West.

The second step provided for the establishment, in slow degrees, of an international inspection system for all the laboratories and industrial plants dealing with the materials used in making atomic bombs.

The third and final step proscribed the construction of atomic bombs by any nation. Under it, existing stockpiles of bombs would be dismantled and their ingredients put into peaceful nuclear power plants; future production of atomic raw materials would likewise go toward producing power for industry and not bombs. Any effort to reconvert this material into weapons would be, Bush argued, discoverable by international inspectors. The only mention of Anglo-American cooperation in the entire memo was Bush's recommendation that current collaboration be suspended except for the sharing of atomic raw materials.

Outwardly at least, the first step of the "Bush plan" resembled Stimson's earlier proposal for cooperation with the Russians—in all, indeed, except the matter of intent. Here Bush's objective of opening up Russia was more in keeping with the idea of the *quid pro quo* which Stimson had abandoned after Potsdam. This was a point that Bush had stressed in the memo, and that was probably not lost upon Byrnes.

Nonetheless, Byrnes' enthusiasm for the "Bush plan" was guarded in a meeting with its author on November 5. He was still concerned with the question of whether the Russians should be approached on the subject of the bomb. Obvious dangers existed. There was yet no guarantee, for example, that the Russians would not exploit a U.S. initiative on the bomb as a pretext for demanding an immediate share in the weapon's control.

This question, coincidentally, was destined to be resolved the following day by the Russians themselves—when Molotov for the first time acknowledged that the atomic bomb was a divisive issue in Soviet-American relations. Warning that America's nuclear monopoly could not last indefinitely, he cryptically declared that "we shall have atomic energy and many other things too." Until that time, Molotov cautioned, exploitation by the United States of a temporary advantage in hopes of political gain could not be expected to "yield positive results."

Molotov's statement was discussed between Byrnes and Truman in a meeting at the White House on November 7. Called to Byrnes' office the following afternoon, Bush found that the attitude of the secretary of state toward his plan had warmed considerably. "He had quite completely shifted his position," Bush wrote to Conant. "[T]his time we were discussing carefully ways and means toward an effective accord rather than merely struggling with the question of whether any accord is possible." But Russia, not Britain, was still the focus of Byrnes' concern at the meeting. "Some discussion but not much revolved around the Quebec Agreement."[42]

With the question of the bomb finally in the open between the United States and Russia, Byrnes had only to select the *dramatis personae* of the American delegation for the Washington conference before the British and Canadian prime ministers arrived in the capital. The Bush plan would be the basis of the American proposal at the conference —but Byrnes had already decided upon one vital change that he did not even tell Bush about. It was not to be a joint Anglo-American overture to the Russians on the bomb; the British were not even going to be consulted on the plan. In a show of Byrnes' growing independence, the plan was to be his private—and personal—initiative.

"A Most Extraordinary Affair"

The British arrived in Washington on November 10, 1945, as suppliants rather than equals. Their loss of influence in the world was a result of the progressive weakening of their empire—a situation which

Churchill's efforts had been powerless to prevent—and the perilous condition of their postwar economy.

An uncomfortable coincidence for the British, therefore, was the fact that while Attlee and his chief adviser on atomic energy, Sir John Anderson, were guests of President Truman, another British delegation was in Washington seeking a $6 billion interest-free loan to rescue the island's economy from inflation and economic stagnation. One member of that delegation, economist John Maynard Keynes, tersely summarized the main problem facing the British: "There was still much kindly concern for Britain. But the war was now over." After some wrangling with residual anglophobia in Congress, the British negotiators left with less than they had expected or hoped for—a loan of $3.75 billion at 2 percent interest.[43]

In the matter of atomic energy, the British negotiating position had become unstuck even before Attlee's plane set down in Washington. The Quebec Agreement—whose main feature pledged the United States and Britain to consult before use of the bomb—was essentially a wartime pact now made obsolete by the conditions of victory, the death of Roosevelt, and the success of the Manhattan Project. The other symbol of past Anglo-American cooperation, the 1944 Hyde Park "Agreement and Declaration of Trust," which promised "full collaboration between the United States and the British Government in developing [atomic energy] for military and commercial purposes" after the war, was, incredibly, known to only a few in Washington—Truman not included.*

The British had also annoyed Truman and Byrnes when an account

---

*The Hyde Park aide-mémoire became an ironic victim of wartime secrecy and of FDR's penchant for personal diplomacy. Since the British code name for atomic energy was Tube Alloys, an unknowing American clerk concluded that the document dealt with torpedoes and filed it accordingly. The only U.S. copy of the agreement was not discovered until 1957. The British gave Truman a copy of the aide-mémoire in June 1945, but the following November he seemed unaware of— or unwilling to believe—its provisions for Anglo-American cooperation. Byrnes, too, remained unknowing or uncaring of prior agreements with the British on atomic energy. Groves' office supposedly forwarded the entire record of Anglo-American cooperation on the bomb to Byrnes at the end of August 1945. But neither Acheson nor another State Department aide was able to find the documents in Byrnes' files that fall. As a secret executive agreement between Roosevelt and Churchill, the aide-mémoire was not in any case binding upon the Truman administration.

FDR himself had inadvertently characterized the perils and pitfalls of his manner of conducting diplomacy in 1943 when he told Lord Cherwell, Bush's British counterpart, that the only thing which could interrupt Anglo-American collaboration on the bomb would be his death and the simultaneous deaths of Cherwell, Bush, and Churchill, since all four men saw "eye to eye" on the subject. By war's end, only Cherwell and Bush remained in their respective governments, and the two men—Roosevelt's opinion notwithstanding—did not see eye to eye on collaboration.[44]

of the so-called "Attlee plan" appeared in U.S. newspapers before the conference began. This "plan"—which simply proposed that the United States, Britain, and Russia share the atomic bomb with the UN—had evidently been leaked to the press by a member of Attlee's delegation in the misplaced hope that it might strengthen Britain's tenuous bargaining position. Yet Attlee seemed unaware of how weak that bargaining position really was. "We were allies and friends," he remarked plaintively when it was over. "It didn't seem necessary to tie everything up."[45]

Byrnes did not share Attlee's illusion concerning America's special relationship with Britain, particularly when it came to the bomb. The delegation of Americans he had assembled at the eleventh hour to negotiate with the British was, by any measure, one most unlikely to promote an Anglo-American entente.

Although Bush had earlier voiced a suspicion that Britain's avowed interest in the bomb really masked her ambition to become America's foremost rival in the commercial development of atomic energy, he was chosen by Byrnes to help in redrafting the Quebec Agreement. Byrnes' other choice—General Leslie Groves—was even more of an anglophobe than Bush. Groves had initially opposed the original Quebec Agreement, only to change his mind when it later became the basis for guaranteeing to the United States the atomic raw materials under Britain's control. His presence at the conference was a reminder to all that America's principal interest in cooperating with Britain on atomic energy had been, and remained, access to the uranium and thorium necessary to make bombs.[46]

Despite the conflicting aims and disparate personalities of the three delegations, the Washington conference began smoothly enough. A first heads-of-government-only meeting took place on the morning of November 11, aboard the presidential yacht *Sequoia* cruising the Potomac. Truman began the talks by expressing the view that "a free exchange of scientific knowledge is necessary for the peace of the world." The eventual control of the bomb, he continued, "should be lodged in the United Nations Organization"—immediately adding a significant caveat: "when we [are] absolutely sure that the confidence of each nation in the good faith of the other is well founded."[47]

Truman had hoped to limit the entire conference to the three men, but ultimately bowed to Attlee's insistence that Britain's experts on the bomb, Lord Halifax and Sir John Anderson, be included in the discussions. A second meeting was held on the yacht that afternoon, when Byrnes and Admiral Leahy joined the President.[48] On this occasion the conversation ranged far afield from atomic energy, but as before, general unanimity characterized discussion on the bomb. All agreed "in principle" with American proposals for the free exchange of scientific knowledge and eventual international control of atomic energy.

Eager to end the summit before news leaked out of the discussions on board the *Sequoia,* Byrnes instructed Bush to join with the British in drafting an official communiqué the following day. This arrangement Bush—who had attended neither meeting on the yacht—properly found "extraordinary."[49]

Extraordinary too was the fact that missing from this communiqué —and the conference—was any mention of cooperation with the Soviet Union. Far from being the "great question" at the conference, Russia was barely discussed at the meetings. There would be no Anglo-American overture to the Soviet Union, as Bush had proposed. While this undoubtedly seemed curious to him, it was perhaps only part of what he had come to call, wonderingly, "a most extraordinary affair." "He had never participated in anything so completely unorganized or so irregular," Bush wrote to Conant.[50]

Real problems did not arise at the Washington conference until Bush and Groves approached the British and Canadians on renegotiating the Quebec Agreement. Groves wished the British to agree to put all of the Commonwealth's atomic raw materials at the disposition of the United States in exchange for abrogating the clause of the original agreement that disclaimed Britain's interest in the commercial application of atomic energy. In effect, the British—who were in the position of having fuel but no furnace—were asked by Groves to surrender the fuel for a promise that the United States would not hinder construction of the furnace.[51]

Understandably, the British balked, preferring, they said pointedly, not to resolve the question of a renewed Quebec Agreement "at this time or at this level."

What promised to be a sour ending note for the Washington conference, however, was avoided by the signing of a secret Anglo-American "memorandum of intention" on November 16. This compromise, worked out between Groves and Anderson, was meant to serve only as a guideline for some future renegotiation of the Quebec Agreement. It was, as well, a masterpiece of ambiguity—providing for

Anglo-American cooperation on "such ad hoc arrangements as may be approved from time to time . . . as mutually advantageous." Another secret accord, signed the same day by the President and the two prime ministers, expressed the simple desire of all three "that there should be full and effective cooperation in the field of atomic energy between the United States, the United Kingdom and Canada."[52]

Like Bush, the British privately complained about chaos at the summit. In a diary that he kept on "Archer"—the British code word for the conference—diplomat Ian Jacob confided his feelings: "I do not feel any satisfaction with the outcome. . . . I do not feel that something good has been accomplished. . . . [O]n the yacht the three big men parted with no clear cut idea of the next step, and each side began independent drafting." "Mr. Attlee managed to stave things off for a short time," Jacob noted, but Truman had ultimately forced the prime minister's hand. Fear of news leaks had dictated the hurried pace of the meetings. "The American Press is one of the greatest menaces of our day," Jacob concluded.[53]

Still, the agreements reached at the Washington conference seemed to signal a return to the earlier days of close Anglo-American cooperation on atomic energy. The Agreed Declaration—the public communiqué that Bush had drafted and which the three leaders announced at the end of the summit on November 15—seemed to symbolize a revival of the "special relationship" by its implicit treatment of atomic energy as a shared possession of America, Canada, and Britain. Equally, the two secret accords held out the prospect of future collaboration in applying atomic energy to industry, a development which Attlee expected to be a help in bolstering Britain's faltering economy.

Yet what Attlee saw as unanimity was more apparent than real. In exchange for continuing to surrender their atomic raw materials to the United States, the British had received only a vague promise of cooperation—cooperation which, as Groves had been careful to add in a passage to the new agreement, while "desirable in principle," would not be forthcoming in practice. Remarkably, Byrnes remained unaware of the contents of the two secret documents. Truman, as events would later show, was oblivious of the importance that Attlee attached to them.

The renewed era of good feelings in Anglo-American relations which the Washington conference seemed to portend for the British was based, therefore, upon a perception of common interest not shared by the Americans. It would not be long before the British were disabused of their illusions.*

"Byrnes Had Changed His Attitude"

With the departure of the British and Canadian delegations from Washington, Byrnes could once again turn his attention to the Russians. Indeed, his concern had never wandered far from the subject of Russia and the bomb throughout the conference. On the day that Groves and Bush had drafted the secret agreements with the British, for example, Byrnes was in Charleston, South Carolina. He had traveled there to deliver a message that was seemingly directed as much to the Kremlin as to his American audience. Titled "The South in International Relations," Byrnes' speech was really aimed at countering the latest Soviet attacks upon his foreign policy.

American policy on the atomic bomb was now the focus of those charges. Incited by the appearance of Anglo-American solidarity at the Washington summit, the Soviet press alleged that the United States and Britain had formed an "anti-Russian bloc" engaged in "atomic diplomacy" and were attempting "to use the atomic bomb in the game of foreign power politics."[55]

In his speech, Byrnes rejected the idea that the United States would use the bomb in diplomacy as a threat. But concerning the Soviet claim that the Agreed Declaration marked a tacit Anglo-American alliance against Russia at the UN, he remained circumspect. Byrnes was doubtless aware that the Washington conference might be seen by the Russians as an Anglo-American nuclear cabal, and that pious denials would not convince them otherwise. Also, since the Russians themselves had already broached the subject of the bomb as a serious obstacle in Soviet-American relations, the timing for an approach to the Soviets on this issue was propitious. The opportunity for such an approach, Byrnes realized, was quickly passing.

As Stimson had warned the previous September, it would be too late for a direct approach to Russia on the bomb when the United

---

*The first shock would come within a month. That December the British were bluntly refused help in building a nuclear power plant by Truman, who told Byrnes—according to the latter's recollection—that "there was little discussion at the time of the signing of the agreement" as to what "full and effective" cooperation really meant. But Truman did not interpret it as meaning the furnishing of "full information as to the production methods developed by the United States."[54]

Nations convened a commission to study the control of atomic energy
at the beginning of the year. The public exposure of Russian and American bargaining positions would thereafter make substantive agreement
impossible. Byrnes had already taken the first step toward another meeting with the Russians when he pledged to work for a second Council of
Foreign Ministers, at Moscow, during the dying throes of the London
council. Yet the last time the idea of a second meeting had come up,
at a Cabinet meeting in late October, both Truman and Byrnes himself
had dismissed it. Since then, the notion of a mission to Moscow had
apparently lapsed.

Nor did Truman change his mind. In a press conference at the end
of November, he expressed disdain for and opposition to any more
"special conferences," adding that no further meetings of the Big Three
would occur before the meeting of the UN General Assembly in January.
Although Byrnes was later to explain that the President's statement
applied only to heads of state and not to foreign ministers, he, too, had
seemed to foreclose the possibility of another council by announcing on
November 20 that the United States would not consult with Russia until
the first meeting of the United Nations' atomic energy commission.[56]

In fact, Byrnes had already privately decided upon a bold new initiative
to Russia on the bomb.[57] His apparently last-minute decision to ignore
Russia in the Washington conference communiqué, therefore, had not
been meant as a slight to the Soviets but was, rather, an indication that
policy on the bomb was now moving in another direction. That direction
became clear on November 23 when Byrnes proposed to Molotov that
the Council of Foreign Ministers hold a second meeting in Moscow the
next month. The following day—before he had even received a reply
from Molotov—Byrnes directed a special staff in the State Department
to begin drafting a proposal for cooperation on the bomb to present to
Molotov and Stalin at the Kremlin. In its essentials, the State Department plan would resemble the direct approach to Russia that Stimson
had initially proposed, Byrnes had first decried, and Truman had ultimately rejected. The vital difference now was that Byrnes' offer would
be a distinctly personal initiative. As such, it was meant to gain for him
the credit of bringing order out of what Bush had characterized at the
outset of the Washington summit as "a thoroughly chaotic condition"
—American policy on the bomb.

Certainly no part of the impetus for this initiative had come from
Truman. On December 4 the President told Forrestal that though "he

was trying very hard to come to an agreement with the Russians," he lacked "the confidence that an agreement reached with the Russians would be lived up to. . . . There is no evidence yet that the Russians intend to change their habits so far as honoring contracts is concerned."[58]

Three days later, Byrnes publicly announced his intention to meet with the Russians in Moscow before Christmas.

On December 11—exactly three months after Stimson had written his memorandum to Truman, and as Byrnes was packing for his trip—the retired secretary of war received a letter from a former aide concerning the details of Byrnes' proposed mission to Moscow. American policy on the bomb, the aide reported, "had entirely changed in the last few days and . . . now Truman [is] following [the] Stimson plan exactly."[59]

For Stimson, events had seemingly gone full circle. He wrote in his diary of the news: "If so, this must mean that Byrnes has changed his attitude on the first point, the secrecy point, and second that the president had changed his views on the method of carrying out the sharing."

As events would show, Stimson was only half right.

4

Moscow:
The New Atomic Diplomacy

"Much to everyone's surprise, the Russians did not argue or talk back."
Vannevar Bush to James Conant, December 1945

"Byrnes had taken it upon himself to move the foreign policy of the United States in a direction to which I could not, and would not, agree."
President Truman, letter, January 1946

"Stalin Was Very Anxious for the Conference"

Byrnes set out upon his mission to Moscow on December 12, 1945, with cautious optimism.[1] The omens had been good. Molotov had waited only two days before responding to his initiative by inviting the secretary of state to the Russian capital—an abnormally short reaction time for Soviet bureaucracy in general and for the methodical foreign minister in particular. Truman, too, took Stalin's quick and positive reply to his letter of the 12th as an indication that the Soviet leader "was very anxious for the conference."[2]

The proposal which Byrnes carried to Moscow was designed to avoid the mistakes made at London. Most important—for Byrnes—the plan to be offered to the Russians was entirely an American initiative, and peculiarly his handiwork. Moscow would be his own show, he believed and—no less important—he hoped it would be the scene of his vindication in the eyes of a growing number of critics.

What Byrnes intended at Moscow was little short of a coup in the administration's foreign policy. Rather than approaching the Russians furtively with the atomic bomb in his pocket, as he had done at London, Byrnes meant to lay the bomb on the negotiating table at Moscow. The bomb, in fact, would be the centerpiece of the negotiations in Russia, but an agreement concerning control of the weapon might be the breakthrough by which other disputes could also be resolved. The Moscow meeting would be the scene of an entirely different sort of atomic diplomacy than that practiced at Potsdam and London. Thus it was not as a threat but as a promise that the bomb would make its diplomatic debut in Moscow—the promise of closer Soviet-American relations through mutual cooperation on atomic energy.

Such a course, Byrnes realized, was inimical to the wishes and disposition of many in the administration and in Congress, and ran counter to the President's declared policy. The resentment of allies who had not been consulted or whose interests were not considered in this move was inevitable. It also meant giving the reins to a group of government planners whose ideas had previously received little attention in the administration—advocates of cooperative control for the atom. And, finally, it signaled a sudden and complete turnaround from Byrnes' own earlier thoughts and attitudes on the bomb. But these were all risks or drawbacks that Byrnes clearly thought acceptable, for the sake of the country as well as for his own place in history.

It was a vision, moreover, that Byrnes would believe he came tantalizingly close to realizing. The fatal opposition to his bold initiative, ironically, would come not from the Kremlin but from Washington.

"Action . . . Whenever It Is Likely to Be Fruitful"

As Stimson had been the first to realize in urging a direct approach to Russia, no less important than the content of the proposal that Byrnes would take to Moscow was the way in which it would be offered. Concerning tactics and procedure, Byrnes wished the meetings at Moscow to be less formal than those at London, with greater flexibility on issues that were tangential to the interests of the Big Three. Byrnes had already told Davies that a resumption of negotiations on the peace treaties and clarification of control of the bomb were his two major concerns at the conference.[3] Of the two, Byrnes' initiative on the bomb would mark the more complete and significant break with previous policy.

Actually, the first inspiration for this break had come not from Byrnes himself but from two men in the State Department, Benjamin Cohen and Leo Pasvolsky. Cohen was the department's chief counselor as well as Acheson's aide; Pasvolsky had played a significant role in drafting the plan that created the United Nations. Both men had joined with Acheson in supporting Stimson's cooperative approach on the bomb. Their concern had grown as this approach was ignored in the Truman administration, and they had finally decided to approach Byrnes on their own.

The initiative they outlined for Byrnes in broad detail during early December was essentially the same as the course he was then considering, founded upon the "Bush plan." Both Bush and the State Department group, however, stressed the point of consulting with the British before making any agreement with the Russians on the bomb—a diplomatic nicety which Byrnes felt he had already satisfied at the Washington conference, and which he would ignore at Moscow.

Enthusiastic at suddenly being included in planning on the bomb, Cohen and Pasvolsky created a committee in the State Department of experts on diplomacy and atomic energy for the detailed drafting of their proposal. Significantly, among those included were representatives of the informal and "reluctant lobby" for international control of the bomb—the atomic scientists.*

The most striking feature of the State Department proposal was its flexibility. Whereas the "Bush plan" had only recommended that the United States extend an invitation to the Soviets to join with the West in controlling the bomb at the UN, the Cohen-Pasvolsky draft provided for Soviet-American agreement on the workings of the UN commission before approaching that public forum, as Stimson had urged. The State Department version also followed the "Bush plan" and the Washington conference communiqué in its recognition that progress toward cooperative control of the bomb would have to proceed incrementally, by measured steps. But it differed crucially from both—and came closest to Stimson's original intent—in its provision that progress on any one step need not be a prerequisite for progress on others, but that "action should be taken whenever it is likely to be fruitful," even on Soviet counterproposals.[5]

The implications of this provision belied its modest wording. Thus it removed the Agreed Declaration's ban upon the interchange of scien-

---

*The scientists were a "reluctant lobby" in part because many were politically naive. Indeed, one of the reasons they were generally ignored in the government was their reputation for woolyheadedness. The typical scientist's reaction to the atomic bomb, one satirist wrote, was that it was "just too terrible, too dreadful, too everything. We must do something about it. What are you doing? What am I doing? We must all get together right away and do more."[4]

tific information with the Russians and deemphasized the importance of prior safeguards, which had seemed paramount in the Anglo-American agreement. Further, the plan included a means by which Byrnes could prove to the Russians the seriousness of his intent. Appended to it was a recommendation that Byrnes begin Soviet-American cooperation on the bomb with agreement at Moscow on a symbolic exchange of atomic scientists, basic scientific information on atomic energy, and radioactive isotopes useful in medical research. To that end, Byrnes was advised by the State Department to include a scientist in his entourage to Russia.

Despite its ostensibly radical origins, the State Department proposal, in keeping with the spirit of Stimson's suggested approach, would give nothing of substance to the Russians. Like its progenitor, its importance was a symbol of beginning Soviet-American cooperation. The department proposal resembled Stimson's in the vagueness of its wording as well. That lack of precision was perhaps purposeful. Thus the State Department committee was ever "careful," one of its members wrote, "that what we are offering can in fact be offered." Any hint that their proposal might violate the sanctity of atomic secrets, they realized, would doom the cause of cooperation with the Russians.[6]

"Christmas in Russia Isn't till January 6th"

Symbolic also of his departure from previous policy was Byrnes' decision to yield on the question of representation at Moscow—one of the issues that supposedly had led to the breakdown in London. The French and Chinese foreign ministers would simply be excluded from the conference.*

Nor did the British fare much better at Byrnes' hands. Bevin learned of the proposed meeting with Molotov from the Russian himself —a point which underscored for him the extent to which the British

---

*"Chip" Bohlen recounts that this decision occasioned some anxiety on Byrnes' part when the delegation's plane had an unscheduled layover in Paris. Because he had neglected even to inform the French of his plans before making the overture to Molotov, Byrnes feared a scene at the airport. The incident did not occur, but other problems were to plague the secretary and his delegation on their flight. The Russians, Bohlen writes, were playing waltzes on the frequency the Americans had been given for landing; the plane eventually set down on a snow-covered runway at the wrong airport.[7]

were now excluded from making policy on the bomb despite the Agreed Declaration. Bevin's first reaction to this slight—a refusal to accompany Byrnes on the latter's mission to Moscow—was soon overcome by his realization that the American would rather go alone than cancel the meeting. The British, in fact, had little choice but to follow the American lead. Halifax had even recommended such a move earlier, when he suggested that an effort be made to enlist Russian support for the Agreed Declaration. But, he now complained, Byrnes' action in calling the meeting unilaterally had "got us in a bit of a hole."[8] Bevin, too, could hardly afford to damage the image of Anglo-American solidarity which the Washington conference had spread—and which the Attlee government had already taken political risks to defend in Britain.

Byrnes' reason for approaching the Russians alone is clear. He hoped in this way to dispel the illusion of what Molotov had since called an anti-Soviet Western "bloc" at the Council of Foreign Ministers. "It would not have looked good to the Soviets for the United States and Britain to jointly propose such a meeting," Byrnes explained to "Ernie" Bevin by teletype in late November. The real reason he had notified the Russians "before wiring Bevin," Byrnes told Walter Brown, was "to make Molotov feel good." Byrnes also admitted to Davies that "he would not have been disappointed if [Bevin] had not gone."[9]

Bevin's sensibilities aside, another incident showed that in a choice between offending either British or Russian feelings, Byrnes would henceforth sacrifice the British. The result was disingenuousness, if not outright duplicity, on his part. Even a small concession to Bevin at this time—an agreement to announce the Moscow meeting as an Anglo-American initiative—was thus withdrawn in the State Department's press release.

The British were not inclined to be gracious in bowing to the inevitable and accepting the offhanded Soviet-American invitation to Moscow. He would go to Moscow—"in deference to your strong views" —Bevin telegraphed Byrnes. But, in a parting shot, the foreign secretary made light of Byrnes' avowed hope that a settlement might be made with the Russians before Christmas. "Christmas in Russia," he pointed out, "isn't until January 6th so they'll be in no hurry themselves."[10]

Byrnes' effort to gain the confidence of the Russians by these concessions and by his snub to Bevin was, nonetheless, apparently unavailing. Although the Russians evidently understood Byrnes' intention—Molotov asked Harriman wryly if a Soviet invitation to attend the conference would come as a "surprise" to Bevin—they were not outwardly impressed by the maneuver. Stalin, in fact, informed Byrnes—in an Orwellian twist of logic—that America's slighting of Britain "was obviously only a cloak to hide the reality of the [Anglo-American] bloc." Equally, Byrnes' exclusion of the French needlessly offended that ally. In an early meeting with Byrnes, Stalin—perhaps to outdo the secretary of state at his own game of compromise—magnanimously offered assurances that the French would be welcome at future conferences.[11]

"Trouble Threatens Behind Byrnes' Back"

Byrnes did not have to look overseas for critics of his intended trip to Russia—or even, indeed, beyond his own delegation. Disconcerted by the secretary's personal brand of diplomacy, Bohlen thought Byrnes' plans for the conference "hastily improvised" and "thoroughly disorganized," and believed Byrnes carried "much of the foreign policy . . . [within] his head." The charges of George F. Kennan—the future American ambassador to Russia and ranking State Department Soviet expert—were more serious. Deeply skeptical of summit diplomacy, Kennan questioned Byrnes' motives. The purpose of the visit, he suggested, was only "to achieve some sort of agreement, [Byrnes] doesn't much care what." Further, the real aim of the meeting, Kennan wrote in his diary, was "its political effect at home. And that the Russians know. . . . They will see that for this superficial success he pays a heavy price."[12]

The most threatening opposition to Byrnes' plans, however, came from within the administration and from Congress. Reading a State Department draft of the initiative on the bomb, Secretary of the Navy Forrestal promptly informed Byrnes of his feeling "that the proposed basis of discussion goes too far." Forrestal's recommendation was, in effect, that the United States simply invite the Russians to ratify the Anglo-American Agreed Declaration. A note from General Groves, forwarded to Byrnes by Robert Patterson, was more direct. Groves expressed his "hope" that the negotiations in Moscow "will not at this time discuss the raw materials situation"—a provision, in fact, that the State Department plan encompassed as a second stage.[13]

Foremost in the congressional opposition to the Moscow mission was Arthur H. Vandenberg, Republican leader of the bipartisan consensus in the Senate. Vandenberg had gained a reputation as a flamboyant champion of the administration's foreign policy since his sudden conversion from isolationism to internationalism over the issue of the United Nations. That remarkable eleventh-hour metamorphosis, Vandenberg's detractors pointed out, had surely been as politically expedient as it was timely, in the aftermath of the Second World War. But it had also not changed his consistently hard-line attitude toward the Soviet Union. Now as an avowed internationalist, Vandenberg continued to inveigh in the Senate against Russia's "blackout curtain of secrecy."

A particular target of Vandenberg's ire in the fall of 1945 was Byrnes, who, he charged, "helped surrender at Yalta." "Jimmy Byrnes is a grand guy (for any *other* job down here)," Vandenberg wrote his wife after Byrnes' confirmation as secretary of state, "But his whole life has been a career of compromise."[14]

There was a personal element, as well, to Vandenberg's vocal displeasure with Byrnes. The secretary had pointedly overlooked the Michigan senator when he assembled the delegation to accompany him to London, choosing Dulles as the Republican representative instead.[15] The selection had assured Byrnes greater control over the delegation, but the political cost in alienating Vandenberg was great—as would soon become clear.[16]

Dulles, too, had joined the ranks of Byrnes' critics by mid-November 1945. He "had the impression," Dulles told Byrnes, that "nothing was being done and that it was going to be difficult for me, or anyone like me, to carry on."[17]

Byrnes had even begun to make enemies within his own party because of his insistence upon conducting foreign policy on his own. Not only Vandenberg but Tom Connally, the chairman of the Senate Foreign Relations Committee, had been piqued when Byrnes sought to include him in a picture of participants at the Washington conference —after he had been excluded from taking part in the conference itself. Neither senator posed for the photograph.

In a vain attempt at political fence-mending, Byrnes had invited Vandenberg, Connally, and other critics in Congress to his office before departing for Moscow. Unwilling in that interview, however, to give any specifics on the proposals he meant to introduce at the Kremlin—his State Department experts informed him that to do so before the conference would be "unwise"—Byrnes found his guests were hardly reassured by his presentation. Far from defusing their criticism and enlisting their support for his venture, his vague explanations of the initiative on atomic energy created fresh doubts in their minds. Connally voiced the view that "complete secrecy should be maintained" in dealing with the Russians on the bomb. Vandenberg, protesting that what Byrnes had presented was a *fait accompli* rather than a briefing, dismissed the trip to Moscow itself as "sheer appeasement." Both men were upset that no important member of Congress would accompany Byrnes to Russia. Leaving the meeting convinced that he and the other senators "had made little impression on the secretary," Vandenberg privately vowed to go to Truman with his objections.[18]

Thus far the President had given solid—if unenthusiastic—support to his secretary of state, despite the growing sentiment against Byrnes within Truman's own circle of advisers. In a meeting of Truman and Byrnes on December 11, the eve of the latter's departure for Moscow, the President expressed no complaints, and he willingly granted Byrnes' request for a letter to Stalin. Since then, Truman's attention had been diverted by crises evolving in China and Iran. But there were already disturbing indications, as Joseph E. Davies recounted in his diary, that "trouble threatens behind Byrnes' back." And Truman, in a private forum, had begun to protest the independence of his secretary of state.

Taken aside by Truman aboard the *Sequoia* on December 8, Davies was "amazed" to hear the President speak of the secretary of state as "a 'conniver.' " Truman, Davies recalled, "was greatly concerned and . . . asked me to see Byrnes without fail before Byrnes got away."

Reflecting upon this incident later that day, Davies wrote in his journal: "This was a complete change in [Truman's] attitude. Someone quite obviously had been needling him against Byrnes. I fear Jim has not maintained his lines of communications with the Commander-in-Chief sufficiently active," Davies continued. "I did the best I could as to Jim's good judgment and fidelity to him. But it couldn't be done. He has been poisoned and his mind was quite set. Jim is through, and it is a pity."[19]

Davies' assessment of Byrnes as "through" was surely premature, but his attempt to warn the latter of the "palace guard" scheming against him was even then too late. Here, as well, it is likely that Davies was reluctant either to spoil Byrnes' ebullient mood upon leaving for Moscow or to discourage the initiative which Davies thought long overdue—for his visit seemed to have little effect upon Byrnes. In what may have been another effort, therefore, to convey a warning to Byrnes,

Davies had Benjamin Cohen take a letter to his chief just as the plane was preparing to take off for Moscow. The contents of that letter, however, suggest that Davies, like Truman, was unable to confront Byrnes directly with the evidence of his growing unpopularity in the administration, or to recommend that he restrain his independence at Moscow.[20]

Whereas Davies' letter and the abortive meeting with Vandenberg and Connally could not have left Byrnes entirely unaware of the difficulties he was facing at home, neither prepared him for the extent or the effect of the domestic opposition he would encounter to his purpose at Moscow. What he hoped to accomplish there was opposed, in varying degrees, by elements of the administration, the Congress, and the President himself. But Byrnes' mind was also undoubtedly preoccupied with thoughts of his coming meeting with Molotov and with the hope that the results of the conference would justify its risk. It is likely, therefore, that Byrnes' determinedly optimistic attitude in setting out for Moscow was a result less of insensitivity than of the desperate, driven nature of his hopes.

"The Byrnes Formula Must Be Stopped"

Upon arriving in Moscow on December 15, Byrnes soon had proof that he had not left his problems behind in Washington. His buoyant mood promptly received two unexpected shocks—one from Molotov and another from Truman.

First was Molotov's insistence that the subject of atomic energy, which Byrnes had put at the head of the conference's agenda, be relegated to the end of the list. Instead, the Soviet foreign minister wished to discuss U.S. involvement in the Chinese civil war and British intervention in Greece—both increasingly bitter points of controversy in Russia's relations with the West. This was especially disappointing for Byrnes, since he had hoped that an agreement on the difficult question of atomic energy at the outset would set the tone for the rest of the meeting. Molotov's gesture, Byrnes later wrote, was designed to show him that the Russians still viewed the subject of the bomb "as one of little importance." In London, Molotov had sought to discount the diplomatic importance of America's atomic advantage by making light of it; in Moscow, he aimed at the same effect by ignoring it.

Another reason Byrnes may have wanted to bring the bomb up immediately in the conference—in addition to his desire to defuse it as an issue between the two countries—was his hope that an agreement with the Russians might be signed before the ground was cut from under him by opposition at home. If so, there was awaiting him in Moscow a sign that he was already too late: a memorandum from the President. Its presence there was the result of a drama that had taken place in Washington after Byrnes' departure.

While the secretary of state was en route to Moscow, Truman had met with members of the congressional Joint Committee on Atomic Energy, at Vandenberg's insistence. Vandenberg and his colleagues were newly upset at the discovery that Byrnes, upon the recommendation of the State Department committee, had taken James Conant along to Moscow, presumably to aid in establishing a program of scientific interchange with the Russians.[21] This was only further evidence, Connally complained, of Byrnes' "secretive" nature.

Of even greater concern to the assembly in the President's office, however, was the order of the four steps for cooperative control of the bomb contained in the State Department's draft proposal.

Those steps envisioned, first, an ever widening exchange of scientists and scientific information; second, the development and exchange of knowledge concerning atomic raw materials; third, the exchange of technological and engineering information on atomic energy; and last, safeguards against and control over military use of the bomb.

The order of the steps, Vandenberg protested to Truman, should be reversed. Safeguards should be established before cooperation with the Russians. Otherwise, he argued, Byrnes' plan would make it "possible for the Secretary to prematurely give away, while in Moscow, at least half of all our 'trading stock.' "[22]

Truman's attempt to soothe the delegation by reading them a "directive" he had sent along to Byrnes was unavailing. "To our amazement," Vandenberg later recounted, "we found that the 'directive' would fully justify the precise sort of plan which Byrnes told us he intends to pursue." Truman, however, refused to be swayed by Vandenberg's imprecations. The President "seemed to fail to grasp our point in regard to the 'directive,' " the senators complained. Frustrated by Truman's apparent inability—or unwillingness—to understand their objections, Vandenberg and the others retreated from the Oval Office. But they had hardly conceded the battle. "It is our unanimous opinion that the Byrnes formula must be stopped," Vandenberg wrote Dulles after the meeting.[23]

Although Vandenberg obviously did not know it, he had already carried his point with the President, for Truman would side with the senators against Byrnes. Prior to his meeting with the congressional delegation, Truman had defended Byrnes and his initiative in a Cabinet meeting. "The President," Wallace recollected of that meeting, "said he was convinced they [the senators] were wrong; that the Russians had just as good scientists as we had; that the scientific information was now available to everyone and that it was important that we help create an atmosphere of worldwide confidence." Earlier, Truman had also championed the State Department proposal against Wallace's charge that the emphasis of the plan upon separate stages meant "Russia would have to pass the first grade in moral aptitude." "Truman said that this step-by-step procedure was best for dealing with the Russians," Wallace noted.[24]

Throughout this time, however, Truman had shown an increasing sensitivity to other problems with Russia, spurred perhaps by the current tension over the situation in Iran. By the winter of 1945, Iran had become the focus of the latest Soviet-American clash, with Russian troops still in that country months after the war's end. On December 16, while Byrnes was in Moscow, the President unburdened himself of these concerns to his press secretary, Charlie Ross: "Of Russia, [Truman] said they confront us with an accomplished fact and then there is little we can do. 'Now they have 500,000 men in Bulgaria and some day they are going to move down and take the Black Sea straits and that will be an accomplished fact again. There's only one thing they understand.'

" 'Divisions?' Ross asked.*

"The President nodded and added that we can't send any divisions over to prevent them from moving from Bulgaria. 'I don't know what we're going to do,' he said."

One thing Truman decided to do three days later was to get tougher with the Russians—reminding the Soviets of their wartime debt to the United States. Just as the Moscow conference had gotten under way the President had Samuel Rosenman release to the press a report on the lend-lease program which stressed America's contribution to the Russian

*Obviously, Ross had heard the story before. His reply was an insider's reference to one of Truman's favorite anecdotes about Stalin at Potsdam. According to the President, Churchill's concern that the Pope might be displeased with the fate of Poland's Catholics was met with a retort from Stalin, who, tugging nonchalantly at his mustache, asked Churchill: "How many divisions did you say the Pope has?"[25]

war effort. He made the same point in a comment to Eben Ayers: " 'If it hadn't been for our supply line, they'd all have been licked,' Truman said, and added that Stalin admitted as much at Potsdam."[26]

Regardless of how the Russians behaved, Truman could hardly afford to alienate the two senators who were the foundation of his foreign-policy support in Congress. This point was impressed upon him anew with the White House visit of the chairman of the Joint Committee on Atomic Energy, Senator Brian McMahon, shortly after the President's meeting with Vandenberg and Connally. Equally, Truman's own growing resentment of Byrnes may have figured in his subsequent move to restrain his secretary of state.

Perhaps a last straw in this regard had been Byrnes' early December speech on U.S. postwar economic policy toward Germany. That speech, like others before it, had not been previously cleared with Truman. "The President said it seemed to him he should not have to read the newspapers to get . . . U.S. foreign policy," Ayers wrote on December 12.[27]

Two days later, while the delegation of senators was in the President's office, signs of Truman's anger surfaced in his decision to side with Byrnes' critics. "Jimmy's already on his way," Truman told Connally. "I'll get in touch with him en route and have him change the order [of the stages]."[28]

Even now, Truman was reluctant to discipline Byrnes directly, but assigned that task instead to someone known to be sympathetic to the latter's goal at Moscow—Under Secretary of State Dean Acheson. Like that of Davies' last-minute letter to Byrnes at the airport, the point of Acheson's memorandum to his chief in Moscow was virtually lost by his desire not to jeopardize Byrnes' mission. Almost oriental in his obeisance in that telegram as a result, Acheson still tried to convey the point that the President, under congressional pressure, was drawing back from his earlier sanction of Byrnes' trip. Importantly, the memo instructed that the first step of the State Department proposal—the exchange of scientists and scientific information—would only be discussed, and such discussion would pertain solely to the known fundamentals of atomic energy. Further, Byrnes was told, "any proposals advanced would be referred here before agreement was reached." Acheson informed Byrnes that Truman "had no intention of agreeing to disclose any information regarding the bomb at this time or unless and until arrangements for inspection and safeguards could be worked out."[29]

For Byrnes, the significance of Acheson's message was clear despite its deference. He was being instructed to pull back from the ambitious program he had taken to Russia. This was a disappointing, and even ominous, development at such an early stage of the conference. But it did not yet mean an end to his plans at Moscow.

"Somewhere in the Middle"

Byrnes' return telegram to the President on December 17 showed a substantial retrenchment from the position he had initially taken at Moscow. He assured Truman that he would make no proposals "outside the framework" of the Washington conference's Agreed Declaration. Indeed, the final version of the "United States Proposal on Atomic Energy" which he included with his message was a document considerably changed from the original State Department draft.[30]

Specifically, the amended version dropped the appeal that the Soviets join in sponsoring the upcoming UN commission on atomic energy and merely "suggested" instead that all five permanent members of the Security Council sponsor the commission. More important, left out was the heart of the State Department plan—the idea that agreement need not wait upon the accomplishment of separate steps but should be attempted whenever it appeared likely of success. Finally, deleted was the proposal for Soviet-American scientific interchange and the U.S. offer to discuss atomic energy outside of the UN. In its place was a statement borrowed from the Agreed Declaration which proclaimed that cooperation could not begin before "effective enforceable safeguards" had been devised.

On paper, this was a headlong retreat from the principle of the direct approach. Apparently assured by this answer that Byrnes was now back in line, Truman sent McMahon a copy of the telegram to demonstrate that fact to his committee.

In reality, Byrnes' retreat had been more apparent than real. Despite his assurances to Washington, he had abandoned neither the principle of his original plan nor his intention to act independently at Moscow. Nor, for that matter, had Byrnes been deserted by his allies at the State Department. Cohen and Pasvolsky continued to send the secretary additional proposals for discussion with the Soviets, ignoring the growing signs of trouble for him in Washington and the waning prospects for success at Moscow.[31]

The proposal that Byrnes actually laid before the Russians on De-

cember 18 was thus not the one he had sent to Truman only a day earlier.
Without informing the President, he had decided to omit the all-impor-
tant passages on "separate stages" and "enforceable safeguards" in the
final document. By their exclusion the possibility of an informal agreement remained, and Byrnes had at least theoretically left the door open
for wider-ranging talks with the Soviets on control of the bomb.

This had not been achieved without cost, however. In submitting
his proposal on the 18th—only a day after Bevin had asked for more time
to study it—Byrnes further strained relations with the British at the
conference. His evident haste in putting the plan forward may have been
to forestall any further revisions, or to present his critics with a *fait
accompli* at the conference.

In either case, the purpose of Byrnes' clandestine maneuver was
wasted. Unsatisfied—or unconvinced—by Truman's promise that he
would control Byrnes at Moscow, one or more of the congressmen in the
President's office the previous week had decided to take their case to the
newspapers. On December 20, as he awaited a response to his proposal
on atomic energy from Molotov, Byrnes learned from Acheson of press
reports detailing the disastrous meeting with Vandenberg and the others. With the dispute over stages made part of a public debate, he
realized that there could be little hope of avoiding the same issue at
Moscow, even with Truman's support. Further, fresh evidence was
forthcoming that he no longer enjoyed such backing. Byrnes probably
already suspected the truth behind the *New York Times'* report on the
20th that the administration "now finds itself on the atom question
somewhere in the middle between the liberal atomic scientists and the
conservative [congressional] committee." Indeed, Truman had already
sided on that issue with the senators. On the same day, therefore, as the
Times headlined "Senators Demand Russian Atom Vow," Byrnes belatedly introduced the missing passage on stages into the U.S. proposal at
Moscow—explaining somewhat contritely to Molotov that it "had been
omitted by mistake."[32]

"The Russians Did Not Argue or Talk Back"

In the aftermath of what he now knew to be hostile opposition at home,
Byrnes proved to be more cautious than his critics. Even a sign that
Truman was having second thoughts about his earlier instructions—in
a telegram on the 21st suggesting that Byrnes reinstate the proposal for

Soviet-American discussions outside UN auspices—was simply ignored by him.

Byrnes perhaps had not entirely given up hope for positive results at Moscow, however. His optimism seemed to return when the Russians conditionally accepted the basic proposal on atomic energy three days before Christmas. He was not the only one in the U.S. delegation unprepared for this sudden evidence of Soviet cooperation. "Much to everyone's surprise, the Russians didn't argue or talk back," Conant wrote Bush.[33]

Any celebration of this unexpected turn of events would have been premature, nonetheless. The conditions demanded by the Russians were on vital issues. The first concerned establishment of the UN commission on atomic energy—the Russians wanting it to come under the direction of the Security Council, while the American proposal specified control by the General Assembly. Though this dispute was superficially over procedure, it absorbed the next several days of meetings, and actually lay at the basis of Soviet-American differences. Hence, control of the commission by the General Assembly—with the majority of its members either sympathetic or politically indebted to the United States—meant dominant American influence in that body. Control by the Security Council, however, would allow the Russians to veto any decision of the commission which they found objectionable. On the difference between the two approaches might depend the future of international control.

The second condition concerned, predictably, the matter of separate stages of cooperation. Asking for Soviet approval of the passage on stages, Byrnes realized, was tantamount to requiring that the Russians endorse the results of the Washington conference—a conference from which they had been excluded, and which Molotov had branded "anti-Russian." But Soviet acquiescence to the provision on stages was also necessary if Byrnes was to have any hope of disarming his domestic critics before he returned home. As Molotov remained unyielding on either issue—and as his own self-imposed Christmas deadline approached—Byrnes' despair of achieving some tangible success in the conference grew.

It was to break this deadlock that he decided to play his last card at the conference. Accordingly, Byrnes requested a meeting with Stalin for December 23.

Stalin, according to Bohlen, was "listless" at that late-night interview in the Kremlin, doodling the heads of wolves on a piece of paper while he talked—as he had at Potsdam. But the Soviet leader was also no less blunt than at Potsdam in stating his views. The Russian government, he told Byrnes, "had accepted nine-tenths of the American proposal and had only proposed one-tenth for their side"—establishment of the UN Atomic Energy Commission (UNAEC) under the Security Council. When Byrnes objected that Soviet-American differences on Iran would then come under public scrutiny, Stalin was matter-of-fact in his reply: "This will not cause us to blush."[34]

To Byrnes' distress, even a second late-hour meeting of the two men—on Christmas Eve—failed to produce any concessions from Stalin. As Bevin had predicted at the outset, it was Byrnes and not Stalin who made the first move toward compromise. Though missing his Christmas deadline by one full day, Byrnes succeeded in getting Stalin to accept the clause on stages in exchange for U.S. approval of Security Council control over the future UN commission—a concession that would later have major, and unforeseen, consequences for Byrnes' diplomacy at home.

But compared to the disappointment of London, the Moscow conference had been an overwhelming success, in which Byrnes could cite his meetings with Stalin as a highlight. The joint Soviet-American communiqué, released to the press upon the eve of the new year, might well have symbolized for him a new beginning in relations between the two countries. There had been several other settlements to come out of the meetings as well. Both sides reached agreement on holding a future European peace conference with French and Chinese representatives included, thereby erasing one of the bitter disputes at the previous Council of Foreign Ministers. Stalin had also agreed that Byrnes' proposal of a four-power treaty against German military resurgence would be discussed at that conference. Finally, Russia was invited to join a multinational control commission for Japan—another point of contention at the ill-fated London conference, and a personal victory for Byrnes over Truman's earlier objections.[35]

The great questions of Soviet-American diplomacy, to be sure, remained unresolved at the conference. No settlement was reached on differences concerning Greece and Iran, for example, or leading to U.S. recognition of the communist governments of eastern Europe. Rather than the cause of a breakdown as in London, however, discussion of these disputes was in Moscow simply deferred when the two sides agreed to disagree.

As important for Byrnes as the substance of the contrast between the London and Moscow councils was the difference he perceived in the cooperative spirit of the latter. His experiment with a different sort of atomic diplomacy had proved to his satisfaction that the bomb would accomplish more in the guise of a promise than as the embodiment of a threat.

Byrnes could even point to tangible cases where he believed his cooperative approach on the bomb had engendered a like response from Stalin. The controversial issue of the African trusteeship was only briefly raised by Stalin in their Christmas Eve meeting, and then as quickly dropped. Of greater symbolic importance was an incident that same evening which recalled for Byrnes the London conference and his nemesis there, Molotov. At a dinner party where Stalin was host, Molotov had joked that this time it was Byrnes' associate, Conant, who had an atomic bomb in his pocket. Some years later, Byrnes thought Stalin's stinging reproof of Molotov significant: "He had said nothing before, but now rose and said he thought Mr. Molotov was wrong in speaking so lightly about the American scientist; Stalin said he himself was no scientist and had no knowledge of physics, but he thought Conant and his associates deserved the plaudits of all peoples."[36]

Leaving Moscow after the signing of the joint communiqué, Byrnes was clearly less concerned with the compromises that his eroding position at home had necessitated than with what he viewed as the positive accomplishments of the conference. Foremost among these had been his agreement with Stalin on the establishment of the UN atomic energy commission, which might still redeem his efforts in the eyes of his American detractors.

It was, further, perhaps reasonable to hope that those things which had not been accomplished at the meeting might yet be the subject of agreement at the UN. For Byrnes believed that the Russians—and especially Stalin—had seemed earnest in their desire for continuing cooperation with the West.

Finally, it was not the least of his accomplishments, Byrnes might reflect, that this had been achieved despite the obstacles put in his way by the British, the Russians, and—most serious of all—by the President and domestic critics.

"One More Typical American 'Give-Away' "

Byrnes was wrong, however, if he thought the agreement at Moscow had mollified the most formidable of his critics. Before Byrnes' plane had even touched down in Washington, Vandenberg was attacking the resolution on atomic energy contained in the conference communiqué.

Vandenberg's objections to the agreement were—if nothing else—ironic, for the specific target of his attack was the very paragraph on stages which Byrnes had taken such pains to add to the final resolution. As before in his meeting with Truman, Vandenberg objected to the order of the four stages. Those stages, he argued, still put agreements before safeguards. At the same time, he mistook what had been one of Byrnes' major concessions at Moscow—Security Council control of the UN commission—as an American diplomatic triumph.[37]

This difference in perception was perhaps symptomatic of the divergent attitude that Byrnes and Vandenberg had toward the prospect of cooperation with Russia. Byrnes saw in Security Council control the chance that the Soviets might veto American proposals. Vandenberg saw in it the opportunity for the United States to veto Russian proposals. America's atomic monopoly was "a wasting asset" to the former, the nation's "trading stock" to the latter. Obviously, the Michigan senator did not share Byrnes' vision of the Moscow conference as a step toward better relations with the Russians. He saw it instead as a possible threat to America's continued nuclear hegemony. It was, Vandenberg wrote his wife, simply "one more American 'give-away.'"

For a time it even seemed likely that Vandenberg's opposition would prevent Senate approval of the Moscow accord. In another meeting with Truman just after Christmas, he threatened to resign from the United States delegation to the forthcoming UN meeting in London. His resignation would be a protest to the establishment of the UNAEC without, as he believed, adequate safeguards. Vandenberg's threat undoubtedly impressed the President, since the Republican's defection would split the delegation along partisan lines and set a precedent dangerous for the administration's foreign-policy consensus.

Fortunately for both Truman and Byrnes, Vandenberg's touchy sensibilities were assuaged by an ingenious solution originating with Acheson. This was a statement—which the senator then issued to the press under his own name—specifying that the four steps of the communiqué were to be read together rather than in order, "all being finally subject to Congressional approval." The compromise seemed both to repair Vandenberg's wounded ego and to assure his future cooperation. "Under the circumstances," he wrote subsequently, "I feel that I can now proceed to London without impairing my obligations to my Senate colleagues. Indeed, the circumstances *now* probably *demand* that I go. . . ."[38]

For Byrnes, this was only the weathering of the first crisis on the Moscow accord; and, for Vandenberg, only a superficial sign of unanimity.

Despite Vandenberg's apparent conversion to the Moscow agreement, Truman remained plainly miffed at Byrnes. One reason was the latter's failure to keep him informed of events in Moscow. Even after Acheson's warning telegram on the 15th, Byrnes' dispatches to Washington continued to be both infrequent and imprecise. Truman was particularly incensed, therefore, to learn of the end of the Moscow conference—and even the contents of the official communiqué—from radio reports rather than from his secretary of state. Compounding this insult was Byrnes' public announcement of a nationwide broadcast on the conference upon his return. This cavalier attitude, and the evidence that he was now accustomed to issuing statements without consulting Truman, had caused the President, Davies wrote in late December, to go "sour on Jim." "There will be a change there before long," he predicted.[39]

Informed of Truman's angry mood by Acheson once back in Washington, Byrnes was "disbelieving, impatient, and irritated." Yet in a meeting with Truman later that same evening, he characterized their discussion as "cordial." Byrnes was apologetic about the communications problem which, he said, had made consultation with the President impossible.[40]

Truman—even if disbelieving—chose once again not to confront Byrnes with his displeasure. Indeed, in his radio address the following day, Byrnes betrayed only a slight sign that his enthusiasm was now tempered with caution when he reported on the Moscow accord. That speech stressed, therefore, the importance of safeguards in the Soviet-American agreement.[41]

On New Year's Eve, Byrnes joined Truman and his advisers aboard the yacht *Williamsburg.* To no one's surprise, Leahy used the occasion to denounce Byrnes generally and the Moscow agreement in particular. Truman, however, did not join in the attack. "We spent a pleasant evening," Byrnes, undaunted, wrote of the episode, "all the group joining in singing the old year out." On January 2, Truman and Byrnes met for two hours, with the President evidently approving the speech the latter had given on the radio. Seemingly, the most important obstacles in the way of approval of the accord had been overcome. When Byrnes explained that his remarks had not been cleared with Truman only because of a subordinate's error in the State Department,

Ayers heard Truman vow to "rake" the aide "over the coals."[42]

But the appearance of peace was deceptive. In fact, the incident which would finally bring about the long-delayed showdown between Truman and Byrnes was one which the latter, in his eagerness to appease Congress over the matter of stages in the accord, had entirely overlooked.

"I'm Tired of Babying the Soviets"

The President's receipt in early January of a State Department report concerning the curtailment of political liberties in eastern Europe—prepared upon Byrnes' order but forgotten during the Moscow conference itself—again brought to the fore all of Truman's old resentment. Byrnes, Truman discovered, had taken the document to Moscow with him but had neglected to give him a copy until his return. The so-called Ethridge Report symbolized for Truman not only the casual disregard which Byrnes had for his authority, but also a trend in the secretary's conduct of foreign affairs which he thought dangerous.

Byrnes learned of Truman's renewed anger over the Ethridge Report when he arrived at the White House later on the afternoon of January 6. Speaking from notes for a letter that he had originally intended to send Byrnes, Truman said that he considered the latter's accomplishments at Moscow "unreal," and "no more than a general promise" from the Russians. Byrnes had made no progress at the conference, the President charged, in areas where genuine American interests were involved—the liberalization of the regimes in eastern Europe and the removal of Soviet troops from Iran. Instead, Truman claimed, he "had taken it upon himself to move the foreign policy of the United States in a direction to which he could not, and would not, agree." "I'm tired of babying the Soviets," the President snapped.

Surprised—if not stunned—by this criticism, Byrnes' defense of his actions at the conference was perfunctory. Moscow had been "simply another effort to provide means for securing compliance to . . . previous agreements," he said. Adding—in what might have been an implicit criticism of Truman's handling of foreign policy—"It might not be successful but it could not be any worse than the previous situation."[43]

While he never publicly admitted to the split with Truman, privately Byrnes speculated at length on its cause. In material that was never used in his memoirs, Byrnes wrote of his "deduction . . . that someone of [Truman's] friends on board the ship" that New Year's Eve had turned the President against him.[44]

In point of fact, Byrnes had surely become aware much earlier of the maneuverings of what Davies had termed Truman's "palace guard." The captain (or, actually, admiral) of that guard was Leahy, who characterized the Moscow accord in his diary as "an appeasement document which gives to the Soviets everything they want and preserves to America nothing." Leahy had even earlier muttered that Byrnes was influenced by "communistically-inclined advisers in his department." Another conservative member of that guard, Samuel Rosenman, agreed with Leahy that the Moscow communiqué contained "nothing of value to the U.S." Almost certainly, Leahy and Rosenman had shared their views with Truman on board the yacht. Yet the storm these two might have created on that occasion had passed over without incident. Truman's criticism of Byrnes did not come until a week later.[45]

It is possible that Truman's outburst on the yacht reflected a certain sympathy with the Republican opposition to Byrnes. However, it is hardly true that the President abandoned Byrnes because of the senators, since the crisis over Vandenberg's threatened resignation was resolved before Byrnes stepped on board the yacht. Nor was Truman's claim that Byrnes at Moscow had departed from his instructions entirely convincing, since Truman had issued no detailed instructions to his secretary of state.

In reality, the reason for the dispute with the President over the Moscow accord was one which Byrnes was either too close to see or too reluctant to admit.

That rift originated in the differing conceptions of the two men concerning what the Moscow conference was to have accomplished. Truman and his "palace guard" had expected that Byrnes' meeting with Molotov and Stalin would be conducted along the same lines as the wartime conferences at Yalta and Potsdam, where the major territorial questions of the peace settlement were discussed. As his reaction to the Ethridge Report showed, Truman was still preeminently concerned with the Russian presence in eastern Europe, and with such other apparent evidence of Soviet encroachment as their continued occupation of Iran. He had shown no real interest in—or understanding of—Byrnes' initiative at Moscow on atomic energy. Truman's earlier disregard of the Stimson proposal, and this latest rebuff to Byrnes, indicate that he considered Soviet-American cooperation on atomic energy intangible—"unreal." Believing that he had settled the question of U.S. policy on the bomb the previous October, Truman viewed Byrnes' December initiative in Moscow—understandably—as dangerous insubordination. The President's message on "babying the Soviets" had made that clear. By it, Truman also made it clear that there would be no change in policy on the bomb and no rapprochement on what he considered minor issues—including scientific interchange on atomic energy—until the outstanding territorial and economic issues between the United States and Russia were settled.

For Byrnes, however, the lesson of the Moscow conference was entirely different. The story of postwar dealings with the Soviets up to that point was one of failure. Not having attended either the London or the Moscow councils, Byrnes believed, Truman could neither comprehend the atomic bomb's limitation in diplomacy as a threat nor appreciate its positive contribution as a promise of cooperation. With the Soviet-American agreement on the UNAEC, there had perhaps begun the kind of cooperation that could be substantive rather than just symbolic. Not least important for Byrnes himself, of course, was his hope that this cooperation would be a personal victory of major proportions, with its own rewards at home.

Ultimately, Byrnes's vision of the Moscow accord was more consistent with the diplomacy of Roosevelt than with that of Truman. But the fact that the temper of the later administration proved hostile to Byrnes' initiative was perhaps not so much the fault of Truman as of Byrnes. For his had remained too private a vision throughout.

In one sense, Byrnes' approach at Moscow had been exactly the opposite of his approach at the London Council of Foreign Ministers. At London, he had sought to use the bomb as a means of achieving America's ends in diplomacy—including, foremost, the liberalization of the regimes in eastern Europe. At Moscow, the end became an agreement on the bomb itself, apart from and even subordinate to U.S. concern with eastern Europe. Byrnes' deliberate decision to keep Truman in the dark regarding his plans in Russia, however, not only forfeited the possibility of support from the President and Congress, but also substantiated the charges made by Vandenberg and Truman's "palace guard" that he was seeking to turn U.S. foreign policy in a new direction. The price that the "secretive" Byrnes would pay for this show of independence would be made evident as the UN convened in London at the start of the new year.

"We Retrieved Some Ground at London"

Having learned directly from Truman of the President's loss of confidence in him, Byrnes almost immediately came under attack by the disgruntled senators and Dulles. At London the shared resentment of Vandenberg, Connally, and Dulles toward his conduct of foreign affairs united in a bipartisan consensus against Byrnes. The three men told him that his earlier assurances concerning safeguards in the Moscow accord were now insufficient. They demanded in addition that the statement which Acheson had drafted on separate stages be included in the formal agreement.

This demand amounted to requiring that Byrnes renegotiate the accord with Russia—a move that Moscow could only interpret as an indication of bad faith, and would certainly reject. Hoping to salvage his agreement with the Soviets, Byrnes agreed to fly to London in order to intercede personally with the opposition. Privately, he suspected that the real motivation behind the demand to amend the agreement was a desire to humiliate him. London was meant to be his own private Knossos, Byrnes believed, for there was little substance in his critics' apparent change of heart. At the airport, about to leave for the British capital, Byrnes defended the accord to a sympathetic Davies. The communiqué, he noted, said nothing about "tackling the problem of how the atomic bomb was produced. . . . [The] secret was safe."[46]

Once in London, Byrnes again displayed his talents as a "troubleshooter" and "compromiser"—and also confirmed his own suspicions about the motives of Vandenberg, Connally, and Dulles. Speaking at length with the two Republicans, he tactfully emphasized the role that the Security Council veto might play in protecting American interests in the UNAEC. Byrnes suggested to Vandenberg a compromise agreement which upheld the latter's insistence upon four discrete stages but kept the way clear for scientific interchange in the future. His own show of contrition, Byrnes recognized, was more a matter of style than of substance. But it was, apparently, enough. Vandenberg, Connally, and Dulles subsequently agreed to withdraw their demand to amend the Moscow accord. "Thank heaven Jimmy Byrnes hates disagreements,"

Vandenberg wrote his wife from London, "because I don't know where I would be if he decided to continue this fight." In a letter to Dulles, Vandenberg was more explicit. Byrnes' trip to Moscow had been a "humiliating pilgrimage," he charged. "But we retrieved some ground at London this winter."[47]

"This Period . . . Had Passed"

The final victory at London belonged to Byrnes' critics. Newly concerned about his health, harried by the continued criticism, and now plainly convinced of the President's disaffection—Truman announced on January 8 that he did not consider himself bound by the provisions of the Moscow communiqué concerning eastern Europe—Byrnes decided to retire from the administration. After he had informed Truman of that decision, he agreed to stay on in the government until the conclusion of the next Council of Foreign Ministers, later that year in Paris.[48]

It was while at that conference in Paris, in fact, that Byrnes would confess the reason for his conversion to a "hard-line" approach toward Russia. "He, himself," Byrnes told French Foreign Minister Georges Bidault, "had gone to the extreme where he had been subjected to considerable criticism for 'appeasing' Russia and yielding too much. This period, however, had passed, and American opinion was no longer disposed to make concessions on important questions."[49]

With Byrnes' departure, the idea of the direct approach to Russia was allowed to lapse. Enervated by opposition since its inception nearly four months earlier, that approach, first suggested by Stimson but ultimately undertaken by Byrnes, was abandoned in Washington as the new year began. With the imminent shift of discussions on atomic energy to the highly visible arena of the United Nations, its time had passed. And with it had passed also the purpose of Byrnes' stroke at reversing American policy on the bomb through direct diplomacy.

Could the outcome of Byrnes' initiative to Russia have been otherwise?

He later thought it could—at least so far as it concerned the American side. "I am confident," he wrote some years after his retirement, "that if Vandenberg had been with us at Moscow there would not have been any misunderstanding on the subject [of the Moscow accord], and from that day to the end of my service as Secretary I insisted upon his accompanying us to every international conference."[50]

Indeed, Vandenberg's performance at the London UN meeting had been petty and vindictive, though to some degree excused by a legitimate grievance. Specifically, the rekindling of his objections at London—after he had declared himself satisfied with the text of the Moscow communiqué the previous week—justifies the suspicion that the presence there of his two disaffected colleagues, Connally and Dulles, may have emboldened him into a revolt against the Truman administration in general and Byrnes in particular. The demand to change the Moscow accord had perhaps been fair warning to the secretary of state. And the relative ease with which first Acheson and then Byrnes were able to defuse Vandenberg's "irreconcilable" differences with the Soviet-American agreement further substantiates the presumption that the senator's stubbornness at the UN meeting was only tactical, and was aimed at Byrnes personally rather than his policies. "He was not engaged in strategy," Acheson would observe somewhat sarcastically of Vandenberg. "[R]ather he was a prophet pointing out to more earthbound rulers the errors and spiritual failings of their ways."[51]

It is conceivable, therefore, that Byrnes could have gained the support of Vandenberg—and perhaps others among his critics as well—had he taken Congress into his confidence regarding the intended approach to Russia and its aims. For example, had the Michigan senator been courted as assiduously by Byrnes on the matter of Soviet-American cooperation concerning the bomb as he had been earlier by FDR on the UN (or later by Truman regarding the Marshall Plan), Byrnes' experience at Moscow and subsequently at London might have been substantially different. Instead, Byrnes' apparent hope that the Senate might ratify his coup after the fact actually proved fatal to the success of his mission.

It is less likely that Truman would have opposed the initiative to Russia if it had had the support of Vandenberg, Connally, and Dulles. Distracted as Truman was by other matters demanding his attention—and given both his own apparent belief that the bomb was peripheral to the peace settlement and his rejection of Stimson's direct approach—it was all the more probable that the President would have yielded to pressure from these three and from Byrnes. Nor would the British have represented any serious obstacle to an early Soviet-American rapprochement on the bomb. The objections of Attlee and Bevin to Byrnes' diplomacy had clearly concerned its method rather than its content.

This is not, of course, to argue that the direct approach to Russia would ultimately have succeeded, or that it could have substantively affected the cold war. But the true test of such an approach was never made. Instead, with the convening of the UNAEC in late January 1946, its prospects became moot. The brief era of diplomacy in which the bomb, directly and indirectly, had played such a large role ended. Future progress toward the cooperative control of atomic energy would be made through the United Nations—if at all.

In this, Byrnes would have no further role. Until his retirement in 1947, he, like Vandenberg, would go along with the prevailing political current in the Truman administration. That current, clearly, had moved away from a policy of diplomatic accommodation with the Soviets to a policy of monopoly and exclusion. In that policy the implicit threat of the atomic bomb and not the explicit promise of its mutual control would henceforth have the larger role.

BOOK TWO

The Atomic Curtain
Domestic and International
Consequences of Atomic Energy,
1945-1947

Pax Atomica:
The Myth of the Atomic Secret

"If there was ever a time for secret diplomatic agreement, secretly arrived at, this is the time."

General Groves to his staff, February 1945

"One man in the War Department, General Groves, has, by the power of the veto on the grounds of 'military security,' really been determining and almost running foreign policy."

David E. Lilienthal, journal entry, January 1946

"General Groves Tells Me
There Is No Uranium in Russia"

Ultimately abortive, the direct approach to Russia undertaken by Byrnes was still not entirely without results—even if they were unanticipated by him at the time. Prior to his humiliating encounter with Vandenberg and Dulles at London that January, Byrnes had seemingly struck a final blow for his own independence by creating a "Secretary of State's Committee" on atomic energy. The committee's task would be to study the problem of the bomb's international control. The fact that the Senate had already announced it intended to open hearings on international control, and the timing of Byrnes' announcement—at the airport upon leaving for the meeting with Vandenberg at London—suggest that his panel of experts was intended to be a parting shot to his enemies in Congress, and a way of preserving the State Department's autonomy in making policy on the bomb. Yet it was also a move destined to shed light upon a subject previously cloaked in mystery—the atomic secret.

The Secretary of State's Committee would be the first governmental body to look into the atomic secret outside of the Manhattan Project. Appointed to head that committee by Byrnes and Acheson, former TVA Director David Lilienthal wrote in his journal of the opportunity this task presented: "Inevitably (as I see it), the assignment would force an examination of the crucial question: _What is there that is secret?_ If my hunch that in the real sense there are no secrets (that is, nothing that is not known or knowable) would be supportable by the facts, then real progress would be made. For then it would be clear that the basis of present policy-making is without foundation." Lilienthal was also openly skeptical of what he termed "the Army-sponsored thesis that there are secrets." He continued, "And since it is in the Army's hands (or, literally, Gen. Groves') to deny access to the facts that would prove or disprove this vital thesis, there has been no way to examine the very foundation of our policies in the international field."[1]

It was, of course, not only the issue of the bomb's international control that was affected by the mystery of the atomic secret, but domestic policy as well. By early 1946 a debate was underway in Congress concerning a national commission for the domestic control of atomic energy. The outcome of that debate, and the future of international control, would depend in large measure upon the answer given to the "crucial question" of Lilienthal's inquiry: "_What_ is there that is secret?" This question lay at the heart of the decision about what to do with the atomic bomb once the direct approach to Russia had been rejected.

By early 1946, Lilienthal was hardly the first in the government to wonder what the Manhattan Project had created besides the bomb—but he was perhaps the first to demand an answer. The anatomy of the atomic secret was a subject discussed by Stimson and Groves at Truman's first briefing on the bomb, in April 1945. "A great deal of emphasis was placed on foreign relations and particularly on the Russian situation," Stimson wrote of that briefing. "The steps taken by us to secure control of raw materials were discussed at considerable length."[2]

The matter of secrecy had next come up at an Interim Committee meeting in mid-May 1945. There the question of when the Russians might get the bomb—considered crucial to the decision of whether to tell them of the weapon before its use—was again left unresolved. At that meeting, Conant, the only member of the committee proper with training as a scientist, voiced the almost unanimous opinion of those who had built the bomb that the Russians would catch up with the United States in three to five years. Groves was the sole dissenter, claiming that it would take the Soviets up to a generation—as long as twenty years—to duplicate America's achievement. While he deemed this accounting "highly unsafe," Conant was apparently unable to persuade the others on the committee to accept his shorter estimate. In testimony some months later, Groves declined to comment on the "striking discrepancy" between his estimate and that of the scientists.[3]

Questions concerning the nature of the atomic secret and the monopoly's likely duration had received no answer, therefore, by the time the bomb was dropped on Hiroshima. For Stimson, they had lost their earlier importance. "Whether Russia gets control of the necessary secrets of production in a minimum of say four years or a maximum of twenty years is not nearly as important to the world and civilization as to make sure that when they do get it they are willing and cooperative partners among the peace loving nations of the world," he argued in his September memo. In his radio address of the previous month, Stimson had explicitly rejected "any long term policy of secrecy."[4]

Events would show that Stimson's rejection of continued secrecy was no more popular an idea in Washington than his proposal for a direct approach to Russia on the bomb. Indeed, by fall 1945, other members of the Truman administration—including Truman himself—seemed to consider the question of when Russia might get the bomb as of principal significance, and to accept the word of Groves rather than that of the scientists on the subject. It was upon Groves' advice, therefore, that Truman chose to reject the State Department's warning that America's monopoly would be short-lived. More than one reporter listening to Truman's announcement of atomic policy at Linda Lodge later that month was left with the impression that the President believed the Russians might never get the bomb.[5]

Byrnes, by this time, also supported a continuing policy of secrecy, and believed that the monopoly would be enduring. At a meeting late in spring 1945, the atomic scientist Leo Szilard had been "completely flabbergasted" by Byrnes' attitude toward secrecy and the Russians. When Szilard pleaded for Byrnes to endorse international control of atomic energy because the Soviets would otherwise soon have the bomb, the secretary of state had matter-of-factly replied: "General Groves tells me there is no uranium in Russia."[6]

Even after Byrnes' experience at the first Council of Foreign Ministers had disabused him of the notion that the threat of the bomb would be America's master card in diplomacy, his faith in a long tenure for the U.S. atomic monopoly remained. In a meeting with Patterson and Forrestal only two weeks after the London conference debacle, Byrnes complained that an "overemphasis" had been put on the views of the scientists in discussion of what should be done with the bomb. Byrnes "said that he bowed to [the scientists] in their ability to develop the bomb but on the question of giving information to others he thought the scientists were no better informed than he was on the construction of the bomb." Besides, he concluded, "General Groves knew more about the problem than any of the people from Dupont, Union Carbide or Eastman."*

Like Stimson, Byrnes departed from the policy of secrecy and exclusion despite his estimate of the monopoly's lengthy duration. It was not from a position of weakness but from strength that he had launched his ill-fated initiative on the bomb. Byrnes' was a faith founded upon assurances from Groves of the atomic secret's relative inviolability and lasting duration. Shared by Truman and many others in the administration, this common belief in a prolonged monopoly safeguarded by secrecy was one of the greatest miscalculations of the cold war.

It was a miscalculation with fundamental consequences at home and abroad. Concern for the atomic secret had been a confirming factor in the decision to exclude rather than approach Russia on the bomb. The attitude that it would be some time before the Russians could develop their own bomb—together with some element of plain wishful thinking —undoubtedly reinforced what has been seen to be the administration's existing inclination to exclude Russia in the matter of the bomb.

"The Postwar Position . . . Would Not Be Unfavorable"

The myth of the atomic secret had its beginnings in the realities of the project to build the atomic bomb. When General Leslie Groves inherited the Manhattan Project from Roosevelt's Office of Scientific Research and Development early in 1942 he also began to shape the earliest expectations and assumptions concerning the bomb's use. The unique strictures of secrecy connected with the Manhattan Project even facilitated Groves' independence as director. Groves himself wrote immod-

---

*On June 1, 1945, representatives from these three companies—the prime contractors for the Manhattan Project—had advised the Interim Committee of their opinion that it would take no more than five years for the Russians to build an atomic bomb.[7]

estly—but not inaccurately—in his memoirs that "the command channels of the [project] . . . had no precedent"—a fact which meant that he soon became involved in "matters of extremely high-level policy, including international relations."[8] Nor did Groves consider himself bound by the probable duration of the war in his role as planner. Upon his appointment as Manhattan Project director he immediately set about the task, he later wrote, of "insuring that the postwar position of the United States in the field of atomic energy would not be unfavorable."[9]

What Groves meant by this cryptic remark was that he sought a means of guaranteeing the atomic bomb as an exclusive American possession not only during the war, but for some time after as well. His personal contribution to the Manhattan Project was to be strategic rather than scientific—not only to supervise the building of the weapon but to retain control over it subsequently by keeping the necessary ingredients for its construction from other nations. This was to be accomplished by a monopoly of the world's atomic raw materials, a monopoly that was meant to be—in Groves' term—"preclusive," insofar as the Russians would be unable to build atomic bombs until they had somehow gained, or been given, access to such raw material.

Groves' gargantuan task began in fall 1942, when he overturned the decision of his civilian predecessors, Bush and Conant, against bringing additional uranium ore under government control.[10] Along with stockpiling uranium, Groves initiated a clandestine program of identifying and purchasing uranium ore around the world. Code-named the Murray Hill Area (in keeping with the nomenclature of the Manhattan Project), this top-secret adjunct of the bomb project came under his personal direction and received sanction from President Roosevelt and Secretary of War Stimson. Even the money for the purchase of the ore—ultimately amounting to several million dollars—was channeled from the project's budget through Groves' own bank account so as to avoid detection by spies and, he wrote in his memoirs, a later "change of heart on the part of Congress."[11]

The eventual purpose of this effort to corner the market on uranium was made plain by Groves at the time to the hand-picked staff he put in charge of the Murray Hill Area: "When the war is over, there will be diplomatic exchanges between the victorious nations, possibly even another Versailles Conference. . . . I am determined that any American negotiators after the present war will have available to them all possible information concerning the sources of fissionable materials."[12] In a

September 1944 report to Stimson, Groves predicted that the United States would control, directly and indirectly, some 90 percent of the world's high-grade uranium ore by war's end.[13]

Groves found his task eased somewhat by the cooperation of Edgar Sengier, a Belgian national who was also a representative of the African Metals Corporation (Afrimet) and a director of Union Minière, a mining consortium with control of the world's largest deposit of uranium ore, in the Belgian Congo. Sengier had fled Belgium just prior to the 1940 German invasion, arriving in New York with a substantial quantity of uranium ore, which he had stockpiled in a Staten Island warehouse. Wartime secrecy and the German occupation of Belgium guaranteed Sengier virtual autonomy in his direction of Union Minière, and an independence equal to that of Groves in the Manhattan Project. A close bond subsequently developed between the two like-minded men.[14] The Murray Hill Area not only purchased all of Sengier's ore but signed an agreement with the Belgian government-in-exile late in 1944 for "effective control now of all the uranium in the Belgian Congo without reference to review at the end of the war."[15]

Groves, of course, realized that even control of the Congo's uranium was not sufficient to guarantee a preclusive monopoly of the ore. Guided by its own comprehensive survey of world uranium resources, the Murray Hill Area thus initiated negotiations under his direction with seven foreign governments for the atomic raw materials in their possession. The discovery by Manhattan Project scientists during these negotiations that thorium—an element some ten times more plentiful in nature than uranium—could also be used to sustain an atomic chain reaction did not discourage Groves and the Murray Hill Area staff, but only caused them to widen the scope of their activities.[16]

Throughout 1944 and 1945 this clandestine bargaining between the Murray Hill Area and foreign governments proceeded apace, usually without the knowledge of the U.S. State Department. Since these governments remained ignorant of the destiny of their uranium—the ore's principal prewar use being in the manufacture of glass and as a ceramic pigment—first-refusal contracts were easily and cheaply arranged. Occasionally, the secret nature of these negotiations resulted in some embarrassing and even ludicrous incidents which may actually have hindered rather than helped Groves toward his final goal.*

---

*One such episode occurred in the course of the Belgian negotiations. Sengier's involvement with the Manhattan Project was apparently unknown to his own government, for he joined the Belgian negotiators as a neutral "adviser." The arrival of Sengier on the Belgian side delighted Major

The spirit of this monumental undertaking was best summed up by the general himself in a memorandum to his staff early in 1945, one which recalled Versailles as Groves' *idée fixe:* "If there was ever a time for secret diplomatic agreement, secretly arrived at, this is the time."[18]

Whereas they were always arranged in secrecy, the raw-materials purchases of Groves and the Murray Hill Area had been authorized at the highest level from the very beginning. In June 1943 the Military Policy Committee of Stimson's War Department approved Groves' request that he "allow nothing to stand in the way of achieving as complete control as possible" of the atomic raw materials. Indeed, as late as the winter of 1944, President Roosevelt took a personal interest in the progress of the Murray Hill Area and the methods by which it acquired ore, asking a briefing officer to point out to him on a map the location of uranium deposits in the Congo.[19]

It had also been clear from the beginning that the task of achieving a preclusive monopoly of atomic raw materials was not one that the United States could accomplish on its own. The prospect of a preclusive monopoly had only been made possible, in fact, by the 1943 Quebec Agreement, one provision of which created a Combined Policy Committee to oversee the purchase of uranium from the exile Belgian government in London. In keeping with his role as creator and director of the Murray Hill Area, Groves became an influential participant in this committee. Characteristically, however, his role there remained a secret. He explained in his memoirs that it "would not have looked well if I had been officially appointed to serve on a committee of civilians."[20]

Groves also supported the Quebec Agreement and later defended it to skeptics in the Truman administration solely for its part in assuring that the British would not gain exclusive control of the Congo's uranium ore. For him, even America's wartime alliance with Britain was not to stand in the way of the West's raw-materials monopoly. The Quebec Agreement, he believed, was only a marriage of mutual convenience which could be annulled by the United States at war's end.

The revelation in the summer of 1944 that thorium could also be

---

H. S. Traynor, Groves' man at the talks; as Traynor wrote, "[Sengier's] presence during the negotiations would be an insurance against delay and unfortunate questions." Such questions probably did arise, however, when Traynor, introduced to the Belgians at the outset as a civilian, forgot his role and later appeared in uniform alongside Sengier. To compound the farce, Sengier opposed the American proposal, holding out for a higher price—until Traynor discreetly pointed out that his association with them left Sengier vulnerable to charges of treason from the Belgian government, thereby clinching the deal.[17]

used to make atomic bombs required that the honeymoon with the British be prolonged beyond Groves' original estimate. This was provided for shortly thereafter by the Hyde Park "Agreement and Declaration of Trust," which created the Anglo-American Combined Development Trust. The purpose of the trust was to assure joint control of uranium and thorium ore under British dominion but not yet in the stockpile of the Manhattan Project.

The existence of the Combined Policy Committee and the advent of the Combined Development Trust late in 1944 did not compromise the independence of Groves and the Murray Hill Area, but actually had the reverse effect. As a *de facto* member of the committee, Groves worked behind the scenes to assure that real control of atomic raw materials would not be shared with the British. Appointed chairman of the newly established trust, Groves was able to make decisions on the procurement of uranium and thorium independent of the committee. It was at Groves' insistence that a provision for review had been appended by Roosevelt to the original "Agreement and Declaration of Trust." This "escape clause," as Groves termed it, provided that the trust itself could be dissolved by either of its members at the end of hostilities. By such means he meant to assure that the lion's share of uranium and thorium, like the bomb itself, would stay with the Manhattan Project after the war.

Thus it was primarily to revise the Hyde Park aide-mémoire and to renegotiate the Quebec Agreement that the British had insisted upon meeting with Truman in Washington the previous November. The original Quebec Agreement had provided that the British would surrender their equal share of uranium to the United States during the war "on the basis of need"—a tacit recognition that only the Manhattan Project was likely to produce a bomb before the end of the war. As a result, Britain was essentially without any uranium by war's end, despite her partnership in the trust. Expecting the United States to agree to an equal division of the ore in peacetime, the British had calculated that the annual American need for uranium would be some six hundred tons. Instead, the British were shocked to learn at Washington that Groves now proposed the allocation of ore on "an actual use basis," and that his estimate of the Manhattan Project's needs in peacetime was some four times their own—*or nearly all of the Congo's annual production*—for each of the next five years. To the British this meant that Groves intended no slowdown in America's production of atomic bombs after the initial crash effort, and that he meant to preclude them from developing their own atomic-energy program.[21] They were right on both counts.

"Russia Was Our Enemy"

When, at the beginning of 1945, it became obvious that time was about to run out for his effort to corner the market on the world's atomic raw materials, Groves initiated a project of a different sort. The war had given the Murray Hill Area a unique advantage that was unlikely to be continued in peacetime. The ability to conduct negotiations with foreign governments in secret was no small part of this, as was the fact that Allied armies then occupied the majority of land outside Russia to be surveyed or mined for uranium and thorium. Determined not to be at a disadvantage when that occupation ended, Groves arranged for the ore mined overseas to be moved to and stockpiled in the United States.

Yet the Murray Hill Area's greatest asset—the fact that the final destination of the ore it purchased was unknown to the nations selling it—would unavoidably end with the first use of the bomb as an instrument of war. No nation could ignore that a binding contract for uranium and thorium was, in the atomic age, less a short-term economic arrangement than a long-term military alliance. The contracts already signed with Belgium, for example, guaranteed exclusive American rights to the uranium and thorium in the Congo for from ten to thirty-three years. But it was doubtful that such arrangements could be reached with other countries once the existence of the bomb was known.

A source of atomic raw materials beyond the reach of the Murray Hill Area and Groves' checkbook was occupied Europe. Fear of an atomic arsenal in Hitler's hands had originally compelled many American scientists to join the Manhattan Project, since little was known during the war of German progress toward an atomic bomb. In order to fill that gap in strategic intelligence, Groves had ordered the establishment in late 1943 of the Manhattan District Scientific Intelligence Mission—Operation Alsos (fittingly, the Greek term for "grove"). During the liberation of Europe in 1944, Alsos agents followed in the wake of advancing Allied armies, collecting information on German scientists and capturing apparatus used in experiments on atomic energy.[22]

By early 1945, with the war and Alsos both approaching an end, the nature of this mission changed. Growing evidence from Alsos that the Germans were still far from producing an actual atomic bomb redirected the focus of the mission from the wartime to the postwar world. Consequently, Alsos was assigned the task of keeping the scientists and atomic raw materials of the nascent German bomb project out of the hands of the Russians.

With the invasion of Germany in the spring of 1945, an Alsos spinoff, Operation Paperclip, was undertaken to capture German scientists in the American zone, offering them asylum in the United States.* On Groves' premise "that nothing that might be of interest to the Russians should ever be allowed to fall into French hands, Operation Harborage was mounted at the same time, as American troops swept into what would become the French zone of occupation in Germany. Perhaps the dramatic finale of Alsos, Harborage involved the recapture of Belgian uranium ore from the Germans at an atomic-research facility between the rapidly converging lines of American and Russian troops. On at least one other occasion, involving a German atomic laboratory beyond the reach of Alsos in what was to become the Soviet zone, Groves ordered that the facility be bombed to prevent its capture by the Russians.[24]

The Russians, in fact, were never far from the attention of the Murray Hill Area and Alsos once the specter of a German atomic bomb had been banished. For Groves, a concern with Russian motives and Russian progress toward the bomb went much further back. "There was never, from about two weeks from the time I took charge of this Project any illusion on my part but that Russia was our enemy," he would claim some years after the war. "I didn't go along with the attitude of the country as a whole that Russia was a gallant ally. I always had suspicions and the project was conducted on that basis."[25] The Manhattan Project's chief of security also later disclosed that his investigations were aimed not at enemy sympathizers but were "primarily concerned with . . . who were or were not Communists in the loyalty sense in the Army."[26]

The closed nature of Soviet society continually frustrated American attempts to learn more about the Russian atomic-bomb project. As a

---

*Paperclip was followed by Project 63, a Defense Department plan to deny German and Austrian scientists to the Russians. To that end, the U.S. State Department in 1951 sent a list of such scientists to the governments of certain Latin American countries "for the purpose of encouraging German scientists' emigration to the relatively safer areas of the Western Hemisphere in order to positively deny their services to the Soviet Union."[23]

result, some of the operations authorized by Groves in order to penetrate the shroud of Soviet secrecy were, at best, bizarre.

Among these were efforts in 1943 and 1944 at what a Groves aide termed "smoking out" Russian knowledge of uranium and its uses. This involved the shipment to Russia of more than half a ton of uranium salts and slightly more than two pounds of low-grade uranium metal under the lend-lease program. The apparent aim of this curious loan was somehow to identify Russian sources of uranium ore, to gauge Soviet progress in atomic research—the Russians had asked at least for the uranium salts—and possibly also to sabotage their first nuclear "pile." Though it obviously did not bring the hoped-for results, this lend-lease "giveaway" of uranium ore to Russia did prove an acute embarrassment to Groves when it was uncovered late in 1949 and spurred a congressional investigation that unwittingly exposed the wartime activities of the Murray Hill Area. "Every bit of uranium that could be located was secretly bought up by the Government to prevent its possible export anywhere," an aide to Groves confirmed in those hearings. Concerning the prospect of sending usable or high-grade uranium to Russia, the same aide protested that he and his staff "did their darnedest to see she got none."[27]

Equally strange was a proposed effort to have an American scientist visiting Moscow in June 1945 question his Soviet colleagues about atomic energy. Groves was so concerned such inquiries might alert the Russians to American progress in atomic energy that he decided against contacting the scientist. Chemist James Conant, who accompanied Byrnes on his mission to Moscow the following December, privately assured the government of his opinion that "they know nothing" about the bomb.[28]

Of a more serious nature were covert operations conducted inside Russia with the aim of uncovering the extent and quality of uranium and thorium deposits. However, those operations—which remain under a cloak of secrecy even today—apparently did nothing to contradict the glib assurance which Byrnes had offered physicist Leo Szilard in April 1945, that "there is no uranium in Russia."*

---

*The reason for such confidence is unclear. As late as February 1945 an updating of the Murray Hill Area's "World Index Map" of uranium and thorium deposits showed that surveying work was not yet completed for Germany, and was limited to only a bibliographical search for Russia. Moreover, an accompanying memorandum on world uranium resources noted of Russia: "potential possibilities could be great."[29]

To be sure, the strident warning of the Russian threat which Groves and his associates sounded was both fashionable and politically expedient after 1949, when the nation was caught up in a fevered search for culprits in the alleged theft of the atomic secret. Groves' testimony in the case of wartime uranium shipments to Russia—"We were not worried about Germany or Japan. . . . We were worried about Russia"—therefore gave him a reputation for prescience in 1950.

Such postwar grandstanding aside, the creation of the Murray Hill Area and the subsequent world-ranging operations of Alsos leave little doubt that the real target of these adjuncts to the project to build the atomic bomb was neither Germany nor Japan, but Russia.

"We Danced Warily Around . . . the Russians"

Roosevelt's death and Truman's accession to the presidency in April 1945 did not interfere with Groves' effort to corner the atomic-raw-materials market. That summer Truman was briefed on and approved Groves' progress in "making the arrangement whereby we would have as nearly exclusive long term rights as possible to the thorium production of the world's major deposits." Because of thorium's relative abundance, its postwar control was more difficult than that of uranium, Groves acknowledged. But, he assured, provided that the United States contracted for the supply of the ore available in India and Brazil and "we're not criminally careless, we will dominate the situation."[30]

The surrender of Germany on May 8, 1945, intensified the sense of urgency surrounding the procurement of uranium and thorium ore by the Murray Hill Area. In the frenetic atmosphere of the Nazi *Götterdämmerung,* the pace of the remaining negotiations quickened. As the war's end approached, the Combined Development Trust simultaneously conducted talks with the governments of Sweden, Holland, Brazil, and India for the ore in their possession.

The negotiations with Sweden were especially touchy. Sweden's longstanding neutrality and its government's recent shift toward socialism were complications that Manhattan Project negotiators had not previously encountered. Groves feared, moreover, that the scheduled mid-July test of the first atomic bomb, if it became known to the Swedes, would end any chance of an agreement.[31]

It was, of course, not Alamogordo but Hiroshima that was the undoing of Groves' plan to gain control of additional uranium. The intervention of the U.S. ambassador to Sweden, Hershel Johnson, and of two troubleshooters from Groves' personal staff on the eve of the atomic bombing came too late to facilitate an agreement, for the political implications of the negotiations they were engaged in became apparent to the Swedes the following day. "We danced warily around the subject of the Russians," Johnson reported to Groves on August 7. Although the negotiations with the Swedish government continued up to and after the surrender of Japan, there was little hope remaining for success. When the talks were finally broken off by the Swedes in early September 1945, the reason for their failure—as well as a subtle new reality of the atomic age—was evident in the Swedish government's announcement that "political considerations make it . . . impossible . . . to put an option relating to uranium materials, by means of a secret agreement, in the hands exclusively of two of the great Powers of the world."[32]

"We Are Now in a Favorable Position"

The surrender of Japan and the end of the Second World War did not occur before Groves believed that he had attained his goal of a preclusive monopoly of atomic raw materials. Some in the Truman administration —including the President, Stimson, and Byrnes—obviously knew much earlier the secret behind America's unique atomic advantage. But it was not until four months after the war that Groves officially reported to members of the Combined Policy Committee and administration representatives on the results of Alsos and the Murray Hill Area. Cautioning that his comments "were of the highest order of secrecy," Groves disclosed to this assembly the substance of America's real atomic secret.[33]

His effort to corner the world market on atomic raw materials had been even more successful than he had hoped in his prediction to Stimson more than a year before. The Combined Development Trust nations controlled at war's end some 97 percent of the world's high-grade uranium ore from countries presently mining the mineral, Groves reported on December 3, 1945. Of the lower-grade ore deposits capable of early development, most were either under British dominium or in neutral Sweden. "Looking ahead ten years or more to large tonnage low-grade deposits which might be developed if no consideration is given to costs," the trust retained control of 35 percent, with the remainder divided between Russia and South America.

Groves also made the significance of these figures clear in the briefing. Of the two countries, Sweden and Russia, in a position to challenge the "dominant position of the Trust" concerning raw materials, only Russia could be considered a threat. Yet "Russian resources of raw materials are far inferior to those of the Trust group of nations," containing no high-grade uranium and probably requiring a "revolution in extraction techniques" to develop low-grade deposits.

Though unstated, Groves' conclusion was plain. It might take the Russians as long as twenty years to build a single atomic bomb, and even then its raw materials would give the West a substantive advantage in a nuclear arms race.

If an atomic scientist had been present at Groves' December briefing—none was invited—the scientist would almost certainly have contested the claim that the West had monopolized the world's atomic raw materials. Ironically, among the first to believe that atomic energy might be controlled by a monopoly of raw materials was Leo Szilard— the scientist who had been "flabbergasted" by Byrnes' assurance in 1945 that there was no uranium in Russia. By late 1942, however, Szilard had abandoned the idea of a raw-materials monopoly as impractical.[34]

In September 1944, Vannevar Bush and James Conant wrote to Stimson on the same theme: "We do not believe that over a period of a decade the control of the supply [of uranium and thorium] could be counted on to prevent such secret developments [as the bomb] in other countries."[35] With Stimson's espousal of the direct approach to Russia a year later, Bush and Conant may have considered the question moot.

A June 1945 report to the government by a panel of distinguished atomic scientists had been emphatic on the fallacy of a raw-materials monopoly. The authors of the Franck Report put their conclusion in italics: "[W]e cannot hope to avoid a nuclear armament race either by keeping secret from the competing nations the basic scientific facts of nuclear power or by cornering the raw materials required for such a race."[36]

Perhaps most remarkable about the unheeded warnings of Bush, Conant, Szilard, and the other scientists was not "why" they were ignored but "how." One reason had to do with the organization of the Manhattan Project itself. The unprecedented secrecy of the bomb project meant, as Stimson once told Truman, that "many of the people who are actually engaged in the work have no idea what it is." This fact was exploited by Groves, who once disdainfully characterized the project's scientists as "the greatest bunch of prima donnas ever assembled in one place." Because the scientists had literally no "need to know," they remained unaware not only of the real purpose behind the Murray Hill Area and Alsos, but even of those organizations' existence.[37]

Additionally, those few in the government who knew the truth of the atomic secret—and who might have been the natural allies of the scientists—were, like Stimson, either gone from the administration by the time of Groves' presentation; or, like Truman and Byrnes, of a mind to prefer Groves' vision of an enduring monopoly. Indeed, for this group the idea that the Russians might not have the bomb for as long as a generation was both a comforting notion in early 1945 and another reason to exclude the Soviets from sharing in America's knowledge of atomic energy in later months.

Finally, Groves was in a unique position as an adviser on the bomb —perhaps the only person to know all the Manhattan Project's secrets. Dubbed the "Atom-General" in frequent press accounts after Hiroshima, he henceforth showed that he intended to use his reputation for expertise on the bomb to advise the government in the realm of diplomacy as well. Significantly, that advice would consistently stress a theme that was also recurrent in Groves' wartime correspondence and postwar memoirs: America's lost chance for a lasting peace at the end of the previous world war.

Even as Truman and his Cabinet met at the White House on September 21, 1945, to discuss Stimson's proposed direct approach, Groves spoke before an assembly of International Business Machine executives in New York on the bomb and the future. "We have a spirit in the United States that is not duplicated elsewhere," he told the receptive audience.[38]

It was not "spirit," however, but the "relative industrial weakness" of other nations compared to the United States that Groves argued was really the key to America's atomic advantage. He opposed sharing that advantage "until such time as we feel and know that the other nations are willing to go along with our ideas as to keeping the peace. I mean they must be anxious for peace in their hearts, and not merely by speech or by signature to a treaty they do not intend to honor." The question of postwar control was so vital, he explained, because the bomb was "complete victory in our hands" while we alone had it, and because "it can be used also as a diplomatic bargaining point to lead to the opening up of the world so that there will be no opportunity for a nation to arm secretly. . . . If this nation controlled the atomic bomb for a few years until other nations are prepared to share it we will go a long way toward preserving peace."

Naturally, Groves did not allude to America's preclusive monopoly of atomic raw materials in his speech to the IBM executives. Nor did he repeat the ten-to-twenty-year estimate he had given the Interim Committee for a Russian bomb the previous May. But his testimony before a closed congressional hearing in October 1945 was more candid about the source of that estimate: it was based on what Groves calculated would be the time required by the Russians to solve the technical problem of utilizing low-grade uranium ore and to build the plants necessary to manufacture a bomb.* Groves had assured War Secretary Patterson in September 1945 that the Russians "would not be able to work on the scientific and the industrial problems simultaneously" due to a lack of trained scientists and technicians.

In other private and secret forums, Groves was equally blunt about what he thought were the postwar political implications of America's atomic advantage. In a January 1946 memorandum for Congress entitled "Our Army of the Future—As Influenced by Atomic Weapons," he foresaw only two alternatives for the United States in the matter of the bomb: "Either we must have a hard-boiled, realistic enforceable world agreement ensuring the outlawing of atomic weapons or we and our dependable allies must have an exclusive supremacy in the field." If "there are to be atomic weapons in the world," he concluded, "we must have the best, the biggest and the most." Significantly, Groves included here the possibility of a preemptive nuclear strike against foreign atomic-research facilities to guarantee such supremacy.[40]

Supremacy in a world order had been Groves' theme as well at a discussion in the War Department some months before concerning postwar strategic planning. "We are now in a favorable position . . . We should get our bases now and plan not for 10 years but for 50–100 years ahead."[41]

---

*During an interview in February 1979, former Atomic Energy Commission Chairman David Lilienthal observed that "a whole miasma of misunderstanding" surrounded the idea of the atomic secret—in no small part because of General Groves. "Groves thought that the idea of a single 'atomic secret' was a joke." His attitude, Lilienthal suggests, was "not a downgrading of the Russians generally" [but] "a downgrading emotionally of the Russians' technical capacity . . . as an ignorant, clumsy, backward country. He overdid that."[39]

Indeed, Groves envisioned at the end of the Second World War nothing less than an American-administered Pax Atomica—an atomic league of nations, founded upon the West's supposed technological superiority and the secret, preclusive monopoly of atomic raw materials.

Certainly Groves' suggestion of establishing the Pax Atomica by a preemptive nuclear attack upon Russia did not receive much backing in the Truman administration at this time. Truman, in fact, had rejected Groves' design by October 1945 when he dedicated the government to pursuing international control of the bomb. In the "sacred trust" which the President had announced on that occasion remained, nonetheless, the possibility of a *de facto* atomic league. The machinery for that league was already in existence. Because of the policy of exclusion, close secrecy would be maintained after the war in the Combined Development Trust, and Russia would continue to be excluded from even symbolic cooperation on the bomb. At the heart of America's atomic trusteeship was the assumption of an enduring monopoly of the bomb—an assumption which faith in the atomic secret made possible. Until the atomic secret was exploded as a myth, that assumption would play an important, even decisive, role in determining American policy on the bomb beyond 1945—first in Congress, then in the United Nations.

"Atom Spies" and Politics

"The war psychology has gotten into their blood and the ends justify the means. I am expecting them to circulate the most absurd stories."
Commerce Secretary Henry Wallace, journal entry, November 1945

". . . I have a feeling that there is a desire at Washington that this information should get out. . . ."
Canadian Prime Minister Mackenzie King, journal entry, February 1946

"The Secret Is Safe"

As was the case with international control, a national atomic energy commission became a concern in the government well before the first bomb exploded at Alamogordo. It was recognized at the premier meeting of the Interim Committee, in May 1945, that the responsibility for safeguarding the bomb as well as for developing the future nonmilitary application of atomic energy would require a new sort of governmental agency.

The exigencies of war had deferred any serious consideration of domestic control by the Interim Committee until the end of hostilities, however. And the issue was again almost immediately submerged by the debate within the administration over Russia and the bomb. The seeming resolution of that controversy by the end of 1945 with the abandonment of the direct approach and adoption of the policy of monopoly, as well as Byrnes' preemption of the international-control issue by his Secretary of State's Committee, meant that Congress finally seemed about to settle the question of domestic legislation on atomic energy as 1946 began.

Initially, the matter of domestic control seemed uncontroversial—at least compared to the portentous questions of Russia, international control, and the bomb itself. Truman, in fact, had announced that neither he nor his administration would take any part in congressional deliberation upon the nature of the proposed commission or the extent of its powers. Byrnes, too, had tacitly ignored the issue of domestic control in his preoccupation with how to approach Russia on the bomb. Taking advantage of this lack of leadership on the part of the administration, drafters of an atomic-energy bill in the War Department that would have given the military strong influence—if not outright dominance—over the proposed commission very nearly succeeded in securing passage of their bill through Congress by January 1946.

Yet a belated recognition of the dangers inherent in such a bill dramatically reversed sentiment favoring the original proposal and reopened the whole question of domestic control. Domestic control and the atomic energy commission thereafter became the subject of public as well as congressional debate. Throughout this debate, the President and his administration followed rather than led popular opinion. That opinion, by early February 1946, had come increasingly to side with a coalition of atomic scientists, State Department proponents of international control, and liberal senators in favor of a rival bill which specifically provided for civilian preeminence in the establishment and operation of the commission.

Passage of this rival bill seemed assured by mid-February. Significantly, it would have taken control of the bomb and of the decisions concerning its future away from the army and the Manhattan Project. No small part of the sudden impetus behind this alternative legislation, indeed, had been a desire to ensure that the AEC would help rather than hinder the prospects for international control of the bomb.

The policy of monopoly, if not the trusteeship itself, was also under attack at this time from the British. The now insistent demands of the Attlee government that the Truman administration make good on its secret promise of "full and effective cooperation" in the matter of atomic energy meant that Groves and the Manhattan Project might have to begin sharing not only scientific data but even the prized "know-how" of the bomb with the British.

The eruption of an international espionage scandal at this precise moment, culminating in the arrest of Canadian and British "atom spies" allegedly in league with Russia, immediately stopped the momentum toward a civilian-dominated atomic energy commission and the international control of atomic energy. In the wake of that spy scare this momentum was reversed, with both public and congressional opinion now favoring military-style security and the close safeguarding of all information concerning the bomb.

The result of the "atom spy" scandal and its attendant hysteria by early summer of 1946 was passage of a bill on domestic control that not only guaranteed a strong military voice in the commission, but also severely restricted the extent of international cooperation possible through the exchange of information on atomic energy. In significant ways this final bill was even more security-conscious than the original War Department–sponsored bill. Further, the fact that British scientists and Canadian citizens were implicated in the spy scandal fatally weakened Attlee and King's argument for future cooperation with the United States on atomic energy, and ultimately guaranteed an even stricter policy of exclusion.

In the excitement of the moment's preoccupation with communist "atom spies" in the Manhattan Project, few suspected a truth that was, in any case, only verified in the light of subsequent events. Thus the spy scandal was certainly exploited—and even largely created—for reasons which were plainly political. Specifically, its purpose was to ensure passage of domestic legislation that would provide for significant military representation in the atomic energy commission and preclude the sharing of information on atomic energy with other nations, including even America's partners in creating the bomb, Great Britain and Canada. Indeed, America's only real "atomic secret"—the supposedly preclusive control of atomic raw materials and her technological "know-how"—by its very nature *could not* be seriously threatened by Soviet espionage. Consequently, Russian spying was not and had never been a serious concern in the Truman administration. By early 1946, however, it provided a convenient rallying point for the new, tougher policy toward Russia that the administration had adopted.

"An Atomic Bomb Bill"

On the day that the atomic bomb was dropped on Nagasaki, President Truman pledged that he would soon submit a plan to Congress for the domestic control of atomic energy. What he intended that plan to be apparently remained vague even in his own mind more than a month later, however. In a meeting with senators on September 18, 1945,

Truman, according to the recollection of one legislator, simply advocated that the army's Manhattan Project be "re-implemented" in the postwar world, and that the military be allowed responsibility for atomic energy in peacetime as well.[1]

The Cabinet debate later that month on the bomb sidetracked the issue of postwar legislation on atomic energy and further delayed the President's declaration of a policy on domestic control. This continuing delay, to be sure, did not seem the cause of any particular anxiety for Truman. He wished to play no personal role in the drafting of the necessary legislation. As he told Dulles the following March, he "proposed to leave this matter to Congress and only give it attention when Congress had passed a Bill which would come to him for signature."[2]

Truman did not need to worry about drafting such a plan, for that task had already been accomplished elsewhere, even before it was known that the atomic bomb would actually work. In July 1945, two government attorneys in the War Department, Kenneth Royall and William Marbury, had written a domestic atomic-energy bill. Because of the war and the urgent need to decide upon the use of the atomic bomb, the Royall-Marbury draft was largely ignored by the Interim Committee until after the Japanese surrender. Moreover, aware of the stigma that would be attached to a "War Department" bill, two of the plan's earliest and most enthusiastic proponents—Groves and Patterson—proposed that it go to the President and then to Congress after approval by the State Department. The fact that Byrnes raised no obstacle to this scheme was likely an indication less of uncritical approval than of his preoccupation with the coming Council of Foreign Ministers in London.

While Byrnes was at London, Dean Acheson, the acting secretary of state, found the Royall-Marbury bill objectionable on several counts. Foremost of his objections was to the sweeping powers that the bill would grant a part-time government commission of four military and five civilian members. Both the civilians and the officers as a group would have final veto power over the commission's majority decisions. Members would be appointed by the President to a term of indefinite length; would have custody of all nuclear facilities and materials; and would thus also control the direction of atomic research and development.[3]

Behind Acheson's concern with the Royall-Marbury bill was his fear that such a commission would jeopardize Stimson's proposed direct approach, then before the Cabinet. He worried, too, that exercise of the veto by military representatives might prevent the exchange of scientific information on atomic energy with other governments—an obstruction which could prove fatal to the prospects for cooperative control of the bomb.[4] In the long run, finally, Acheson believed that the unlimited tenure of commissioners posed a potential challenge to presidential authority. This last, at least, was a point to which almost any president seemed likely to be receptive.

The subtle way in which the Royall-Marbury bill compromised presidential authority and might jeopardize the possibility of international control Acheson emphasized to the President in a briefing on September 18. Truman, however, suggested no revisions in the bill, and he reiterated his intention to remain apart from any struggle in Congress.[5]

To Groves and Patterson, Acheson's interference with the domestic-control issue seemed to be deliberate foot-dragging. By late September the two men were eager to get the draft bill out of the State Department and before Congress.[6] Indeed, Acheson's insistence that the President's promised statement on domestic control contain an endorsement of international cooperation had led to an unexpected delay. Another delay had been caused by the preoccupation of the Cabinet with Stimson's proposed direct approach to Russia, a preoccupation which also steered the Cabinet away from a planned discussion of domestic control in a meeting on September 25.

The diverse origins and conflicting purposes of Truman's long-deferred speech—which had its roots in recommendations from Groves, Rosenman, and Acheson and others at the State Department—meant that it represented more a statement of noble intention than a program for legislative action. But the fact that the Royall-Marbury draft was introduced into the House only the day after Truman's speech by its congressional sponsors—Congressman Andrew May and Senator Edwin Johnson—undoubtedly relieved and encouraged Patterson, Groves, and the other proponents of military representation on the AEC.

Introduction of the bill before Congress hardly meant that its passage was assured. But opposition to it—Acheson notwithstanding—was neither vocal nor united. The measure itself affected a variety of complex and often conflicting interests. Cast, for example, in the role of lobbyists against the bill—renamed the May-Johnson bill for its sponsors—was the newly formed Federation of Atomic Scientists. The scientists feared, with reason, that the bill would simply establish a peacetime extension of the Manhattan Project. They were especially wary of the effect that a commission of military careerists and nonspecialists might have upon scientific freedom in postwar research. And, like Acheson, they remained skeptical that the issue of domestic control of atomic energy could be divorced from that of international control of the bomb.[7]

Some notable scientists, including Robert Oppenheimer and Enrico Fermi, preferred to support the May-Johnson bill as a known and lesser evil. According to Oppenheimer, "it was safer to trust the commission and the administrator to use their powers wisely than to risk the chance that Congress, subjected to multiple pressures during a long debate, might produce something very much worse." Secretary of War Patterson made this point more directly when he warned that the scientists "did not realize that by delaying action and raising all sorts of objections to the present bill, they may very well end up with a much more stringent measure."[8] Patterson professed not to understand the "well-nigh hysterical criticism" of the bill by the scientists. He saw no conflict between cooperation on the bomb and the strictures to be imposed by the May-Johnson bill. His failure to perceive a paradox between the two may have been a result of Patterson's view, shared by the other service secretaries, that international control was properly a State Department preserve and that control of atomic energy on the home front should remain where it had been since 1942— in the hands of the War Department. Most scientists chose to ignore such threats and warnings.[9]

By late fall 1945 there was a sense that time was running out for supporters and opponents of the May-Johnson bill alike. The question of authority over atomic secrets had to be resolved before the sharing of information could begin. Since the end of the war, the return of Manhattan Project scientists to civilian life and the nation's rapid demobilization had made the need for action on domestic control even more urgent.

Among opponents of the May-Johnson bill, however, there was the suspicion that another desire made the bill's supporters anxious to see it quickly through Congress. Groves and Patterson seemed eager, therefore, to achieve its passage before the provision for military representation became controversial, and before rival legislation could be introduced to restrict the War Department's role. In fact, much more than the domestic control of atomic energy was involved, as the two men certainly realized.

The previous July, Groves had expressed his opposition to international cooperation on atomic energy in a memorandum to the Interim Committee. Cooperation, he wrote, "can only be justified if we are to accept the hypothesis that all nations concerned will act in good faith at all times. . . . Current trends indicate that a safe course cannot be steered if historical precedent is ignored. . . . To follow the proposals advanced would be to invite disaster to the U.S. unless my lack of belief in the good faith of other nations proves to be without justification."[10]

Some months later, Groves would be even more blunt, writing of international control that "it would be an easier task to outlaw war itself."[11]

The suspicion that at least some degree of support for the May-Johnson bill was motivated by a desire to hobble international cooperation on the bomb was one factor beginning to unify the opposition to the bill by mid-October. Nobel Prize–winning atomic scientist Harold Urey perhaps summarized this sentiment for a number of his colleagues when he complained that the May-Johnson bill should be "primarily what it purports to be, namely, an atomic energy bill for power purposes and not primarily what it actually is—an atomic bomb bill."[12]

By this time as well, opposition to the bill had gone beyond the special interests of the scientists. *The Nation,* in an editorial of October 20, attacked the May-Johnson bill for its endangerment of international control. Noting both the "indecent haste" with which the bill was being pushed in Congress and its origins in the War Department, the magazine objected that the measure "actually represents the commitment of the United States to a particularly vicious form of isolationist foreign policy. Such a policy would tend to emphasize rather than heal the rifts in international society today—particularly the rift between Russia and this country allied with Britain. . . . The more firmly we insist upon unilateral control of the atomic bomb, the more difficult it will be to persuade others that our faith in a world organization is genuine."[13]

This dissent by liberal pundits and disaffected scientists notwithstanding, opponents of the May-Johnson bill were still plainly a minority approaching year's end, when they gained three important allies. The three were unlikely political bedfellows. Illinois Senator Scott Lucas' support reflected a vocal constituency of scientists at the University of Chicago. Senator Arthur Vandenberg's opposition to the bill was not yet voluble, and was motivated more by his concern with Johnson's chairmanship of the rival Senate Military Affairs Committee. Brian McMahon, a freshman Democrat from Connecticut, was a spokesman for the cause of civilian supremacy. Together, with McMahon as their eventual leader, these three joined with the scientists in launching a successful revolt against the May-Johnson bill.[14]

The seeds for such a revolt had been sown some time before. Indeed, on the day that the Royall-Marbury draft had been introduced in the House, McMahon sponsored the resolution creating a special Senate Committee on Atomic Energy, later becoming its chairman. McMahon's eleven-member committee became the rallying point for opposition to the May-Johnson bill, and the start of rival legislation.

Puzzled by the lost momentum of the cause, May made an ill-advised attempt to ramrod the bill through the House on October 22 in five hours of hearings—during which the scientists were pointedly not invited to testify—thus actually aiding his opponents. Johnson's effort to wrest control of the Senate Committee on Atomic Energy from McMahon also brought attention to the heavy-handed methods employed by the bill's sponsors in their desperation.[15]

A final blow to the bill's chances for quick passage was struck that same day with Budget Director Harold Smith's letter to Truman, informing the President that Patterson had publicly claimed the May-Johnson bill represented "the views of the Administration as well as of the War Department."* Patterson's claim may have been true weeks earlier, but it was no longer the case in the wake of the public's increasing disaffection. Privately, the President had withdrawn his support of the bill once it was clear that the opposition to it reflected more than just the special pleading of the scientists, but he was not yet willing to attack it publicly.[17]

Emboldened by the growing sentiment in Congress against the May-Johnson bill, McMahon opened hearings on a rival bill in late October. In this forum the scientists were allowed to play a conspicuous part. The focus of the opposition to the May-Johnson bill there became

---

*Smith had become aware of how the cold war would be like other wars when Groves' 1946 budget request for the peacetime Manhattan Project matched that of what the wartime project had received in 1945. Smith found this request "ridiculous." In fact, the Manhattan Project ultimately received the money Groves requested, concealing its budget, like that of the modern CIA, in appropriations for other government agencies.[16]

the charge, made repeatedly by those testifying, that the original measure threatened the establishment of a "military state," since the proposed part-time commissioners could by their veto exercise a power equal to that of the President. As the testimony of scientists and other experts on the bomb continued into and through much of November it became clear that the purpose of the hearings was actually to delay a vote in Congress until an alternative to the May-Johnson bill could be made ready.

Work had begun on drafting rival legislation in mid-October, when it appeared that quick passage of the May-Johnson bill was impossible. A month later, the authors of an alternative bill had rallied the support of May-Johnson opponents behind the concept of a nine-member, full-time civilian AEC, closely tied to the executive branch and without the power of the veto. The drafters of this bill believed they had resolved the conflict between secrecy and freedom by giving a civilian commission rather than the military complete authority over refined uranium and thorium. This arrangement would allow the peaceful uses of atomic energy as well as international cooperation through the sharing of information, and would also safeguard the government's control of the bomb.

Although the aim of the McMahon committee was cooperation and not monopoly, its solution to the domestic control of atomic energy unwittingly borrowed an idea from Groves' plan to keep the bomb in American hands. As the draft bill itself proclaimed: "Fissionable material is the core of the control problem."[18]

Eager to test this hypothesis against the facts, McMahon and his committee asked Groves in late November for detailed information on the atomic bomb. They wished to know everything about the bomb, from its genesis in the acquisition of raw materials to its role in postwar Anglo-American relations. By their request the drafters of the McMahon bill were unknowingly asking for information at "the core" of the atomic secret—the monopoly of atomic raw materials. The McMahon bill, moreover, would have transferred jurisdiction over that monopoly from the army to the civilian commission—a provision which Groves was certain to reject.

Groves' categorical refusal to release any information on the bomb or the monopoly to the committee angered and surprised its members. That refusal seemed, indeed, a demonstration of the kind of military obduracy that was a target of the McMahon bill.[19] This feeling was confirmed when an appeal to Patterson by McMahon proved unavailing.

Evidently expecting that Truman might share his outrage at Groves' willfulness, McMahon approached the President, who agreed to meet with the principals in the controversy on December 4. The timing is especially ironic, since this was the day after Groves briefed the Combined Policy Committee as well as Byrnes and Patterson on the success of the Murray Hill Area and Alsos.

McMahon's hope that the President would force Groves and the War Department to back down on the question of secrecy was forlorn. Instead, Truman supported Groves' refusal to cooperate with the Senate, citing the need for secrecy while the Russians remained uncooperative. McMahon had allowed the hearings in his committee to get "off on a tangent," he complained. While eventually agreeing with the committee that there should be no military representative on the proposed commission, Truman still refused to publicly disavow the May-Johnson bill.[20]

Truman's defense of Groves and secrecy also betrayed, if not timidity on his part, at least a surprising ignorance about the bomb. During a Cabinet meeting a week later, Wallace was shocked to hear that Truman did not know how many atomic bombs the United States had, and that he "didn't really want to know either." When Wallace objected that the President *should* know, Truman "retreated in some confusion and said he guessed he should know and then covered up by saying, 'I do know in a general way.' " Patterson, who also claimed ignorance as to the number of bombs, finally answered Wallace's original question by admitting that Groves was in control of the bombs. Wallace was hardly comforted by this disclosure. "I thought it utterly incredible that Patterson and the President should be willing to trust full information and responsibility on this to a man like Groves and his underlings without knowing what was going on themselves."[21]

By the first weeks of 1946, the momentum favoring the May-Johnson bill—and, by extension, military dominance in the postwar commission—had been slowed but not stopped. At the same time, the rival McMahon bill was stalemated by the refusal of Groves and the War Department to grant access to the secrets that would confirm or refute its viability. The President had taken no active part in this controversy. But, simply by inaction, he had sided by default with Groves and the existing system of secrecy.

The diehard proponents of the May-Johnson bill, particularly

Groves and Patterson, showed no inclination to compromise as this deadlock continued—even at the cost of direct opposition to Truman. Hence a memorandum sent by Truman to Patterson at the end of November had listed what the President termed four amendments "essential" for him to support the May-Johnson bill. Most important of these was that military representation in the commission be dropped. Patterson had nonetheless rejected this concession outright in a return letter to Truman on December 12, 1945.[22]

Faced with a weeks-long standoff in the Congress, and undoubtedly also spurred by such insubordination, Truman publicly threw his support behind the McMahon bill at the end of January. He reaffirmed his intention to abandon the May-Johnson bill with a letter to McMahon which endorsed the principle of civilian supremacy. Together with the impressive public support the McMahon bill had begun to receive, Truman's act seemed to doom the May-Johnson bill.[23]

Certainly the unprecedented resistance of May-Johnson supporters in the administration and Congress to any substantive change in the bill that affected military representation in the commission was an indication of the earnestness of their belief. Since fall 1945, Groves, in contravention of his oath as a military officer, had openly campaigned for the May-Johnson bill with speaking engagements around the country. In a press conference in early November, for example, he had been characteristically frank in urging that the bomb be kept in American hands, and used to bring about a stable, durable peace: "We may never get another chance. We must make the most of this one."[24] Some weeks later, Groves made plain how far he was willing to go to guarantee that America retained the upper hand with the bomb. "With atomic weapons a nation must be ready to strike the first blow if needed. The first blow or series of blows may be the last," he told Congress.[25]

The obvious devotion on the part of Groves and Patterson to the cause of ensuring military representation on the AEC had finally angered Truman and alarmed Wallace. The latter's diary entry at this time, indeed, would seem prophetic in light of subsequent events: "After noting the way in which the Army has spread rumors about Pregel, Szilard, and Condon, I am inclined to think they will knife anybody who, directly or indirectly, fights the legislation which they are pushing. . . . The war psychology has gotten into their blood and the ends justify the means. I am expecting them to circulate the most stories."*

"Some Sort of Magic Formula"

Soviet espionage directed against the Manhattan Project was certainly nothing new by 1945. According to his own later testimony, Groves learned of Russian spying upon American atomic research as early as the fall of 1942, only two weeks after he assumed command of the Manhattan Project. Secretary of War Stimson acknowledged that he knew of Soviet efforts to obtain details on the bomb by September 1943, and that he told President Roosevelt of them at that time. Groves also gave FDR a report on spies in 1944. Truman was informed by Groves of Soviet espionage during his April 1945 briefing. This was the reason that Truman was neither shocked nor alarmed by Prime Minister King's revelation the following September that the Canadian government had uncovered a Soviet spy ring seeking information on the procurement and refining of uranium. "The President did not seem surprised," nor inclined toward any action against the spies, King recollected of that meeting. Truman even advised him to take no steps "which might result in premature action in any direction." King again brought up the subject of Russian espionage at the Washington summit the following November. Neither this nor a secret memorandum that same month from FBI director J. Edgar Hoover to the White House concerning Soviet spying in the United States prompted any special measures on Truman's part.[27]

Nor, logically, was there any particular reason for Truman to be concerned about Russian spying on the bomb project. For if the real atomic secret consisted of a preclusive monopoly of atomic raw materials and America's technological "know-how," there was little or nothing of value that the Russians *could* steal. Groves himself acknowledged as much in a 1948 magazine article, in which he claimed that the Russians would be unable to build atomic bombs "in quantity" before 1955—

---

*A friend of Wallace's, Boris Pregel was president of a Manhattan Project subcontractor, the Canadian Uranium Corporation. Pregel, Wallace writes, had earlier warned that "Groves is slightly pathological," and that the latter believed in the importance of excluding foreigners (including Jews) "from the uranium business." The Canadian also knew a secret, the significance of which neither he nor Wallace could appreciate at the time: "Pregel says the Army doesn't realize that Russia has vast stores of uranium."[26]

even if they had stolen a complete set of blueprints for the Manhattan Project.[28]

Indeed, considering the furor that would later erupt over "atom spies" in the Manhattan Project, the project's own declassified intelligence and security files indicate that foreign espionage there was of a small and amateurish order. The scant three-page segment allotted to espionage and sabotage investigations in the project's multivolume official history contradicts the subsequent popular image of massive and successful infiltration of atomic-bomb plants by crafty Russian master spies.* The most serious breach of security involving American citizens and recorded in FBI and Manhattan Project files, therefore, was a thwarted attempt by six former U.S. servicemen in 1946 to sell photographs of the first atomic bomb to an American newspaper. Real espionage, to be sure, occurred outside the Manhattan Project, but within it—the army history claims—"prompt action and . . . activity in each case prevented the passing of any substantial amount of Project information."[30]

Another tacit acknowledgment that the real atomic secret was believed to be in no danger came with the release—only six days after the destruction of Hiroshima—of a detailed account of the scientific and technical principles behind the bomb. The Smyth Report, so named for its Princeton physicist author, shocked many Americans with its open exposition of the bomb's step-by-step development, but it actually revealed nothing of the manufacturing "know-how" behind the bomb's construction.[31] Praised by scientists as in the spirit of intellectual freedom—and condemned by some congressmen as going too far in that direction—Groves' decision to release the Smyth Report had little to do with either freedom or science. It was in order to "backfire" critical and "reckless" statements by the atomic scientists about his leadership of the Manhattan Project that he had decided to publish the report, Groves told Stimson a week before the bombing of Hiroshima. While it did not "take the stage away from the others" as the general had hoped, he would use the controversy over secrecy engendered by the report to discredit individual scientists—who had, he subsequently claimed, pressured him into releasing the document.[32]

---

*The army's history of the project recounts incidents replete with the paraphernalia of counterespionage: miniature cameras, hidden microphones, disguises, and agents masquerading as "electricians, painters, exterminators, contractors, gamblers, etc." One agent with cover as a bellhop at a large hotel, the history boasts, performed so well in his role that within a few months he was promoted to bell captain by his unsuspecting employer.[29]

Even before publication of the Smyth Report, just the notion of an atomic secret made most Americans acutely security-conscious. The spurious debate that September about giving the atomic secret to the Russians, for example, had begun to unify popular opinion behind the necessity for strict security as early as fall 1945. The "mood for clutching the secret tightly, rather than letting out a single phrase of it, appeared wholly predominant," one newspaper observed of popular sentiment. This view was also reflected in public-opinion surveys, which showed that some 85 percent of those polled were opposed to sharing "the atomic-bomb secret" with Russia.[33]

Popular misconceptions concerning atomic secrets frustrated the scientists' lobby for civilian control of the atom, and were not limited to the public. Vannevar Bush thought Admiral William Leahy typical of the problem. "[Leahy's] view was like the postwar attitude of some of the public and many in Congress: There was an atomic bomb 'secret,' written perhaps on a single sheet of paper, some sort of magic formula. If we guarded this, we alone could have atomic bombs indefinitely." Physicist Chester Barnard was equally amazed to learn that even members of McMahon's Senate Committee on Atomic Energy believed the United States "could retain the then existing monopoly almost indefinitely" by holding on to a mysterious secret. However, the increasing emphasis upon secrecy did not yet preclude the possibility of cooperation with the Soviets and others—in the public's mind, at least. Hence a majority of Americans in late 1945 still supported the effort to achieve international control of the bomb.

Given the nature of the real atomic secret, it is hardly surprising that this public concern with secrecy was not reflected in official attitudes to the same extent. Informed of Russian attempts to obtain information from scientists at Berkeley and the University of Chicago, Groves took no extraordinary measures to stop or even restrict such spying. Conceivably, this was with the intent of uncovering or entrapping the agents themselves. But Truman, too, remained unconvinced of any urgent need to capture the spies, as shown by the fact that he had cautioned Prime Minister King against exposing their operations too soon. There was, in fact, "no precious secret" for the Russians to steal, the President confided to former Secretary of State Edward Stettinius in October 1945.[34]

The remarkable complacency on the part of Groves and the Truman administration continued even amid signs that the foundation of the atomic monopoly was crumbling. Ignored were the Soviets' own oft-repeated warnings, like Molotov's in November 1945, that the Russians "would soon have atomic energy and many other things too." More ominous was a secret report sent to the White House by FBI director Hoover the month before, detailing information obtained from a member of the Soviet legation in a South American country. Hoover's source indicated that Russian experiments in atomic fission had begun in 1940 and had resulted in an "accidental explosion" by 1943. "They have valuable deposits of uranium and thorium, especially of the latter in Tashkent (in Turkestan)," the FBI agent wrote, adding that the Russians had received help in nuclear research from German scientists. Perhaps most disturbing of all, however, was a portentous single-sentence memorandum of November 19, 1945, from an official at the U.S. embassy in Moscow to Byrnes, and relayed by him to Groves: "From a reliable government source I have learned that the Czechoslovak government has been officially requested to furnish uranium ore to the Soviet government." There is no evidence that Groves even acknowledged receipt of the message.[35]

Disregarded as well were the repeated warnings of American scientists that the atomic monopoly could not endure. In a February 1946 edition of the *Bulletin of the Atomic Scientists,* the newly formed publication of dissident scientists at Chicago, one warning took the form of an article entitled "The Distribution of Uranium in Nature." The article concluded that "any country can secure as much uranium as would be necessary for atomic warfare." A layman's version of the same article appeared in the *New York Times* later that month, with its conclusions implicit in its headline: "There Are Abundant Sources of Uranium for Those Who Are Willing to Pay a High Price."[36]

As with previous and subsequent warnings, these signs that America's atomic monopoly might be slipping away—entirely independently of efforts by Soviet spies—went unheeded by Groves and others in the administration best able to interpret them.

Confident in its special knowledge of the real atomic secret, the administration maintained an attitude of apparent unconcern for the security of the monopoly, despite the known activities of Russian agents. While more worried about secrecy, the public—which still favored international control and opposed the May-Johnson bill—seemed willing to accept a balance between freedom and secrecy. One explanation for this seeming paradox is the fact that the public remained unaware of the supposedly preclusive U.S. monopoly of atomic raw materials, and thus believed that the Russians would soon have atomic bombs anyway —and might have them already.[37] If so, the events of early February 1946 would fundamentally tilt that balance in the popular mind toward secrecy and away from freedom.

"A Fellow Like Groves"

On February 3, 1946, Americans were stunned to learn on commentator Drew Pearson's evening radio show of the Soviet spy ring operating in Canada. Pearson's dramatic disclosure contained no details about the size of the ring or the real target of its activities, but noted that official —though unidentified—sources could verify its existence. In the next few days, newspaper stories about the rash of postwar labor strikes, the continuing imbroglio in Congress over domestic control of atomic energy, and the growing rift between Truman and Byrnes were gradually displaced by journalists' accounts of what was soon perceived to be a burgeoning espionage scandal. On February 8 the issue came closer to home at a State Department press conference in which Byrnes was asked what damage the Canadian spies might have done to security. Byrnes' attempts at reassurance neither satisfied the journalists nor ended the controversy.[38]

Instead, the case of the "atom spies" became a public *cause célèbre* just over a week later, with the Canadian government's announcement of the arrest of twenty-two suspected agents. The arrests had been forced, Prime Minister King admitted, by the publicity the case received from Pearson's "scoop," and had had to be carried out before the months-long investigation by Canadian police was completed. Since Truman himself had earlier cautioned against just such a premature disclosure, King had strong suspicions as to the motivation—if not the source—of the leak to Pearson. He saw the spy story as having been "in some way . . . inspired": "I may be wrong but I have a feeling that there is a desire at Washington that this information should get out; that Canada should start the enquiry and that we should have the responsibility for beginning it and that the way should be paved for it being continued into the U.S. . . . This may be all wrong, but I have that intuition very strongly. It is the way in which a certain kind of politics is played by a certain type of man."[39]

King's "intuition" that the Pearson leak represented only a prelude to events extending the spy scandal into the United States was confirmed when a second revelation about Soviet agents appeared the same day as the Canadian arrests. Washington columnist Frank McNaughton disclosed from a "confidential source" that the Soviet spies in Canada had had as their real target atomic scientists and information in the United States, and that a second ring of Russian agents was even then operating in America. The FBI, McNaughton's informant claimed, would have moved earlier to break up this second, American-based spy ring "but for the arguments of state department men—who [the source] will not name—that to do so would upset our relations with Russia."[40]

McNaughton's story of espionage on the home front, subsequently embellished in Pearson's syndicated newspaper column, signaled the start of what would become, in successive weeks of headlines, a near-hysteria over communist "atom spies" in America. Unable to judge the validity of disclosures about Russian spies in the bomb project, or even to identify their source, Americans reacted with understandable frustration and anger to the unfolding story—a frustration compounded by the lack of anyone in particular to blame.

Nor was the situation improved when the Russians, for reasons that may only be guessed at—but that certainly reflected a misjudgment of U.S. public opinion—made an unprecedented, and never repeated, admission that they had received "insignificant secret data" through espionage. This confession was tempered with the backhanded justification that the postwar duplicity of the Western allies had made such espionage necessary, and it was excused as not having yielded anything that wasn't already in the Smyth Report in any case. Predictably, the Russians' strange and unrepentant admission occasioned in the popular mind not relief but renewed suspicions concerning the scientist-contributors to the bomb project and the Smyth Report. Ironically, the Russians were probably telling the truth when they dismissed the results of their spying as "insignificant."

The specific aim of Soviet espionage in Canada had been to acquire samples of enriched uranium—some low-grade samples of which they had already received, gratis, from Groves in 1944—presumably in hopes of achieving a better insight into industrial enrichment techniques. This they had failed to do, although they did get a certain amount of slightly enriched uranium ore from British physicist Alan Nunn May, the alleged master spy of the Canadian case. The value of this to the Russians was, at best, questionable. Groves himself later acknowledged that the Canadian spy ring learned no secrets of the bomb's manufacture, since it was "very doubtful" that May had "anything but a general knowledge of the construction of the atomic bomb." The Canadian government also subsequently confirmed in its report on the case that "the Soviets failed to obtain details on the structure of the atomic bomb"; May, in fact, ultimately defended his actions on the grounds that the information he furnished the Russians was "mostly of a character which has since been published or is about to be published." Nor was the Canadian case quite the cloak-and-dagger operation portrayed by Pearson and McNaughton. Incredibly, the Russian "spies" in Canada had even tried to purchase up to half-a-million dollars' worth of uranium ore on the open market from a subcontractor to the Manhattan Project, Eldorado Mines Limited.[41]

The fate of the celebrated Canadian spy ring was equally undramatic and anticlimactic. Since prosecution of at least some of the ring's members would have required the testimony of Edgar Sengier concerning the value of uranium to the Russians—and would thus have exposed continuing efforts to keep it from them—Groves recommended that those cases involving Soviet efforts to obtain uranium not go to open court. As a result, only half of the original alleged "atom spies" were eventually convicted, on the reduced charge of "giving unauthorized information" and largely upon the evidence of their own confessions.[42]

The principal information of value which the Russians might have received in the Canadian case concerned the way in which they had been systematically excluded from sources of uranium outside Russia. They might have learned as well something of the rate at which the United States was able to enrich uranium and, hence, to build atomic bombs. But the former certainly did not come as news to the Russians, and the latter could only have confirmed information they had probably already obtained—and would continue to receive, unknown to the West—from much better sources than May: Klaus Fuchs and Donald Maclean.[43]

These facts, of course, would remain hidden to the public for some years to come. As late as 1955, in the wake of a resurgent spy scare, the idea that the earlier atom spy scandal was really an atom spy hoax failed to receive serious attention.[44] At the time, evidence that a foreign (albeit British) scientist had been the key figure in the Canadian spy ring tended to cast doubt upon the wisdom if not the viability of the cause of international control, for which the scientists themselves had become spokesmen by 1946. But surely the most rapid and telling effect of the spring spy scandal was upon the continuing congressional debate over domestic control of atomic energy. As one observer of that debate noted, the "tide" of mail from constituents favoring the McMahon bill before the Pearson and McNaughton stories subsided to a mere "trickle" in their aftermath.[45]

Lurid notions of Russian agents in the Manhattan Project dissolved virtually overnight the popular consensus in support of civilian supremacy in the proposed atomic energy commission. The first postwar nuclear test by the United States, which coincided with the February revelations, drew additional attention to the espionage drama and seemed to underscore the importance of the stakes involved. Supporters of the McMahon bill, who had seemed assured of victory at the start of February, found themselves at month's end on the defensive against a renewed attack by advocates of the May-Johnson bill. Bowing reluctantly to pressure from within his own committee, McMahon called Groves before the Senate on February 27 to testify on the escalating spy scandal. The hearings on domestic control had actually been completed the week before, but the espionage disclosures caused them to be abruptly reopened.

Presenting what he termed "his personal views as divorced from the War Department," Groves argued for military representation in the proposed commission and even suggested the names of specific officers he considered suitable for the post.* Patterson had made the same argument before the McMahon committee on February 15, a day before the spy arrests in Canada, and received little attention. Groves' testimony, however, coincided with a "get-tough-on-the-Russians" speech by Vandenberg that same day in the Senate, and took place in an atmosphere altered by the news of spies. His message inspired a spontaneous and affirmative response from the committee. Indeed, an indication of the changed mood in that forum—and of the way in which the initiative there had been reversed—came from one angry exchange at the hearings. When McMahon sarcastically observed that Groves' testimony on military representation had "drawn a bill of particulars . . . which you could pretty well fit," the latter re-

---

*Groves could hardly presume to speak for the military, since the armed services' two highest-ranking officers, General Dwight Eisenhower and Admiral Chester Nimitz, supported the McMahon bill and the principle of civilian supremacy in the AEC.

sponded that he would now have to be urged to fill a spot on the proposed commission.[46]

There was no doubt a private satisfaction for Groves in being called before the reconvened hearings on domestic control—since it was he who was the "confidential source" that McNaughton cited in his stories tying the Russian spy ring to the United States. McNaughton's private papers at the Truman Library, opened to researchers some thirty years after the original spy scare, tell the story of that celebrated leak. Although the journalist was not in a position to evaluate the information Groves gave him, even at the time he had a suspicion that "Groves obviously knows more than he tells." The possibility that Groves in fact knew *less* than he told apparently did not occur to McNaughton until he asked the general to identify the Americans in the spy ring. Of the 1,700 Russian-directed agents that he had said were targeted against atomic secrets, none that he knew of was in the American government, Groves admitted. Groves also later discounted the spies' effectiveness and importance in talks with McNaughton.[47]

In March there was a further decline in support for the McMahon bill, and for the principle of civilian supremacy, in the fight over domestic control. It became increasingly evident, indeed, that the bill's proponents were fighting what was at best a rear-guard battle in their attacks on Groves and the War Department for "excessive security"; in the wake of the spy stories, "excessive" secrecy seemed impossible. The steady erosion of public support for the McMahon bill made the fight for it a progressively more one-sided struggle. "If the people of the United States are awake they will realize that they have a quarrel too with the Manhattan District, as indeed, the whole world has a quarrel with that organization," scientist Harold Urey complained forlornly in early March.[48]

The report by a *New York Times* correspondent that May-Johnson advocates in Congress had begun to use the spy scare aggressively to promote passage of their bill, and to argue against civilian supremacy, failed to slow the downward spiral of the McMahon bill. Instead, a charge by McMahon and Urey on March 19 that military representation would eventually lead to military domination of the commission prompted Groves to drop yet another spy-scandal bombshell in a letter to one of his congressional allies, conservative Republican Senator Bourke Hickenlooper. Hickenlooper read the letter on the floor of the Senate the following day. Invoking the "Pilgrim fathers, who went to church with their muskets loaded," he dramatically announced that British physicist Alan Nunn May, arrested two weeks earlier on espionage charges, had had access to secrets concerning American "knowhow" and the bomb.[49]

Groves' letter, however, was perhaps only the *coup de grâce*. Even before his inaccurate claims concerning May's value to the Russians, the McMahon committee had decided—against the single opposing vote of its chairman—to amend their original bill in the military's favor. The "Vandenberg amendment," which represented the sort of last-minute conversion for which the Michigan senator had become justly famous, delighted May-Johnson supporters by establishing a "military liaison board" which would review and appeal the decisions of the civilian commissioners directly to the President.[50]

Bereft of administration support, rejected by a Congress now plainly in favor of a substantive military role in the commission, and shaken repeatedly by scandals evidently involving scientist-spies, the last remaining opposition to a military presence in the commission weakened and collapsed as March ended. Only able to lament that efforts "to rid themselves of military control and of security regulations have been identified in the public mind with international control of the bomb and with 'giving the secret to Russia,'" atomic scientists reluctantly gave their approval to the amendment in the hope that by so doing they would speed passage of a final bill on domestic control that was "40 to 50 percent agreeable to us."[51]

Unlike the scientists, however, McMahon remained unreconciled to the Vandenberg amendment. On March 28 he sent Truman a bitter note charging that it "is not a compromise between the supporters of the Vandenberg amendment and the supporters of the principle of civilian supremacy," since it gave the military, in effect, the sole veto power in the commission. Wallace, too, was unmollified by the resolution of the domestic-control question, and resolute as to where the blame for the spy scare lay. He wrote in his diary on March 26: "It was very clear to me that Groves could use the plea of protecting against Russian spies to do anything he wants to. . . . A fellow like Groves, using the Russian phobia as a screen, can, if the military is given the power it desires, go to almost any excess."[52]

One reason for the bitterness felt by McMahon and others after their defeat was the fact that perhaps the only person who could have stopped

the spy-scare momentum and championed the cause of civilian supremacy in Congress—Truman—had throughout remained apart, even aloof,
from their struggle. Worse, the President, after finally throwing support
to the McMahon bill at the end of January, had deserted it less than a
week later, when the espionage stories began to appear on radio and in
the press.

Truman, to be sure, had vowed not to participate in the domestic-
control debate. But his actions at the beginning of February marked a
reversal of the stand he had finally taken against military representation.
In fact, his failure to discipline Patterson after the latter publicly endorsed the May-Johnson bill on March 9 is remarkable. Patterson's
action constituted direct insubordination following his rejection of the
"essential" amendments to the May-Johnson bill. Nor did Truman react
to a proposed directive from Groves which, Eben Ayers wrote, "would
make it almost impossible to give out any information or for scientists
to exchange information. . . . [Patterson] said it would even put the
President below the War Department."[53]

Privately, Truman denigrated the spy scandal and the scare that it
had aroused. In a letter to Patterson, he angrily rejected the war secretary's claim that there had been a "dangerous trend toward breakdown
in security of the Atomic Bomb Project," pointing out that "careful
investigation by the Department of Justice and other government agencies . . . reveals no breach of security on the part of any official of the
United States Government or any of the scientists engaged in the Manhattan District Project."[54] Publicly, however, he was circumspect.

Truman's refusal, despite McMahon's plea, to reaffirm support for
the principle of civilian control bewildered opponents of the May-Johnson bill and caused some confusion as well among the public concerning
his stand on that issue. A *New York Times* editorial of March 17 entitled
"Wanted: Atomic Policy" observed that the President had endorsed
both the May-Johnson and the McMahon bill. Truman himself did not
resolve this confusion by a statement on domestic control so ambiguous
that it was cited by each of the opposing camps in Congress as supporting its position.[55]

The President's decision to back away from support of the McMahon bill is, indeed, curious. Certainly one reason might have been an
unwillingness on his part to risk alienating Vandenberg and other key
Republicans in Congress, whose support was necessary to the passage of
his administration's legislative program—then stalled in the Senate. But

this would not explain why Truman did nothing to defuse, or even diminish, the growing and unnecessary hysteria over "atom spies." Clearly, fear of tipping off the Russians to the nature of America's atomic advantage in raw materials and "know-how" was not a part of this, for the Soviets were well aware of their handicap and its causes. If there was any doubt remaining after the Canadian spy arrests that the United States intended to retain its grip on atomic raw materials, that doubt should have been removed when the State Department embargoed the sale to Russia of any equipment useful in the mining or refining of uranium ore.[56]

The rationale for keeping the supposed monopoly of atomic raw materials at "the highest order of secrecy" thus almost certainly had more to do with domestic public opinion than with the Russians. So too, it seems, did Truman's acquiescence in the spy scare. At home, the unconfirmed stories by Pearson and McNaughton had had a profound effect. Already in awe of atomic secrets before the spy scandal, many Americans afterward were for the first time reluctant even to consider the prospect of cooperative control for the bomb. The attitude of most citizens, one congressman reflected in midsummer 1946, was "to lock the bomb in a burglar-proof safe and not discuss it."[57]

It is equally true that the Truman administration by this date had decisively moved away from the idea of cooperating with the Russians on the bomb, compared to its position of just a year before. The disclosures concerning May and the Canadian spy ring coincided with—but did not provoke—a conscious toughening of the administration's policy toward Russia. The new policy had begun after Byrnes' abortive trip to Moscow, and was already well advanced, in rhetoric at least, by spring 1946. The exaggerated threat of communist "atom spies," in addition to a real Soviet-American crisis in Iran, produced the necessary psychological justification for gathering public support behind this developing policy, and also provided the backdrop against which the Truman administration evolved its long-term strategy for countering Soviet communism.

7

The Atomic Curtain Descends

"Are we not asking Russia to raise the 'iron curtain' at the same time that we keep the atomic curtain down tight?"

A. J. Muste, letter to Dulles, July 1946

"Resort by Soviet leaders to measures of forceful coercion has been characteristic for nearly 30 years within the Soviet Union, and long preceding the atomic bomb. . . ."

John Foster Dulles, letter to A. J. Muste, July 1946

"Paris Was Munich in Reverse"

Since it coincided with the government's new and tougher approach to Russia, the 1946 spy scare initially met the purposes of the Truman administration as conveniently as it served those advocates of continued secrecy who had created and exploited it. Confronted with the prospect of exorcising the useful but false specter posed by "atom spies," and thereby also revealing the truth of what Groves held at "the highest order of secrecy," Truman and other initiates in the real atomic secret chose, instead, to remain silent on the insubstantial threat of Soviet espionage. Not surprisingly, given the developing hysteria of the popular mood, the repeated but unspecific public disclaimers of administration spokesmen like Byrnes that "the secret is safe" were unconvincing.

Ultimately the bogus espionage scandal and the real hard-line policy toward Russia combined to promote a national attitude of fear which, in the long term, would engulf both the administration and the progenitors of the spy scare. In the short term, that fear had already begun to compromise the prospect for the international control of the bomb, even before formal talks on the subject in the United Nations had gotten under way.

Since the October Revolution of 1917, the American government had made an attempt to understand—and to counter—Russian communism.

The Soviet Union's rise to great-power status in the aftermath of the Second World War had given this effort at understanding an importance and an urgency it had not had before. An initial effort to analyze Soviet policies in terms of their motivations, in fact, was the aim of Ambassador Averell Harriman's April 1945 telegrams to Truman. It was those telegrams that had persuaded Stimson to abandon the idea of a *quid pro quo* with the Russians at Potsdam. Harriman—an early if amateur Kremlinologist—espoused a hard-line, self-professed "realist" policy toward the Soviets.[1]

Since the war's end, however, the official appraisal of the Russian threat by American experts on the Soviet Union had been considerably more optimistic than Harriman's bleak assessment of the chances for peaceful coexistence. A December 1945 study by the intelligence chief of the State Department's USSR division concluded, for example, that "the United States need not be acutely concerned about the immediate current intentions of the Soviet Union" and that Russia's monumental task of postwar recovery meant the United States "enjoys a considerable latitude in determining its policy toward the USSR . . . between a moderate and deliberately reassuring policy, [or] the policy of developing a maximum alignment of power against the Soviet Union" for the day when the capabilities of the latter would constitute a real danger. Expanded upon and circulated within the government by Charles Bohlen, Byrnes' special assistant and translator, this view expressed the professional view of the State Department's Soviet experts.[2]

A similar assessment of postwar Russia, but from a different source, was the navy's secret intelligence memorandum on "Soviet Capabilities and Possible Intentions" of January 1946. The Russia portrayed in this assessment was "exhausted" physically and economically by the war; her industry and transport "in an advanced state of deterioration." Far from scheming world domination, Russian policy toward the outside world in this view was defensive in nature and aimed only "to establish a Soviet Monroe Doctrine for the area under her shadow, primarily and urgently for security, secondarily to facilitate the eventual emergence of the USSR as a power which could not be menaced by any other world power or combination of powers."[3] A report by the Joint Chiefs of Staff the following month essentially concurred with the navy's perception of the Russian threat—or, rather, the lack of a Russian threat for the short term.[4]

Ironically, this sanguine view of Soviet-American relations may even have been shared by Truman himself at the beginning of his administration. The President's rejection, therefore, of Stimson's direct approach had ultimately been for reasons more of psychology than of security, with the purpose of showing that he could be a "direct action fellow," too. Truman's subsequent and frequent expressions of hope for getting along with the Soviets should, for the same reason, not be discounted as insincere. A sign that his—and his administration's—attitude toward Russia might be changing, however, was evident at year's end with the President's chastisement of Byrnes for allegedly "babying the Soviets." The Soviets' consolidation of their position in eastern Europe had been a further cause of distress for Truman.

In other ways as well, things since then had gotten worse, from Truman's perspective at least. In early February, Stalin announced a series of five-year economic plans for the postwar reconstruction of Russia. His boast that Russian industrial capacity and scientific prowess would match that of America's before many more years was interpreted in the administration as a challenge far from peaceful in its implications. Indeed, as one observer commented, it seemed a virtual "declaration of World War III."[5] Finally, Stalin's refusal to evacuate Red Army troops from Iran after the joint Anglo-Russian occupation of that country was to have ended suddenly seemed evidence to the United States of a dangerous expansionism whose aims were just becoming clear.

In fact, neither the continuing Soviet presence in eastern Europe, nor Stalin's pronouncement of a plan for domestic recovery, nor Russian policy in Iran marked a contradiction of what American intelligence assessments had concluded was a historic—and understandable—Russian mania for security. But all were apparently interpreted by Truman as confirming evidence that his administration, if it was to guarantee the freedom of the rest of Europe, had to get tougher with the Russians. On February 20, accordingly, the President told Leahy that he intended to take a much stronger attitude toward the Russians in the very near future.[6]

Any public expression by Truman of this hard-line policy was preempted, however, by Senator Arthur Vandenberg's speech only a week later. The timing of that speech hardly seemed coincidental. Calling for a "positive" foreign policy to counter communism, Vandenberg rather than Truman sounded the keynote for the tougher attitude toward Russia. The following day, in an address before the Overseas Press

Club that used "unusually forceful language"—and was so similar in theme to the senator's as to be dubbed the "Second Vandenberg Concerto" by journalists—Byrnes, too, declared his allegiance to the administration's new policy toward Russia. Byrnes' speech, indeed, had been personally edited by Truman the night before. Truman considered it, Ayers noted, "even better than Vandenberg's."[7]

While Byrnes would later cite Stalin's five-year plan and the situation in Iran as the twin inspirations for his hard-line speech, another reason for his sudden turnaround on Russia was less dramatic. "The President said he had told Byrnes to stiffen up and try for the next three months not to make any compromises," Ayers wrote in his journal on February 28. Perhaps in line with that advice, Byrnes, less than a week after his speech to the press club, sent an uncharacteristically strong diplomatic note to the Russians on Iran.[8]

Truman decided to follow words with action on the 28th: he ordered the battleship *Missouri* to Turkey, a nation whose strategic significance at the opening to the Mediterranean rivaled that of oil-rich Iran. Although the *Missouri* was ostensibly sent as a tribute to the death of Turkey's ambassador to Washington, the true purpose behind the President's gesture was probably as clear to the Russians as it was at the time to the assistant press secretary: "[Truman] said the U.S. was sending the battleship *Mo* and a task force to Constantinople . . . 'to honor a dead Turk.' (And impress Russia?)"[9]

The speeches of Vandenberg and Byrnes notwithstanding, the government's mobilization behind a "get tough with Russia" policy in the spring of 1946 was begun substantially without a battle plan. Indeed, for as long as the attitude of the State Department, the military chiefs, and the public continued to discount the existence of an objective Russian threat, no such rallying of an anticommunist consensus was possible. The words and deeds of February and early March 1946—and the spy scare —did much to bolster the notion of a Russian threat at this time. But the administration was still without a comprehensive strategy for dealing with Soviet communism, even as the symbolic call to arms was sounded.

Aware of this gap was the American chargé d'affaires at Moscow, George F. Kennan—a silent critic of Byrnes' summit diplomacy the previous December. Kennan's famous "long telegram," sent to the State Department on February 22, 1946, was actually in reply to a government query concerning Soviet economic policy. Rather than respond directly to that question, however, Kennan had composed a primer on the relationship between communism and Soviet conduct in foreign affairs.[10]

The "long telegram" represented, as well, a substantially different analysis of Russia from that which had seemed the accepted wisdom only a month before. Far from being a nation preeminently concerned with postwar domestic recovery, the Soviet Union was, in Kennan's assessment, motivated by "a political force committed fanatically to the belief that with [the] U.S. there can be no permanent *modus vivendi,* that it is desirable and necessary that the internal harmony of our society be disrupted, our traditional way of life be destroyed, the international authority of our state be broken, if Soviet power is to be secure." The suspicious, even "neurotic" leaders of Russia, Kennan argued, were from the same mold as the autocratic tsars. "Marxism," he wrote in a memorable phrase, was but "the fig leaf of their moral and intellectual respectability."[11]

The effect of the telegram upon Washington was, in the author's own term, "sensational." Circulated within the government—and later released to the press—by administration supporters of the hard-line approach like Navy Secretary Forrestal, Kennan's image of Russia quickly supplanted the cautiously optimistic assessment of the State Department and the joint chiefs. "Six months earlier this message would probably have been received in the Department of State with raised eyebrows and lips pursed in disapproval," Kennan wrote. "Six months later, it would probably have sounded redundant, a sort of preaching to the convinced." Arriving only days after the spy arrests in Canada, however, it constituted the rationale for a new and emerging policy toward Russia.[12]

Later that same spring, the administration's new policy was put into practice at the Paris Council of Foreign Ministers, meeting April through May. Significantly, though the Iranian crisis had by that time faded as a symbol of the Soviet threat, the hard line itself continued. Nor was U.S. policy toward Russia any longer riven by dissent. In a move apparently intended to show the recently achieved unanimity of view among former antagonists, Truman gave the members of the American delegation to that conference—Byrnes, Vandenberg, and Connally— what Ayers termed "a good send-off" in the White House rose garden, and then accompanied them to the airport.[13]

Ironically, the chief practitioner at Paris of the new and tougher approach was Byrnes, the former "great compromiser." Literally flanked at the Paris meetings by Vandenberg and Connally, the secretary of state refused to give ground to the Russians on the postwar peace settlement with Germany, or even on an issue of agreement at the Moscow summit the year before—the four-power treaty against German military recrudescence that Truman had meant as a "test case" of Soviet-American relations. This change in attitude—and the reason for it—was noticed by others at the conference. "Byrnes is an admirable representative of the U.S., weak when the American public is weak, and tough when they are tough," an aide to Bevin observed.[14] The inspiration for this new toughness was also not far away. "Byrnes has 'stood up' 100%," Vandenberg wrote Dulles from the meeting. "He only 'almost weakened' once —at which point I put on one of my well-known exhibitions." Vandenberg reassured his fellow Republican that Byrnes and American policy toward Russia had truly changed: "Paris was Munich in reverse."[15]

While Vandenberg and Connally were undoubtedly a contributing cause of Byrnes' toughness at Paris, it is also true that the latter apparently felt a need to show new resolve at that meeting. "No longer," Byrnes would write some years later, "was there any wisdom in minimizing [Soviet-American] differences because no longer was there any justification for the belief that we were animated by the common purpose of an early peace." At the same time, Byrnes remained eager not to make relations with Russia needlessly worse. A month before the Paris meeting he wished to postpone upcoming U.S. nuclear tests in the Pacific on the grounds that they "might have a bad effect upon the already disturbed world situation." For the same reason, Byrnes worried that release then of a Canadian report on the spy investigations, meant to reassure the public, might be interpreted instead as a deliberate swipe at Russia. With publication of the report, Prime Minister Mackenzie King noted that "Byrnes had made no comment to the reference which the report contained to what information had been sought in the U.S. . . . What he seemed more concerned about was how everything was focussing up pretty strongly these days against Russia, so much so that it might be thought matters might be prearranged."[16]

Byrnes' words and actions at Paris, therefore, underscored the complex—and often contradictory—role that he played in the administration. But his new caution in that role demonstrated that he now knew enough to express whatever doubts he might still have about the hard line in private.

"The Honeymoon . . . Was Coming to an End"

Neither Kennan's "long telegram" nor the hard-line approach of Byrnes and Vandenberg at Paris suggested the means by which the new, tougher approach to Russia could be made to achieve America's aims. Kennan's analysis had changed the American image of Russia, but it provided no answer to the problem that it defined. Certainly the Soviet expert's genial advice—in Acheson's interpretation, "to be of good heart, to look to our own social and economic health, to present a good face to the world"—was of little practical value in a crisis.[17]

The potentially fatal flaw of the administration's new policy was that nothing of substance stood behind the hard line. America's wartime six-million-man army by spring 1946 had melted away in the course of peacetime demobilization, and was yet to be replaced by what the administration hoped would be congressional approval for universal military training. Even the gesture of sending the *Missouri* to Turkey had been a tacit acknowledgment of weakness rather than of strength, since there was no more militarily appropriate (or politically acceptable) means of responding to the distant crisis in Iran.

A solution of sorts to this dilemma was proposed by Winston Churchill in the course of his famous speech at Fulton, Missouri, in early March 1946. Expanding upon both the rhetorical and geographical boundaries of the cold war by his declaration that an "iron curtain" had descended from "Stettin in the Baltic to Trieste in the Adriatic," Churchill's speech essentially called for a revival of the wartime Anglo-American alliance against a new enemy—Russia. Such "a fraternal association of the English-speaking peoples," he predicted, would mean "there will be no quivering, precarious balance of power to offer its temptation to ambition or adventure."[18]

Apart from its rhetoric, most noteworthy about the speech was that, while Churchill's view of Russia's "expansive and proselytizing tendencies" would seem to have accepted Kennan's long-telegram thesis of the previous month, his proposal of a revised Anglo-American entente recognized a fact that Kennan's theorizing had steadfastly ignored: the atomic bomb would necessarily be at the center of the West's stand against Russia. Indeed, the bomb and not the communist "iron curtain" was subtly at the center of the speech. Churchill thus branded it "wrong and imprudent to entrust the secret knowledge or experience of the atomic bomb" to the UN, and "criminal madness to cast it adrift in this still agitated and ununited world."[19]

Reporters present at the occasion rightly assumed that Truman's presence beside Churchill on the dais constituted tacit administration approval for the former prime minister's message. Privately, some of the British were as disturbed by this connection as by the hard line and its implications. Despite later White House denials, the President was not only aware of the contents of the speech but had read a copy prior to its delivery.

The generally negative popular reaction in the United States to Churchill's speech was perhaps a surprising indication to Truman that public opinion, though tending increasingly toward the hard line, still continued to follow rather than to lead the administration in this direction. Henry Wallace—expressing what may have been a popular sentiment—denounced the speech and sarcastically deplored "any recrudescence of imperialism even under enlightened Anglo-Saxon atomic bomb auspices."[20]

It is likely that Truman merely acquiesced in Churchill's bid for an Anglo-American union as a means of uniting public opinion behind the hard line with Russia—a tactic that backfired in this case, however. For it is clear that the President himself intended no such alliance, especially as it might relate to cooperation on the atomic bomb. Even as Churchill spoke of future Anglo-American collaboration on atomic energy, American policy on the subject was moving entirely in the opposite direction.

The British members of the Combined Policy Committee chose the suitable date of Groves' presentation on the success of the Combined Development Trust in establishing a shared monopoly of atomic raw materials to revive the dispute over the meaning of the Washington conference's agreement on "full and effective cooperation." However, just as McMahon would be refused on his request for information on the bomb that day, so the British, too, were frustrated in their appeal. The unsettling news received by them this time was that the ubiquitous Groves had been appointed to a three-member American committee meant to resolve the problems surrounding Anglo-American cooperation on atomic energy. Not surprisingly, the meetings of this joint committee dragged on from December through mid-February without agreement.

Privately, Groves was frank about his reasons for opposing a renegotiated Quebec Agreement. Cooperation of any sort with the British, he later wrote, "was felt by me to be decidedly against the best interests of the United States."[21]

At the committee meetings, Groves proved a quiet but efficient obstructionist. Just how far he was willing to go to preclude a second Quebec Agreement was made clear on February 13—two days before the scheduled meeting to discuss final proposals for the agreement—when, in Acheson's words, Groves "threw a monkey wrench into the machinery" of the negotiations.*

Groves' "monkey wrench" was a letter to Byrnes which claimed that Anglo-American cooperation on atomic energy "could well be considered as tantamount to a military alliance," and as such was in violation of Article 102 of the recently signed UN Charter, the stipulation forbidding secret executive agreements between member states. Groves also insinuated that later public disclosure of the Quebec Agreement might have adverse political repercussions at home. He reminded Byrnes of the secret nature of Anglo-American cooperation: "The true relationship and the basis of collaboration between the United States and the United Kingdom has been kept from the American people and the Congress."[23] Never sanguine about the prospects for collaboration with the British on the bomb, Byrnes, Patterson, and Bush also seized upon Article 102 as a way out of that dilemma, and supported Groves in his unyielding stand against a renewed agreement.[24]

"Increasingly pressing," Acheson wrote, "and rather indignant" upon learning of Groves' intention to scuttle a new Quebec Agreement, the British recognized this sudden insistence upon Article 102 for what it plainly was—a convenient legal pretext for abrogating the terms of the agreements reached during the Washington conference and for ending future Anglo-American cooperation on atomic energy. Nor were they soothed by Acheson's effort to mollify them a month later with a frank memorandum which admitted that "it was quite impossible to fulfil the obligation of the arrangement." "If a secret arrangement were carried out, it would blow the Administration out of the water," Acheson reasoned. "[The British] must just resign themselves to the fact that, although we made the agreement, we simply could not carry it out; that

---

*According to Acheson, Groves came to the State Department in late February "a very scared man. 'This is the mess we are in,' Groves said, quite upset; 'you have got to get us out of it.' " "Groves' agitation," Lilienthal noted, "came from the fact that now the British wanted action on the promise of cooperation."[22]

things like that happen in the Government of the U.S. due to the loose way things are handled, and they would have to face the problem of their own country's feelings of being let down, just as we would have to face our problems."[25]

This avuncular counsel did not dissuade Attlee from intervening personally with Truman in mid-April, as the stalemate in Anglo-American dealings on atomic energy continued. Plainly skeptical of American excuses, Attlee reminded Truman of the commitments made at the Washington conference, adding, "it seems to me that this cannot mean less than full interchange of information and a fair division of the materials." The President, however, was not to be swayed from his stand in opposition to substantive cooperation with the British. "The language 'full and effective cooperation' is very general," Truman wrote back to Attlee. "We must consider what was the intention of those who signed the secret agreements at Washington." Truman's own intention, the remainder of this message left no doubt, was to abandon such cooperation altogether.[26]

It is equally true, of course, that Britain's case for cooperation had already been seriously damaged by the spy scandals, and particularly by the arrest of Alan Nunn May. The story of May's arrest had first appeared in American newspapers—on the same day, in fact, as Churchill's "iron curtain" speech—and an exaggerated account of May's importance to the Russians had been the point of Groves' letter to Hickenlooper in mid-March. The fact that May's arrest had been prompted by the leaks to Pearson and McNaughton on the Canadian spy ring, and the fact that Groves' supposed revelation of May's treachery coincided with the deadlock over renewal of the Quebec Agreement, may have given rise to suspicion among the British that the spy scandal—and May's case in particular—was being manipulated to their loss, though only Canadian Prime Minister King actually expressed such a view. Their hope of "full and effective" cooperation with the United States on atomic energy seemed beyond redemption in any case. Recognizing this, the Canadian government—now embroiled in its own espionage scandal—abandoned the expectation of cooperating with the United States.[27]

A settlement of Anglo-American differences seemed to have been reached in mid-May, when the British, forced to play their last card, threatened to pull out of the Combined Development Trust and to stop shipment of the Commonwealth's ore to the United States. The resulting compromise provided that the United States and Britain would share equally in the future distribution of uranium ore. Though it was strenuously resisted by Groves, the American members of the Combined Policy Committee admitted that their concession had been necessitated by fear that "a failure to reach agreement on this basis will threaten the future of the Combined Development Trust and of our mutually-advantageous collaboration with them in the field of raw materials."[28]

Hardly the Anglo-American nuclear entente that Churchill envisioned in his "iron curtain" speech, this last-minute settlement on raw materials seemed to offer at least the prospect of continuing cooperation with the United States. For the British, there was even some expectation of receiving American help in exploiting atomic energy's commercial uses to revive their failing economy. Yet even this faint glimmer of a brighter future in Anglo-American relations was deceptive. The severely amended McMahon bill, still being debated in Congress by April 1946, would eventually so restrict the interpretation of scientific interchange as to make it meaningless, and would outlaw sharing U.S. technology on atomic energy's "industrial uses" with foreign nations by 1947.

"The honeymoon of Anglo-American relations existing during the war," Acheson observed, "was coming to an end, and some of the commitments of the marriage seemed to be causing pain to one of the spouses." More accurately, it might be said that the British, having accepted a junior position in the atomic partnership with the United States during the war, had later become but a mere poor relation in that arrangement—and were now about to be disinherited altogether.*

"The Atomic Curtain"

A final consequence of the spy scare and of the Truman administration's hard line toward Russia was the transmogrification of the McMahon bill. Passed by Congress in the summer of 1946, the McMahon Act, one War Department aide observed, *"guarantee[d]* greater military participation

---

*Gordon Arneson, an early and constant participant in Anglo-American negotiations concerning atomic energy, now believes that the McMahon bill was the "real watershed" in that diplomacy. Initially puzzled as to why the Truman administration neglected to tell Congress about previous Anglo-American cooperation on the bomb, and neglected also to inform the British about the McMahon bill's restrictions upon future interchange, Arneson came to believe that the McMahon bill was seen by the administration as an easy, tacit way to end the relationship begun by Roosevelt and Churchill.[29]

than [did] the May-Johnson bill."[30] Symbolic of the changes the original bill had undergone was the retitling of one section concerning "Dissemination of Information" to "Control of Information." The difference was substantive as well. According to the official history of the U.S. Atomic Energy Commission, "the declaration establishing free dissemination as the cardinal principle in the information field" was abandoned in the amended version of the bill, along with the distinction between " 'basic scientific' " and " 'related technical' information." "Now the emphasis was on restrictions."[31]

The compromises necessary to secure the final passage of the McMahon bill in the House by that July meant that the principal aims of May-Johnson supporters were ultimately achieved—not only military review of the decisions reached by the civilian commission, but also such restrictions on the sharing of information as effectively to scuttle Anglo-American interchange and to dim even more the prospects of international control.

The most significant provision of the completed bill, however, was that which left in the hands of the War Department two vital tasks. In an amendment to the original bill, the army would continue to have responsibility for the stockpile of uranium and thorium, as well as authority for collecting and assessing intelligence on foreign progress toward an atomic bomb. This meant that Groves retained his role as the key figure behind America's supposedly preclusive monopoly of atomic raw materials, and that he would also still have the task of estimating the duration of the atomic monopoly. By a special provision of the McMahon Act, both these responsibilities would remain outside the purview of the civilian Atomic Energy Commission when the latter came into existence in January 1947. Significantly, these fateful concessions—seemingly minor at the time—had been brought about as a direct result of the national spy scare.

With the resolution that summer of the congressional fight over domestic control, the behind-the-scenes exclusion of the British from continued cooperation on atomic energy, and the gradual fading of the spy scandal from newspaper headlines—if not the public's consciousness—the attention of the Truman administration returned to the still-unresolved question of international control of the bomb.

Since February 1946, that question had been under consideration by Lilienthal and other members of the committee chosen to draft the

American proposal on international control to be presented at the UN. International control did not become a popular concern, however, until the selection some weeks later of the delegation to represent the United States at the UN. It was in the comparatively new forum of the United Nations that the matter of international control—now further complicated by the cooling of relations with Russia and the stringent restrictions of the McMahon Act—would be resolved.

In the minds of some Americans, the outcome at the UN seemed previsioned by the approach the United States had already adopted on domestic control, Russia, and the bomb. In each case, therefore, the Truman administration had followed a policy of monopoly and exclusion. The effect that these policies might have upon the prospects for international control was a particular topic of concern between two famous and unlikely correspondents—pacifist A. J. Muste and foreign-policy expert John Foster Dulles—through an exchange of letters that summer. "So long as we have our tremendous military establishment and the atomic bomb," Muste wrote Dulles, "they determine our relations with Russia and they determine also Russia's estimate of our intentions and our methods." The Soviet Union's evident hostility toward the West, he explained, was motivated "in large degree by fear of us and our atomic bombs."

"Resort by Soviet leaders to measures of forceful coercion has been characteristic for nearly 30 years within the Soviet Union," Dulles rejoined, "and long preceding the atomic bomb. . . . The objectionable feature of their foreign policy is that they are attempting in foreign affairs to do precisely what they have been doing at home for nearly 30 years."

It was Muste who had initiated the correspondence with Dulles and who now intended to have the final word in their exchange: "You speak of 'the secrecy which surrounds what is going on within the Soviet Union.' What but secrecy surrounds the atomic bomb stockpile? Are we not asking Russia to raise the 'iron curtain' at the same time that we keep the atomic curtain down tight?"[32]

Neither then nor later in his career did Dulles seem bothered by the question that Muste had posed. By summer 1946, the passage of a severely restrictive law for the domestic control of atomic energy—itself the product of a genuinely more aggressive policy toward Russia and of the not-so-genuine spy scandal exploited to promote that policy—had isolated the subject of atomic energy and the bomb not only from a traditional ally, but from the attention of a frightened and unsettled domestic audience as well. In this setting of communist "atom spies" and the "iron curtain," the bomb itself became sacrosanct. As the exchange of letters between Muste and Dulles shows, the lines were already firmly drawn on the question of secrecy and the bomb. Overseas, the iron curtain had been brought down. For Muste, as for other advocates of international control since before the destruction of Hiroshima, the upcoming negotiations in the UN represented the best—and perhaps also the last—hope for raising the atomic curtain between the United States and the world.

Scientists, Soldiers, and Diplomats

"[T]he atom bomb will . . . be one of the very first real tests of our ability to understand the Russian problem . . ."

David Lilienthal, journal entry, March 1946

"Searls said that in this way we would find out what is going on in Russia. And if the Russians refused to accept this proposal, then we would know that they would not go along on any international scheme, and . . . he didn't finish the statement, but his eyes indicated what he thought should then be recommended, and it was anything but pleasant."

David Lilienthal, journal entry, May 1946

"Anyway, We've Got the Bomb!"

In their study of the prospects for international control of the atomic bomb, David Lilienthal and his committee had remained isolated from —though not unaware of—both the spy furor and the congressional struggle over the McMahon bill throughout the winter and early spring of 1946. Central to their study remained the question that Lilienthal, as head of the committee's Board of Consultants, had posed at the outset: *"What* is there that is secret?" Operating from a suspicion "that the basis of present policy-making is without foundation," Lilienthal had assigned to his prestigious panel of experts and scientists the task of devising a workable plan for international control that would, until its final stage, preserve America's atomic advantage.

Despite the passive resistance—and occasional active opposition— of Groves to the efforts to answer that question, Lilienthal's Board of Consultants had devised by the end of spring an ambitious but seemingly feasible scheme for distinguishing between "military" and "harmless" applications of atomic energy. The key to this involved "denaturing" fissionable materials, a process that would render uranium useless in weapons but still usable in industry.

Endorsed by Byrnes, the "Acheson-Lilienthal Report," as it became known, seemed the brightest hope since Stimson's proposed direct approach for advocates of a cooperative approach to Russia. Pleased at the favorable reception accorded the plan when it was made public that March, the members of the Secretary of State's Committee were yet dismayed at the administration's choice of the man to "translate" their plan into the American proposal at the United Nations.

Bernard M. Baruch had been Byrnes' recommendation to fill the role of U.S. representative to the UN Atomic Energy Commission. Baruch had two qualifications of especial importance in the wake of the "atom spy" scandals—public prestige and good relations with Congress. But the native conservativism of Baruch and of the business associates he chose as advisers made them seem particularly poor choices as sponsors of the idealistic Acheson-Lilienthal plan. The further decision of the Baruch delegation to oppose any infringement of private enterprise by the plan and their selection of General Groves as a key consultant appeared additional reasons to question the depth and extent of their attachment to the cause of international control.

In fact, Baruch and his associates effectively transformed the original Acheson-Lilienthal plan, in scope if not in purpose. Its transformation into the Baruch plan did nothing, therefore, to safeguard the arrangements for international control but was a needless provocation to the Russians, and focused attention unnecessarily at the outset upon the negative aspect of punishment for violators rather than, as did the original, upon the positive aspect of mutual cooperation.

Lilienthal saw in some of these changes a cynical and self-serving attempt not only to gain unilateral advantage for the United States, but to "open up" Soviet society to change—a suspicion given credence by the words and actions of at least one member of the Baruch delegation. Indeed, in private and secret meetings before the convening of the UN commission, Baruch and his advisers considered abandoning the idea of international control altogether and substituting in its place the Pax Atomica envisioned by Groves. In an atomic league threatening the nuclear destruction of future aggressors the United States would inevitably play the dominant role. Failing to find support for such a proposal among military leaders or in the Truman administration, the delegation nevertheless persisted in a vain effort to turn the Baruch plan and the bomb itself to diplomatic advantage. Indicative perhaps of the attitude that the atomic monopoly engendered in Baruch was his glib dismissal of McMahon's doubts that the Russians would accept his plan: "Anyway, we've got the bomb!"[1]

"One of the Very First Real Tests"

Appointed chairman of the Secretary of State's Committee by Byrnes, Dean Acheson from the beginning interpreted his role and that of his committee to be more than simply advisory. Part of this wider latitude was Acheson's reaction to the way policy on the bomb had been handled by the administration. "Byrnes and Truman didn't understand anything about the bomb," he confided to Lilienthal upon appointing the latter to head the committee's Board of Consultants. Byrnes in particular was discussing atomic energy "without a knowledge of what the hell it is all about—literally."[2]

Acheson agreed with Lilienthal that the problem had been not only Byrnes and the State Department but "the War Department, and really one man in the War Department, General Groves [who] has, by the power of the veto on the ground of 'military security,' really been determining and almost running foreign policy." Frustrated by his failure to affect policy up to this time, Acheson now looked upon his role of chairman as an unequaled opportunity to bring the bomb and the policy toward it back under the control of the State Department, and also into the realm once more of international cooperation. Acheson realized as well that Byrnes had picked a strong group for the committee—having learned from Senator Arthur Vandenberg that the source of policy on the bomb was almost as important as its content. Besides the unavoidable Groves, the other members were the familiar Vannevar Bush, James Conant, and a former Stimson aide later to achieve fame in Washington, John J. McCloy.[3]

It was probably no surprise to Acheson when serious disagreements arose at the committee's first meeting. Troubled by his own lack of technical expertise on the subject, and inevitably mindful that three of his four colleagues on the committee were advocates of the May-Johnson legislation he opposed, Acheson urged that they appoint a team of scientific consultants to educate and advise them on atomic energy. Vocal in opposition to this idea was Groves, who argued that the members of the committee already "knew more about the broad aspects of the problem . . . than any panel that could be assembled."[4] Even more ominous to Acheson was the general's next suggestion—that the committee rely for advice upon the War Department's Technical Committee on Inspection and Control, a body which Groves himself had established after the bombing of Hiroshima.

Acheson won the first round. Overruling Groves' objections, the committee agreed upon Lilienthal as head of the advisory group and empowered the former TVA director to appoint the remaining members of the Board of Consultants: J. Robert Oppenheimer, the senior scientist on the Manhattan Project; Chester I. Barnard, president of New Jersey Bell and a veteran of wartime cooperation between government and industry; Charles A. Thomas, vice-president of Monsanto Chemical Company and an expert in the area of plutonium chemistry; and Harry A. Winne, in charge of engineering for General Electric. Winne's selection was an apparent concession to Groves, for he had worked with the latter on the Manhattan Project. Acheson's aide, Herbert Marks, served as liaison between the committee proper and the board.[5]

Acheson recognized in Lilienthal a kindred spirit, for his instructions to the board and its chairman were far-reaching. Their task was to define the methods of control available to a cooperative, international plan for preventing the future military use of atomic energy. Appended to this responsibility was that of judging the potential of other countries —specifically Russia—for developing an atomic bomb. In all of this, Acheson stressed, the board was under no restriction as to the form its advice could take; its members were to have both free access to the innermost secrets of the bomb and a free hand in making policy recommendations.

Like Acheson, Lilienthal believed that the importance of such a challenge went even beyond the significance of meeting it successfully. Control of the atomic bomb would "be one of the very first real tests of our ability to understand the Russian problem . . . and also of our own willingness . . . to face the implications of international organization."[6]

In both form and function, therefore, the Secretary of State's Committee and its Board of Consultants exceeded their initial charter as an advisory body. This seemed neither to surprise nor to displease Byrnes, however. The extension of the committee's role was justified by Acheson as in the spirit of the President's statements committing the administration to explore the prospects for international control; and excused by Lilienthal for the reason that their report would be "based on facts not now known by our political officers."[7]

But it is also likely that both Acheson and Lilienthal realized Byrnes would be in sympathy with their efforts to bring the bomb back into the purview of the State Department and out of the reach of Groves in the War Department or of Vandenberg and Connally in the Senate.

A blow for independence, in fact, would seem to have been the point of Lilienthal's recommendation at the board's first meeting in late January 1946 that they consider as one step the four steps outlined in the UN General Assembly resolution on atomic energy. The order of those four steps assuring safeguards Vandenberg had made a *cause célèbre* in London earlier that month. By this one motion Lilienthal and the board rejected the concession that Byrnes had had to make to appease Vandenberg and Connally, and regained the initiative—or so they hoped—to make policy on the bomb.

Lilienthal's recommendation on the order of steps was also a subtle indication that he and the scientists had serious doubts about what he categorized as "the Army-sponsored thesis that there are secrets." Throughout the last part of January and early February, Lilienthal and the other members of the board were educated in the facts of atomic energy by a collection of experts, including Robert Oppenheimer and scientists from Groves' headquarters. Faring better than McMahon's committee had in this regard, Lilienthal and the Board of Consultants heard from George Bain, the senior geologist for the Murray Hill Area, and Captain Joseph Volpe of Groves' staff about the wartime effort to corner the world market of uranium and thorium. The message of the two men at this briefing was apparently the same as that of Groves to Byrnes more than a year before—there was no uranium in Russia.*

By mid-February the board's thinking had coalesced around what was being called the "Oppenheimer plan." Robert Oppenheimer had suggested a simple but elegant way to achieve control of the bomb. Under his plan the "dangerous" or military uses of atomic energy would come under the jurisdiction of an international authority responsible for overseeing the mining, refining, and utilization of the world's atomic raw materials. Atomic energy's so-called harmless uses—in research, medicine, and commercial power plants—could safely remain in national

---

*In an interview more than thirty years after this briefing, Lilienthal spoke of it with amusement. "What we now know is that the mineral people were dopes. . . . It never occurred to them to drill." He confirmed, however, that "the information . . . the State Department consultants' group had came from those reports."

hands, however, after the fissionable material had been "denatured" by
the international authority and rendered useless for the clandestine
manufacture of bombs.[8] By this plan the Lilienthal group believed it had
hit upon a workable solution to the problem of the bomb, rejecting the
fatuous "outlawry of war" that had undone many previous efforts to
restrict arms. At the same time this expedient would preclude the prospect that some on the board feared most: leaving control of the bomb
solely in the hands of the military.

Among the other attractions of the Oppenheimer plan was the
evidence that "denaturing," believed to be an irreversible process, would
not require extensive safeguards to ensure that the use of radioactive
material remained "harmless." This meant as well that "security through
cooperative development"—the board purposely avoided the negative
term "control"—could be achieved without the need of establishing a
modern police state at home and an empire overseas to enforce the
agreement. It was the prospect of just such "a totalitarian type of control," the consequences of which "would be almost as horrible as the
effects of atomic bombing itself," that had caused some initial pessimism
in the board concerning an international authority.[9] The Oppenheimer
plan, therefore, seemed to meet the twin criteria that Lilienthal had
given the board for its recommendations—that they "work" and that
they have a reasonable chance of acceptance by the Russians.[10] Those
consultants with corporate backgrounds were encouraged by the precedent for an international authority in the early success of private companies doing business in Russia. Some possible sticking points with the plan
—the nature and timing of punishment for violations of the international authority, for example—were intentionally left for the UN
Atomic Energy Commission to resolve. The emphasis of the board
throughout was upon cooperation and harmony.*

However, the introduction of the Oppenheimer plan to Acheson's
committee in early March was destined to meet with greater resistance.
Lilienthal realized that the report to the committee was the combination

---

*Typical of the positive spirit that guided the consultants' group was the sign that Conant put up
in their meeting room: "Behold the turtle . . . he only makes progress when he sticks his neck out."
More than a generation later, Lilienthal defended the idealism of the consultants: "This was a rare
period which led to an elevation of feeling in the country that impossible things can be done. It
took something bold and amateurish. It was a supreme example of what should be more often
possible in human affairs to bring people together at a level of anticipation and idealism that makes
impossible things not only tryable but possible." The analogy, he said, is that of a twenty-foot chasm
to get over, "where the only previous effort has been ten feet, but not jumping will be disaster.
. . . You are confident you can make twenty because the alternative is so bad."[11]

of a thorough scientific study with a partisan plea for international control. Convinced of their arguments, the members of the board must nonetheless have been aware that their principal recommendation, to abandon the U.S. atomic monopoly in favor of cooperative control, required a considerable leap of faith. And yet, interestingly enough, the key to the Oppenheimer plan was the same idea of controlling the bomb by control of atomic raw materials that Groves saw as the foundation for a U.S.-dominated Pax Atomica. The conclusion of the board's report— "Absolute control of uranium would . . . mean adequate safeguard regarding raw materials"—was entirely in line with Groves' own thinking.[12] But there the similarity of thought ended. Groves' conception was an atomic league to punish aggressors. The board envisioned an international authority to abolish nuclear weapons.

In this light, Groves' objection to the consultants' report and the Oppenheimer plan is especially curious. He argued that the proposed international authority could be circumvented by nations exploiting previously undiscovered or low-grade deposits of uranium ore—a prospect that did not seem to concern him in the case of the atomic league, however. In a turnabout, Bush dismissed Groves' idea outright; Lilienthal thought it "shallow."[13]

Bush's own objection to the plan was more political than technical in nature. The atomic bomb remained, he reminded the board, America's principal counterweight to Russia's immense land army. Rather than attempting to remove the weapon suddenly from power politics that goal should be approached deliberately, by a series of stages. The process of separate stages toward an international authority would not only make the board's plan more acceptable at home, Bush concluded, but could also aid American interests if Stalin were made to "open up" the Soviet Union to the West as an initial sign of good faith. In a reprise of the argument he had made to Byrnes the previous November, he urged that such a *quid pro quo* would cost America nothing but might yield impressive results in the transformation of Soviet society.[14]

Throughout meetings between Acheson's and Lilienthal's committees during the first half of March, the notion of a *quid pro quo* grew in popularity with Bush, Conant, Groves, and McCloy. Unable, even with Acheson's support, to convince the other members of the committee that Russia's sudden transformation could not be brought about by the United States, Lilienthal was increasingly skeptical too of some of the motives behind the proposal to "open up" Russia. Reluctantly, he agreed to put the idea of separate stages back into the plan for international control.

Becoming "belligerent" at one meeting when Bush and Groves wished the plan to specify the timing of each stage, Lilienthal had begun to despair of achieving any agreement by mid-March. He even felt it necessary to remind the members of the Acheson committee that the President had committed them to an effort at achieving cooperative control of the bomb. In near despair, he resubmitted the board's report to the committee on March 17 with an ultimatum that it be approved or rejected in its entirety. To Lilienthal's surprise, all five members of Acheson's committee endorsed the Oppenheimer plan.[15]

Newly dubbed the Acheson-Lilienthal Report, the plan still required the sanction of Truman, Byrnes, and the still-to-be-chosen American delegate to the UN Atomic Energy Commission. But the very existence of such a plan seemed a signal accomplishment to its authors. Accordingly, Acheson urged Byrnes that it be promptly made public. While changed fundamentally from the original Oppenheimer plan by the addition of transitional stages and provisions for punishment, the report itself left the exact timetable for those stages and the nature of those sanctions open to future negotiations. The public release of basic information on atomic energy as a gesture of good faith by the United States also remained a prospect, subject to a resolution of the struggle over domestic control in Congress.

Indeed, most remarkable of all is that the Acheson and Lilienthal committees were able to devise a plan while that bitter congressional debate continued, in the presence of the scandal over "atom spies," and despite the administration's hard line toward Russia. For the drafters of that plan, it was a time seemingly of the brightest hope that atomic energy could be made an agency of peace rather than destruction. Subsequent events would prove this a fragile and perhaps even futile hope—and certainly one destined to disappointment.[16]

"It Is the Old Crowd"

Initially, Lilienthal's optimism about the Oppenheimer plan seemed well founded. Byrnes cautiously averred that he was "favorably impressed" by the report. The members of McMahon's committee in the Senate, still caught up in the dispute over domestic control, announced that they were giving it careful study.

Before an official reaction to the still-secret report could be gauged, however, a summary of the Oppenheimer plan was printed in Washington newspapers on March 26. The apparent aim of this leak was to arouse popular enthusiasm for the report and for the idea of international control; but its real effect was more nearly the opposite. In a political atmosphere hypersensitive to charges of espionage, Truman and Byrnes were obliged to decry the unauthorized disclosure of classified information. Privately, members of the administration resented what they rightly suspected was an effort to pressure the government in the direction of international control.

The leak of the Acheson-Lilienthal Report also revealed that the sudden and unexpected conversion to the plan of former irreconcilables on the Acheson committee like Groves had been more apparent than real. In a secret memorandum to Secretary of War Robert Patterson the day following the report's appearance in newspapers, Groves dismissed the feasibility of "denaturing" uranium and predicted that Byrnes "will issue a statement that the report does not represent the policy of the Government and has not been endorsed by the State Department Committee of which I am a member."[17]

The fact that no such disclaimer was forthcoming suggests, indeed, that Byrnes was not a disinterested party in the report's release. Groves, in any case, blamed the leak upon the State Department.[18]

Groves' defection aside, the authors of the Acheson-Lilienthal Report recognized that they had suffered their greatest setback in Byrnes' choice of Bernard M. Baruch as the chief American delegate to the UN Atomic Energy Commission. Byrnes had been considering candidates for that position since late February. By the end of the month he and Truman had settled upon Baruch, a seventy-five-year-old financier who made his first fortune in the stock market, and who during two world wars had established a largely self-promoted reputation as a close confidant of several American presidents. This reputation, combined with an equally well-publicized philanthropic bent, gave Baruch's appointment immense popular appeal. Perhaps typical of press reaction to the appointment was the comment of the *Chicago Tribune* that "we can all sleep better at night knowing . . . clear-eyed Bernie Baruch is on guard."[19]

The selection of Baruch inspired little enthusiasm among the members of the Acheson and Lilienthal committees—or even from Truman or Byrnes himself. Acheson had tried to dissuade the latter from this choice, specifically citing Baruch's age and vanity but probably mindful as well of the septuagenarian's innate conservatism. Lilienthal's objections in his journal were more direct. "When I read this news last night, I was quite sick. . . . We need a man who is young, vigorous, not vain, and who the Russians would feel isn't out simply to put them in a hole, not really caring about international cooperation. Baruch has none of these qualifications."[20]

An ominous forewarning of the trouble ahead was Baruch's threatened resignation only three weeks after his appointment over the premature release of the Acheson-Lilienthal Report. Sensitive to the danger of becoming only a "messenger boy" for the report, Baruch on that occasion sought assurance from the administration that he would not be bound by the plan it contained. Accordingly, he inquired of the President who was responsible for drafting the American proposal. Truman replied heartily, "Hell, you are!" Not content with this vote of confidence, however, Baruch approached Byrnes in mid-April for an endorsement. Significantly, Byrnes' response was somewhat more qualified than Truman's. While he and the President would continue to determine policy on the bomb, Byrnes announced, "as a practical matter" the two men would seek Baruch's views on the subject. The administration's early suspicion of Baruch was reciprocated. When Baruch sent an aide to confer with Acheson, the aide reported back that the under secretary of state had on his staff "an internationalist . . . who needs continuous watching."[21]

Following confirmation by the Senate in only two days of hearings, Baruch was free to choose what he termed his "team" on the delegation. Banker John M. Hancock had worked with Baruch on industrial mobilization during the Second World War. Herbert Bayard Swope had been Baruch's assistant on the War Industries Board during the First World War, and later became a journalist and public-relations specialist. Ferdinand Eberstadt was an investment banker and a former aide to Navy Secretary Forrestal. Fred Searls, Jr., in many ways Baruch's most important appointment, was a mining engineer and a long-time personal friend.

Baruch's choice of advisers occasioned new dismay among supporters of the Acheson-Lilienthal Report. Disconcerted by the absence of scientists on the delegation, Bush derisively tagged the aides "Wall Streeters." Lilienthal was, as usual, even more blunt in his assessment: "It is the old crowd: Hancock, Eberstadt, Swope (Herbert Bayard) and that familiar bull in the china closet, Searls. God! Isn't this something."[22]

Not surprisingly, Baruch received an unenthusiastic response from most of the members of the Acheson and Lilienthal committees to his request that they stay on as advisers to the delegation. Bush acidly informed Baruch that he considered him and his coterie the "least suited" for the job. Acheson politely excused himself from participating in the delegation, claiming too much work in Washington. Acheson, like others, was doubtless made wary by the prospect that Baruch would attempt to use his presence in the delegation as an endorsement of its work.[23] Doubts surfaced also in the Acheson-Lilienthal group over how extensive would be Baruch's modification of their report. As yet there had been no real indication of what changes he and his delegation intended to make in the original Oppenheimer plan. But many atomic scientists had seen as a portent Baruch's early announcement that for counsel on the technical aspects of the bomb he would "look to . . . Groves and those in American industry who have made a success of the use of atomic energy."[24]

Years later Baruch bitterly complained that "the scientists had run off and had refused to serve." At the time, however, there was no indication that he actually sought—or would have accepted—their advice. While the scientists proved resistant to wooing, it is true that Baruch was—at best—a reluctant suitor. He assured Lilienthal in late March, therefore, that he "could smell his way through" the problems of international control without scientific or technical advice. Baruch's comment to Bush, also in March, was revealing: "I concluded that I would drop the scientists because as I told them, I knew all I wanted to know. It went boom and it killed millions of people and I thought it was an ethical and political problem and I would proceed on that theory."[25]

Baruch's belated attempt in early April to enlist Oppenheimer as chief scientific adviser to the delegation was no exception to his general disregard of scientists. A meeting then with the physicist in which Baruch attempted to persuade Oppenheimer to join his "team" had the reverse effect, as the latter told Lilienthal. "Don't let these associates of mine worry you," Baruch had cajoled. "Hancock is pretty 'Right,' but (with a wink) I'll watch him. Searls is smart as a whip, but he sees Reds under every bed." Most disturbing of all to Oppenheimer had been the tenor of Baruch's remarks: He spoke of "preparing the American people for a refusal by Russia."[26]

Suspicious of the delegation's motives and convinced by the interview that Baruch wished to use him only as window dressing, Oppenheimer diplomatically but firmly refused the offer. He had, in any case, already settled upon an alternative course of action that he hoped would put pressure upon Baruch from outside the government.

Oppenheimer gave some indication of his real feelings and plans in a telephone conversation of early May with a fellow scientist. Unknown to him, his telephone had been tapped by the FBI, which suspected him of communist associations. A transcript of that call was forwarded to Byrnes (and presumably Baruch) by J. Edgar Hoover "as of possible interest to the President and you." Concerning Baruch and his plans for the Acheson-Lilienthal Report, Oppenheimer confided to his colleague: "I just want to watch this side of it and see if anything can be done. I think that if the price of it is that I have to live with the old man and his people, it may be too high. . . . I don't want anything from them and if I can work on his conscience, that is the best angle I have. It just isn't worth anything otherwise. . . ." Undoubtedly of principal interest to Hoover was the evidence of this conversation that Oppenheimer considered contacting European colleagues in order to form a scientists' lobby for international control: "It is very hard for me to tell if there is harm, little good, or some good, in my getting in touch with those European scientists. . . . And I don't know, I have to play it a little bit by ear, I'm not close enough to it. . . . The general philosophy I have now is about this, and that if there is any way in which I can make an effective contact with the few people from Poland, France, England, and Holland, I will try to pursue that, but I will not pay a price for it that is out of all proportions."*

Having excluded the scientists, Baruch did not seem any more responsive to other sources of advice on the bomb. Indicative of this insensitivity was the show that Baruch made of turning off his hearing aid when reporters asked his opinion of the Acheson-Lilienthal Report.

*Although Oppenheimer evidently did not suspect the tap on his phone, others at this time were more suspicious. Some weeks after this incident Dean Acheson wrote to Baruch inquiring whether his calls were being recorded. Baruch responded that the phone was not tapped; nor were stenographic records kept of the conversations. The "Acheson" file among Baruch's personal papers nevertheless contains apparently verbatim transcripts of telephone conversations between Baruch and the under secretary of state.[27]

Few if any of the vast number of letters supporting the report were acknowledged by Baruch or his staff; letters critical of the report, however, were answered promptly with a sympathetic note of concern. Thus either deserted by or in voluntary isolation from the atomic scientists as well as the authors of the Acheson-Lilienthal Report, Baruch and his staff began the drafting of the American proposal for international control of the atomic bomb, preparatory to the convening of the UN commission in mid-June 1946. Still silent on the nature and extent of the changes he intended to make in the Acheson-Lilienthal plan, Baruch, by his initial approach, had already substantially diminished the support he could expect for any changes.[28]

"Some of It Was Mischievous in the Extreme"

The first confirmation that Baruch intended a major divergence from the Acheson-Lilienthal Report came in his letter to Byrnes at the end of March concerning the need for "extensive amendment" of the Oppenheimer plan. In a series of meetings held throughout May between the Baruch delegation and members of the Acheson-Lilienthal group, the latter learned how substantial those changes would be. Lilienthal remained the most critical of Baruch's intended approach. "They have a fancy set of ideas and think, or say at least, that they are in pursuance of our Report," he wrote after one meeting. But "the gravest danger is that they will put forward proposals in a spirit that will insure their refusal."[29] Privately, he suspected that Baruch and his associates were already well along in preparing a case against the Acheson-Lilienthal plan.

Lilienthal's suspicion was, in fact, well founded. At the beginning of May, Baruch and Hancock had secretly decided that the delegation would present its own plan to the UN. Significantly, the two men had also resolved on this occasion not to make any substantial concessions in their plan during the subsequent negotiations, for fear that such would be seen by Congress and the public as a "retreat."[30]

The outline of this new proposal was revealed to the Acheson-Lilienthal group in mid-month. The Baruch plan represented four major changes from the Oppenheimer plan. First would be a call for total disarmament, rather than a focus just on control of nuclear weapons. "This would hopelessly confuse and mix issues, and obscure the hope of working out something on the atom bomb," Lilienthal objected.[31] Second was a new emphasis upon punishment—including atomic attack—for violators of the plan. This was an idea that the Board of Consultants had initially considered but ultimately rejected as premature in the first phase of negotiations, and as possibly "fatal" to the plan's chances for acceptance in the UN. Third was a deemphasis of the role of the proposed international Atomic Development Authority, and a corresponding shift of responsibility for the mining and refining of fissionable materials back to private industry. Baruch's businessman associate, Hancock, was particularly adamant on this change, fearing the Authority envisioned would be "the first start to an international socialized State." But the most controversial revision concerned the Baruch plan's proposal to abolish the veto power in the United Nations Security Council, a power guaranteed by the UN Charter to each of the nations of the council. The veto, Baruch argued, would allow the Russians to withdraw from the Atomic Development Authority at any time on the pretext of disagreement over some minor point, presumably after they had already gained valuable information on the bomb.[32] Byrnes had finally gotten the Russians to agree to abolition of the Security Council veto at Moscow, but subsequently abandoned the agreement at London as a concession to Vandenberg. Even more ironic is the fact that the Security Council veto was originally an American proposal for the UN Charter, and had been only reluctantly accepted by the Soviet Union in the founding of the United Nations.

Lilienthal and the Board of Consultants remained unalterably opposed to each of Baruch's suggested revisions. The Baruch plan's emphasis upon punishments and abolition of the veto, Acheson objected, added nothing to the security of the arrangement, since any violation of the plan would inevitably be accompanied by the collapse of cooperation in the UN and the imposition of sanctions by individual nations. Thus the plan needlessly emphasized the prospects of failure. But Baruch, too, stood unyielding. Indeed, he may have suspected that proponents of the Oppenheimer plan meant to blackmail him into adopting the Acheson-Lilienthal Report by withholding their support from his plan. Earlier in the month Baruch was probably advised by Byrnes or Hoover of another tapped conversation Oppenheimer had had with a colleague concerning this meeting being "an attempt to box the old guy in."[33]

For Lilienthal, it was not the revisions that were most disturbing about the Baruch plan, but the motivation behind them. He thought a proposal that Searls made at one meeting for a preliminary survey of world fissionable materials had been especially revealing of the direction that Baruch and his associates were headed: "Searls said that in this way we would find out what is going on in Russia. And if the Russians refused to accept this proposal, then we would know that they would not go along on any international scheme, and . . . he didn't finish the statement, but his eyes indicated what he thought should then be recommended, and it was anything but pleasant." In fact, Searls gave a better idea of what he was thinking at this meeting when he suggested that "each nation be permitted a stockpile of bombs, as a deterrent against atomic warfare; and that the UN also have a stockpile of bombs for retaliation." What Searls proposed was not cooperative control of the bomb but the atomic league of nations originally promoted by Groves. Certainly this seemed to Lilienthal a curious plan for international peace. The real aim of the initial raw-materials survey, he suspected, was plainly not cooperation, but espionage. He was inclined consequently not to take Searls' ideas seriously. The latter's presentation, Lilienthal wrote in his journal, was "unrealistic, silly, but time-consuming. . . . Some of it was mischievous in the extreme."[34] These last few meetings between the Baruch delegation and the Acheson-Lilienthal group, Acheson dryly observed in his memoirs, "made clear that others would not be profitable."[35]

"Bernie Is Like an Elephant at a Bridge"

Remarkably, apart from the civilian secretaries of the individual services, the leaders of the nation's armed forces had had little to say on or about the atomic bomb since the surrender of Japan. Indeed, with the notable exception of General Groves, most high-ranking officers had shown a studied reluctance to volunteer advice on the bomb to civilians, perhaps from a fear of seeming to take too political a role.

It was Baruch who made the first move, telling the Joint Chiefs of Staff in early April 1946 that he desired their views on international control before submitting his own plan to the United Nations. When a response was not forthcoming from the joint chiefs by mid-May, Baruch sent Searls to speak with members of the Military Staff Committee, the military's representatives on the U.S. delegation to the UN. Baruch also protested to the Pentagon that he was "considerably upset by the difficulty of obtaining military views."[36]

Searls was surprised to learn at the outset of his meeting with the

Military Staff Committee that its members had never discussed the bomb. The committee was perhaps equally surprised to discover that what Searls and Baruch desired was not advice but an endorsement of their idea for a Pax Atomica.

Searls' notion of an atomic league was apparently not his own, but that of Army Air Force General Henry (Hap) Arnold, to whom the Baruch delegation had turned for advice in early April. Arnold's plan, now the "idea of the Baruch group," Searls told the committee, "was that the member nations [of the UNAEC] conclude a treaty among themselves agreeing to outlaw the use of the atomic bomb and further agreeing that if any one nation, whether a signatory or not, violated this treaty, the others would automatically and with the least possible delay, employ the atomic bomb against the offender." Searls suggested that a total of five key bases with four to six atomic bombs each be established in the Azores, Cairo, Karachi, Burma, and the Philippines. UN commanders there would have sealed orders to retaliate against the first nation using an atomic bomb.[37]

Searls found little encouragement from the committee for his remarkable plan. Its admirals and generals deferred comment on the proposal until June 7, and only then made the restrained observation "that the United States would not desire to have foreign powers near . . . with atomic bombs at their disposal to drop on us without notice." A belated study by the joint chiefs on the military implications of international control—which did not reach the Baruch delegation until late July—observed more directly that if the atomic league was established by the United States outside the UN it "would greatly weaken the position of the United Nations and might lead to its eventual dissolution." While this study did not reject outright the Baruch delegation's concept of bases overseas for the purpose of retaliation, it noted an additional fact that Searls had neglected to mention but surely had not overlooked in his presentation: "[their] locations are all too obviously pointed at the U.S.S.R."[38]

This study and others sent to Baruch represented the official view of the joint chiefs as a group. Collectively, the latter remained circumspect about the Baruch plan.[39] Privately, and as individuals, they were more candid. Each of the military men Baruch requested advice from in May—Army Chief of Staff Dwight Eisenhower, Chief of Naval Operations Chester Nimitz, Army Air Corps General Carl Spaatz, and Truman's military aide, Admiral William Leahy—argued in personal replies that the atomic monopoly put America in a preeminent bargaining position with regard to the Soviet Union, and that such an advantage should be exploited at the UN. "It will be desirable," Nimitz wrote, "for international agreements concerning the atomic bomb to follow the European peace treaties and definitely to precede the time when other countries could have atomic bombs." As the officer whose service would deliver the atomic bomb, Spaatz saw an even more ambitious place for the weapon in diplomacy. "Our monopoly of the bomb, even though it is transitory, may well prove to be a critical factor in our efforts to achieve first a stabilized condition and eventually a lasting peace."[40]

To Baruch's undoubted disappointment, however, the military leaders were considerably less encouraging about his call for general disarmament, and attacked the wisdom of its provisions for penalties. Nimitz' letter was particularly perceptive. "I do not believe that the people of this country are prepared now to enter into an agreement for automatic punishment of other nations for acts which do not directly concern the United States. . . . If such punishment is dependent solely on the actual use of the bomb by a violator, the world catastrophe has already occurred; . . . we face the incongruity that the atomic bomb is necessary to enforce an agreement to outlaw its use." Eisenhower, too, expressed himself as "uncertain of the attitude of the people of the United States toward automatic retaliation against nations which may violate international agreements."[41]

While the joint chiefs, therefore, proved generally supportive of the Baruch plan where it followed the lead of the Acheson-Lilienthal Report, Baruch clearly lacked their imprimatur for his more expansive vision of a worldwide Pax Atomica. Indeed, even their much more limited endorsement arrived *after* Baruch's deadline for the announcement of his plan before the United Nations. The delay in submitting their views, ironically, had been occasioned by one final show of caution by the military men. They had first wanted assurance from President Truman that their opinions would not conflict with civilian policy on the bomb.

Disappointed by the reluctance of the joint chiefs to sanction his ideas, Baruch turned to General Groves as a source of advice for the final drafting of the American plan. Groves, in fact, had begun working for Baruch in April as liaison between the delegation and the Military Staff Committee, with the blessing of the latter. As what Baruch termed his "interpreter of military policy," Groves increasingly came to supplant that committee and the joint chiefs themselves as an adviser to the delegation, particularly when it became clear that the military careerists would not endorse the atomic-league concept. The fact that Groves represented himself in this role and not the military did not seem to disturb Baruch and the delegation. When Acheson warned Hancock of his feeling that Groves "would be speaking without the support of the military authorities," for example, Hancock demurred. Acheson "was pleasant but firm in restating his position," the Baruch aide noted.[42]

Groves' role in the delegation proved to be substantial. Not the least of this influence was his choice of advisers for the delegation. Brought to the United Nations from the Manhattan Project was physicist Richard Tolman to serve as Baruch's scientific consultant. Like the selection of the "Wall Streeters," Tolman's appointment occasioned little joy among the other atomic scientists. In a tapped telephone conversation before the choice of Tolman had been announced, Oppenheimer charged that "if Richard sits with [the delegation], one can just write it off as hopeless."[43] Groves also influenced other appointments. His deputy in the Manhattan Project, Major General Thomas Farrell, was assigned the vital responsibility by Baruch of estimating how long it would take other nations to build atomic bombs. Predictably, Farrell's estimate of twenty years for a Russian bomb coincided with Groves'. Groves' important wartime ally, Edgar Sengier, joined Searls as a raw-materials expert in the delegation. Like Hancock, Sengier was vocal in his opposition to an international Atomic Development Authority. Such an organization, he protested, would "upset wages [and] dissatisfy people" in the uranium mines.[44]

Indicative of the influence his appointment had upon the Baruch plan was Groves' recommendation, subsequently adopted by the delegation, that the phrase promising "prompt and certain" punishment for violators of the control plan be amended to "immediate and certain" punishment. The word "immediate" removed whatever doubt might have existed before that the Baruch plan intended atomic attack as the penalty for violations.[45]

The relationship of aid between Baruch and Groves was also reciprocal. At the end of April, Groves had called upon Baruch and Hancock to oppose the British request for a renegotiated Quebec Agreement. Later, Searls joined with Groves in using the delegation's UN auspices to purchase uranium and thorium ore not already acquired by the Manhattan Project's Murray Hill Area.[46]

With the help of Groves, Farrell, and Sengier, Baruch and his associates began putting the finishing touches on their plan in late May and early June 1946. Baruch now believed that he had sufficient backing —apart from suspected "internationalists" and the circumspect military leaders—to propose severe penalties and the abolition of the Security Council veto in that plan. He obviously also believed that compromises were not necessary in the UN—or with the administration.

Last-minute efforts by Acheson, Byrnes, and even Truman to amend the Baruch plan were consequently rebuffed by Baruch. A State Department suggestion that he reconstitute the original Board of Consultants for technical advice during the upcoming negotiations was now dismissed for reason of the scientists' "inelasticity," although Baruch himself had initially proposed such an arrangement. Byrnes' effort to get Baruch to abandon his proposed preliminary survey of world atomic raw materials, for the reason that it would be "worthless" and "would invite an early breakdown without a clear and adequate basis for such a breakdown," was equally unavailing. Instead, these belated efforts to force a moderation of the plan prompted another threat from Baruch to resign. "I have lost confidence in my being able to work this out with the President and you satisfactorily," he telephoned Byrnes on June 6. As before, this threat apparently had its intended effect, for both Byrnes and Truman backed down on the changes in a meeting with Baruch the following day. Baruch accepted only one alteration in the plan: the phrase "prompt and certain" was reinserted in the penalties provision, thereby leaving the nature of punishment for violators still in some doubt. But Truman assured Baruch that he would support the delegation's demand for abolition of the Security Council veto and penalties, and that the former "special relationship" of the United States with Britain and Canada in the matter of atomic energy would no longer apply at the UN negotiations.[47]

Baruch's approach in drafting the final version of his plan was characterized by Herbert Swope: "Bernie is like an elephant at a bridge. . . . He tests every board with the utmost care, and after he is fully satisfied that it will bear his weight, sits down on the bank and waits for somebody else to cross first." Swope's analogy characterized as well Baruch's approach to the pending negotiations in the UN. The proof of good faith, the true test of intentions, deliberately lay with the Russians in the Baruch plan. There was perhaps no longer any other alternative to that plan as the date of the negotiations approached. The "time has passed,"

Henry Stimson wrote Baruch in June, "for handling the bomb in the way I suggested to the President last summer." To the drafters of the Acheson-Lilienthal report, however, the changes that Baruch had made in the Oppenheimer plan seemed at best a dubious emphasis for the negotiation and were more likely, they suspected, a manifest provocation to the Russians, if not an implicit invitation to failure. The Baruch plan's provisions for an initial raw-materials survey, penalties, abolition of the veto, and the protection of national economies against "interference" by international authority had each transformed the original Oppenheimer plan.[48] But not less important than these was the change in attitude that the Baruch plan represented. Thus it was the potential costs of cooperation and not cooperation's benefits that dominated the concern of Baruch and his associates. The creators of the Baruch plan guaranteed that international control would be entirely on American terms—or not at all. In the immediate aftermath of the nation's "atom spy" hysteria, and during the progressive deterioration of Soviet-American relations over Iran, Greece, and eastern Europe, there surely could be little reason for optimism even among members of the Baruch delegation themselves.

Indeed, in the two months since Baruch's appointment the buoyant hopes of the Acheson-Lilienthal group had given way to despair. Byrnes, too, had come to share this pessimism. On the eve of the UN General Assembly's convening in New York he confessed to Acheson that choosing Baruch was "the worst mistake I have ever made. . . . But we can't fire him now, not with all the other trouble."[49]

The Winning Weapon
in the United Nations

"America can get what she wants if she insists upon it. After all, we've
got it and they haven't and won't have for a long time to come."
    Bernard Baruch to David Lilienthal, December 1946

"In time in America your plan will be seen as unfair."
    Vyacheslav Molotov to Bernard Baruch, August 1946

"Our World"

Baruch's proprietary feelings toward what he termed America's "winning weapon" inevitably affected the way that he and his delegation
approached the negotiations on international control, and tempered
their eagerness to work for a reasonable settlement with the Russians.
His faith in the stronger bargaining position of the United States because of the bomb made him more willing to abandon those negotiations, therefore, if the Soviets did not embrace the Baruch plan. Had
they accepted the plan, the Russians would have been compelled to
abide by its provisions for stages toward the cooperative control of the
bomb, the first step being an unrestricted survey of Russia's resources of
uranium and thorium. The actual end of American nuclear hegemony
would not have come until the final stage, when the U.S. stockpile of
bombs would be destroyed or surrendered to the United Nations. A
suspected violation of the control plan by the Russians at any time in
the intervening stages held the prospect—implied though not stated in
the plan—of a devastating atomic attack upon the Soviet Union. Thus
the Baruch plan did not differ in substance from an ultimatum the
United States might have given Russia to forswear nuclear weapons or
be destroyed.
    A lengthy but indefinite continuation of the U.S. atomic monopoly
followed by a Soviet-American nuclear arms race was always thought by

Baruch and his aides to be the most likely alternative to international control. Whether the Baruch plan was accepted or rejected they believed that the United States would continue for some time to have a decisive advantage in its "winning weapon."

When the Russians decisively rejected the Baruch plan in late summer 1946, the attention of Baruch and his aides returned to the idea of the atomic league, or nuclear consortium, that they had considered the previous spring. As the UN talks dragged on into the fall without result—and as domestic and foreign criticism of the Baruch plan increased—an informal atomic league was preferred by them to any further attempt at cooperating with the Russians. A formal, international Pax Atomica no longer seemed possible, since the UN stalemate and the increasing enmity of the cold war showed that there was no practical circumstance under which the Soviet Union could be included in what one Baruch aide had begun to call *"our* world." Indeed, the alternative to international control—the continuing U.S. trusteeship of the bomb —resembled the atomic-league idea. The threat of a U.S. atomic attack against Russia remained implicit in the "sacred trust," therefore, whereas it would be explicit in the league concept. The final exclusion at this time of Britain and Canada from cooperation with the United States in any area of the bomb but atomic raw materials meant that America constituted, in effect, a nuclear consortium of one.

With abandonment of the last hope for atomic energy's cooperative control, and the consequent recognition that the U.S. nuclear trusteeship was henceforth open-ended, the era of direct diplomacy involving the bomb came to a close.

"We Had the Right as Well as the Power on Our Side"

For a subject concerning the potential obliteration of humanity, the presentation of the Baruch plan before the UN General Assembly on June 14, 1946, was appropriately dramatic. "We are here to make a choice between the quick and the dead," Baruch intoned at the beginning of his speech, which had actually been written by aide Herbert Swope. The plan Baruch introduced followed the essential lines of those changes in the Oppenheimer plan of nearly two months before. "Condign punishment," he emphasized, "lay at the very heart" of the American plan, since before a country would be "ready to relinquish any winning weapons . . . it must have more than words to reassure it." Inspection would take the place of an international Atomic Development Authority. And there could be no veto of any of the plan's provisions.[1]

One of Baruch's pet ideas, the outlawry of war, was purposely understated in the speech, presumably as a concession to the State Department, which had requested that he omit the idea entirely. The final version of the Baruch plan acknowledged that progress toward the wider goal of disarmament would first depend upon abolition of the atomic bomb.

In a forum already becoming accustomed to rhetoric, the speech was nonetheless remarkable for what it left implied but unstated about the Baruch plan, Baruch's vague allusion to the bomb as America's "winning weapon" being just one example. The vital timing of stages was left entirely unresolved, as were the prerequisites for the initial stage of cooperation and the type of punishment to be meted out to violators of the plan. A memorandum by the Joint Chiefs of Staff observed that it "is not clear from [Baruch's] address . . . whether or not he proposed employment of the atomic bomb as a retaliatory weapon against violators." Baruch, in fact, dropped any mention of the atomic-league idea from his remarks, though a multinational consortium in sole possession of atomic bombs was one outcome envisioned in the plan's final stage.[2]

Despite, or possibly because of, this ambiguity, reaction to the Baruch plan in the United States was overwhelmingly favorable. The *New York Times'* military correspondent, Hanson Baldwin, described the proposal as "thoughtful, imaginative and courageous."[3] Most newspaper accounts were more fulsome than Baldwin in their praise. Nor was Baruch unmindful of or indifferent to the paean of enthusiasm with which his plan was greeted. A survey of newspaper editorials by his staff claimed to show that 98.5 percent of press opinion was favorable to the report.[4]

The public vote of confidence this survey seemed to reflect may have been misleading, however. Certainly there was no acclamation for Baruch among sources who viewed the plan either as a surrender to the Russians or as a mask for atomic diplomacy. Hearst papers blasted him for giving to "FOREIGN MASTERS the AMERICAN SECRET of the atomic bomb." The *Daily Worker* dismissed the plan as "atomic blackmail."

More moderate critics based their objections upon Baruch's tactics at the outset of the negotiations.

One such early critic was journalist-commentator Walter Lippmann. Lippmann argued in his syndicated column the week following the UN speech that Baruch had chosen a spurious issue in abolition of the veto, since the history of the League of Nations had proved that the prospect of a war to punish aggressors was only more likely to deter states from enforcing sanctions. Privately, Lippmann was even more direct. Baruch "had hardened U.S. opinion behind ideas that made no sense" and unnecessarily irritated the Russians, he told scientist Chester Barnard.[5]

The initial response of the Russians to the Baruch plan was silence. On June 19, however, Soviet UN delegate Andrei Gromyko replied with a comprehensive counterproposal. Gromyko called for an international convention prohibiting the production, possession, or use of atomic bombs. The "Gromyko plan" provided neither for inspection nor for sanctions against violations occurring at the outset. Instead, in the Russian plan safeguards would be established concurrent with scientific interchange on the bomb, and both together would constitute a second step after initial agreement on the weapon's control. "[T]he veto," Gromyko declared pointedly, "must be retained under any circumstances."[6]

Less than a week after presentation of the Baruch plan, the differences between the American and Russian positions at the UN seemed clear—and unbridgeable. As Acheson and Lilienthal had predicted, the negotiations immediately became bogged down in a dispute over abolition of the veto. The hope that Baruch might be made to yield on the veto, or at least defer its discussion with the Russians, was abandoned when he remained adamant despite the efforts of Oppenheimer, the State Department, and the heads of the Canadian and French UNAEC delegations. Baruch justified his intransigence to former aide D. F. Fleming on moral grounds. Fleming's suggestion that Baruch should postpone a confrontation with the Soviets was rebuffed by the latter in a labored biblical reference which boded ill for the spirit of compromise: "We can agree with them as we did with the Germans, but what profiteth a man if he gaineth [sic] the whole world and yet loseth his own soul?"[7]

Baruch could also point to Truman's approval for a tough stand on the negotiations. Thus the new hard line was in accord with Baruch's stand on the veto, and with his demand for an unrestricted survey of world atomic raw materials. "[W]e should stand pat on our program," Truman wrote to Baruch. "We must have assurance that the raw materials from which atomic energy can be released are controlled at the source and I am of the opinion that we should not under any circumstances throw away our gun until we are sure the rest of the world can't arm against us. . . . I think we understand each other on this subject," Truman volunteered.[8]

Confident that the public and the President would support his stand on the veto, Baruch informed Molotov on July 5 that he rejected the Russian proposal as well as a French-Soviet request that the United States cease manufacturing atomic bombs until safeguards against their use could be agreed upon.*

Baruch's formal rejection of the Gromyko plan may have seemed unnecessary to the Russians. Only four days before there had been what some Americans, and probably most Russians, considered a more forthright exposition of U.S. policy than anything said at the United Nations —the first postwar test of an atomic bomb.

There had been no atomic explosion in the world since the destruction of Nagasaki. The army and the Manhattan Project had wanted to test an advanced version of the Nagasaki-type bomb the following May, but that test had been delayed. Byrnes had played a role in the decision to postpone the test. "Secretary Byrnes said that from the standpoint of international relations it would be very helpful if the test could be postponed or never held at all," Henry Wallace noted at the Cabinet meeting where Truman approved the delay.[10]

Truman's reasons for wanting to postpone the tests only incidentally involved the Russians. In late March Patterson had told a War Department aide that the President urged delay "in view of the very increased expenditures that were required, the large number of personnel to be committed to it . . . the unsettled conditions of the times and

---

*Baruch's refusal to consider an "atomic truce," a temporary moratorium on U.S. bomb production as a sign of good faith, had brought about the resignation the previous May of an idealistic member of the delegation's staff. The young staffer, Cord Meyer, Jr., afterward observed in an essay pointedly entitled "Hope and Illusion" that it "must be clear by now that other nations do not regard our bomb monopoly as the exercise of a sacred trust but as an imminent threat to their existence." Meyer's subsequent career represents a fascinating intellectual and political conversion —from a leader of the World Federalists when he worked for Baruch, to the CIA chief of station in London during the early 1970s.[9]

the fact that the tests were not conclusive." There was apparently still another, more prosaic, reason for the postponement. Three days before the decision to delay, Henry Wallace records, the "President was very happy to agree" to wait until July for the tests, since he "didn't want a lot of Democratic congressmen out witnessing the test when their votes were needed here in Washington."[11]

Truman's political motives and Byrnes' concern with appearances may have led to a tactical error in the timing of the tests as they affected the UN negotiations, nonetheless. Certainly Soviet-American relations were not improved by the summer, when the first test bomb was exploded. The lack of progress in the UN talks at that juncture made the timing of the experiment seem deliberate even to outsiders. And yet, though various congressmen lamented the coincidence of the tests with the negotiations in the UNAEC, Byrnes seemed almost alone in the administration for his concern with their effect upon the Russians.

However coincidental the timing of the atomic tests was with the UN stalemate, the Russians capitalized on the event. "If the atomic bomb did not explode anything wonderful," *Pravda* observed, "it fundamentally undermined the belief in the seriousness of American talk about atomic disarmament."[12]

Unconcerned with the atomic test, Baruch also felt no reason to be defensive about the lack of progress at the UNAEC. As the deadlock there continued throughout July, he acknowledged the Baruch plan itself to be a principal cause of the standoff. Others in the delegation shared Baruch's attitude of "no compromise." Noting "some people are already thinking about compromises on minor aspects of the problem," Hancock wrote to Searls that he had "frowned" on such suggestions "in every way I can. . . . I fear that if we once start even an orderly retreat on minor points, we may well be facing a rout later on."[13]

Baruch may have been trapped in an unyielding position by his own rhetoric. One of the delegation's defenders outside the UN, John Foster Dulles, confessed to Chester Barnard in 1947 that Baruch had once agreed to a compromise on the veto sponsored by the UNAEC's Australian delegation. But he had subsequently reneged when it came time to actually endorse the motion. Barnard surmised from Dulles' anecdote that Baruch had "so successfully sold the country on the veto as being a vital matter that he could not, as a practical matter, reverse his position. . . . It certainly will be a tragedy if the whole thing fell through because of a created popular emphasis upon . . . a false approach."[14]

Dulles' suggestion that Baruch at least clarify the type of penalties envisioned by the plan—and thereby exclude preemptive atomic attack—was rejected by Baruch. Significantly, the latter confided to Lilienthal that the real stumbling block in the negotiation for the Russians was not the veto "but rather the whole idea of permitting their country to be subjected to the inspection from without."[15]

As the summer of 1946 wore on without progress in the talks, Baruch seemed more concerned that his plan receive support from Americans than from the Russians. Consequently, the wholesale rejection of the plan on July 24 by Gromyko, whose previous objections had only been in detail, apparently left Baruch and his associates undaunted. There was "no real cause for disappointment at the progress to date," Baruch told his staff on August 1, for "we had the right as well as the power on our side." Additionally, "there has been a tremendous change in public opinion toward Russia," he confided to the Canadian delegation later that day.[16]

Clearly, Baruch's optimism did not concern the prospects for an agreement with the Russians. Only hours before Baruch spoke of the change in public opinion, a candid meeting between Eberstadt and Gromyko had ended with the consensus of the two men being that "our only problem is when to quit." Advised by Eberstadt that the negotiations were "a short sale," Baruch nevertheless rejected his counsel that they should "get out" of the talks: "We must go on until the people generally come to the opinion we have." Hancock concurred in Baruch's assessment the following week: "We can break off any day but if we were to start drawing lines at this moment, I think we would lose every bit of American support which I think we now enjoy."[17]

Having concluded by early August that the vital question was when, not whether, to break off the negotiations in the UN, the U.S. delegation seemed still uncertain about the timing of that break. "We haven't decided yet that we want to press the matter to an issue," Hancock wrote to Acheson in mid-month. He admitted he was then preparing "a coolly analytical statement" on the shortcomings of the Soviet proposal, and "the timing of the use of this analysis is probably almost as important as its contents." It would be a mistake to prompt a break too soon, Baruch observed later in the month, since "the tide of public opinion is running very strongly against the Soviets," and the "so-called liberal groups" had been alienated by Gromyko's obstreperousness.[18]

Eberstadt was perhaps the only one of the delegation worried that the American public would later accuse them of adopting a plan "obviously unacceptable to the Soviets with the full realization that they would reject it and then . . . proposing an atomic alliance against them."[19] Eberstadt's concern, however, appeared groundless by late summer 1946. The lasting effects of the previous spring's spy scare, as well as the signing of the McMahon bill into law in early August, seemed to secure Baruch's domestic flank against serious criticism.

Overall, the delegation seemed to view the atomic bomb in a new light once Russian rejection of the Baruch plan seemed a near-certainty. The proprietary attitude the delegates had taken toward America's "winning weapon" had been borne out in the subsequent negotiations, but the phrase itself acquired a double meaning as the stalemate at the UN continued. As hope for international control faded, the mere existence of the bomb seemed to reinforce Baruch and his associates in their conviction that compromise with the Russians was unnecessary. Baruch made this explicit when he told Gromyko that he would rather abandon the negotiations than submit an alternative plan. Hence the "winning weapon" guaranteed success on American terms either if the Russians finally accepted the plan, or, if diplomacy failed, in the perhaps unavoidable war that would follow. Baruch seemed unmoved by Gromyko's rejoinder at this meeting: "In time in America your plan will be seen to be unfair."[20]

By the end of August, the alternative to cooperation on the bomb was a topic discussed with increasing frequency in the delegation. In private, Eberstadt speculated upon "the difficulties of determining what nations would have to be excluded from *our* world" after abandonment of the Baruch plan. Groves' deputy, Farrell, advised Hancock that the United States needn't wait for a collapse of the negotiations but "should at once undertake a great expansion of its atomic weapon program, so as to have at the earliest possible date an overwhelming superiority in such weapons. . . . They should be dispersed at widely separated bases . . . [so] the bombs could be delivered in crushing numbers any place in the world. . . . I like Mr. Baruch's idea of calling the bomb our 'winning weapon'—a weapon which we give up only when we are sure the world will remain safe. . . . If we cannot be sure, we must arm to the teeth with the winning weapon."[21]

It must also have seemed to the delegation that the bomb now constituted America's only real weapon against the Russians. Thus Baruch rejected another suggestion that the United States temporarily stop producing bombs as a sign of good faith during the negotiations. The "U.S. should retain its winning weapon as a means of maintaining its security," he objected, since "if we were to stop making bombs we would be almost defenseless and would certainly have only a modicum of military power with which to stand up to the USSR." Groves pointedly reminded the delegation also "of the reliance now placed by the United States on the atom bomb as a counter-balance to the enormous military establishment maintained by Russia."[22]

In this atmosphere of expectation and anxiety, discord continued within the U.S. delegation as to the timing of the decision to abandon the negotiations, which remained in September essentially where they had been at the end of June. There was, however, a growing consensus to speed things toward an end. All were agreed, therefore, that a final vote on the Baruch plan would have to come before the end of the year. In January the three Western nations supporting the United States in the Security Council would be replaced by eastern European states, and another Soviet ally, Poland, would chair the UN Atomic Energy Commission. With these changes, the United States would lose the margin of ten votes in favor and two votes opposed to the Baruch plan.

Emphasis now was clearly upon the form rather than the content of the talks. "It must be clear that Russia had been given every possible chance to understand and to accept," Groves told the delegation, adding that "this sort of procedure was essential whether we felt that the Russians would accept it or not." Yet there was also a danger that too much delay might forfeit the initiative of the talks. "By prolonging negotiations we play into the hands of the Russians," Swope warned.[23]

In fact, a public-opinion survey conducted by the delegation in early September showed that Baruch's mandate from the American people was somewhat diminished, but essentially still intact. Some 76 percent of those polled indicated support for Baruch's uncompromising stand. This slippage was a cause for sudden concern for Baruch in a memo to his aides: "We have lost the initiative to Russia and other nations are beginning to waver more and more. . . . The longer we hesitate and the more we retreat, the more other nations will shift away from us. . . . We are losing ground every day."[24]

Baruch was overreacting to the polls. An independent survey at the end of June 1946 revealed that nearly three-quarters of those questioned had never heard of his plan. But the polls showed that the sensitivity of Americans to threats against the "atomic secrets" persisted. Whereas a majority (69 percent) of those who were not familiar with the Baruch plan still favored international control even when it was explained that this would involve eventual destruction of the U.S. nuclear stockpile, control achieved at the price of surrendering the "atom bomb secret" to the Russians was disapproved by 72 percent of those questioned in August 1946.[25]

Baruch's concern with public opinion notwithstanding, he acknowledged the necessity not to appear precipitate in forcing a vote in the Security Council. On September 10, Hancock argued that the delegation "cannot afford to let the issue come to a head in the Atomic Energy Commission before the middle of November."

Hancock's concern was apparently with public opinion as well. Two weeks before, Senator McMahon had told him that the negotiations would have to continue for a year before the delegation could count on American public opinion.[26]

Another reason for delaying a final vote became clear in the letter that Baruch wrote on September 9 to the State Department concerning his delegation's "strong desire to make sure that what they are doing and will do is in line with over-all foreign policy considerations." Specifically, he was concerned that the showdown on international control in the UN coincide with the hard-line approach toward the Soviets then being taken by Byrnes at the Paris Council of Foreign Ministers. "It is obvious that the AEC negotiations are now only a sideshow in the international picture," Baruch told his aides in early September. "The sideshow must be tied in with the main rings of the circus."[27]

" . . . *the* 'Showdown' with Moscow"

Eager to have the President's approval for the coming showdown, Baruch sought a meeting with Truman for September 18. "A new phase is about to begin," Baruch intended to tell Truman. His goal was to ensure that "our efforts may become a positive, rather than a passive, factor in the overall foreign policy of the United States."[28]

Fatefully, neither the UN negotiations nor Russia was the main topic of discussion at this meeting with the President. In fact, the instructions Baruch sought were virtually forgotten there. Displacing these was the subject of a letter Henry Wallace had written to Truman the previous July, published that day in the newspapers. The Wallace letter was generally critical of the administration's new hard-line policy toward the Soviet Union, and specifically attacked the Baruch plan. Wallace's letter, Baruch fumed, was a frontal attack against his efforts in the UN, and "an irresponsible opinion which could only divide American opinion and give comfort to people who are trying to tear down America's objective." For the third time since his selection as chief U.S. delegate to the UN Atomic Energy Commission, Baruch threatened to resign unless he could be assured of administration support against his critics.[29]

The "Wallace affair," as it would become known, had had its origins in the commerce secretary's progressive disillusionment with the administration's foreign policy. Throughout the spring and most of the summer of 1946, when that policy took a decided swing to the right concerning Russia, Wallace had refrained from commenting at length upon his own growing disaffection. Toward the end of July, finally spurred on by what he believed was a steady drift toward war with Russia, Wallace penned his long and rambling letter to the President.

The first part of the letter was an appeal that Truman try to understand Russian motivations. "How would it look to us," Wallace asked rhetorically, "if Russia had the atomic bomb and we did not, if Russia had 10,000-mile bombers and air bases within a thousand miles of our coastlines and we did not?" He was especially critical of "a fatal defect" in the Baruch plan—the clause that required the Russians to suspend atomic research "and to disclose their uranium and thorium resources while the United States retains the right to withhold its technical knowledge of atomic energy until the international control and inspection system is working to our satisfaction." "In other words," Wallace chided Truman, "we are telling the Russians that if they are 'good boys' we may eventually turn over our knowledge of atomic energy to them and to the other nations. . . . Is it any wonder that the Russians did not show any great enthusiasm for our plan?"

Wallace charged further that the Soviet Union had only "two cards which she can use in negotiating with us: (1) our lack of information on the state of her scientific and technical progress on atomic energy and (2) our ignorance of her uranium and thorium resources. These cards are nothing like as powerful as our cards—a stockpile of bombs, manufacturing plants in actual production, B-29s and B-36s, and our bases covering half the globe. Yet we are in effect asking her to reveal her only two cards immediately—telling her that after we have seen her cards we will decide whether we want to continue to play the game."[30]

Truman decided to ignore the letter. Yet, amazingly, he approved an amended version of the same message in Wallace's speech on September 12 to an assembly at Madison Square Garden. Truman evidently now paid attention neither to Wallace's spoken nor to his written word, for he subsequently endorsed the controversial speech in a press conference as "exactly in line" with U.S. policy toward Russia.*

The confusion over Wallace's stand and Truman's support of it culminated on September 17 with publication of the original letter by the President's press secretary in an effort to head off speculation concerning its contents.

Baruch was certainly not the only one in the government besides Truman to be discomfited by Wallace's remarks. Since April, Byrnes had been pursuing his own "get tough" line toward Russia at the Paris Council of Foreign Ministers on the issues of war reparations and trusteeships. Understandably, he saw Wallace's letter and speech as undermining that policy. Joining Baruch, Forrestal, and a multitude of senators and congressmen in condemning Wallace's views, Byrnes pressed Truman to fire the mercurial commerce secretary. Truman had been at first hopeful that Wallace could simply be enjoined from speaking out on foreign policy until the end of the Paris conference. But this arrangement had seemed to please no one, Wallace included. The President, therefore, demanded the latter's resignation on September 20. For Byrnes, Wallace's firing was the end of the affair.[32]

Not so for Baruch. Upset at having his work compared to a rigged poker game, Baruch also feared that Wallace's attack might have done lasting damage to the domestic support his plan had always enjoyed. Gromyko had given grounds for that fear, and further wounded Baruch's dignity, when he quipped that the Russians were unaware of differences in opinion on the Baruch plan before the Wallace letter. Baruch appar-

---

*Wallace had earlier remarked that he suspected "there had never been a President who could move in two different directions with less time intervening than Truman." Of a meeting with Truman on September 12 he noted in his diary: "The President apparently saw no inconsistency between my speech and what Byrnes was doing—if he did he didn't indicate it in any way." Truman's deference to Wallace was probably motivated more by his hope that the latter's liberal political ties would be of help in the upcoming midterm elections. The President in any case showed no disposition to change his "get tough" attitude toward the Russians.[31]

ently concurred with Hancock's assessment "that it was the Russian plan to propagandize and undermine our position." Wallace, Hancock hinted darkly, may even have been consciously aiding the Soviet cause.[33]

Indeed, this evident paranoia on the part of Baruch and his associates might have been prompted by the surprisingly accurate information that Wallace seemed to possess concerning their plans. The arrangement on stages to international control had been finally worked out between Hancock and Groves only in mid-August—weeks after Wallace's letter to Truman. Yet what Wallace had termed the plan's "fatal defect," the initial requirement that Russian resources of atomic raw materials be made known to the West, was the first step required in that plan.

So sensitive was Groves to this proposal on stages that he had personally supervised its preparation. In a secret memorandum to the delegation, he noted that the raw-materials survey would "not require any material change in the special position of the United States," since America would not reveal her own thorium and uranium resources until the second stage.[34] Groves had already taken steps to ensure that the existence of the Combined Development Trust would not become known to the Russians in the course of the UN negotiations.*

Since there was no time limit for the raw-materials survey, this initial stage could as well constitute a hidden veto of the Baruch plan by the United States—a fact that Wallace pointed out in his letter. This detail had not become clear in the course of the negotiations only because Groves' document on stages had not been circulated beyond the U.S. delegation by the end of August, and had never even been discussed there, so certain were its members of a rejection by Russia. Accordingly, Baruch and his aides suspected treachery. Since the raw-materials survey had been discussed the previous spring "under State Department auspices," Hancock concluded "that somebody there had leaked and had assumed what we were going to do."[36]

Ultimately, it was not Wallace's letter but Baruch's pride that almost revealed the hidden veto to the public at large. Intent upon discrediting Wallace, Baruch had Groves draft a point-by-point rebuttal of the original letter for the President. That rebuttal was itself disingenuous. "We have not asked others to disclose their own material resources

---

*Here Groves was already too late, since the British representative on the trust, Donald Maclean, almost certainly informed the Russians of its work.[35]

and would not do so unless we were prepared to disclose our own," it protested. While accurate in that the delegation had not yet demanded Russia be opened to inspection, this statement's implied promise that the United States would reveal her uranium and thorium resources at the same time as Russia was contradicted by the precise terms of the stages arrangements.[37]

Not stopping with this "rebuttal," Baruch at a meeting in late September demanded that Wallace retract his criticisms of the plan. Instead, Wallace advised Hancock that "a clear statement of our position on stages would go a long way to rally additional support for our proposals." When Eberstadt weakly averred in response that "we have not yet spelled out our ideas on the substance or timing of stages," Wallace refused to back down from his initial criticism. Enraged, Baruch finally brought their feud into the open with the charge in early October that Wallace had willfully damaged his bargaining position at the UN. Wallace correctly pointed out that Baruch had never refuted his criticism of the plan's "fatal defect concerning stages."[38]

The Wallace-Baruch feud had an anticlimactic ending. With Wallace's dismissal from the government, his opinions no longer carried weight. The feud thus gradually faded that fall from newspaper headlines and from the public's consciousness; and with it too went the chance that the Baruch plan's "fatal defect" would be exposed.

Baruch was right in believing that his credibility and that of the plan had been damaged by the affair. But he was wrong in ascribing the cause of the damage to Wallace. In his eagerness to deny Wallace's charges, Baruch cast himself in the role of the aggrieved party who protested too much. By denying to Wallace, therefore, that the delegation had ever considered the approach on stages—which they had in fact already secretly adopted—Baruch unwittingly focused attention upon his own methods and motives at the UN.[39] Indeed, what Baruch actually intended there was evidently now open to question in the public's mind. An opinion survey of October 1946 showed Americans equally divided on whether U.S. policy on atomic energy was aimed at "making the United Nations strong," or at "trying to keep ahead."[40]

Not only the substance but also the style of Baruch's dispute with Wallace undermined his case. Even Vannevar Bush, increasingly a hardliner with respect to Russia, complained that Baruch was being too "stiff-necked" in his approach to the Soviets. In a letter to James Conant, Bush observed that "[w]e are asking a great deal indeed when we ask Russia, in the first stage, to lift the iron curtain. In return, we've given them only information as to our supplies and our knowledge of world supplies, a considerable fraction of which they probably already know."[41]

Predictably, the greatest effect of the Wallace incident upon Baruch and his aides was to accelerate their efforts toward bringing the American plan to a final vote in the UN. Ignoring the requests of the French and Canadian delegates that he prolong the negotiations in the hope of an eventual agreement, Baruch decided on October 5 to press a vote before the delegate shuffle began with the new year.

Meanwhile, he turned a deaf ear to indications that the Russians might be seeking a way out of the impasse. Stalin had given the first indication of a change in the Russian attitude toward the Baruch plan in an unusual interview with an American journalist that September. The Soviet leader struck a conciliatory note concerning the negotiations that seemed, in spirit at least, a reversal of his earlier belligerence toward the West. A meeting of Richard Tolman's Scientific and Technical Committee with its Soviet counterpart in late October also produced an unexpected concession by the Russians to the principle of an early raw-materials survey, which they had specifically ruled out in the Gromyko plan. A subsequent leak by a member of the Soviet delegation to an American newspaper stressed the view that the differences between the two countries on atomic energy were negotiable.[42]

The U.S. delegation's reaction to this sudden show of Russia's willingness to cooperate was unconciliatory, however. Questioned by a Soviet delegate as to why America refused to halt even temporarily its production of atomic bombs, Eberstadt retorted "that approximately six weeks ago he had come to the conclusion that the Soviet government did not wish to reach an agreement for the international control of atomic energy." A final suggestion by the Russian delegate that Byrnes and Molotov meet privately to discuss a compromise on atomic energy was rejected outright by Eberstadt, though he had proposed just such a meeting the month before. "[F]urther discussion would merely serve to take the focus off the Commission's work as such," Eberstadt told the Russian.[43]

The decision as to "whether the Atomic Energy Commission is to proceed or stall" would have to be made "pretty soon," Baruch reminded Truman by telephone at the end of October. "Time is running out against us."[44] Baruch was not alone in his concern that the UN negotiations be brought to the sort of ending that would reflect well upon America's image. In mid-October 1946 the Paris Council of Foreign Ministers had broken up with recriminations between Byrnes and Molotov concerning blame for this latest failure of Soviet-American diplomacy. The collapse of the Paris talks was not a particular cause of concern for Senator Arthur Vandenberg, however. "Baruch's report to the UNAEC is far more important to the peace of the world than anything that happens here," he wrote from the French capital. "It is *the* 'show-down' with Moscow."[45]

"Another, Less Openly Belligerent Route"

There could no longer be any serious doubt as to what Truman's response to Baruch's request would be. As Eberstadt's remark of late October revealed, the U.S. delegation had abandoned hope for the negotiations some time before. The Wallace episode had also demonstrated, to Baruch at least, the peril of additional delay. That peril was underscored for Baruch when Molotov publicly condemned the Baruch plan on October 29 and proposed an alternative—general disarmament. Fearing that this had given the initiative to the Russians, Baruch wrote a bitter and self-justifying letter to Acheson: "The Soviets have taken advantage of our indecision, have moved in, and now apparently have become the advocates of disarmament. . . . As you may recall, I strongly advocated that we should do it first."[46]

Molotov's proposal was the final spur to action. Byrnes gave the U.S. delegation tentative approval for the decisive vote on November 5. Two days later, Truman approved the final showdown in the UN. Though too late to bring the matter to a test by mid-November as Baruch had originally hoped, the President's sanction would still allow the climactic vote before year's end.

Perhaps the first of the delegation to acknowledge that their official efforts had failed was Fred Searls. He resigned on November 10 with the explanation that remaining work would be just "shadow-boxing." A little more than two weeks before, Searls had written a candid account to Byrnes of what the alternative to the Baruch plan would inevitably be: "It is assumed very generally indeed, not only by Mr. Wallace and the Communist-Scientist group, but by almost everyone else who has spoken or written on 'The Atomic Bomb,' that failure to reach an agreement by the Atomic Energy Commission or some other creature of the United Nations, means acceleration of an atomic armament race, which most —but not all—of the writers and speakers believe will lead to war."[47]

Searls' work with Groves and the Manhattan Project had convinced him that "there is perhaps another, less openly belligerent route, that we can follow—indeed are following—which, if handled with great wisdom and not made subject to interference by radicals, can accomplish years of delay in competitive atomic weapon production, even if the Atomic Energy Commission fails of agreement." Searls' alternative route was, in fact, the atomic league of worldwide bases that he had unsuccessfully championed to military leaders the previous June. The "continuation and stimulation of preclusive and cooperative contracting in the field of raw materials" was an activity that "may become of surpassing importance . . . in the event of the UNAEC's failure," he argued.*

An international nuclear consortium had always been considered as perhaps a final stage of the Baruch plan by its authors. But what Searls now had in mind was a league of a more exclusive sort. Recent observations at the UN concerning "the attitudes, questions, desires, and general behavior of the Russians" had persuaded him "that it may well be ten years before they can become possessed of an adequate supply" of atomic raw materials, "if we can prevent their obtaining it from other countries." And ten years "may well mean everything in relations with the Russians since, surely, it is only a question of time before internal opinions will force a change in their government's behavior to its own people and to foreign nations"—a point, indeed, that George Kennan had made in his "long telegram."

It was vital, therefore, that Byrnes not allow the "most delicate and important series of negotiations" that would follow the failure of international control in the UN to "fall into the wrong hands," Searls pleaded. Were that to happen, "we can probably fold up the new-born hope that little by little we can draw other nations in with the United States, the United Kingdom, and Canada, to form a group that will control atomic energy through possession of such an overwhelming proportion of the

---

*As if to underscore this point, Groves wrote to Byrnes the same day requesting that he arrange for "additional trained observers" to be sent to the Belgian Congo under the guidance of "an officer who, preferably, speaks French and who has a working knowledge of mining or geology." While the "situation in Belgium is thoroughly and accurately covered," Groves informed Byrnes, he was "concerned that political unrest in the Congo might threaten the deliveries of uranium ore."[48]

raw materials, that those nations left without the circle must pay the price of admission—real arrangements for permanent peace—or, failing that, realize that they will be hopelessly behind in an atomic energy race for many years to come." While not a permanent solution to the arms race, since the Russians would eventually be able to build at least a few bombs, "if the work initiated by the [Manhattan Engineer] District and furthered by the Trust is let alone and wisely handled, it could provide the way to peace."

Another purpose of the letter had been to urge Byrnes to intercede with Truman in blocking the appointment of David Lilienthal as chairman of the U.S. Atomic Energy Commission. Lilienthal, Searls contended, was "the most stubborn advocate of international ownership of atomic energy ores," and was "fairly certain to take over, or at least, interfere with the quiet, helpful work that has been going on." At a minimum, Byrnes and Truman should guarantee that the procurement of uranium and thorium by Groves and the trust could not be halted by the new commission and its chairman.

In fact, Truman apparently harbored some doubts about the choice of Lilienthal. He had written to Vannevar Bush in early August, "I like him very much myself but he is doing a grand job where he is and I don't want to take the chance of getting a dud in that place." However, Searls' missive came too late. Three weeks before, Truman had finally decided upon Lilienthal as AEC chairman.[49]

Byrnes himself was certainly aware of the "quiet, helpful work" that Searls had accomplished to ensure the groundwork for a Western Pax Atomica. As early as mid-July, Searls had joined another of the delegation's technical advisers, Franklin Lindsay, in purchasing thorium-bearing ore for the government. The two men had even used Baruch's contacts with the Indian delegation in the UN to arrange the purchase. "[Y]ou will find the State Department ready to be of any assistance within their jurisdiction," Searls had promised the sellers. Occasionally, this work went on entirely outside of the Combined Development Trust. Exasperated by the breakdown of the promised interchange on atomic energy with the United States, the British government embargoed the shipment of thorium ore to America from India in September. Yet, Searls and Lindsay remained undaunted. The duo thus arranged for the purchase of Brazilian thorium through a member of that country's delegation to the UNAEC.[50]

.   .   .

Confident that even the outright rejection of the Baruch plan in the UN would mean the vindication of their efforts, the U.S. delegation looked forward to the Security Council vote with a new assurance. At worst, Russian rejection would result in the indefinite continuance of America's nuclear monopoly; as Searls had indicated to Byrnes, the ultimate outcome would still be "the solution of an important segment of the world's difficulties" through America's supremacy in nuclear arms and the West's preclusive hold on atomic raw materials. Weeks earlier Eberstadt had speculated upon "the difficulties of determining what nations would have to be excluded from *our* world." Russia's unconditional refusal to accept the Baruch plan made that determination much easier.[51]

As November approached its end, the energy of Baruch and his aides was focused less upon the negotiations themselves than upon the task of consolidating domestic support behind their plan. For that purpose, Hancock began drafting a memorandum which he hoped would answer criticism of the Baruch plan at home.[52] Baruch was unwilling to be put off from a year-end vote even by some last-minute Russian concessions. He rejected a proposal by Molotov to suspend the veto in the day-to-day operations of a world disarmament authority once such a body had been established by the Security Council. Ignored by the delegation too was the evidence of progress in a Soviet-American committee dealing with the technical problems of enforcement and control. Indeed, on the day of these concessions Baruch's attention was centered upon a test vote in the Security Council in which all but Russia and Poland sided with the American plan. The result had encouraged him to hope that a final vote might come by early December. A last effort by the French and the Canadians to delay the vote dashed that hope, however.

Instructed by Byrnes in mid-December to force a vote at the earliest occasion, Baruch henceforth would not be stayed—even, he told his aides, if he was assured of support from only a bare majority of the UNAEC's members in the Security Council. A direct appeal from the Soviet delegation for a meeting between Molotov and "someone equally empowered" on December 14 was rebuffed, as was Gromyko's proposal of a late-night private interview with the American delegation.[53] Perhaps sensing that the American delegation's obvious eagerness for a vote had diminished its support in the UN, Gromyko chided: "Why is it necessary to rush along and try to reach hasty decisions?"[54]

Gromyko's barb hit its mark. An eleventh-hour rebellion by the

British, French, and Canadian delegates—who sought a change in wording on the plan's provisions for the veto that would save face for both sides—provoked an ultimatum from Baruch on December 28. With three days remaining before the year-end deadline, he told the delegates: "Gentlemen, it is either-or."[55] Baruch received support for his unyielding stand in a telegram that day from Vandenberg, who observed that the Senate was unlikely to ratify any plan that would "paralyze even temporarily the application of effective sanctions."[56]

With the exception of the British, the incipient revolt against the Baruch plan in the UNAEC collapsed the following day when Vandenberg's telegram was published in American newspapers. With only one day remaining till the deadline, Baruch warned the head of the British delegation "that if Britain walked out on us, I would denounce her in terms that would make 'perfidious Albion' sound like words of praise."[57]

Suspecting that the British stand was only a bluff, Baruch called for a vote on the plan in the Security Council on December 31.[58] The results met with his expectations. Of the twelve-member council, ten nations endorsed the Baruch plan; only Russia and Poland chose to abstain rather than vote against it.

The overwhelming endorsement of the Security Council, Byrnes told the press, was "a great victory for Baruch and his associates." Baruch had candidly revealed his own attitude toward the vote some days before when he told Lilienthal, "America can get what she wants if she insists upon it. . . . After all, we've got it and they haven't and won't have for a long time to come. I don't know how long, but it will be some time."[59] The fate of the Baruch plan did not prompt any substantial changes in the American negotiating position. While pro forma negotiations in the UN on revision of the plan would continue for another two years, a secret State Department appraisal of the talks in August 1947 conceded that "no modification in detail can, under present circumstances, conceivably make the U.S. proposals acceptable to the USSR."[60]

Baruch resigned from his UN post at the start of the new year. Significantly, his parting recommendation to Truman was in line with the advice he had received from Farrell some weeks before: the United States should dramatically increase its production of atomic bombs.

By the first week of 1947, American policy toward the bomb had finally been decided both at the UN and at home. For America's allies, for the Russians, and even for citizens at home, the atomic curtain had been firmly rung down just as the new year began. Abroad and in the UN, the collapse of international control made U.S. policy one of rigid exclusion and monopoly, anticipating a long tenure for American nuclear hegemony based upon "know-how" and a secret, supposedly preclusive supply of atomic raw materials. At home, the advent of a civilian Atomic Energy Commission actually signaled no substantial change from wartime policy toward the bomb, since the passage of the amended McMahon Act and the aftermath of the spy scandal had ensured that the commission's task would remain that of safeguarding the atomic secret and the nuclear monopoly. Groves relinquished his stewardship of the bomb to Lilienthal only after the latter agreed to continue the activities of the Combined Development Trust and to leave foreign intelligence on atomic energy to the army, subject only to review by the new atomic energy commission. These were, in fact, the two conditions that Groves had found Senate support for in the wake of the spy scare, and that Searls had urged upon Byrnes in his October letter.[61]

The Baruch plan left its own legacy. While it is difficult to imagine that the Russians were sincere in their desire to continue talks in the UN on the American plan, except to gain the obvious advantages of delay, the final impetus for ending those negotiations had clearly come from the United States. The Truman administration's abandonment of interchange with the British, and the disregard that Baruch had shown for friends of the United States in the UN, certainly did nothing to dispel the suspicion of America's allies that they, too, might ultimately be left out of what Eberstadt had called *"our* world."

In that world, the earlier goal of Stimson and Byrnes to use the bomb as a positive force in diplomacy and as a focus for cooperation rather than conflict was forgotten. It was in another guise that the bomb assumed a new importance. Henceforth, America's strength would increasingly—and of necessity—reside in the military threat of her "winning weapon."

BOOK THREE

Diplomacy and Deterrence
The Military Dimension,
1945-1950

10

Strategy and the Bomb

He stood upon that fateful ground,
Cast his lethargic eye around,
And said beneath his breath:
Whatever happens,
We have got
The Maxim gun
And they have not.   *Hilaire Belloc, The Modern Traveller, 1898*

"Our safety is their undoing. Let us remember we have the greatest
weapon ever devised by man. It is the atomic bomb and we have it
alone."

   Bernard Baruch, speech at the National War College, June 1947

like Burnham

"Sudden Death Out of a Clear Sky" — *Groves thought same*

Postwar American military planning was already well advanced when the
atomic bomb made its debut. But the advent of the bomb after most
services had begun to finalize their plans for the postwar world, and the
traditional conservativism of many military leaders, meant that the revolutionary potential of this weapon would not be fully appreciated—or
integrated with American strategy—more than two years after the destruction of Hiroshima.

   Among the most vocal in dissenting from this conservativism, and
also in promoting the counterargument for an "air-atomic" strategy,
were the representatives of the service most affected by the development
of this terrible new technology—the air force. The persistent and ultimately successful lobbying of these air-power proponents—the latter-
day adherents of Douhet—was in part an effort to secure larger appropriations for their service and a role independent of the army.
But their principal motivation was a vision of the world changed by
the bomb. The consequence of unpreparedness in the atomic age,

one such visionary warned, was "sudden death out of a clear sky."[1]

The proponents of an air-atomic strategy for the United States were represented to some extent in every service. But in each, including the air force, they constituted a distinct minority. The strategy which these enthusiasts promoted would not have gained the ascendancy it eventually did in U.S. defense planning had it not been for the absence of any real alternative. The rapid demobilization of America's wartime armed forces, budgetary constraints, and the *de facto* rejection of peacetime universal military training by Congress and public opinion, however, assured the victory of air power by default.

In retrospect, the increasing importance that the bomb attained in American military planning between fall 1945 and spring 1947 seems unjustified, particularly in view of the U.S. nuclear arsenal's minuscule size throughout that time, and of the problems in delivering even this small number of bombs effectively. Indeed, because of excessive secrecy and bureaucratic rivalry, neither President Truman nor the joint chiefs would discover how few bombs the United States had or learn of the other serious weaknesses in American nuclear strategy until April 1947. U.S. military planning up to that date had been done in a vacuum; war plans had been based upon bombs and bombers that did not exist. By summer 1947, however, what had always been an implicit assumption of some theorists became an explicit principle of U.S. military planning when the bomb was recognized as the centerpiece of American security.

"Shock Was Apparent on Truman's Face"

After only four months in his role as chairman of the U.S. Atomic Energy Commission, David Lilienthal was already alarmed by what he considered to be that agency's lack of preparedness for the realities of the atomic age. Citing "serious weaknesses" in the program the commission had inherited from the Manhattan Project for the production of atomic bombs, Lilienthal's first report to Truman reflected his own surprise upon discovering what conditions were on the inside. "The present supply of atomic bombs is very small," he informed the President.* None of the bombs in America's nuclear stockpile was then

---

*In an interview with the author, Lilienthal recollected his own shock at discovering how militarily unprepared the United States was when he went to Los Alamos in January 1947 as head of the AEC: "Probably one of the saddest days of my life was to walk down in that chicken-wire enclosure;

assembled, and the atomic mechanism of the most important type of bomb being produced "is new and has never been tested by explosion."[3]

The number of atomic bombs in America's possession was perhaps the premier secret of the Truman administration during the U.S. nuclear monopoly. The importance of this figure was underscored by the fact that it was never written in reports but was always supplied verbally by the briefing officer, even to the President. Indeed, the revelation of how few bombs were in the stockpile invariably came as a considerable surprise to the hearer.* The "shock was apparent on Truman's face," Lilienthal wrote of his report's effect.[5]

Truman had told Henry Wallace in 1946 that he already knew "in a general sort of way" the number of bombs in the arsenal—and disclaimed any interest in knowing more of the frightful subject. At a Cabinet meeting in October of that year, the President confessed to Eben Ayers that "he did not believe there were over a half dozen [atomic bombs] in the United States"; but, he was quick to reassure Ayers, "that was enough to win a war."[6]

It was this assumption that Lilienthal called into question in his report. Despite Truman's easy assurance to the contrary, the existence of probably no more than a dozen atomic bombs by spring 1947—none of them ready for immediate use—and of a production rate that completed perhaps two weapons per month was not "adequate to meet the security requirements of the U.S.," Lilienthal concluded. Another thing prompting his report had been his surprise discovery of how little the administration or the service chiefs knew concerning America's perilous state of atomic readiness. A "preliminary study" of the vital production rate of fissionable materials by Manhattan Project plants, begun at the instigation of presidential military adviser Admiral William Leahy, had

---

they weren't even protected, what gimmicks there were. . . . I was shocked when I found out. . . . Actually we had one [bomb] that was probably operable when I first went off to Los Alamos; one that had a good chance of being operable." A major problem the AEC had inherited from the Manhattan Project was that the few individuals trained to put together the bombs had returned to civilian life at the end of the war. A team of twenty-four men required nearly two days to assemble a single bomb. Lilienthal commented of this predicament: "The politically significant thing is that there really were no bombs in a military sense. . . . We were really almost without bombs, and not only that, we were without people; that was the really significant thing. . . . You can hardly exaggerate the unreadiness of U.S. military men at this time. . . ."[2]

*After repeated requests, Senate Atomic Energy Committee Chairman Bourke Hickenlooper finally induced Truman to show him the highly classified figures on bomb production in early 1947. Hickenlooper was "visibly shaken," according to Truman. He told the President: "I now wish you hadn't given me this thing to read. I'd rather not have known anything about it."[4]

not been undertaken until February 1947—more than eighteen months after the bombing of Hiroshima. That study had warned that even if all the fissionable material produced by those plants was put in bombs during 1947 it would still "fall far short of the total military requirement." Even "extraordinary efforts in terms of money, materials, equipment and human energy" begun "at the earliest possible moment" would result in too few bombs to meet the needs of existing U.S. military plans. "Indeed," Leahy's study concluded pessimistically, "it appears that the atomic bomb and future military requirements of fissionable materials cannot be met for a number of years." Technical problems with the plants that enriched uranium and political unrest in the Belgian Congo made the supply of fissionable material for the future problematical as well.[7] Most astonishing of all was Leahy's discovery, confirmed by Lilienthal, "that the Joint Chiefs of Staff had not been informed of the foregoing facts."[8]

What seemed either blissful ignorance or a dangerous unconcern on the part of U.S. military leaders regarding the number and production rate of atomic bombs in America's arsenal was, in fact, the result instead of excessive secrecy and of the divisive rivalry that by 1947 had become characteristic among the military services. As much as a year after the atomic bombing of two Japanese cities, the future commander of the air force's Strategic Air Command, Curtis LeMay, would complain that "agencies of the Air Staff and other units of the AAF [Army Air Forces] concerned with the atom bomb find themselves hampered in the proper execution of their duties because of a lack of knowledge of the subject." They remained ignorant, therefore, not only of the number of bombs the United States had, but also of their physical effects upon a variety of targets. In fact, most AAF officers had yet even to see an atomic bomb.

LeMay also objected that it was almost impossible to learn more about the bomb, since the War Department's interservice advisory group—the Armed Forces Special Weapons Project—had purposely excluded the Army Air Forces from a role in deciding military policy on the weapon, even though LeMay and the Air Staff were instructed at this time to prepare the AAF's plan for a nuclear attack upon Russia. The frustration of LeMay and of the Air Staff at the limitations put upon knowledge of the bomb was reflected in their guarded advisory "that if *sufficient* force were applied in a short enough period of time against the major cities of a modern nation, a morale collapse would end the war."[9] There was, however, as of that time no way for Air Staff planners to know if such a sufficiency then existed—or would exist in the foreseeable future.*

Thus the air force and LeMay were equally zealous to safeguard their own special relationship as it concerned the atomic bomb. The navy had begun making plans for an aircraft-carrier-launched atomic bomber in summer 1946, but had to defer construction of that plane when the air force refused to release to its sister service the dimensions of the bomb.[11]

The fact that the individual services, because of these constraints, remained almost entirely ignorant about the number and capabilities of atomic bombs in the stockpile did not prevent some military planners from making a tentative effort to assess the impact of the new weapon upon old doctrines. The earliest and most ambitious of these assessments was begun only two months after the Japanese surrender. Part of an intelligence report commissioned by the Joint Chiefs of Staff, it was entitled "Strategic Vulnerability of Russia to a Limited Air Attack." Assuming "that the atomic weapon used against Japan will be used against the USSR," the study selected twenty Soviet cities for nuclear attack in the event of war. The choice of targets was determined by their importance as industrial centers, military research and development facilities, and locations for "key government or administrative personnel." Significantly, since the number of bombs then existing was not known, no consideration was given in the study to the number of bombs that would be required for such a task, or to the difficulty of delivering them against Russia. The study was meant to be a basis for future planning rather than an operational plan itself.[12]

Possibly one reason this study was presented only as a guide was its authors' concern with how the other services would have received it had

---

*The public had already been given—inadvertently—some clues to the slow rate of production for atomic bombs, if not to the actual size of the stockpile. A *Newsweek* article appearing only weeks after the surrender of Japan disclosed that a third atomic bomb, "Big Boy," would have followed the first two bombs had the war not ended by the close of August—a "scoop" that prompted Groves to order an investigation into the author's sources. An article by Stimson in the February 1947 *Harper's* confirmed that there had been only two bombs in the American arsenal, and that the rate of production of bombs was "very small." This inadvertent disclosure of a military secret by the former war secretary caused anxious moments for both Groves and Baruch. The two men were relieved when the disclosure went unnoticed by the press.[10]

it been introduced as an actual military plan. Certainly the figure of twenty Soviet cities destroyed was not considered "decisive" in concurrent but separate studies undertaken by the army and navy in their planning for a future war. In fact, there was very little—if any—unanimity of view among the services in such planning. Another intelligence study by the joint chiefs predicted, for example, that it would probably take only five years for the Russians "to develop effective transoceanic missiles." A contemporary War Department symposium on "foreseeable new developments and countermeasures" concluded that intercontinental ballistic missiles were at least twenty years away, and might never be feasible.[13]

Perhaps most striking about these early postwar assessments was how small a role most military planners ascribed to the bomb in a future war—even when they erroneously assumed that the United States had many more bombs than actually were in the stockpile.[14]

While fighting had continued in Europe and Asia, little emphasis was placed upon planning for future wars. As a result, the long-range planning staffs of the army and navy were undermanned during the war, and their reports virtually ignored even within their own services. Partly for that reason, too, the theorizing on modern war that took place at the dawn of the atomic age proved substantially at odds with the reality. The initial ideas of some planners—like the predictions concerning missiles in the joint chiefs' study—were far off the mark, and sometimes simply bizarre.

Unquestionably in the latter category was the assumption of planners in the Army Air Forces' "postwar division" concerning the future basing requirements of long-range bombers. Dominated by a zeal to make the air arm organizationally independent of its parent service, the army, these early architects of the postwar air force nonetheless accepted uncritically what one analyst has termed the "Mercator-projection thinking" of their land-based progenitors. The initial planning that originated from the office of the AAF's "Air Staff, Plans" proposed basing intercontinental bombers not along the polar route, which would be the most direct path for an air offensive launched from—or against—the United States, but on either coast of the United States. In effect, this presumed a flat world, or one at least where air technology made distances utterly unimportant.[15]

The peculiar myopia of early air force planners was not limited only to bomber basing, but extended to grand strategy as well. Such planners demonstrated a remarkable degree of political insularity even for 1944, therefore, by their assessment that Germany and Japan would be the nations most likely to threaten the United States in the postwar world, and they showed a flair for dubious realpolitik in their prediction that the United States and Great Britain would together develop a postwar sphere of influence in Africa. Significantly, AAF planners virtually dismissed at this time the idea of a Russian threat because of their mistaken premise that the Soviet aircraft industry was "primitive" and unlikely to constitute a challenge to U.S. capabilities in less than a generation's time.[16]

In fairness, the authors of early air force planning suffered under a variety of handicaps. Among these was a lack of direction from above, a dearth of actual military experience, and an understandable reluctance to presume upon their civilian superiors by offering political advice. As with all forecasters, moreover, the last obstacle in the way of their predictions was also the most significant—the intrusion of the unforeseen.

One such unforeseen development had been the rapid deterioration of Soviet-American relations toward the very end of the war. Last-minute reassessments by the AAF Air Staff at the approach of Japan's surrender halfheartedly tried to put the changing Russian equation into perspective. A July 1945 air force intelligence estimate concluded, for example, that with "the advent of peace concerted efforts will be directed [by Russia] toward complete development of air power." The military analysts thus predicted, in their truncated argot: "Country poses threat to security of United States." Whereas during the war AAF planners had dismissed the Soviet bomber force as a threat for the foreseeable future, by fall 1945 they saw it as challenging the United States for air supremacy in from five to ten years.[17]

This view that Russian industrial recovery would be rapid was unique to the air force. Even so, it occasioned no real change in AAF plans. Unencumbered by any responsibility to the War Department or Congress, air-power advocates on the planning board had long before decided to meet the largest possible threat with the largest possible air force. The "Initial Post War Air Force Plan" devised by them called for a peacetime air armada consisting of 105 aircraft groups and one million men—considerably more than the wartime AAF's maximum strength.

Foremost among the surprises to air force planners near the end of the war, of course, had been the atomic bomb. The advent of the bomb would, like the developing perception of the Russian threat, fundamentally change all that had gone before in military planning. But it arrived on the scene too late—and too suddenly—to be incorporated into the Air Staff's vision of the future.[18]

Predictably, the postwar world envisioned by the navy was widely different from that of the air force. The assumptions on which the navy's future planning would be based were formulated less by that service's planning staff than by its forceful civilian secretary, James V. Forrestal. A principal reason for Forrestal's continuing concern for military preparedness was his conviction that the Second World War had been brought about in large part because of the weaknesses of the West's democracies. For Americans, Forrestal complained in 1943, history was "something that occurred on another planet." By 1946 he believed the aggressive nature of Soviet intentions had become so evident that he professed amazement when others admitted difficulties "preparing for the war just over the horizon."[19]

The date of Forrestal's conversion to Russophobia is uncertain, but Stalin's behavior at Yalta would seem to have been one cause for his doubts about the amiable future of Soviet-American relations. Subsequently, Forrestal would play a major role behind the scenes in promoting Kennan's July 1947 "Mr. X article," an updating of the latter's famous "long telegram."* Forrestal's influence upon the navy's perception of a Russian threat was earlier, and more direct.

Forrestal's navy hoped to assure for itself a global role in postwar U.S. military plans. In promoting that goal, Forrestal himself would encounter a variety of obstacles, not the least of which was the conservative tradition of the navy's own "battleship admirals," who continued to favor the funding of obsolete dreadnoughts over the creation of a modern air arm for their service. Another barrier was Forrestal's own emphasis upon postwar fiscal responsibility for the navy. At once too grandiose

---

*It was in early 1945, therefore, that Forrestal underscored in his diary this comment by Harriman: "[W]e now have ample proof that the Soviet government views all matters from the standpoint of their own selfish interest. . . . [W]e must clearly realize that the Soviet program is the establishment of totalitarianism, ending personal liberty and democracy as we know and respect it." Some months later Forrestal had resolved that the problem in Soviet-American relations was whether "we are dealing with a nation or a religion." In an attempt to answer that question he commissioned a War Department researcher, Edward Willett, in December 1945, to determine if Stalin had a blueprint for conquest similar to Hitler's *Mein Kampf*. Kennan's article also grew out of that search.[20]

in conception and too miserly in appropriation, the navy of Forrestal's dreams was immediately open to attack on the basis of both economy and utility.

But by far the largest dilemma facing Forrestal was the task of justifying how an expanded navy could accomplish the aims of American postwar security—prevention of a world war and deterring Soviet advances in Europe. Unlike the army, the navy could play no direct part in safeguarding the European landmass. Nor could it, like the air force, realistically expect to strike deep inside Russia in the event of war. Since Russia in 1945 was not a major naval power and seemed to have little ambition in that direction, there appeared little justification for the force that Forrestal envisioned. He himself seemed implicitly to acknowledge that fact as late as February 1946 when he observed that there "is today, fortunately, no prospective enemy." It was perhaps because Russia posed no immediate threat to U.S. sea supremacy, therefore, that navy planners assumed the wartime alliance of the United States and Russia would continue after the war, and even at the start of 1946 saw Soviet motives as primarily defensive in nature.[21]

As was also subsequently the case with the air force, the atomic bomb and the growing anticommunist consensus in the United States ultimately resolved Forrestal's problem in promoting an expanded navy. Yet Forrestal and the navy both initially resisted adapting to the new weapon. In September 1945 he objected to the Cabinet that it was "dangerous to depend on documents or gadgets, as these instruments do not win wars," and a January 1946 navy memorandum on warfare in the future neglected even to mention the atomic bomb. But Forrestal would later become among the most enthusiastic advocates of integrating the bomb into U.S. strategy. The same month as his deprecating comment on "gadgets," for example, he told the House Naval Affairs Committee that the atomic bomb would "give this nation and the world a swift and effective means of dealing with arrogance wherever it might raise its head."[22]

A belated champion of the bomb, Forrestal joined with the naval heroes of the war just ended—Admirals Chester Nimitz and Arthur Radford—as a spokesman for the "new navy": a world-ranging fleet of "supercarriers" capable of launching atomic bombers to strike at the heartland of Russia. The argument for the "new navy" was founded upon what these spokesman viewed as the inherent limitations of land-based, long-range bombing. In order to hit Russian targets from bases in the United States, naval enthusiasts argued, the air force would have to rely either upon untested refueling techniques or one-way "suicide" flights into Russia. An air-atomic offensive launched from the open ocean might be the "only means by which this nation could retaliate promptly and effectively, should we be attacked, and the only means by which we could take early action to blunt the enemy's offensive . . . before our own war-making capacity could be seriously crippled."[23]

Despite the earnest efforts of Forrestal and other "new navy" proponents, the implications of the bomb for military strategy would not be appreciated by the old navy until well after the Second World War. For the navy and for the other services, the true integration of the bomb into strategic planning was still far away.

More conservative than the navy or the air force in its reaction to the bomb, the army faced the challenge of atomic energy by virtually ignoring the new weapon. With the exception of Groves, army planners discounted the notion that the bomb had revolutionized or even greatly changed warfare. The army's "Special Planning Division" based its assumptions for the next war upon the experience of the last. A third world war, the army believed, would be of five years' duration and would be preceded by a year-long warning of its eruption, allowing the United States sufficient time to mobilize its manpower and industry. This complacency, of course, seems especially stunning in light of the army's own woefully inadequate state of preparedness on the eve of the Pearl Harbor attack—a story then being told in newspaper headlines of congressional inquiries into the debacle.

Army planners believed that the atomic bomb would play some role in the ensuing battles, but presumably only as an adjunct to the conventional air offensive against the enemy. As in the Second World War, final victory would be achieved after a protracted campaign. Unlike the air force or the navy, the army identified no specific enemy in its planning but, in the tradition of its "Rainbow plans" predating the Second World War, prepared for the contingency that the United States might be attacked from any side.[24]

Thus, despite the fact that the mammoth Red Army presented the most obvious threat to U.S. security interests, army planners dissented from Forrestal's early distrust of the Russians and the air force's belated concurrence in that view. Whereas in September 1945 Forrestal would characterize the Russians as "oriental" in their thinking, Army Chief of

Staff Dwight Eisenhower one month before had praised the Russians as "naturally a friendly race," perhaps mindful of the triumphant meeting between Soviet and American troops at the Elbe.*

Of course, one possible reason for the army's relative equanimity concerning both the Russians and the bomb may have been its easy confidence that tradition assured its position in American military strategy, regardless of technology or politics. While the bomb might necessitate a reduction in the size of combat units because of the new vulnerability of large troop concentrations, General George Marshall reasoned, that very vulnerability would demand a corresponding increase in the number of supporting troops, so that no overall reduction in the size of the army would be required.[26]

Army planning, in fact, seems the best example of what one historian has termed the "preparedness ideology" shared to some extent by all of the services at the end of the war. This ideology was a modern adaptation of the classical injunction "To have peace, prepare for war," since it held that future wars would be won—or, better still, prevented —only if America was prepared to fight them. The atomic bomb made this task more manageable, but it did not lessen the need for preparedness itself.[27]

Caught in the middle by and also representative of these disparate views on the Russian threat and the bomb were the Joint Chiefs of Staff. Since the establishment of their organization during the Second World War, the joint chiefs had been given the responsibility for coordinating American planning and strategy. Aware of the need to unify the conflicting opinions of the army, navy, and air force, the individual members of the joint chiefs nevertheless held differing perspectives on the problem, insofar as each man represented as well his own branch of the service.

The joint chiefs' collective view of the prospects for cooperating with the Russians, for example, reflected the roller-coaster course of military attitudes during and after the war. A "Revision of Policy with Relation to Russia," written shortly after the Yalta summit of February 1945 by the head of the U.S. military mission there, had advised that American cooperation with Russia cease, and that the United States

---

*There were, to be sure, exceptions within the army to Eisenhower's magnanimous view of the Russians. General George Patton, for example, considered them individually and altogether a "scurvy race," "Mongolian savages," "an all out son of a bitch, a barbarian, and a chronic drunk."[25]

"wait for Russia to come to us." A JCS intelligence study of postwar Soviet capabilities and intentions, however, argued at this same time that Russia's security concerns were legitimate, and motivated in part by "fear of capitalist encirclement." The joint chiefs' statement on "United States Post-War Military Policy," finished only days after the Japanese surrender, also concluded on a positive note: "In the last analysis the maintenance of world peace will depend in a great measure upon mutual cooperation between Britain, Russia, and the United States, especially between Russia and the United States." The breakdown of cooperation and the need for the United States to take unilateral action were here viewed as an unfortunate prospect: "Such an eventuality presents the most difficult problem from the military point of view . . . [since it] is recognized that the maintenance of overwhelmingly strong forces in time of peace is politically and economically unacceptable to the people of the United States."[28]

The task of reconciling the divergent viewpoints of the individual services might have been made simpler had the joint chiefs not also been charged with responsibility for persuading the services to accept two ideas that the Truman administration hoped would save money and streamline the nation's peacetime armed forces at no loss of security. The first of these, universal military training (UMT), had been tirelessly promoted throughout the war by Stimson, who looked to it as a means of avoiding the hasty and chaotic conscription that seemed to always precede America's entry into war. UMT had even initially received a warm reception from the Pentagon's admirals and generals, who saw it as a way of guaranteeing combat readiness in peacetime. But the end of the war and the return of peace made its reception by Congress and the public problematical.

More controversial than UMT was the unification of the services that Truman proposed shortly after taking office. Designed to prevent waste and duplication as well as, the administration hinted, to ensure close civilian control of the military, unification was the one common issue on which all of the services would eventually agree—to oppose. At first, most military leaders supported the idea of unification, each believing that his own service would eventually become preeminent. It was not the prospect of tighter civilian control but the slow realization that peacetime unification could lead to cutbacks in each of the services that turned the military as a group against the concept.[29]

Among the most apprehensive about the effects of unification was

Forrestal, who feared, correctly, that air force proponents might use it as a new justification for their longstanding goal—abolition of the navy's air arm. Alerted to the coming storm during the war, Forrestal had commissioned his friend (and subsequent Baruch aide) Ferdinand Eberstadt to conduct a study of unification's likely impact upon the services. So tendentious were the subsequent hearings that when the Eberstadt Report surfaced in September 1945 its findings did more to discredit than promote the idea of military unification. Such, indeed, may have been Forrestal's original intent. Congressional hearings on unification in fall 1945 also made no progress toward resolving the issue, but only showed the depth of the division between the services and the administration.[30]

Confronted with the need to incorporate two new elements—the bomb and Russia—into its contingency planning by late fall, and faced also with conflicting requirements from the individual services, the Joint Chiefs of Staff decided to retreat into abstractions. Hence the Pentagon's first postwar assessment of the atomic bomb's effect upon military strategy, drafted in October 1945 by the Joint Strategic Survey Committee, began on a remarkably cautious note. The panel conceded that the bomb would make the defense of military bases more difficult in the future, but rationalized that the great expense and probably limited availability of the weapon would also severely restrict its effectiveness in warfare. "This limitation will dictate its use only against targets of major importance. . . . Thus, only exceptional circumstances would justify its tactical employment in support of conventional land, sea, or air operations."[31]

The implications of this first study were elaborated upon some months later in another report by the same committee, prepared for the benefit of the nation's political and military leaders. This second assessment spelled out in language tailored to the nonspecialist the experts' view of the impact of atomic weapons upon warfare. Here again the emphasis was more upon the limitations of the bomb than upon its potential. These restrictions—the bomb's great expense, its limited availability, and its very destructiveness—"at this time profoundly affect the employment of this new weapon and consequently its influence on the future conduct of war. The present bomb is primarily a strategic weapon of destruction best suited for employment against large industrial centers, ports, supplies, or other targets vital to the war potential of a nation and therefore worthy of the bomb."[32]

The impact of the atomic bomb upon military strategy, therefore, was represented by the joint chiefs as a change in degree but not in kind. They ultimately agreed with the army that the advent of the bomb did not lessen the role of existing conventional forces but actually justified an increase in those forces, which would now be needed to secure and protect the bases that could launch atomic attacks against the enemy. Significantly, they believed too that the conduct of future war would not differ importantly from the pattern of the past: "The enemy resources for war, diminished by atomic warfare and by naval and air blockade, must then be reduced by actual capture and occupation of the homeland, to the final point where resistance is no longer possible."[33]

This eagerness on the part of Pentagon planners to discount—if not dismiss—the impact of the atomic bomb upon warfare was probably meant in part as an antidote to the naive idea, popularized after the destruction of Hiroshima, that the bomb had so changed military affairs as to make the traditional services obsolete. "There is a vague thought in the popular mind that the advent of new weapons, particularly the atomic bomb, will somehow replace or greatly reduce our army, navy, and air forces," asserted a report by the Joint Strategic Survey Committee in October 1945.[34] Concern with such thinking had actually prompted one air-power advocate to urge that the AAF abandon its plan for a single wing of atomic bombers, since the public might consider this one wing all that was necessary in the way of an air force. But the curious depreciation of the bomb by the joint chiefs was surely also a reflection of what they believed to be the conflicting pressures upon them. Their thinking elsewhere had already shown the effect of those pressures. A fall 1945 report on secrecy and the bomb, for example, had been sent to the President only after they had deleted all references to Russia and had rewritten the report both to avoid the "appearance of pessimism with respect to the UN" and to express "a military interest in political discussions looking toward international control [of atomic energy]."[35]

A more subtle but no less important consideration on their part was the need to avoid antagonizing the individual services during the transition from war to peace. Their official pronouncements on the bomb, it seemed reasonable to hope, had satisfied the interests of all the services by reiterating the need for a "naval and air blockade" to follow the inevitable atomic attack but precede the army's invasion of the enemy's homeland. This omnibus description of the services' individual roles in a future war—coupled with the fact that the joint chiefs had depicted the bomb as a strategic weapon more effective against civilian than military targets—seemed a conscious effort on their part to reach a compromise in thinking about the bomb that would neither threaten the *raison d'être* of one service nor show favoritism to any other.

But the joint chiefs' caution was unavailing. Already begun in the services was a substantial and growing rebellion against the prevailing view that downplayed the importance of the bomb. The leaders of this rebellion in military doctrine, many of them young officers in the three services, not only challenged the plans and assumptions of the Pentagon concerning the next war in detail, but sought to redirect American military thought itself toward a new postwar strategy whose principal element would be the atomic bomb.

"The Tail Will Wag the Dog"

Not surprisingly, the earliest and also the most vocal criticism of the view that deprecated the importance of the atomic bomb came from within the AAF.

Schooled in the classic doctrine of air power by the writings of the Italian theorist Giulio Douhet—and by such of his modern disciples as the Hungarian-American Alexander de Seversky—the officers of the AAF were eager to apply the lessons of the war just ended to the postwar world. Yet, despite the lives and heroic effort devoted to strategic bombing during the Second World War, the experience of that war had hardly made the case for air power. It seemed to show instead that the theories of Douhet and de Seversky did not apply in practice. Far from having been decisive in the struggle for Europe and Asia, the Allied strategic bombing of Germany and Japan appeared only an adjunct to final victory once the war was over. To the embarrassment of air-power advocates, the AAF's own *Strategic Bombing Survey,* published in 1946, showed that the strategy of bombing "bottleneck" industrial targets in daylight precision raids had been too costly in terms of casualties for its dubious effect. The peak of the strategic-bombing offensive against Germany had coincided with the peak of German industrial production. Equally, the famed "carpet bombing" of the war, although it resulted in fewer military losses than precision bombing, had killed a vast number of German and Japanese civilians without significantly affecting industrial production or breaking the enemy's morale.[36]

Indeed, the *Survey* concluded that the indiscriminate bombing of cities apparently increased the enemy's resolve to fight on—a phenomenon to which Londoners could attest—and that strategic bombing may even have ultimately delayed victory in Europe by slowing the advance of Allied troops, who found their way blocked less often by German resistance near the war's end than by bomb-created rubble.

Perhaps most surprising was the *Survey*'s opinion that not even the atomic bomb had proved decisive in the Second World War: "Certainly prior to 31 December 1945, and in all probability prior to 1 November 1945 [the planned date for Operation Olympic, the U.S. invasion of Japan], the Japanese would have surrendered, even if the atomic bomb had not been used, and even if no invasion had been planned or contemplated."[37] These words were plainly seen as a challenge by some of the bomb's proponents. Groves rejected the *Survey*'s conclusion outright. Secretary of War Robert Patterson personally interceded with army historians in 1946 to ensure that the bomb, and not Russia's entry into the war, would be represented in official postwar accounts as decisive in Japan's surrender.[38] For defenders of a traditional role for the army and the navy, however, the *Survey* was undoubtedly viewed as a welcome vindication.

Nor were traditional air-power advocates necessarily discomfited by the *Survey*'s conclusion on the bomb. Its ambivalent view of the bomb's role in ending the war presented no challenge to existing air-power doctrine, which relied upon an enormous air-force-in-being rather than upon a small, specialized striking force meant to carry the bomb. This latter concept was, in fact, anathema to the classical air-power theorists who continued to dominate AAF postwar planning. Paradoxically, the bomb was felt by these traditionalists to threaten air-power doctrine insofar as it seemed to obviate the need for a large peacetime air force.

As yet unrecognized either by these air-power traditionalists or by the authors of the *Survey*, of course, was the transforming effect that the atomic bomb would have upon the role of the postwar air force. The conclusions of the *Survey*, like the earlier predictions of the AAF's Air Staff, Plans, had been founded upon assumptions of a protracted and costly air offensive similar to that of the previous war, ignoring the possibility of a small airborne striking force armed with atomic bombs. Because the big bomber was the strongest single argument for an independent air force, AAF planning even well after Hiroshima—like army planning of the same vintage—represented another curious twist upon the adage that military thinking lags one war behind. For the sake of autonomy the air force was planning to fight the next war not only with the last war's weapons and tactics, but with weapons and tactics which had proved ineffectual in that war.

It was the atomic bomb that would revive the discredited theories of Douhet and de Seversky after the war by realizing for the first time that which air-power advocates had sought since the 1920s—the ability to project great destructive power at a considerable distance. The bomb, and the very-long-range bomber necessary to carry it to the target, thus finally made feasible a sudden and decisive blow from the air.

Recognizing this, there was already within the AAF by 1945 a small group of officers intent upon adapting the classical theory of air power to the changed realities of the atomic age.[39]

Foremost among promoters of the new doctrine in the air force was General Carl Spaatz. During the Second World War, Spaatz had been the architect of American bombing raids against Germany. He was also one of the few senior AAF officers who had no difficulty adapting air power to the bomb. On October 17, 1945, the top-secret "Spaatz Board Report," an unabashed brief for building the modern air force around the bomb, was circulated within the AAF. Prevailed upon by the army at war's end to trim his appropriations request for the AAF from 105 aircraft groups to seventy, Spaatz' vision of the air force's future was in no way diminished. Even before the "Spaatz Board Report," a briefing paper of which he was principal author predicted that unification en-sured the army and navy too would "come under the new medium, the air. At first the tail will wag the dog, then become the whole dog."[40]

Spaatz, of course, was certainly not unique even among high-rank-ing AAF officers for his virtually limitless faith in the potential of the new service. Unlike Spaatz, however, General Henry Arnold was as much concerned with the threat posed by air power as with its promise. He particularly worried about the period facing the United States once a prospective enemy possessed a modern air force. While professing not to be a fanatic on the subject of preparedness, Arnold delivered a nation-wide radio message the day after the destruction of Hiroshima that could hardly have been meant to engender complacency. In an oblique refer-ence to Pearl Harbor he warned that the "next sneak attack may not come two thousand miles from our shores," and "may be centralized on Michigan Boulevard, Biscayne Boulevard, Sunset Boulevard or on Main

Streets in your home town. We may not have a comfortable cushion of time to plan and build and train."[41]

The bomb would be at the center of this transformation of the air arm. To Spaatz and Arnold the postwar air force was meant to be an aerial *gendarmerie* with worldwide range—in conception a composite of FDR's vision of the United Nations' "Four Policemen" and the omnipotent "airmen" of H. G. Wells' futuristic novel *Things to Come.* [42]

Already looking ahead to the time when atomic bombs would be launched from earth-orbiting satellites, Arnold's immediate vision of postwar air power was detailed in a November 1945 report to Secretary of War Patterson. Coining in that report the term which came to symbolize the synthesis of air power with the new technology of mass destruction—"air-atomic"—Arnold counseled that the future security of the United States depended upon making it "apparent to a potential aggressor that an attack on the United States would be immediately followed by an immensely devastating air-atomic attack on him." With the insistent tone that would subsequently characterize his assessments of the air force's requirements, Arnold declared it "imperative that the United States maintain its present air posture." To accomplish this the nation needed to establish a "worldwide intelligence service" to learn "the capabilities and probable intentions of any possible enemy," and to "remain at the forefront of research on and development of nuclear weapons."[43]

Arnold himself would play no direct role in this process, since he was retiring from the AAF. Appended to his report was a recommendation to the army that Major General Curtis LeMay be appointed deputy chief of staff to the commander of the AAF, to ensure that the new doctrine would be well represented. LeMay was an obvious choice. The man who, as commander of the 20th Air Force, had led the March 1945 incendiary raids upon Tokyo that killed more Japanese than both atomic bombings combined, LeMay was also among the first bomber pilots in the AAF to champion the atomic bomb. Indeed, LeMay and the AAF's deputy commander, General Ira Eaker, dissented from the common wisdom of traditional air-power advocates by their willingness to sacrifice the seventy-group air force for a "small striking force capable of exploiting the atomic bomb and other new bombardment weapons."[44]

Like Arnold, LeMay foresaw the revolutionary effects that modern rocketry would have upon warfare. In November 1945 he proposed a joint army-navy agency for coordinating the adaptation of nuclear weap-

ons to intercontinental-range guided missiles. It was not until the beginning of 1946, however, that LeMay would be granted a forum to express
his views concerning the bomb and air power. Addressing a January
hearing of the War Department's Equipment Board, he testified to his
belief "that the advent of atomic energy will change the fundamental
military concepts of the United States." The army-in-reserve idea that
had allowed previous American victories in war, LeMay charged, would
"no longer guarantee our national security." Of the four elements that
had previously ensured U.S. security—natural resources, industrial capacity, time, and space—the atomic bomb made the last two obsolete
and diminished the importance of the first two. While this fact did not
obviate the need for a "large, well-equipped Air Force"—like Arnold,
LeMay reasoned that the bomb made an expansion of conventional
forces more urgent—the exigencies of modern war dictated that emphasis be put upon a small, nuclear-armed striking force of bombers.[45]

The endorsement by Arnold and LeMay of a conventional air force
was almost certainly a tactical concession meant to ensure unity in the
ranks of that service. As late as 1949, Arnold would publicly question the
need for a seventy-group service. But their collective call for a greater
reliance upon the atomic bomb in U.S. military planning was undoubtedly sincere. Within weeks of LeMay's testimony that appeal was answered with the creation of the Strategic Air Command, the nucleus of
the air-atomic striking force that Spaatz, Arnold, and LeMay had envisioned.[46]

Air force enthusiasts were not alone in advocating a larger role for the
atomic bomb in postwar American strategy, but they found an unexpected ally for this struggle in the army. At the same time that Arnold
and LeMay were promoting the striking-force concept, Army Chief of
Staff Dwight Eisenhower wrote to the joint chiefs decrying their tendency "to depreciate the importance of the development of atomic weapons and to insist unnecessarily strongly that the conventional armed
services will not be eliminated." This attitude, Eisenhower objected, was
too "negative or defensive," and might be "misconstrued by Congress
and the public . . . as an indication of reactionism on the part of the
military."[47]

Founded as it was upon a concern for public relations more than
sound strategy, Eisenhower's was perhaps a curious objection. But the
sentiment behind it could hardly have displeased the air-atomic advo-

cates of the AAF. Certainly, too, the Groves memorandum "Our Army of the Future"—appended by Eisenhower to his criticism of the joint chiefs—was not at odds with the new doctrine in its injunction that "[i]f there are to be atomic weapons in the world, we must have the best, the biggest and the most."[48]

Not only the army but Forrestal and the navy proved a useful—if equally unintentional—ally of air force promoters of air-atomic strategy. Forrestal's growing obsession with the Soviet threat and his continuing concern with the rapid pace of America's postwar demobilization logically dictated an increasing reliance upon the striking-force concept promoted within the AAF. The country was "going back to bed at a frightening rate," and the services would soon be facing another "disarmament wave," he wrote in his diary.[49]

With an increasing number of GIs returning home from Europe and the Pacific, and the return to a peacetime economy, the atomic bomb began to assume a larger role in U.S. military planning than the planners themselves had envisioned. This result was a matter less of strategy, however, than necessity.

By summer 1945 the melting away of America's 10-million-man wartime army was an active concern in each service. While military leaders had known that demobilization would inevitably follow victory over the Axis, the unexpectedly rapid rate at which soldiers, sailors, and airmen were being sent home upset wartime calculations. In an October 1945 "reassessment" of military needs, the joint chiefs tried to put this change in perspective. "Six months ago the United States was the greatest military power in the history of the world. . . . It may be said, without exaggeration, that the primary interest of the American public in our military forces at the present time is to liquidate them to a vaguely defined 'minimum.' " The problems caused by demobilization were "further complicated by the post-war dislocation of our economic life, with resulting strikes and unemployment which, if not gotten under control soon, will not only render our military forces largely inoperative, but, by strange irony, will seriously curtail the demobilization processes now planned."[50]

The steady undermining of America's conventional strength when U.S. relations with the Russians were also deteriorating was an especially ominous development. Yet popular pressure made this trend toward what some critics termed "unilateral disarmament" appear irreversible

—at least for as long as Americans remained unconvinced of a Russian threat. Within weeks of the Japanese surrender, newspaper accounts of decisive battles had been replaced by human-interest stories concerning "Bring-Daddy-Home Clubs," letter-writing campaigns to speed demobilization, and the servicemen's own pleas to return to civilian life.[51]

The cumulative effect of public sentiment was to speed the discharge of men and women from the services. President Truman had promised one week after the bombing of Hiroshima to release 5.5 million of those serving within twelve to eighteen months. Less than eight months after that promise, nearly 7 million had already been discharged. By June 1946 the services stabilized at their intended peacetime level, with approximately 3 million men and women on active duty.[52]

As the joint chiefs had predicted, a common argument confronting those who opposed the headlong rush to demobilize was that the atomic bomb made conventional armies and navies unnecessary. This argument achieved a certain currency in the public mind when it appeared in magazine and newspaper articles some weeks after the war's end. On occasion, some in the military even abetted the belief. *Aviation News*, a publication openly sympathetic to air-power interests, declared in a September 1945 article that soldiers and ships had become "definitely obsolescent in the light of the atomic bomb," and that the next revolutionary weapon would be "a V-2-type rocket with an atomic bomb in the nose." "With such weapons as these war may be concluded overnight," the article's author enthused.[53]

During the adjustment of the country to peace in succeeding weeks, however, many Americans began to see such claims for the bomb as extravagant, or at least premature.

Popular attitudes toward the bomb, moreover, provoked a counterattack by some traditionalists. Air-power advocate Alexander de Seversky, fearing that the bomb would undermine the rationale for a large air force, charged in the February 1946 *Reader's Digest* that an atomic bomb would do no more damage to a modern city than a high-explosive, ten-ton "blockbuster." A similarly erroneous claim by Admiral William Blandy at this time prompted a public disclaimer from AEC Chairman David Lilienthal, who feared that Americans might henceforth come to dismiss the bomb as just another weapon.[54]

Even if not an "ultimate weapon," the bomb was generally believed to have alleviated the traditional need of a democracy for a large citizen army in reserve. As well, its very existence was a ready-made argument against universal military training and a further rationale for hastening demobilization. Finally, since the public had no way of knowing about the lilliputian size of the U.S. nuclear arsenal—and little understanding of the tactical limitations upon the atomic bomb's use—most citizens could no longer see any justification for a military draft or a large peacetime defense budget.

It was not armies and navies *per se* but the idea of long-term preparedness itself that was perceived by many Americans, because of the atomic bomb, as not immediately necessary—and perhaps forever obsolete. Largely as a result of this popular attitude, the Truman administration had had to abandon hope of getting a universal military training program through Congress by the end of 1945—though, paradoxically, public support for the principle behind such a program remained high.[55]

"A Tremendous Advance over Other Weapons"

The result of Americans' reaction to the atomic bomb was a tendency to side with that small number of military theorists who ascribed a revolutionary potential to nuclear weapons, and against the greater number of admirals, generals, and traditional air-power advocates who opposed them. Behind this popular feeling, of course, were also the realities of demobilization and postwar economic reconversion. Compelled, presumably, by these facts as well as by the renewed lobbying of air-atomic advocates, the joint chiefs began a reassessment of the atomic bomb's effect upon U.S. military strategy in early spring 1946. An updated and revised version of the Joint Strategic Survey Committee's original report showed the result of this rethinking. While the Pentagon planners six weeks before had stressed the limitations of the atomic bomb in warfare, they now declared without equivocation that the bomb was "a tremendous advance over other weapons and may influence warfare far more than did gunpowder or the airplane." This new study, completed at the end of March, also reflected the change in emphasis by endorsing General Arnold's earlier recommendation that the United States maintain its supremacy in the air.[56]

By the spring the joint chiefs had begun reassessing other matters besides the bomb. Careful throughout the war to avoid identifying the Soviet Union as anything more than a potential adversary, they apparently no longer felt any need to appear solicitous toward the Russians. Whereas the prevailing military view at the time of the Yalta Conference had seen Soviet aims as essentially defensive, eighteen months later the Pentagon's contingency planning declared Russia's basic objective "to be a limitless expansion of Soviet Communism accompanied by a considerable territorial expansion of Russian imperialism."[57]

Another changed assumption of postwar planning concerned prospects for international control of atomic energy. Because the Joint Strategic Survey Committee had purposely deleted a pessimistic allusion to international control in its October 1945 report to the President, the tenor of that report had been so bland that the army subsequently branded it as "self-serving" and as motivated by political rather than strategic considerations. The attitude of military leaders toward international control since then had fluctuated with the fortunes of the Baruch plan in the United Nations. Though the joint chiefs, for example, declared in March 1946 that the success of the Baruch plan was "earnestly to be desired," their letters to Baruch at this time reveal a common and profound skepticism concerning the prospects for its achievement. This skepticism would, indeed, become progressively less qualified as the UN stalemate continued. By the end of 1946, the joint chiefs joined with Baruch and the State Department in tacitly acknowledging that hope for cooperative control of the bomb had ended.[58]

As this evidence indicates, it was not the experience of the Second World War but the fading prospects for peace immediately thereafter that first turned the attention of America's military leaders to the strategic significance of the atomic bomb.

11

The War over the Horizon

"[F]orbearance in the future will court catastrophe, if not national annihilation. Offensive measures will be the only generally effective means of defense and the United States might be prepared to employ them before a potential enemy can inflict significant damage upon us."

Joint Chiefs of Staff, "Atomic Warfare Policy," June 1947

"As each year goes by in which the Soviets do not solve the practical problems of atomic energy, their possession of even a small quantity of bombs must be advanced further into the future."

JCS Joint Intelligence Committee report, November 1947

"The One Military Weapon"

Less by strategy than by necessity had the atomic bomb begun to assume a major role in U.S. war planning by summer 1946. The growing importance of the bomb in such planning also had an effect upon military thought. While the doctrine of preventing war by the threat of retaliation with atomic bombs—deterrence—remained ill defined in war plans, its slow evolution in postwar strategy represented a subtle but portentous change from traditional American values: first by its emphasis upon preventing rather than fighting and winning a war, and second in its explicit provision for the first use of nuclear weapons against an enemy's civilian population. The wholesale destruction of cities at the outset of a war envisioned by this planning was perhaps but a culmination of the new and gruesome logic that had led to the terror bombings of the Second World War—begun by the Axis but made a science by the Allies.

An increasing reliance upon the bomb characterized U.S. war planning and American military thought in 1946 and 1947. As the joint chiefs wrote Baruch in June 1946, the bomb was "the one military weapon which may for the period until Russia obtains it exert a deterrent effect upon her will to expand."[1]

Along with this reliance was an ironic turnabout in military think-ing—a new complacency founded upon the assumption that atomic bombs, even in small numbers, could be an effective counterbalance to Russia's conventional strength, and a decisive weapon in the event of war. Of equal importance to subsequent American strategy was the predominant view of U.S. military planners at this time that the Rus-sians would be unable to match or even to challenge American nuclear supremacy for another decade—or longer.

"A New Concept of Policy"

The shifting attitude of the Pentagon toward the Russians, the bomb, and the prospects for peace was most graphically portrayed in the first theoretical plan for war with Russia, completed by the Joint Chiefs of Staff in June 1946 under the code name Pincher. The plan posited a Soviet-American war occurring between the summers of 1946 and 1947, with no more than three months' advance warning. It was believed that war might be triggered by a deliberate but limited provocation from Russia which miscalculated American resolve, and thus inadvertently precipitated a major conflict.[2]

Significantly, Pincher was a "tentative" war plan, reflecting in part the joint chiefs' uncertainty about America's ability to respond to a Russian military threat. Concerning one vital point of the plan—the number of atomic bombs available to be dropped on Russian targets—it was specified only that the number would be "limited," since the joint chiefs themselves did not yet know the size of the nuclear arsenal. Russia, it was assumed in the plan, would have no atomic weapons at the time of war.

Carrying uncertainty about the bomb further, Pincher presumed only that it would be a "distinct advantage" to the American war effort, and not the "tremendous advantage" cited in the joint chiefs' 1946 March report, or the "decisive weapon" of their combined assessment to Baruch that June. An indication of the still-unsettled nature of U.S. military thinking as it concerned the bomb is that Pincher's drafters simply appended the fall 1945 targeting study of twen-ty Russian cities for the critical air-atomic component of the plan. Since that study itself had only been intended to provide guidance for an operational plan, and even then assumed capabilities which the United States did not possess, Pincher was hardly a methodical or comprehensive response to the danger of a war with Russia.

But Pincher did serve another, albeit unintended, purpose. Because of it, the joint chiefs discovered that their tentative conception of an air-atomic offensive against Russia was still beyond the present capability of the AAF. The maps prepared for Pincher thus graphically represented its flaws—several of the twenty targeted cities were from three hundred to five hundred miles beyond the maximum operational range of the B-29s assigned to attack Russia from European bases in the event of war.[3] Still unknown to military planners was that the United States had neither the bombs nor the bombers to attack even the cities within range —and would not have for almost another two years.

Most remarkable about Pincher was not its assumption of American military strength because of the bomb, but its tacit admission of relative weakness. The joint chiefs' conservative assessment of the effect of the atomic bomb was a part of this. But their pessimism extended as well to the whole conduct of the war envisioned in Pincher. Though the plan assumed that the United States and its allies would "enjoy a definite superiority in naval forces" and "a qualitative superiority in air and ground forces" in addition to the atomic bomb at the outbreak of war, the emphasis throughout was upon a defensive strategy. Upon the initiation of hostilities, American occupation troops in Europe and Asia would either be immediately withdrawn to unspecified "tenable areas" or evacuated altogether. England would be defended to the last, but Korea and possibly Italy and the Mediterranean area would be given up to the Soviet advance during the first stage of the war.

A mobilization plan that accompanied Pincher was notable for its assumption that the future would resemble, or even repeat, the past. Predicting that the Red Army would quickly overrun "most—if not all —of western Europe" as well as the Middle East and the western entrance to the Mediterranean, this plan offered the qualified expectation that the Russians could be stopped north of Palestine and that Turkey would be used as a staging area for the air-atomic offensive and the eventual invasion of Russia. As such, the mobilization plan also reflected the assumption of U.S. military weakness in Pincher. The air-atomic offensive envisioned would focus primarily upon destruction of Russia's oil industry—a strategy that had been both very costly and ultimately of dubious worth against Germany in the previous war, but one nevertheless dictated by the fact that, unlike other targets behind the Urals, the Caucasus oil fields would be within range of forward-based B-29s.[4]

Before even the initial air-atomic offensive against Russia could be launched, Pincher anticipated a protracted period of Second World War–style conventional fighting, characterized on the American side by a naval blockade of Russia, selective strikes at Soviet submarine pens, and, most importantly, the "establishment and defense of bases in the British Isles, Egypt and if feasible India, Italy, and China." Since these last bases would have to be secured if vital targets beyond the Urals were to be brought within range of the air-atomic offensive, the joint chiefs' qualification "if feasible" seems an implicit admission by its authors of how tenuous their expectation of victory actually was.

Curiously, the single most important factor in American military thinking was never explicitly acknowledged in Pincher—the mammoth size of the Red Army. Yet the geographical and tactical difficulties of striking at that army with the atomic bomb were one reason why American military planners continued to deprecate the practical effectiveness of the bomb, even as they granted its revolutionary potential as a weapon.[5]

Another and more significant reason why the atomic bomb did not play a still larger role in U.S. planning was the continuing failure of military leaders to appreciate its fundamental impact upon strategy and doctrine, particularly upon the strategy and doctrine of deterrence. The importance of the bomb to a strategy of deterring enemy attack was an idea that the joint chiefs had broached in their June 1946 memorandum to Baruch: It was "remotely conceivable that the atomic bomb provides its own deterrent . . . in that fear of retaliation by atomic bombs against a violator who uses them will make the potential violator pause and consider before he decides to go ahead."[6]

Having entertained the idea of nuclear deterrence as "remotely conceivable" in their memorandum to Baruch, the joint chiefs abandoned the concept in Pincher. One apparent cause of the joint chiefs' discomfort with deterrence was their concern with how such a strategy might backfire—the atomic bomb, they predicted, might actually deter the United States from acting against Russian aggression: "A situation dangerous to our security could result from impressing on our own democratic peoples the horrors of future wars of mass destruction while the populations of the 'police' states remain unaware of the terrible implications."[7]

Civilian scientists and strategists by 1946 were well ahead of the Pentagon at understanding how security in the atomic age might be achieved not by fighting or winning a war, but by preventing one. Some civilian strategists believed that future wars might be prevented because of the uniquely horrific nature of the weapon. Vannevar Bush thought that "it would have been extremely difficult, if not impossible, to convince the American people of the potentialities of the atomic bomb had the bomb not found use in the Japanese war." But the memory of Hiroshima and Nagasaki might not be enough. The scientist-authors of the 1944 Jeffries Report had warned that the failure of international control meant "U.S. security would rest upon the fragile hope of deterring enemy attack by the fear of our retaliation." The "fragile hope" of deterrence was also a dominant theme of strategist Bernard Brodie's 1946 book, misleadingly entitled *The Absolute Weapon.* [8]

Brodie and other analysts presented a foresighted vision of the atomic bomb's challenge to traditional military precepts, including the axiom that numerical superiority of forces makes victory more likely. Perhaps most prescient of the essays in the book was that by Soviet expert Arnold Wolfers, who urged that "retaliation must occupy a decisive place in any over-all policy of protection against the atomic danger." Wolfers even anticipated the stabilizing effect of a future nuclear balance of terror: "It would not be surprising . . . if a high degree of Soviet-American 'equality in deterring power' would prove the best guarantee of peace and tend more than anything else to approximate the views and interests of the two countries."

Certainly Wolfers' preview of Soviet-American détente predicated upon strategic equivalence was, in 1946, too ecumenical a vision for the joint chiefs to take seriously.[9] But while the concept of deterring rather than fighting and winning wars was an idea whose time was yet to come in U.S. military doctrine, the bomb had already caused Pentagon planners to depart from other traditions.

In his January 1946 memorandum, "Our Army of the Future—as Influenced by Atomic Weapons," General Groves had urged that the United States initiate a nuclear attack against any "aggressor nation" about to acquire the bomb. Even earlier, in fall 1945, the notion of preemptive attack had been discussed favorably by some military representatives and congressmen at hearings on the unification of the armed services.*

---

*In the course of these hearings, Groves would make the mistake of subsequent thinkers-about-the-unthinkable. He unintentionally chilled his audience with the insight that a future nuclear war with the Soviet Union might result in "only" 40 million American casualties, and that such losses would not preclude ultimate victory.[10]

Publicly, the position of the military seemed unequivocally opposed to the idea of preemptive attack, or "preventive" war. In an apparent effort to dispel concern on just that point, Army Chief of Staff Dwight Eisenhower assured the American people in the wake of the unification hearings, "We are not going to deliver the first blow." While admitting that a preemptive strike in certain circumstances "might be desirable," the joint chiefs had concluded in private that "it is not politically feasible under our system to do so or to state that we will do so." In fact, however, the further, secret deliberations of the joint chiefs—and the provisions of Pincher—left such assurances open to doubt.[11]

Within three weeks of the bombing of Hiroshima, the joint chiefs adopted a navy suggestion that they not rule out striking "the first blow," noting that "this point should be emphasized to make it clear . . . this is a new concept of policy, different than the American attitude toward war in the past." Although there was no consideration on their part of launching a surprise, unprovoked nuclear attack against Russia, they did not rule out the possibility of responding to a conventional Russian attack—or even an unspecified Soviet provocation—with the bomb. Significantly, the joint chiefs' intelligence committee gave some idea of what such a provocation might be when it suggested that Pincher be put into operation if Russia developed the capacity for an "eventual attack against the United States or defense against our attack." Accordingly, the twenty-city targeting plan originally drafted in fall 1945 and later appended to Pincher was designed either to follow or to anticipate a Soviet attack.[12]

The deliberate mass killing of civilians that Pincher contemplated was another foreboding departure from traditional American military thought. However, this marked perhaps the culmination of an evolutionary trend in modern warfare, and represented therefore a change in degree rather than in kind. The experience of twentieth-century wars had surely changed the understanding of the term "enemy," and removed the prohibition against inflicting civilian casualties. The early moral strictures against bombing cities had been overcome even before the outbreak of the Second World War, with the result that by war's end cities and civilians were the principal targets.

But the atomic bomb made a new and vastly more destructive type of terror bombing possible. By the speed of its delivery and the indiscriminate nature of its effects, the bomb was a weapon ideally suited to attacks upon cities aimed at breaking civilian morale or disrupting production, and entirely ill suited to attacks upon dispersed enemy troops or military equipment—a fact explicitly recognized by the joint chiefs in Pincher.[13]

With surprising rapidity and essentially no debate, Pentagon planners had transformed the premises on which American military thought was based. While they had yet to endorse the concept of deterrence, their refusal to reject "striking the first blow" against Russian civilians showed their adaptation to and uncritical acceptance of the new and terrible logic of the atomic age.

"A Source of Embarrassment"

Even if agreed that the atomic bomb had transformed strategy, a considerable difference of opinion still existed among military experts concerning the bomb's likely effectiveness in war. One of the longest and most tendentious of such disputes had begun only eleven days after the destruction of Hiroshima between air-power advocates and the navy over the effect of the bomb upon ships in a harbor.

The army had considered using a nuclear weapon against Japanese ships at Truk, but the July 1945 test at Alamogordo had so impressed observers with "the immense damage that could be done to industrial targets" that a city was chosen instead. Unconvinced of the army's argument, the navy pressed its case for an actual experiment with the bomb after the war. The Manhattan Project, too, had wanted to test an advanced version of the Nagasaki-type implosion bomb in May 1946, but that test had been postponed because of Secretary of State Byrnes' concern with the effect it might have upon the negotiations about to begin at the UN.[14]

The tests finally conducted on and near Bikini Atoll in the South Pacific during the summer of 1946 were consequently perhaps less a scientific experiment than a product of interservice rivalry. Navy Secretary Forrestal and Admiral Bradley Dewey feared that a fizzle in the tests would be a public-relations disaster for their service. Groves took steps to ensure that physicist Robert Oppenheimer—increasingly a critic of air-atomic strategy—would be allowed to observe the tests but not to evaluate their results.[15]

The army's original pessimism regarding an underwater test seemed to be borne out by the results of "Able," the first atomic bomb exploded in a harbor. Dropped by air on July 1, "Able" landed more than two miles off target—an error that prompted some navy officers to suspect the AAF of sabotaging the test. Detonated in relatively shallow water, the bomb sank few of the fleet of mothballed and captured ships brought together for the experiment, though subsequent studies would show that nearly all of the ships were made intensely radioactive. The unspectacular results of "Able" prompted newspaper editorialists and reporters to write disparagingly of the idea that the bomb was a uniquely powerful weapon—a notion that had seemed common wisdom only weeks before.[16]

Suddenly concerned that the disappointing results of the first test might cause the public—and the Russians—to underestimate the power of the bomb, army and navy proponents of the weapon accelerated plans for the second test. The explosion of "Baker" near the end of July, at a greater depth than "Able" and in a setting like that of a deep harbor, was sufficiently impressive to restore the previous image of the atomic bomb in the popular mind as a decisive weapon.

A planned third atomic explosion, "Charlie," was canceled in early August with the official explanation that the success of the earlier two tests had made it "unnecessary." In fact, the real reason for the test's cancellation revealed more about the state of America's atomic arsenal than either of the previous tests: Forrestal informed Truman at the end of the month that he considered a third test inadvisable since "Able" and "Baker" had already delayed research and development programs for new bombs, and because fissionable materials as well as bombs themselves remained in critically short supply.[17]

The subsequent controversy surrounding the atomic tests—dubbed Operation Crossroads by the military—was similar to the prolonged army-navy debate of the 1930s over the vulnerability of battleships to conventional bombing. The tests also resembled that longstanding feud in that they probably changed few minds within the contending factions. Not only pride but the future appropriations of the individual services were at stake. Advocates of air-atomic strategy, therefore, would point to "Baker" as a vindication of their claims; military traditionalists cited the disappointing results of "Able" to buttress their argument that the atomic bomb was a weapon only somewhat more powerful than conventional bombs in its effect.*

---

*Perhaps purposefully, Russian observers invited to Crossroads gave the appearance of being unimpressed by the tests. One American remembers their reaction to the first bomb as being, simply, "Pooh." Not all were so blasé about Crossroads, however. The tests inspired a French fashion designer to create a new article of apparel named after the coral atoll where the bombs were exploded—the bikini.[18]

spring '47 saw advances in atomic thinking

Despite the ambiguous legacy of Crossroads, the atomic bomb had assumed a greater importance in American strategy a year later. Symptomatic of this expanding role was the conclusion of the joint chiefs' June 1947 "Evaluation of the Atomic Bomb as a Military Weapon": "If used in numbers, atomic bombs not only can nullify any nation's military effort, but can demolish its social and economic structures and prevent their reestablishment for long periods of time." While not radically different from their earlier assessments of the bomb, this study possessed a chillingly contemporary ring with its graphic depiction of the world-ending possibilities inherent to the weapon.

More realistic as well was that section of the joint chiefs' report entitled "Atomic Warfare Policy," which warned that "forbearance in the future will court catastrophe, if not national annihilation. Offensive measures will be the only generally effective means of defense and the United States might* be prepared to employ them before a potential enemy can inflict significant damage upon us." In the new context of the atomic age, the joint chiefs argued, it was necessary to redefine the meaning of "aggression." While willing to leave this task to the constitutional authority of Congress and the President, they pointedly included under the rubric of "incipient attack" that might justify nuclear retaliation the "processing and stockpiling of fissionable materials in a certain quantity by a certain nation at a certain time."[19]

In other and more subtle ways, as well, the atomic bomb had come to have a larger and more significant role in American military thinking by early 1947. This fact was evident, for example, in the granting of a "Q," or nuclear clearance, to the entire Eighth Air Force by the Atomic Energy Commission in late spring of that year. A dawning appreciation of the bomb now seemed to extend to the highest levels: "The conclusions as to the effect of the atomic bomb are clearly revolutionary," Secretary Patterson remarked shortly after Crossroads. In March 1947 he advised Eisenhower that the War Department "is already following a policy that assumes the unrestricted employment of atomic energy as a weapon."[20]

There were, of course, still practical restrictions upon the use of the bomb that Patterson had not alluded to, and the joint chiefs did not yet

---

*The odd use of the conditional "might" reflects the joint chiefs' characteristic desire to avoid even the appearance of intruding upon civilian prerogatives in policy-making.

suspect: the "serious weaknesses" of the nation's atomic-weapons program that would be the subject of Lilienthal's report to the President the following month. Ironically, on the same day that the joint chiefs completed their evaluation, AEC Chairman David Lilienthal wrote in his journal of the need to "educate" the military on the subject of the bomb, since they had been kept in the dark while Groves "hoarded" information on and access to the weapon.[21] But there was also for the first time a widespread confidence in the Pentagon that the bomb could be a potentially decisive military advantage for the United States in the event of war with Russia.

This confidence was most impressively displayed in a substantially revised and updated version of Pincher prepared by the joint chiefs at the end of August 1947, and code-named Broiler. An evolution of the earlier war plan, Broiler contained an important change in emphasis that showed the triumph of air-atomic strategy in U.S. military doctrine. Its military significance lay particularly in its new emphasis upon the bomb.

Like Pincher, Broiler anticipated a defensive withdrawal of Allied ground forces in Europe and Asia and a simultaneous strategic air-atomic offensive against Russia. Unlike its predecessor, Broiler conceded that the "success or failure" of the war effort hinged on the "early effectiveness" of the air-atomic campaign. The new plan seemed considerably more sanguine concerning the bomb's effect. Acknowledging that "there will be insufficient Allied forces to ensure carrying out all essential operations," the creators of Broiler reluctantly conceded the need to take "[e]xtremely serious risks" in yielding strategic areas to the enemy. These risks would be made bearable, however, by the "tremendous strategic advantage" afforded the United States in exclusive possession of the atomic bomb. It was assumed that the air-atomic offensive could not only result in the "stabilization" of the Soviet offensive in the first six months of the war, but would also aid Allied forces in recapturing lost territory during the next six months by seriously disrupting Russian war production.[22]

The effectiveness of the air-atomic offensive would be increased in Broiler, furthermore, by staging atomic raids from the Ryukyu Islands of Japan as well as from bases in England, Egypt, and India. The earlier problem of some targets in Russia being out of the B-29s' range was resolved in Broiler by a simple expedient—the bombers would land or "ditch" in friendly or neutral territory on the return flight, as had Doolittle's raid on Toyko. The drafters of the plan reasoned that the "advantage of making the initial attack heavy and of including those targets of major importance . . . more than compensates for the loss of a number of aircraft."[23]

rollback In yet another major departure from Pincher, Broiler envisioned the possibility that the liberation of eastern Europe and the surrender of Russia "may ensue immediately following the initial atomic bomb campaign." To allow for that eventuality, the drafters of the plan urged that "preparations should be made early . . . to enable the Allies to take quick action in case of an early Soviet collapse." Significantly, Broiler was predicated upon the hope of inducing such an early surrender by use of the bomb—a vital difference from Pincher, whose principal goal was the gradual destruction of Russia's war-making capability.

A final new element of Broiler was the explicit admission that selection of targets in the Soviet Union would "be governed in a large measure by political considerations" to produce the "maximum psychological effect of the atomic bomb." Indeed, as the amended targeting list appended to the plan showed, the emphasis of air-atomic strategy had subtly changed since fall 1945 from industrial and military targets such as oil refineries—now to be made the objective of sustained conventional bombing—to "the political, governmental, administrative, and technical and scientific elements of the Soviet nation," or, specifically, "key government and control facilities" in cities.[24]

Here the psychological effect of the bomb was deemed preeminently important. "[I]t seems reasonable to anticipate that the use of this weapon would create a condition of chaos and extreme confusion," an annex to Broiler advised. Not the least of this effect would be "an increased element of hopelessness and shock resulting from the magnitude of destruction; the fear of the unknown; the actual lingering physical after effects of atomic explosions; the psychological effect arising from the necessity to evacuate large densely populated areas; and the attendant psychological state which these factors will create." Whereas Broiler's drafters were unwilling to speculate in detail on what influence these "intangibles" might have toward compelling an early Russian surrender, they deemed it "logical to anticipate that this psychological effect, properly exploited, could become an important factor in the timing of . . . the cessation of hostilities."[25]

With Broiler, modern war became the "sudden death out of a clear sky" that General Arnold had predicted. The new plan seemed as well a long-overdue response to the requirements of U.S. security. The lack

Such thinking lay behind air attacks on NK

of a coherent and workable emergency war plan, Forrestal wrote in 1947, had been a "source of embarrassment to all of the Departments before Congress this year."[26]

Even so, the creators of Broiler acknowledged flaws in their plan. Among these was the continuing uncertainty about how many atomic bombs the United States would have upon the outbreak of war, and how many of these the AAF would be able to deliver against targets in Russia. As a reflection of the bomb's new importance in American strategy, the Joint Strategic Survey Committee informed the Pentagon in October that a "long-term" military requirement existed for approximately four hundred atomic bombs, to be dropped upon a hundred Soviet targets.[27]

But by far the most significant weakness acknowledged by U.S. military planners was their inability to resolve the question that had quietly dominated all efforts at political and strategic planning since 1945: How long would it be until the Russians had the bomb?

"A Special Importance to Us"

The question of when the Russians might get the atomic bomb had been an early concern not only of the civilian policymakers in the Truman administration but of Pentagon planners. Assistant Secretary of War for Air Robert Lovett observed in fall 1945 that the argument against disclosing any information to the Russians on the bomb would be logically strengthened by evidence that it might be years before they could develop the weapon on their own. "This element of time has a special importance to us in the uncertainty of postwar tensions," Lovett wrote.[28]

The question of the Russian bomb had also been considered briefly in Pincher, but the plan's implicit devaluing of the bomb's role in American strategy was reflected in its surprising equanimity toward the monopoly's end. Although Pincher's drafters thought it possible that the Russians might explode a bomb before the end of 1948, they deemed it more probable that the monopoly would not come to an end before 1956 "or even longer." The use of radiological weapons—radioactive dust or gas—by the Russians against Allied troops in the event of war was deemed by them more likely and a more immediate threat than a Soviet bomb.[29]

By summer 1947, the time of planning for Broiler, the increased importance of the atomic bomb in American military thought had given a corresponding urgency to the question of a Russian bomb. Indicative of this new urgency was a report prepared in early July of that year by the joint chiefs' intelligence committee concerning the Soviet atomic-energy program. The joint chiefs had complained the previous November, in fact, that Groves' order excluding them from Manhattan Project intelligence estimates on Russian progress toward a bomb made it impossible to assess the nation's military requirements accurately. Uncertainty about when the atomic monopoly might end cast future planning in doubt, just as the joint chiefs' ignorance about the number of bombs in the nuclear arsenal had made early war plans unrealistic.[30]

The continuing gap in the military's own knowledge of Soviet capabilities was one reason for the joint chiefs' failure to agree in their July 1947 report to the President on the likely date for a Russian bomb. For the same reason, the individual services were unable to reach agreement on that date in their independent assessments. Instead, summarizing these disagreements, the study presented for comparison two widely different estimates. Reflecting a traditionalist bias and a desire to undermine air force claims to the budget, the navy calculated that Russia did not yet have the bomb, was not likely to have one until 1952, and even then would be limited to a production schedule of not more than three to five weapons per year by a shortage of the necessary raw materials. The army and AAF joined in a counterestimate that the Soviets might already have a bomb and would "most probably" have a number of nuclear weapons between 1949 and 1952.[31]

Curiously, the disparate views of the planners and the debate that raged between the services concerning the Russian bomb had not been indicated in Broiler. The apparently greater need for service unity in war plans meant that Broiler's drafters excluded from it any speculation on when the atomic monopoly might end.

In the fall of 1947 there occurred a reminder that the question could not be dodged indefinitely. A speech that November in which Soviet Foreign Minister Molotov bragged that the secret of the atomic bomb had long before "ceased to exist" received widespread publicity in the United States. Members of the State Department's Policy Planning Staff were prompted to a contextual analysis of official Soviet statements on the bomb in the hope of shedding some light on the truth behind Molotov's remarks.*

Two subsequent studies by the joint chiefs in 1947 showed no positive assurance that either of their July estimates for the Russian bomb was likely to be correct. Acknowledging that any projection of Soviet progress in atomic energy to the year 1956 could only be "a good guess," the joint chiefs estimated that the Russians might have "a significant quantity" of bombs by that year, though they thought this "optimistic from the Russian point of view."

Certainly even more optimistic than this, however, was the study's remarkable conclusion: "As each year goes by in which the Soviets do not solve the practical problems of atomic energy, their possession of even a small quantity of bombs must be advanced further into the future."[33]

The guessing game surrounding the Soviet atomic bomb was finally joined—but not resolved—in a year-end study undertaken by the new Central Intelligence Agency and coordinated with the State Department and the Atomic Energy Commission. As the latest and supposedly the best-informed of all the estimates made in 1947, the CIA study was especially significant. It was notable, as well, for the fact that its predictions fell somewhere between the diverging estimates of the military. Upon the premise that technical difficulties and a dearth of atomic raw materials meant that "the USSR could not proceed faster than the U.S. and possibly not so fast" in building a bomb, the CIA declared it "doubtful that the Russians can produce a bomb before 1953 and almost certain they cannot produce one before 1951." The number of Russian bombs manufactured, moreover, would be restricted by these same factors to an estimated eight to fifteen bombs during the first three to five years, while the production rate would decline thereafter because of production problems and raw-material shortages to only one or two bombs a year for an indefinite period.[34]

The fact that the CIA assessment could not give a "probable date" for the development of Russia's first bomb did not seem to worry American military planners. None of these, in any case, apparently challenged the plainly wistful conclusion of the joint chiefs' intelligence committee

---

*No light was shed. The State Department study concluded only that the Russians had probably not yet mastered the "know-how" for making a bomb.[32]

that the evidence the Russians didn't yet have a bomb was a good indication they wouldn't get one soon.

CIA analysts, Pentagon planners, and members of the Truman administration might have been surprised to learn of the skepticism with which the public greeted the idea that the Russians wouldn't have a significant number of atomic bombs for another decade. Just as most Americans privately doubted that the atomic bomb would be decisive in a war, an increasing number of them believed that the Russians already had—or would soon have—nuclear weapons. In a public-opinion poll of June 1946, for example, 20 percent of the respondents believed "some other country may already be able" to make atomic bombs. By August of that year, following the U.S. atomic tests at Bikini, this figure had risen to 24 percent. Another survey found that 42 percent of the citizens questioned in May 1947 believed that some other country or countries were *already* making atomic bombs; more than three-quarters of this group believed the "other" country to be Russia. By October 1947, well over half—59 percent—of the public surveyed thought that Russia was manufacturing atomic bombs in quantity.[35]

Thus, certainly compared to public attitudes, there existed toward the end of 1947 a remarkable complacency in the military and in the Truman administration concerning the durability of the atomic secret and of the U.S. monopoly of atomic bombs. Indeed, the attitude that this complacency had engendered was perhaps best represented in Bernard Baruch's speech earlier that year before the National War College. While what Baruch had once termed the "winning weapon" had conspicuously failed to compel the Russians to accept international control of atomic energy on American terms, he was not discouraged now from claiming another, more direct role for the bomb. Speaking with reference to the Russians, Baruch declared: "Our safety is their undoing. Let us remember we have the greatest weapon ever devised by man. It is the atomic bomb and we have it alone." Privately, Baruch's complacency was assailed by a wavering doubt. He had planned to add in this part of his speech, "and shall have for eight more years." He departed from his text, however, and cautiously substituted for "eight" the more modest and less assured "some."[36]

Not so riven by secret doubt was General Groves. Retired from the Manhattan Project but nonetheless still a semiofficial spokesman on matters concerning the bomb, Groves reaffirmed to a group of newsmen in October 1947 his original contention that it would still be from fifteen to twenty years before the Russians got the bomb.[37]

Monopolistic possession of the atomic bomb, to be sure, seemed to justify a certain assurance, if not complacency, on the part of American military planners at this time. But Pincher and Broiler represented two conflicting directions of strategy and doctrine, and neither resolved the questions this conflict posed: Should the emphasis in military planning be upon fighting and winning, or on deterring, a war with Russia? What is the place—if any—for preventive war and terror bombing in U.S. military doctrine? Should increasing reliance in U.S. strategy be put upon what was necessarily a wasting asset—the U.S. monopoly of atomic bombs?

The fact that the joint chiefs ultimately approved neither Pincher nor Broiler as an operational war plan seemed a tacit recognition that future U.S. strategy and doctrine would, to some extent, wait upon the resolution of these questions.

While the very existence of Broiler marked a transition of sorts by its effort to integrate the bomb into U.S. military planning and by its ominous previsioning of nuclear war's contemporary horrors, even as late as the end of 1947 the United States had no operational plan for a war with Russia based upon actual military capabilities. Lack of planning and the horrors of nuclear war did not, however, diminish the essential optimism expressed by the joint chiefs in their year-end "Review of Certain Significant Assumptions, Summaries, and Conclusions" regarding the state of American security. That security, this review made clear, depended increasingly—and unavoidably—upon the bomb. While they continued to believe that the primary Soviet goal remained "world domination," the joint chiefs concluded that Russia could not pose a nuclear threat of any kind until 1949–52. The greatest danger in the future would be, as in the past, an accidental war brought about by Soviet miscalculation. They believed at least another seven or eight years would pass, moreover, before the size of the Russian atomic arsenal might goad Soviet leaders into a deliberate attack upon the United States. Dissenting from this hardly pessimistic view was the army, which contended that the Russians would not get the bomb for another ten years, and "firmly stated" that even then Soviet uranium shortages would "severely limit" subsequent production.[38]

It is indeed ironic that not only the joint chiefs' year-end review but the CIA's assessment of this time cast the danger of war and the Russian "threat" itself some years into the future. For it was just a few weeks later that this complacency concerning Russia and the atomic bomb would be overturned by events. In those changed circumstances, the evolving attitude that the bomb might prevent a future war and the growing confidence that it, in any contingency, would prove a decisive weapon against Russia were both shadowed by doubt. The notion that the bomb would prove an absolute or a winning weapon in war was openly called into question.

Accordingly, it was not an assurance of victory but the prospect of defeat—despite the atomic bomb—that would dominate American military thinking by early 1948.

The Year of Opportunity:
1948

"The years before any possible power can achieve the capability effectively to attack us with weapons of mass destruction are our years of opportunity."

Secretary of Defense Forrestal, diary entry, December 1947

"It was assumed that we had a stockpile. We not only didn't have a pile; we didn't have a stock."

David Lilienthal, February 1979

"We Are Taking a Calculated Risk"

The new and cautious optimism of America's military planners in the winter of 1947–48 had its counterpart in the confident attitude of some Truman administration officials concerning the course of the now-acknowledged but still-undeclared "cold war" with Russia. "The danger of war is vastly exaggerated in many quarters," George Kennan wrote from the State Department's Policy Planning Staff in a November 1947 résumé of the world situation. Kennan's assurance was due to several encouraging developments in international affairs of the preceding year which he ascribed to American influence, direct and indirect. Among these were a "satisfactory peace settlement" in Europe; the initiation of U.S. economic aid to anticommunist governments; the qualified success of the United Nations (or at least the concomitant failure of the Soviet Union to dominate that assembly); and what the conservative Kennan characterized—with barely disguised relief—as a "natural recession of the wave of post-war radicalism."[1]

Kennan's positive attitude was also engendered by his assessment of Russian intentions. The distinction that he made between capabilities and intentions was, in fact, a hallmark of Kennan's State Department pronouncements. Increasingly it set the latter apart from the worst-case analyses of others in the administration. By the reckoning of its author in this memorandum, the containment doctrine to the end of 1947 was a success.

Indeed, there seemed some objective grounds for Kennan's attitude at year's end. The National Security Act, passed promptly by Congress in July 1947, had supposedly rationalized the process in which foreign and military policy would be made by the creation of a National Security Council to advise the Executive on that subject, and by the establishment of an air force independent of the army. Not incidentally, the act also expanded the President's powers in foreign affairs by founding the Central Intelligence Agency to collect and interpret intelligence, and— more cryptically—to "perform such other functions and duties . . . affecting the national security as the National Security Council may from time to time direct."[2]

As concerned containment itself, the President's announcement of the Truman Doctrine in March 1947, to "support free peoples who are resisting attempted subjugation by armed minorities or by outside pressures" with U.S. military aid, finally gave substance to the strategy that the administration had embraced to combat communism. The extension of the Truman Doctrine three months later to include economic assistance under the Marshall Plan confirmed the government's intention to practice containment with other than military means. The resignation of Secretary of State James Byrnes, and his replacement by former Army Chief of Staff George Marshall, symbolically as well marked the changed nature of the administration's reponse to the Soviet threat at the beginning of 1947.[3]

As early as the fall of that year both the Truman Doctrine and the Marshall Plan had begun to show signs of success in containing that threat, first in turning the tide against the communists in Greece's civil war, and second by slowing the precipitously downward trend in western European economies. Even the normally circumspect Marshall was buoyed by this news in an early-November report to the Cabinet on the international situation, declaring that "the advance of Communism has been stemmed and the Russians have been compelled to make a re-evaluation of their position."[4]

Despite some momentary—and recurring—doubts, this feeling that the United States would be able at the minimum to avoid the worst consequences of the confrontation with Russia extended to Truman himself. Worried that September by the "critical European situation," the President had despaired in a comment related by Eben Ayers that if France and Italy fell to the communists, "then we'll just have to get ready for war." By mid-October, however, with the situation in Europe somewhat stabilized through American military and economic aid, Truman's mood brightened correspondingly. As Ayers noted of an exchange between the President and his adviser Clark Clifford, "[Truman] said he believed that if only Stalin were concerned on the Russian side that everything would be all right now. He said he liked Stalin—the 'old guy' as he referred to him." Truman told Clifford he had asked Stalin at Potsdam to come to Washington and that the Soviet leader had replied he would, "God willing." "God—and the Politburo," Clifford added.[5]

There was perhaps another, pragmatic reason for this change in mood on the part of the civilian and military planners of the Truman administration at the beginning of 1948. By early January at least a short-term solution was found to the AEC's chronic uranium shortage in a special agreement with the British which allowed America access to England's remaining stockpile of atomic raw materials. Just as important, the bottleneck that had previously held up the rate of production of atomic bombs was finally broken in the following month, with the result that the inventory of bombs by midyear began to approach for the first time the number that Lilienthal and the joint chiefs had termed "adequate" for the nation's security in 1947. As the *New York Times* cryptically informed American readers that February, the Atomic Energy Commission was making "majestic and terrible progress" in building the country's nuclear arsenal.[6]

It is paradoxical that a key figure behind the impetus for the raw-materials agreement with the British was James Forrestal, an anglophobe and early skeptic of the bomb's efficacy in military affairs. But, while his attitude toward the British had not changed, Forrestal's perspective on the bomb had. Appointed by Truman in September 1947 to be the nation's first secretary of defense under provision of the National Security Act, Forrestal was also among the first to appreciate the political implications of America's improved military position. He recognized in a letter of early December 1947 to the Senate Armed Services Committee that the administration's policy of emphasizing military and economic aid instead of domestic rearmament meant "we are taking a calculated risk in order to follow a course which offers a prospect of eventually achieving national security and also long-term world stability." Until that better world was achieved, however, he argued that the United States "will continue to have certain military advantages which go far toward covering the risk. . . . As long as we can outproduce the world, can control the sea and can strike inland with the atomic bomb we can assume certain risks otherwise unacceptable in an effort to restore world trade, to restore the balance of power—military power—and to eliminate some of the conditions which breed war. . . . The years before any possible power can achieve the capability effectively to attack us with weapons of mass destruction are our years of opportunity.*

Forrestal's letter to the Senate committee illustrates the extent to which not only American military planning but even the grand strategy of containment itself had become dependent upon the atomic bomb by the end of 1947. Curiously, this was a fact which Kennan, in his contemporary analysis, either overlooked or deliberately ignored. The Russians neither overlooked nor ignored the importance of the bomb at this time, however. The month before Forrestal wrote his letter, Molotov, in a speech commemorating the thirtieth anniversary of the Russian revolution, charged that "a new, peculiar sort of illusion is widespread [among] expansionist circles" in the U.S., where "faith is placed in the secret of the atomic bomb. . . ."[8]

The assumption integral to Forrestal's argument—that stability as well as security was provided by America's unique advantages, foremost of which was the bomb—would be dramatically undermined through a series of crises and setbacks for American foreign policy which began in the early months of 1948. In March, the ouster of the coalition government in Czechoslovakia by a Soviet-supported coup sparked a war scare in the United States and Europe. That summer, the Russian isolation and blockade of Berlin seemed further evidence that the communists meant to actively challenge containment. Throughout this time, the progressive deterioration of America's position in the Far East appeared to belie Marshall's assertion that the communist advance had been halted. Indeed, in the course of these events, it seemed that the "calculated risk" acknowledged by Forrestal had been miscalculated, and

---

*Forrestal expanded on what he meant by a "calculated risk" in a letter of early January 1948 to *New York Times* military correspondent Hanson Baldwin: "It has long been one of my strongly held beliefs that the word 'security' ought to be stricken from the language and the word 'risk' substituted. I came to that conclusion out of my own business experience. . . . The great danger in any country is for people to believe that there is anything absolute about security. Air power, atomic bombs, wealth—by itself none of these can give any security."[7]

that the Russians might even be about to test America's willingness to use the atomic bomb.

"Not a Bit Worried"

The intricacies of military planning and strategy aside, a dominant fact of American preparations for any future war—and one known to civilian and military leaders alike by early 1948—was that America's supposed atomic arsenal was still more promise than substance.* Like this fact itself, the circumstances which would change it were still hidden from the attention and understanding of most Americans.

One of the initial problems plaguing the atomic-weapons program was the necessary changeover from laboratory fabrication of bombs to their assembly-line-style production. But a chronic and ultimately more serious limitation was the amount of uranium available for the production of bombs. Already an end could be seen to the supply of that element from the world's richest deposits in the Belgian Congo. The continuing upheaval of politics in the Congo and what the State Department took to be evidence of Soviet meddling there made the future availability of Congolese uranium a dubious prospect.[10] Difficult and protracted negotiations with foreign governments like that of South Africa lay ahead if the United States was to obtain other sources of uranium.[11]

Aware of the coming crisis over raw materials, the Atomic Energy Commission had begun efforts as early as midsummer 1947 to exploit domestic resources of uranium ore for the bomb plants. Utilization of plentiful but low-grade ore from deposits in Colorado, Wyoming, and Arizona, however, would require—as Groves had earlier predicted concerning the Russians—a long time and the development of an essentially new technology. For the critical interim period ahead the only source of ore was the high-grade uranium apportioned by previous agreement to Great Britain.[12]

Among those urging that the British be approached on allowing American access to their uranium was Forrestal, whose previous words

---

*David Lilienthal observed in 1979 that the size of America's atomic arsenal did not materially increase from 1945 to early 1948: "It was assumed that we had a stockpile. We not only didn't have a pile; we didn't have a stock." A recently declassified document from the U.S. Department of Energy confirms Lilienthal's assertion.[9]

and deeds had put him in the forefront of those opposing closer cooperation with Britain in the matter of atomic energy. But his uncharacteristic
willingness to deal with the British on this occasion was motivated,
Forrestal confided to his diary, by a belief that the need to increase
atomic bomb production was "emphasized by current events" in the
world.[13]

There was as well a more devious motive behind his apparent
turnabout. By reopening negotiations with the British he meant to
remove the last surviving remnant of Anglo-American wartime cooperation: that provision of the Quebec Agreement which called for consultation between the two governments before the use of an atomic bomb.
Though Forrestal's suggestion that the United States make Marshall
Plan aid to the British conditional upon their cooperation regarding the
ore was ultimately overruled by the State Department, his idea of negotiating a so-called *modus vivendi* with the British on uranium was approved by the administration.[14]

Certainly the British—who by this time might have begun to
identify with the earlier plight of the American Indians in their dealings
with the U.S. government—had cause to resist this latest offer to
renegotiate their treaty rights. Perhaps in the expectation that this could
also be an occasion to right past wrongs, however, British representatives
late in 1947 entered into talks at Washington on the *modus vivendi.*

Those talks brought results at the start of the year in a secret
agreement which reserved for the United States the entire production
of the Congo's mines for 1948 and 1949, in addition to whatever other
British-owned uranium would be necessary to meet American needs. In
exchange, the British received a renewed promise from the United
States to aid in promoting England's own atomic-energy program at
Harwell. But since the interchange of substantive technical information
on atomic energy was still proscribed by the McMahon Act, the details
of this latest offer of cooperation remained purposely vague. As before,
this deliberate ambiguity would result in subsequent misunderstandings
and recrimination. For Forrestal and the other American negotiators at
the talks, the overriding feature of the January 1948 *modus vivendi* was
that it guaranteed to the United States for the first time a plentiful
supply of the raw material to make atomic bombs.[15]

There was a further importance to this agreement that may not
have been recognized at the time. The *modus vivendi* was one additional
step toward that consortium of uranium-holding nations which Bernard

Baruch and Fred Searls had envisioned as the preferred alternative to international control of the bomb. With the collapse of hopes for international control, even Acheson had turned to urging such an atomic league the previous year.[16] Held in secret to avoid the appearance of an Anglo-American atomic cabal, negotiations on the *modus vivendi* quickly dispelled any lingering expectation the British might have had that the U.S. monopoly of atomic weapons would become an Anglo-American partnership.*

The possession of sufficient uranium to make a stockpile of atomic bombs was, of course, of no advantage until the obstacles to their mass production that had beset the Manhattan Project were first overcome. Some progress had already been achieved in overcoming one early production bottleneck—fabrication of explosive detonators for the bomb—by the beginning of 1948. But the most significant development occurred in February of that year. Experimentation with an improved bomb design, similar to the weapon dropped upon Nagasaki but more easily constructed and yielding twice the energy for the same amount of raw material, promised to double the size of America's nuclear stockpile in a short time. This new product of U.S. atomic laboratories was to be tested in the Pacific during the coming months.[18]

This breakthrough in weapons development marked a potential rather than an actual jump in America's nuclear strength for the remainder of 1948. Even the doubling of the stockpile in that year left U.S. planners with probably no more than one hundred bombs by year's end —and no means yet of assembling or delivering even that number. But it meant that an arsenal of atomic bombs to meet the nation's declared military needs could now be obtained within the foreseeable future. Evidently in response to this fact, the air force, which at the start of 1948 had only thirty-three bombers capable of carrying atomic bombs, began planning to increase its number of "atomic-capable" B-29s to 120 by the following November. Lagging somewhat further behind, the U.S. Atomic Energy Commission intended to more than double its number of trained bomb-assembly teams from a planned three in June 1948 to seven a year later.[19]

---

*Anglo-American members of the Combined Policy Committee who formed the negotiating group for the *modus vivendi* dubbed themselves the "Insecticide Committee." The appellation, presumedly adopted for security reasons, was singularly inappropriate—among its British members were Soviet spies Donald Maclean and Klaus Fuchs.[17]

Increasingly, the atomic bomb seemed a Faustian bargain. So vital had the bomb become to strategy that progress in the science of mass destruction seemed a guarantee of American security. Whatever ambivalence atomic scientists and technicians might have felt concerning this most recent evidence of skill at their craft, the events of succeeding months would emphasize the importance of their secret and necessarily unheralded achievements.

Perhaps no less significant than these accomplishments for the future of the U.S. atomic-weapons program was General Leslie Groves' retirement from the government. Certainly the departure of the temperamental Groves was not viewed with regret by many in the administration or the Atomic Energy Commission. Lilienthal in particular was aware of Groves' early and persistent opposition to civilian control of atomic energy, and believed—with reason—that the general had tried repeatedly to sabotage his chairmanship and the reputation of the civilian AEC while head of its Military Liaison Committee.

But even this was not the most troubling aspect of Groves' interference with the work of the commission. Since his appointment to that committee against Lilienthal's objections, and also in his role as director of the Armed Forces Special Weapons Project, Groves had lobbied tirelessly to have the custody of atomic weapons transferred to the military—a move that first Lilienthal and then Truman vigorously opposed. As the source of earlier news leaks meant to damage the AEC, finally, Groves seemed the most likely candidate as the "high government official" who had spawned the newspaper sensation of the previous summer concerning secret documents supposedly lost or stolen from the commission. Based upon old and disproved allegations, this claim would nonetheless be the basis for the charge of "incredible mismanagement" leveled at Lilienthal and the civilian commission the following year by Senator Hickenlooper.[20]

Beyond such simple but effective harassment, Groves' role in promoting accounts that the commission practiced lax security and even harbored suspected communist agents seemed aimed at undermining civilian authority. Nor was Lilienthal himself necessarily alarmist in his conviction that this was Groves' real goal. By the end of 1947, largely because of the renewed furor over secrecy, six separate bills were before the House for the repeal of the McMahon Act and a return to military control of atomic energy.[21]

Confronted with this clear challenge to his stewardship of the

AEC, and uncertain how far Groves was willing to go in his campaign to transfer custody of the weapons and restore military control of atomic energy, Lilienthal had begun urging that the general be replaced on both the Military Liaison Committee and the Armed Forces Special Weapons Project after the bogus security scare of the previous summer. While he weathered that storm, Groves' subsequent behind-the-scenes allegations concerning the commission so alienated even his supporters in the Pentagon and Congress that "the Groves situation" occasioned a meeting in mid-January 1948 attended by the service secretaries, Vannevar Bush, James Conant, and J. Robert Oppenheimer. The meeting was for the purpose of deciding how best to ease the former head of the Manhattan Project out of the government. The group's deliberations, however, were cut short when the general, who undoubtedly knew of the growing sentiment against him, announced his intention to retire the following month.[22]

Groves' departure was unlamented by Truman. A letter to Truman of July 1947 from California Senator William Knowland, a noted Groves ally, praising the latter and recommending his promotion to full general, was politely acknowledged but not acted upon by the President.[23]

Groves may have been gone by early 1948 but he was surely not forgotten. Nor was his influence upon U.S. atomic-energy policy at an end. Indeed, debate on the custody issue—which would be a fixture of relations between the military and the Truman administration for the next two years—had just begun, and expectations concerning the future would continue to bear the mark of Groves' supposedly authoritative estimate that the Russians were still as much as a generation away from an atomic bomb. Concerning that prediction, Groves proved entirely consistent even at the end of his career. In response to a reporter's question at his last press conference, he declared that he was "not a bit worried" about the prospects for a Soviet atomic bomb.[24]

"The Suddenly Urgent Immediate Issues"

If not to Groves, the Russians and the prospects for a Soviet bomb were a concern to the Truman administration in the early weeks of 1948, despite the recently upbeat attitude in Washington toward the "cold war." The President's Air Policy Commission had been established the previous summer under the leadership of Washington attorney Thomas Finletter to add a supposedly dispassionate voice to the continuing debate over air power and the defense budget. The Finletter Report was forwarded to the government on the first of the year. Dramatically entitled "Survival in the Air Age," the published report and the public hearings leading up to it amounted to a forum for proponents of the seventy-group air force and a brief for an air-atomic strategy. While never mentioning the Russians directly, the report left no doubt as to either the seriousness or the source of the threat facing America.

But beyond advocating the seventy-group concept—an *idée fixe* with that service which General Spaatz would call an "irreducible minimum" for the nation's security—the recommendations of the commission were vague and confusing. While calling for a "new strategy" in American military planning, its members actually offered a choice of two conflicting strategies without settling upon either one. Unclear from the report's conclusions, therefore, was whether the reliance upon air power it urged was meant to prevent a war by deterring aggression or to win a war when it occurred. Undecided, further, whether they should recommend air defense or a buildup of offensive forces, the destruction of enemy cities or a concentration upon only military targets, the members of the Finletter commission in each case emphasized both.[25]

This confusion as to whether the role of the armed services, particularly the air force, should be to deter a war or to win one was not restricted to the Finletter Report but remained endemic to the thinking of U.S. military planners, as budget and preparedness hearings in Congress at this time also revealed. Perhaps the most anachronistic—and certainly the most chilling—expression of the paradox this thinking represented was Army Secretary Kenneth Royall's comment to Truman in the summer of 1948 that "[w]e have been spending 98 percent of all the money for atomic energy for weapons. . . . Now if we aren't going to use them, that doesn't make any sense."[26]

As long as America's military (and especially nuclear) capability fell short of requirements for even the most limited of U.S. war plans, as long as the unification issue remained unsettled, and, particularly, as long as no imminent threat of war with Russia existed, there was no particular sense of urgency that such contradictions of doctrine and strategy be resolved. "A-day," January 1, 1953—the earliest practical date set by the Finletter commission to expect a Russian nuclear attack upon the United States—was thus still some five years away.[27]

Partly because of this lack of urgency, the Joint Chiefs of Staff had yet to approve as operational any of the war plans devised by their planning committee. Indeed, a contingency plan for the stockpiling of strategic material at the possible approach of war concluded as late as February 1948 that any military conflict with Russia in the near future would resemble in both character and duration the Second World War.

Receiving much less attention in the government was a top-secret study at this time by a committee of intelligence experts from the three services concerning Russian progress toward an atomic bomb. This study concluded that the Russians might have a bomb as early as the middle of 1950, though a more probable date for the first Russian test was thought to be mid-1953. In either case, these analysts believed that the Soviets would have a stockpile of between twenty and fifty atomic bombs by mid-1955—an estimate that placed "A-day" considerably sooner than the joint chiefs' previous estimate.[28]

But the enigma of the Soviet bomb was temporarily submerged in Washington by a more pressing concern.

It was during the relative calm of the international situation in the first few weeks of the new year that the joint chiefs and Forrestal—with Truman's prodding as an added impetus—planned a meeting in Key West, Florida, to discuss and perhaps to resolve the complex matter of the services' unification. Events a world away determined, however, that the Key West conference would be dominated not by the subject of unification but by an urgent reassessment of American military strategy and policy.

The 1948 spring crisis and ensuing war scare did not break entirely without warning. Even in Kennan's November 1947 assessment that— "all in all"—the cold war was going well for the United States, there was a prediction that Russia might soon have "to clamp down completely on Czechoslovakia" because of the danger that that country "could too easily become a means of entry of really democratic forces into Eastern Europe in general." Characteristically, Kennan did not think to stress this eventuality, since he saw it as no direct threat to American interests. A more emphatic warning, and one from a different part of the world, arrived at the Pentagon the month after Kennan's missive from the State Department. In China, Mao Zedong was rapidly winning the civil war. "I want to emphasize that I feel that there is grave danger of war with USSR within a few months," a U.S. Air Force commander in the Far East wrote to Spaatz.[29]

It was the suddenly changed conditions in Europe and not the gradually deteriorating situation in China that actually prompted the first alarms in Washington during early March. While Czechoslovakia —as Kennan's précis had implied—was hardly the touchstone of American security, in the wake of the March coup that country assumed, like Poland ten years earlier, a symbolic importance out of all proportion to its value to U.S. security. "We are faced with exactly the same situation with which Britain and France were faced in 1938–9 with Hitler," Truman wrote to his family on March 3. "Things look black. A decision will have to be made. I am going to make it."[30]

It was appearance that counted more than reality that spring, when the communists consolidated their hold on Czechoslovakia. Only two days after the President's worried letter home the Pentagon received an "eyes only" telegram from the U.S. commander in Berlin, General Lucius Clay: "I have felt a subtle change in Soviet attitude which I cannot define but which now gives me a feeling that [war] may come with dramatic suddenness." The indication of this change, Clay admitted, was simply "a feeling of a new tenseness" on the part of the Russians in Berlin, but "you may advise the chief of staff of this for whatever it may be worth. . . ."[31]

In the shadow of Czechoslovakia's fall, Clay's vague premonition was worth quite a bit. In fact, his remarkable message—like that of his air force counterpart during the previous year—probably had its origins more in a concern for a share of upcoming defense appropriations than in any new or better perception of the Soviet threat. But the war scare that it prompted—spurred on by the apparent murder five days later of Czechoslovakia's pro-Western foreign minister—was undoubtedly genuine.[32]

There remained some serious question in 1948, as ten years before, of what the West could do about the situation in Czechoslovakia—a fact of which Truman as well as Clay was aware. Just two weeks before Clay's telegraphed warning, Major General Alfred Gruenther had briefed the President on the dramatic decline in the strength of America's conventional forces as a result of demobilization. Since the end of 1947 the joint chiefs themselves had been urging the State Department to obtain basing rights for U.S. troops in forward positions overseas. But the plans for bases had then lacked urgency. By the spring of 1948 either these rights were yet to be negotiated or the bases themselves were still unmanned. In the event of a blitzkrieg-style Soviet invasion of western

Europe, the United States as late as March 1948 could neither launch the planned air-atomic strike against the Russian heartland nor evacuate imperiled American forces from the continent.

Reflecting upon this situation in his diary, Forrestal thought it necessary to revise his earlier enthusiasm about "our years of opportunity." He now wrote that "the limitations of our military power to deal with the various potentially explosive areas over the world [were] lamentably clear." Secretary of State Marshall was more blunt. "We are playing with fire while we have nothing with which to put it out."[33]

There was also no immediate prospect that the sorry state of U.S. military preparedness would change in time to deal with the present crisis. Universal military training, which Stimson had once looked to as a surer deterrent of aggression than the atomic bomb, was still stalled by doctrinal divisions between the services and by a cautious Congress. Significantly, when Truman had tried to press for hearings on UMT in the Senate the previous month he was rebuffed by congressmen, whose sensitivity to the unpopularity of conscription with the public was plainly evident. "The effect of the Finletter report and of the Brewster-Hinshaw Board [of congressional air-power advocates]," Forrestal lamented on March 8, "has been to convince the country that by a substantial increase in appropriations for Air, there would be no necessity for UMT. . . ." Indeed, UMT had become a victim of the atomic age.[34] Truman's subsequent effort to promote the idea in a special St. Patrick's Day speech a week later probably occasioned an intensification of the public's fear of war, but did nothing to bring UMT closer to realization. Instead, the overall effect may well have been the opposite of what he intended. As tensions continued to increase in the aftermath of the Czech coup, therefore, attention inevitably focused upon that military area where America's advantage was still unquestioned—the atomic bomb.

Better able than the public to put the crisis over Czechoslovakia in perspective, the nation's civilian and military leaders showed a concern for events there that was far short of panic. It was, Forrestal declared, "inconceivable . . . that even the gang who run Russia would be willing to take on war."[35] The pressure of events, in any case, was not sufficient for the joint chiefs to resolve many of the major issues dividing them at the mid-March Key West meeting, even when that conference was extended two days at the behest of the President in hopes of a reconciliation. The one item of mutual interest and agreement had concerned the immediate, if still unlikely, prospect of war with Russia. Even here, the surprising unanimity of the service chiefs in deciding upon a "short-term emergency war plan"—code-named Grabber*—was qualified by the fact that the plan concerned only forces-in-being and not future doctrine or appropriations. "It is for this reason and this reason only that we are able to submit this Plan without a split," the chairman of the planning committee admitted to the joint chiefs.[36]

Still, the new war plan filled a gap the importance of which had been emphasized by recent events, and reflected an ominous trend in modern warfare. Whereas previous plans had assumed that war with Russia was not likely within five years and would be preceded by a warning period of up to one year, the premise of Grabber was that war could come at any time and would be accompanied by little or no warning.

Grabber differed from its predecessors, Pincher and Broiler, in another important aspect. In a preamble to the plan, the joint chiefs noted that it "emphasizes the current grave military weakness of the United States." Indeed, Grabber implicitly stressed the increasing, necessary reliance of the joint chiefs upon the atomic bomb because of this weakness. With the outbreak of war, U.S. forces would immediately evacuate Germany, Austria, and Trieste to defend a line west of the Rhine. The Middle East would also be given up under pressure to save American troops there for an offensive aimed at recapturing that area and its oil resources during the early part of the war's second year. The vital air-atomic offensive would begin "as early as practicable"—almost certainly within two weeks of the start of war—from bases in England, Pakistan, India, and Okinawa. With the exception of those in England, these bases would be secured by American airborne commandos. As in the Second World War, Britain would be expected to hold out at least initially on her own.[37]

"The shortcomings of this plan," the joint chiefs readily conceded, were that "it does not provide adequate assistance to the countries of western Europe, nor does it provide for the initial retention by the Allies of the Middle East oil resources." But Grabber was, they implied, the most that could be expected with the forces at hand. Grabber's severely limited conditions of victory were also subtly dependent upon a conces-

---

*For a reason that may only be guessed at, the original drafters of this plan for war with the Soviet Union had dubbed it Frolic. Wiser heads—or at least someone with a better sense for nomenclature —settled upon Grabber.

sion from civilian authority that was still pending. Thus the staging of atomic raids against Russia within weeks of the outbreak of war assumed that the air force at that time would already have physical possession of the bomb. Yet this was, at best, a dubious assumption while Truman and Lilienthal refused to grant the military custody of the weapons.

Surely some of the pessimism of Grabber was self-serving, and linked directly to the battle that was to ensue over appropriations and the services' interpretation of their roles. This motive notwithstanding, the plan revealed the extent to which American military strategy was willing—or, as the joint chiefs thought, compelled—to rely upon the security afforded by the bomb. Neither Grabber nor the Key West conference settled, in fact, any of the outstanding theoretical or practical questions dividing the services. But both accentuated, if only unintentionally, the way in which the bomb had come to influence and even to dominate those differences. The "area of disagreement between the Air Force and Navy Air is not necessarily very wide but it is quite deep," Forrestal wrote. "It deals fundamentally with the concepts of so-called strategic warfare, and this boils down to use of the atomic bomb."[38]

Apart from the futile extension of the Key West conference and the hurried drafting of Grabber, the March crisis in Czechoslovakia provoked no direct response from the Truman administration. Perhaps one reason for this lack of reaction, despite the government's evident concern, was the realization that no effective military action seemed warranted—or, indeed, possible. Regardless of what they characterized as fundamental military weakness, the joint chiefs—unlike General Clay and certain other anxious theater commanders—believed the country to be in no imminent danger of war in spring 1948. This was generally true of civilians in the administration as well. A recommendation from George Kennan that the United States consider the evacuation of Korea, for example, was made in response to Korea's unsettled internal politics, and was not a barometer of Washington's fears.[39]

Some in the administration, however, pointed to the Czech coup as an indication that there was still a need to do more to oppose communism. Reflecting this attitude, members of the National Security Council began on their own initiative a reexamination of America's grand strategy in the course of the war scare. Dubbed NSC-7, "The Position of the United States with Respect to Soviet-Directed World Communism," this study—the first administration document to use the term "cold war"—was clearly a product of the crisis atmosphere engendered by the Czech coup. Its opening sentence mirrored its authors' acute concern and set the tone for what followed: "Today Stalin has come close to achieving what Hitler attempted in vain." NSC-7 was a mobilization order for the ambiguous conflict in which America confronted Russia. Eschewing a defensive strategy in the cold war, the members of the National Security Council proposed a broad counteroffensive against communism that included the following elements: the rearming of America through universal military training and the continuance of "overwhelming U.S. superiority in atomic weapons"; a strengthening of American assistance efforts in Europe—including "a coordinated program to support underground resistance movements in countries behind the iron curtain"—and, at home, an unspecified project "designed to suppress the communist menace."[40]

Vague as to both the creation and the implementation of these programs, NSC-7 was yet an indication of the form that American reaction to the Soviet threat might take. It was the latest though not the last suggestion that the home front be transformed to meet the danger from abroad. As such, it was also a proposal to go beyond what some considered the negative and defensive strategy of containment in an ambitious effort to beard the enemy at home and abroad—an effort with plainly ominous implications for domestic civil liberties. Perhaps partly for that reason, NSC-7, after being sent to the White House at the end of March, was still awaiting endorsement by Truman when events in Europe once again attracted the President's attention to the continuing crisis there.*

By the time NSC-7 was completed, evidence was mounting that the United States might already have missed its opportunity to launch a counteroffensive against communism. Thus, by April the Russian political offensive which had precipitated the March crisis seemed about to

---

*Truman's apparent dissatisfaction with NSC-7 was probably, however, not entirely motivated by a concern for the rights of American citizens or by fear that the government might be overstepping its bounds. At this same time, therefore, Truman approved Operation Shamrock, a CIA program to monitor the activities of selected U.S. citizens. In an interview with journalist Merle Miller years after his presidency, Truman professed to have been disturbed from the outset by the latitude allowed the CIA. But he showed no such trepidation while in office, and late in 1950 told the Cabinet that the CIA had been "invaluable in the present world situation." The minutes of the meetings of the National Security Council reveal that the President exploited the "special projects" or covert operations allowed under the CIA charter.[41]

be resumed. The day following the National Security Council's report to the President on NSC-7, Soviet representatives in Berlin began the first harassment of Western traffic into that city, an act which presaged the actual Russian blockade of Berlin some weeks later.

As before, General Clay sounded the tocsin of alarm with another "eyes only" telegram to the Pentagon, announcing his intention "to instruct our guards to open fire if Soviet soldiers attempt to enter our trains." This prospect prompted a quick instruction from Truman and Army Secretary Royall that "our guards not fire unless fired upon." Forrestal, too, had by now grown wary of Clay's nervous flights to the telegraph, noting in his diary that Soviet interference in Berlin "was not as truculent as could be inferred from Clay's first message." Displaying similar caution, Truman decided against convening an emergency session of Congress or sending a special warning to Stalin over Berlin on the plausible grounds that either would add to the growing dimensions of what Forrestal now termed a "war hysteria."[42]

At quickly convened meetings of the Cabinet there remained, as with the Czech coup, the question of what response the United States should—or could—make to Russian provocation. While the extent of the peril facing the United States was again adjudged less by figures within the administration than by the public at large—in early April both the American embassy in Moscow and the CIA discounted the idea that the Russians intended war over Berlin—the threat to American interests there was both more real and more immediate than in the case of Czechoslovakia the previous spring. Consequently, the U.S. response over Berlin would be of an order apart from that of the March crisis. This new sense of concern was especially reflected in the President's order to the joint chiefs that they review existing preparations for war with Russia because of the "suddenly urgent immediate issues" raised by Berlin.[43]

"Our Present Shortcomings, Our Worst Fears"

Coincident with the day that the Russians began applying pressure to Berlin, a committee of the joint chiefs met secretly with British military representatives to discuss a crucial detail of plan Broiler—the transfer of American bombers to England in the event of war. As a result of those meetings, tentative plans for that contingency were agreed upon in early April. Despite the fact that what Forrestal had called "rumors and portents of war" dominated newspaper headlines as early as mid-March, the growing tension over Berlin a month later was plainly a cause of greater concern for America's military leaders.[44]

One other, ancillary result of this planning was that preparations for the dispersion of America's nuclear weapons as a measure against sabotage or Russian sneak attack were accelerated at this time. A sign of one critical weakness still afflicting the U.S. atomic-weapons program was the near-cancellation of Operation Sandstone, a second series of atomic tests in the Pacific proposed for later in the month, lest a Pearl Harbor–style attack kill the critically small number of individuals trained to assemble the bombs. Significantly, an objection to Sandstone that had been determining in the decision to cancel the third test of Crossroads —namely, that exploding even a few bombs would cause a substantial dent in the nuclear arsenal—was not considered important in this case. Part of the difference between Sandstone and Crossroads, therefore, was the greater number of bombs being produced by May 1948.[45] An equally compelling cause to proceed with the new series of tests, however, may have been the fact that the design of the principal weapon then in the arsenal remained untested and hence officially still "experimental."[46] After only one additional postponement—to ensure that the Russians would not be able to learn about the weapons' design by airborne sampling of fallout from the explosions—the three bombs of Sandstone were detonated over Eniwetok Atoll between mid-April and mid-May.

Later accounted a "stunning success" by Atomic Energy Commission historians, Sandstone had a significance apart from physics that went unremarked during the tests. Unlike Crossroads, this latest series of atomic explosions prompted no concern from within the administration of a possibly adverse effect upon Soviet-American relations. Indeed, with the virtual end of diplomacy in those relations, and the resultant tendency toward military display as shown by Berlin, the timing of Sandstone now undoubtedly seemed more an asset than a liability to the Truman administration.[47]

The technical perfection of Sandstone apart, Forrestal had little reason to hope that the outstanding problems of strategy and the bomb would be easily resolved in the wake of the March war scare. In the relative lull following the Czech coup the limited and fragile consensus of military planners at Key West had begun to dissolve. In fact, the appearance of unanimity on the part of the joint chiefs began to fade even before

the so-called Key West Agreement was sent to Forrestal for his approval
at the end of April. Behind this growing contentiousness was a dispute
over money and roles, especially as the latter concerned the use of the
atomic bomb.[48]

The latest round of interservice rivalry had been sparked by publication of a secret navy memorandum highly critical of the air force's
air-atomic strategy in Drew Pearson's syndicated column earlier in the
month. This partisan broadside, which gave voice to the until-then
private criticisms of senior navy officers concerning their sister services,
provoked a counterattack the following month with the first of a series
of *Reader's Digest* articles which extolled the virtues of air power and
belittled the navy's potential contribution in the event of war with
Russia.[49]

A more serious consequence of interservice jealousy, however, was
the navy's behind-the-scenes revolt against Grabber. The country's only
emergency war plan to date, Grabber "incorporates all our present shortcomings, our worst fears, and our most glaring weaknesses," charged
Chief of Naval Operations Louis Denfeld in an April 6 memorandum
to the other service chiefs. The plan, he objected, put an exaggerated
emphasis upon the air-atomic offensive, overestimated Russian military
capabilities, and ignored the potential contributions of Allied armed
forces. Unmentioned by Denfeld in this memo, but in fact at the heart
of his objection to Grabber, was its willingness to abandon the Middle
East and the Mediterranean, from which the navy hoped to stage carrier-
launched atomic strikes against Russia in wartime. Even the temporary
loss of these strategic areas denied the navy a role in an air-atomic
offensive.[50]

The navy's attack upon Grabber was not entirely a gratuitous product of interservice squabbling. Specifically, Denfeld objected to two
previously unexamined assumptions of the war plan—that the President
would automatically authorize the use of atomic bombs, and that Russia
would fold up after the initial atomic attack. These objections touched
upon doubts that were also troubling Forrestal.* They were joined in the
defense secretary's mind by a related concern—the absence of any declared American policy on atomic warfare. Such a policy would state the

---

*Forrestal, for example, took the navy–air force feud personally enough to fume at some length
in a letter over the cocktail-party accusation of an airman that the Marine Corps was "only a bitched
up army talking navy lingo."[51]

conditions under which the United States might initiate an atomic war and the types of targets to be destroyed.

The mechanics by which the military services would be given custody of the atomic bombs and authorization to use them, as well as the way in which they would then carry out a nuclear attack against Russia, had preoccupied Forrestal as early as the March crisis, and they remained unanswered questions in its aftermath. At the same time, Russian actions over the previous six weeks had clearly shaken the earliest assumption of civilian and military planners in the Truman administration that war would most probably come about as the result of a Soviet miscalculation. Recent Soviet moves over Czechoslovakia and in Berlin appeared to directly contradict this thesis, prompting even liberals in the government to speculate seriously that Stalin—as Hitler before him—might have a timetable for conquest.

Beyond strategy and the bomb, an equally urgent problem for Forrestal that spring was his confrontation with the President over defense spending. Convinced of the need to limit the military budget to a level he felt would not overstrain the economy, Truman had already decided to hold defense expenditures for fiscal 1950 under $15 billion —a considerable reduction from the $23 billion that Forrestal and the joint chiefs were requesting. Forrestal's plea in April that Truman reconsider the spending limit was quickly rejected by the President, who later reacted to Forrestal's renewed urging with what Eben Ayers remembered was "considerable feeling": "Truman complained that Forrestal [was] trying to put him 'in the middle,' and he 'was getting damn sore.' " Particularly galling to the President had been the effort of Forrestal and the service secretaries to lobby with the administration's Republican opposition in Congress—"as though they were in control"—for an increase in the defense budget. "[Truman] said the whole thing was back where it was before the Key West meeting held last month by Forrestal and the Joint Chiefs of Staff at which they supposedly threshed out all differences and reached agreement on everything." If Forrestal's insubordination continued, he told Ayers, his next course of action was clear: "I'll get someone else."[52]

As if to underscore his point, the President sent Forrestal a letter in mid-May emphasizing his feeling "that it is necessary to accelerate our national defense program at a steady rate rather than to attempt an immediate very large increase," a point he reiterated in another message to the Pentagon two weeks later.[53]

Truman obviously failed to bring Forrestal around to his view. The day following his stormy meeting with the President, Forrestal spoke to the American Newspaper Publishers Association in New York of the need "to bring our total strength up to the point where it more nearly [meets] the realities of the world situation." Plainly sympathizing with the services in the struggle over the budget, the defense secretary proved unable—or unwilling—to bring them into line with Truman's decision. As late as the following October, therefore, he promised the joint chiefs that he would urge Truman to raise the ceiling on military spending.[54]

Forrestal's seemingly willful failure to control the services—whose unrestricted squabbling was an implicit indictment of progress toward unification—shows that it was he rather than the President who was really caught "in the middle" between military demands and budget restrictions. The effect of this dilemma was also seen at this time in the planning for a successor to Grabber. Because of the budgetary ceiling the new plan, like Grabber itself, lacked enough bombers to carry out the projected atomic raids against Russia, or enough troops to evacuate and move the forward bases from England and Egypt if they were to be endangered by the advance of the Red Army.[55]

Additionally symptomatic of the trouble that Forrestal found himself in between the services and the President was the dispute over custody of the atomic bombs. By early summer, consideration by the National Security Council of the policy on atomic warfare, which Forrestal had been urging for more than two months, was still held up pending resolution of the custody issue by the Atomic Energy Commission. Despite the continued importuning of the military, no settlement of the custody question seemed in sight. Certainly neither Truman nor Lilienthal showed any inclination to budge from their opposition to possession of nuclear weapons by the services in peacetime, on the grounds that such a move might undermine civilian control.

With a rapidity which none of those involved could have imagined, however, the developing crisis over Berlin would draw the custody issue to the fore, resolve in practice the dispute over strategy, and finally bring about the long-deferred consideration of American policy concerning use of the atomic bomb.

13

Beau Geste for Berlin

"Russia would now be at the Dardanelles and in the oil fields of Arabia but for our possession of the bomb."
Former Baruch aide John Hancock, speech, June 1948

"You have got to understand that this isn't a military weapon. It is used to wipe out women and children and unarmed people, and not for military uses. . . .
President Truman to Army Secretary Kenneth Royall, July 1948

"A Terrible Prospect"

The Truman administration's response to the crises of 1948 seemed to restore—at least temporarily—the international stability which the Russians had challenged, and was generally seen as a victory for containment. But no less important than this victory for America in the cold war was the unanticipated effect these crises would have toward resolving the unsettled questions of strategy and the bomb. Specifically, the decision made at the peak of the Berlin crisis to dispatch American bombers to bases in Europe within range of the Soviet Union—a military ruse brought about by America's weakness in conventional forces rather than by any change in strategy—established the practice of nuclear deterrence in advance of its theory for U.S. defense planners.

The necessity of providing for the possible use of nuclear weapons also prompted the first U.S. war plan based upon actual capabilities rather than future requirements. Unexpectedly, this plan pointed up the disparity between America's goals in any war with Russia and the military means for achieving them.

The American response to the crises of 1948 resulted at year's end in the codification of a strategy for fighting and winning the cold war under the terms of what John Foster Dulles called "neither war, nor peace." But the mechanics of how the United States would achieve victory in a war with Russia were as vague as ever. The bombs in the nation's nuclear arsenal, for example, remained in the firm custody of its civilian leadership even at the peak of the year's crises. Truman did not dissent from Budget Director James Webb's sentiment of May 1948 that "[t]he idea of turning over custody of atomic bombs to these competing, jealous, insubordinate services, fighting for position with each other, is a terrible prospect."[1]

If hardly the inauguration of the "years of opportunity" that Forrestal predicted, 1948 at least witnessed the meeting and—it seemed to some—the overcoming of the risks he had outlined. The year signaled as well the final integration of the atomic bomb into America's political strategy for dealing with Russia. As had been the case with war planning, however, this feat was accomplished not so much by rational deliberation and debate as by the urgent pressure of necessity.

"No Time to Be Juggling an Atom Bomb Around"

What Forrestal had earlier termed the "realities of the world situation" did not, of course, await decisions in Washington. While the National Security Council deferred a decision on custody of atomic bombs and the policy on atomic warfare, the Russians in Berlin gradually shut off Western access to the city. The long-threatened interdiction of traffic from the West resulted by mid-June in a limited airlift of military supplies into Berlin, but it was immediately clear that this partial measure could not begin to meet the needs of the civilian population if a blockade became complete. One day before that total blockade began —on June 23—Forrestal suggested, as a possible countermove to Soviet provocation, the transfer of American bombers to bases in England within striking distance of Russia.[2]

There may have been, as some thought at the time, a cynical or self-serving aspect to Forrestal's proposal. It did not escape Lilienthal that this reaction to the emergent Berlin crisis might solve both the outstanding questions of custody and atomic-warfare policy in the military's favor. For on the custody issue the civilian AEC would have to surrender the bombs themselves—if not its authority over them—when the bombers flew overseas. Additionally, once the bombs were at exposed forward bases it was virtually inconceivable that the President would not approve their use in the event of war.

Forrestal, in fact, plainly did see an importance to the bomber transfer apart from the immediate exigencies of the Berlin crisis. In his listing of reasons for the move he did not mention Berlin at all, but cited the forward basing of bombers as an important precedent for future intervention in Europe to counter Soviet aggression.[3]

Even if its timing was advantageous, however, the Berlin crisis did not represent for Forrestal merely the means to an end in his conflict with the administration. In fact, the notion of transferring B-29s to advance bases in a time of crisis—the atomic-age equivalent of gunboat diplomacy—was not new with Berlin. Some weeks previously, Forrestal had urged that the administration send some bombers and their crews to Greece, then in the midst of a civil war, "for training purposes." While thus not unaware of the move's diplomatic significance in the case of Berlin, he also thought the forward basing of bombers was a practical decision long overdue in the nation's preparations for war.

The symbolic step of sending the bomb to Britain may, as well, have been the only action short of beginning such a war that the United States could take concerning Berlin. Since the National Security Council had stopped short of urging actual military mobilization as a reaction to the blockade, and since universal military training was now virtually a dead issue in Congress, the courses of action open to the United States in Berlin were severely circumscribed.

As if to underscore that fact, the Russians sidetracked two trains sent toward Berlin by the American command in a test of the blockade. The trains were forced to withdraw ignominiously after remaining on sidings outside the city for several days. A proposed response to the Soviet encirclement urged by Clay—the sending of an Allied armored column down the principal access road to Berlin—received little favor from the British and the French, and was subsequently rejected outright by the joint chiefs as involving "the grave danger of war" and being "unlikely to succeed." A more ambitious suggestion by General Curtis LeMay to bomb the Soviet troops manning the blockade—presumably with conventional weapons—was considered briefly by the joint chiefs but dismissed.[4]

It was because the United States lacked the means for any more appropriate action in Berlin, and not as any conscious expression of a new strategy, that Truman approved the order sending sixty B-29 bombers to bases in England and a smaller number to Germany at a hastily convened meeting of military and civilian advisers in the Pentagon on June 28. The transfer of the bombers was undertaken along with an expansion of the airlift begun earlier to meet Berlin's minimum civilian needs for food and fuel. Even then, second thoughts on the part of Secretary of State Marshall and others in the administration, who feared that this move might only provoke the Russians, delayed the B-29s' flight across the Atlantic until mid-July.[5]

The symbolic importance of this gesture was not underplayed by the administration, despite the anticlimactic delay. Nor was it lost upon those journalists who chronicled the event. Most newspaper accounts of the bomber transfer, however, either missed or glossed over a crucial point of the story—that the B-29s flown overseas actually carried no nuclear weapons. While pointedly described in government press releases as "atomic-capable," the B-29s sent to Britain and Germany had not yet been modified to carry the kind of atomic bomb that then was the mainstay of America's nuclear arsenal. There was also no indication that the necessary modification was carried out at the overseas bases, or that any of the indispensable bomb-assembly teams was sent overseas with the planes. Additional evidence that the administration's celebrated bombers-to-Britain strategy was a conscious ruse comes from Lilienthal's admission at this time that the AEC had not granted custody of atomic bombs to the military. It is virtually certain, therefore, that whereas the "atomic bombers" went to bases within striking range of Russia in 1948, the atomic bomb did not.*

Certainly this situation was known and approved by the President. Truman had shown a consistently cautious attitude toward actual use of the bomb since the end of the war against Japan. His steadfast refusal to allow military custody of the weapon was part of this, as was his rejoinder, at the height of tension in the Berlin crisis, to Army Secretary Royall's cavalier argument that *not* using the bomb "doesn't make any

---

**Aviation Week was one of the few publications to note that the B-29s were probably not equipped with atomic bombs, although it observed reassuringly that the weapons themselves were only a day away on American soil and that the bombers and their crews were "ready for business." Truman was well aware of the significance of sending atomic bombs outside the U.S. In October 1946 he had angrily branded a "lie" Drew Pearson's report that the U.S. had shipped bombs to England without detonators. He did not deny a similar report during the Berlin crisis, however, even though the non-nuclear as well as the nuclear components of the bombs remained in the U.S. at this time. Budget Director James Webb recommended against sending the actual bombs to Europe since the military could get the weapons from the U.S. "immediately" if necessary. The fact that neither of the two B-29 groups sent to England was the 509th—the bomber group that had dropped the original atomic bombs, and the only one then specifically designated to carry nuclear weapons— suggests that Truman took Webb's advice even further and sent bombers that were not capable of carrying atomic bombs.[6]

sense." "You have got to understand that this isn't a military weapon," Truman told Royall. "It is used to wipe out women and children and unarmed people, and not for military uses. . . . You have got to understand that I have got to think about the effect of such a thing on international relations. This is no time to be juggling an atom bomb around."[7]

Royall was evidently untouched by Truman's appeal. He urged Forrestal to "have several A-bombs available (in England and elsewhere) for immediate use . . . such use [to] be left entirely to the military."[8]

If not the bomb itself, it was at least the explicit threat of the bomb's use that the administration now juggled around in the case of Berlin. But this threat was carefully measured. While allowing "familiarization flights" for the bomber crews over the European countryside, the National Security Council directed that the air force should not conduct "mass maneuvers over Germany or the Mediterranean area." A suggestion that B-29s be used to fly cargo into Berlin was rejected by the council on the grounds that it might be misinterpreted by the Russians and provoke an "actively hostile" response from them. "Soviet sensitivity on this point has been indicated by reports that Soviet air defenses are alerted whenever a B-29 takes to the air in Germany," the army noted.[9]

Whereas the Russians probably knew of the subtle deception being practiced in the skies over Europe, and almost certainly knew by espionage that the U.S. nuclear arsenal remained small, the important feature of the bombers-to-Britain strategy was that it worked—or at least that many Americans believed it worked. By the end of July the absence of any Soviet military countermove to the airlift that had effectively broken the blockade of Berlin was attributed in substantial part to the deterrent effect of the "atomic-capable" bombers within range of Russian cities.

"We Have Won Round One with the Russians"

The success of the Berlin airlift, and the failure of another flare-up in Soviet-American relations to materialize, prompted a new expression of confidence in the administration—even from its critics. "We have won round one with the Russians," John Foster Dulles declared prematurely in late June.[10] For Forrestal and others not normally given to ebullient optimism concerning relations with the Russians, the Berlin crisis had been a sobering experience, one in which tenacity as well as containment had been tested and proven. In many ways Washington's response to the crisis had shown the weaknesses rather than the strengths of the administration's—and America's—position.

Chief among these weaknesses had been the *ad hoc* and even haphazard coordination of views concerning what to do about Berlin. Though Truman apparently had a high opinion of the Joint Chiefs of Staff—at one point during the crisis he claimed that the South would have won the Civil War if it had had such an organization—there was virtually no effort to solicit their opinion when the blockade began. It was only as individuals and not as a group that the country's military leaders gave their professional—often conflicting—views. The stark alternative that the joint chiefs had offered the National Security Council in the crisis—mobilization of U.S. forces for war or withdrawal from Berlin—clearly did not appeal to the council's members.[11]

More disturbing than this bureaucratic confusion had been the frank recognition by military and civilian experts alike of the limits upon what steps the administration could take over Berlin. While both the National Security Council and the joint chiefs agreed that a military probe of the blockade should be only a last resort, there was no unanimity concerning military or other measures to end the encirclement. Among the "quasi-military" moves considered by the council in late July was the arrest of communist leaders in western Germany, and a remarkable "Potemkin village" strategy of increasing "the magnitude of the strategic air threat in the minds of the Russians" by making them think that the United States had more bombers at European bases than it really did.[12]

Forrestal also now feared the prospect of a "dangerous complacency" on the part of the government. However successful the bombers-to-Britain strategy had been as a symbol of American resolve, it had nonetheless failed to break the blockade itself, or even to noticeably moderate the behavior of the Russians in the subsequent negotiations on restoring access to the city. Though the decision to base the bombers in Europe had again emphasized the preeminent role of the bomb in American military strategy—thirty more B-29s were sent to Britain in August, after the crisis had substantially eased—how or even whether the weapons would be used in a future war remained as ambiguous a question after the bomber transfer as before. Significantly, only the shadow of deterrence had crossed the Atlantic. The substance—as insiders like Forrestal were well aware—remained behind.[13] Proof to Forrestal of the complacency the end of the crisis engendered was Truman's adamant rejection of his renewed pleas that the administration bring U.S. capabilities in line with American commitments by increasing the military budget.

Spurred on by the Berlin crisis, Forrestal, joined by Army Secretary Royall, urged the joint chiefs and the National Security Council to complete the independent studies of the nation's military preparedness that they had begun at his request the previous June. He again pleaded with the President to resolve two crucial issues concerning the atomic bomb still outstanding in the wake of the Berlin crisis—the mechanics for transferring to the military actual custody of the weapons, and the administration's policy on atomic warfare.

The prospect that the military might not be able to use the atomic bomb in a war with Russia had haunted Forrestal for some months. An informal poll he had taken of visitors to his office in mid-September indicated almost unanimous agreement that the bomb should be used in a major war. Forrestal was, as well, probably reassured if not cheered by Secretary of State Marshall's opinion that "the American people would execute you if you did not use the bomb in the event of war." A less direful confirmation of public support for use of the bomb was forthcoming in mid-September with a top-secret State Department memorandum which speculated that domestic opinion in wartime "might force the use of atomic weapons, even if the chief executive were inclined against it."*

Despite his remonstrance to Royall about "juggling" an atomic bomb, Truman had never indicated an unwillingness to use the weapon against the Russians. Indeed, he had earlier told Forrestal that his steadfast refusal to grant custody of the bomb to the military was justified on pragmatic grounds—lest "some dashing lieutenant colonel decide when

---

*Marshall himself evidently had some reservations about using the bomb. At the peak of the Berlin crisis, his aide Gordon Arneson suggested to him that the United States use an atomic bomb to break the blockade. According to Arneson, Marshall asked him: "If we were to atomic bomb the Soviet Union, what targets would you choose? Would you bomb Leningrad, with the Hermitage?"

When Arneson conceded that he might spare Leningrad, Marshall objected: "But if you're really serious about this why is there any question?" He advised Arneson "to go home and think about it."[14]

would be the proper time to drop one." But in mid-July he confessed that there were also political considerations behind his decision on custody. The Democratic national convention, meeting that summer in Kansas City, pointedly approved a resolution which emphasized continued civilian supremacy in matters dealing with atomic energy.[15]

As in almost everything concerning the atomic bomb, the custody issue confronted Truman with a difficult choice. Possibly in an effort to placate Forrestal on the subject, he had promised the secretary that his decision against giving the military custody of the weapons could be reviewed after the election. But Truman told a different story, by Lilienthal's account, to adviser Clark Clifford in summer 1948: "As long as I am in the White House I will be opposed to taking atomic weapons away from the hands they are now in, and they will only be delivered to the military by particular order of the President issued at a time when they are needed."*

Since 1945, the problem of custody had kept the atomic bomb in a kind of limbo. Initially stored unassembled in a basement at Los Alamos, the bombs were later moved to an air force base outside Albuquerque, and at one point—presumably to guard against surprise attack or saboteurs—were even kept near the nation's gold at Fort Knox. The time required to assemble and transport the bombs to B-29s capable of carrying them to targets within Russia meant that they were never less than two days from being ready for use, and until 1952 the cumbersome process of granting authorization for their use meant that this delay would probably be considerably longer.[17]

In light of these facts, Forrestal's concern with the mechanics by which the military would be given custody of the bombs in time of war was not unwarranted. Moreover, with the custody issue still in abeyance by fall 1948, members of the National Security Council announced themselves unable to decide on a policy concerning atomic warfare.[18]

---

*Truman was almost able to keep his promise to Clifford. In response to the outbreak of the Korean War, an agreement was reached for transferring custody to the military in summer 1950, under a plan worked out between the AEC and the Pentagon. According to another arrangement made in June 1952, authorization to use the weapons would be given by the President directly to the AEC chairman or a commissioner. If all of the above were killed by a surprise attack upon Washington, custody would be transferred by the AEC's manager of operations in Albuquerque to the military upon notice from the commanding general of the Armed Forces Special Weapons Project that the President had previously authorized the bomb's use. It was not until July 1950 that Truman allowed even the non-nuclear components of atomic bombs to be sent overseas.[16]

However, at least one pressing question was finally approaching resolution at this time—whether Truman would authorize use of the atomic
bomb in war.

"The Chiefest Weapon in Europe's Arsenal"

As late as May 1948, Truman had instructed the joint chiefs that
military planning was not to foreclose the possibility that nuclear weapons would come under international control in the United Nations, and
hence would not be used in a war. By mid-July the Joint Strategic
Planning Committee had consequently prepared an "alternative medium-range emergency war plan," code-named Intermezzo. Before Intermezzo was completed, however, the administration had all but conceded
that it would never be used.[19]

Even those entrusted with pursuing international control in the
UN now privately acknowledged the hopelessness of their task. Efforts
in 1947 and 1948 by Albert Einstein and Niels Bohr to rekindle direct
negotiations with Russia on controlling the bomb had been politely
acknowledged but privately derided by the State Department. Bohr's
proposal for "openness" was essentially similar to the recommendation
that he had made to Roosevelt and Churchill in the entirely different
setting of 1944. Einstein's more ambitious idea of a world government
prompted a State Department official to comment that the famous
scientist "seemed naive in the field of international politics and mass
human relations. The man who popularized the concept of a fourth
dimension could think in only two of them in considerations of World
Government."[20]

Since Russia's rejection of the Baruch plan at the end of 1946,
American efforts in the United Nations Atomic Energy Commission
had been directed at preventing the Russians from merging the issue of
international control and disarmament, thereby scoring a propaganda
coup.[21] The early proponents had, for the most part, long since abandoned the cause. Dean Acheson, exhausted, embittered, and about to
return to his private law practice, had suggested that the United States
join with the other Western nations possessing uranium in an atomic
consortium directed against the Soviet Union. Taking over the question
of international control from Acheson in early 1948, George Kennan
likewise advocated abandonment of the Baruch plan, but recommended

that it be replaced by the sort of direct and secret negotiations with Russia once intended by Stimson and Byrnes, and later sought by Einstein and Bohr.[22]

The previous summer the joint chiefs had decisively rejected the atomic-league idea first proposed to them by Bernard Baruch and Fred Searls. Part of their objection was that such a league would not work and that American atomic secrets would flow to Russia through its member states, particularly France. "Even the possible benefits to be derived from world opinion are discounted since the United States has already served world opinion incredibly well by appearing as a supplicant in a seller's market when we have the only stock to sell," they concluded. A more fundamental problem foreseen by them was the barely disguised purpose of a nuclear consortium: "From the security point of view the realistic reason for forming such an Atomic Development Authority would be that we intended to initiate atomic warfare against the nonmembers of the ADA as quickly as we could accumulate sufficient atomic weapons to give a reasonable assurance of success. It is, however, highly unlikely, if not impossible that the American people could be conditioned to accept the initiation of such an offensive war."[23]

Nothing either in American opinion or Russian behavior had changed since 1947 to alter this view. Indeed, even the most benevolent interpretation of the rationale behind an atomic league—to reform Russia for admission to what Conant had termed the "nuclear union" —no longer made sense in light of the growing evidence that Russia did not share enough common ground with the West for a compromise, and was not intimidated by exclusion from the Anglo-American atomic club.

It was by default that Russia had been excluded from the nuclear club with its rejection of the Baruch plan. In May 1948—just as Truman directed the joint chiefs to prepare for the possibility of a nuclear-free future—the UN Atomic Energy Commission itself abandoned the pretense that Russia might ever be admitted to that club by adjourning *sine die*. Initiated by the American representative on that committee, this move spared the United States the opprobrium of unilaterally breaking off the UN talks. Thus the interim "sacred trust" which Truman had announced in the weeks after Hiroshima would be ended only when Russia got the bomb.[24]

The drafting of the non-nuclear Intermezzo had actually underscored that it was now international control and not atomic warfare that had become unthinkable. Intermezzo ironically showed the degree to which the bomb had become virtually indispensable in U.S. military planning. While its authors conceded that greater use of Allied troops might somewhat offset the strategic disadvantage of not being able to employ nuclear weapons, therefore, they agreed that victory would almost certainly require eventual use of the bomb in quantity.[25]

Beyond Intermezzo, there was another subtle but significant shift in the joint chiefs' war planning toward increasing reliance on the atomic bomb. Partly as a response to navy objections concerning Grabber, the joint chiefs had begun work on a replacement emergency war plan. This latest plan, Fleetwood,* not surprisingly envisioned a much larger role for the navy than Grabber in blockading Russia's coastline and bombing Soviet cities. But there were other important departures from previous planning as well. Under Fleetwood, an effort would be made to hold Russian forces at the Rhine instead of at an unspecified line west of that river. A major counteroffensive would be launched no later than the second year of the war to regain the Middle East oil fields on which the navy and U.S. mobilization depended. But perhaps the most significant part of the new plan was its understanding of the role to be played by the air-atomic offensive. Thus Fleetwood finally acknowledged what had only been implied in Broiler or Grabber—a sudden nuclear attack against Russia might be decisive, and could obviate a protracted, quasi-conventional war.[26]

The changes contained in Fleetwood also reflected the rapidly increasing size of the American nuclear arsenal. Whereas Pincher provided for attacking twenty Russian cities with fifty atomic bombs, Fleetwood would destroy seventy cities with 133 bombs in a single massive attack, emphasizing "the destructive and psychological power of atomic weapons." The key role of the bomb in Fleetwood showed how U.S. military planners had now made a virtue of necessity. An industrial mobilization plan for the war envisioned by Fleetwood concluded that even if the necessary manpower and matériel were available at the outbreak of war, there would still be a 40 percent shortage of aircraft in the second year of hostilities. A short, decisive nuclear attack upon Russia was not only desirable from the American standpoint, therefore,

---

*As with other war plans, Fleetwood went through a series of name changes—as Halfmoon and Doublestar, for example—even though the plan itself remained fundamentally unchanged in its conception. Here the original title will be used through various updatings and revisions of the plan.

but a requirement for victory. As if to underscore the importance of Fleetwood's departure from earlier military thinking, it was quickly approved by the joint chiefs and circulated to the various services on September 1. Conversely, the ratification of Intermezzo even "for planning purposes" was indefinitely deferred. On September 13, 1948, the joint chiefs instructed their planning committee that all future emergency war plans were "to have Fleetwood concept."[27]

In addition to the administration's open abandonment of international control and the military's promulgation of Fleetwood, there was still another—albeit indirect—indication of how the atomic bomb and expectations concerning its use had come to dominate American strategy after the Berlin crisis.

While the wellsprings of the future North Atlantic Treaty Organization can be traced to a June 1948 Senate resolution allowing U.S. participation in regional security arrangements for Europe, it was not until the following month that talks began in London on the establishment of the so-called "Western Union" defense pact that would become NATO.

The American vision of that treaty fell far short of realization at London because of a now-familiar block—the lack of any declared U.S. policy on atomic warfare. In a study prepared by the National Security Council for the guidance of American representatives at the NATO talks, U.S. delegates were admonished not to mention either "the policy or plans of the United States with respect to the employment of atomic weapons in warfare." For as long as that issue was undecided, NATO itself remained a concept only.[28]

The London talks tacitly acknowledged what the administration itself had yet to announce—that the atomic bomb had become the key to U.S. guarantees of European security, as a counterweight to Russia's massive military manpower.

This was a fact widely recognized, if not openly admitted in the administration. Though no longer in the government, Baruch was expressing a view certainly dominant there when he wrote to Secretary of State Marshall in fall 1948 that the "atomic bomb—in American hands —may well be all that protects the peoples of Europe and the Near East from another war. It is the chiefest weapon in Europe's arsenal." The day before writing the letter to Marshall, Baruch had been even more emphatic on this theme in correspondence with Dulles: "The only thing that stands in the way of the overrunning of Europe today is the atomic bomb. . . . When once we outlaw that, there is nothing to stop the Russian advance." Baruch shared this view with a former aide. "Russia would now be at the Dardanelles and in the oil fields of Arabia but for our possession of the bomb," John Hancock had told a Bryn Mawr graduating class two months before.[29]

"Russia Has Few Cities to Lose"

The hiatus of decision-making on the bomb which followed in the wake of the Berlin crisis was finally ended in September 1948, with completion of NSC-30, the long-awaited-and-delayed "Policy on Atomic Warfare." The custody issue that had initially held up the drafting of the policy was itself deferred for later resolution following an August meeting of military leaders with Forrestal at the Naval War College in Newport, Rhode Island.[30] Another cause of delay had been the need of its air force authors to coordinate this policy with a multitude of interests in the administration—including the State Department, the National Security Resources Board, and the CIA. Perhaps because of its varied origins, NSC-30 did not provide answers to all the questions that had preoccupied Forrestal since the spring, and that still to some extent held U.S. military planning in thrall.

Notably, it dodged the issue of whether the U.S. government should publicly declare its willingness to use nuclear weapons in the event of war. Acknowledging that "public opinion must be recognized as a factor of considerable importance" in that decision, the National Security Council concluded that such a declaration in peacetime would be both premature and politically inadvisable. The authors of NSC-30 feared not only that prior announcement of an intention to use the bomb in war might occasion a misguided public discussion—one in which questions of morality rather than of security would become preeminent —but that such a debate during peacetime could create enough doubt in the minds of Russian leaders "to provoke exactly that Soviet aggression which it is fundamentally U.S. policy to avert." The Russians "should in fact never be given the slightest reason to believe the U.S. would even consider not to use atomic weapons against them if necessary."[31]

In other matters concerning the bomb, there could be no mistaking the administration's intention. NSC-30 finally recognized that American plans for the defense and even the economic recovery of Europe relied first upon the bomb. That weapon, it noted, "offers the present major counterbalance to the ever-present threat of . . . Soviet military power." There was equally a new frankness—and a reflection of the administration's recent decision to abandon international control—in NSC-30's conclusion that any "attempt now or in the future . . . to prohibit or . . . to qualify the employment of atomic bombs could result catastrophically."

While the language of NSC-30 was vague on how a nuclear war could—or should—be fought by the United States, it at least answered a fundamental question worrying the nation's military leaders. As one State Department analyst wrote of NSC-30's implications: "If war of major proportions breaks out, the National Military Establishment will have little alternative but to recommend to the Chief Executive that atomic weapons be used, and he will have no alternative [but] to go along. Thus, in effect, the paper actually decides the issue."[32]

As if to underscore that point, Truman told Forrestal at a Cabinet meeting three days later that "he prayed . . . he would never have to make such a decision [to use the bomb], but that if it became necessary, no one need have a misgiving but that he would."[33]

Truman's personal assurance aside, there were still major uncertainties concerning the interpretation by future Presidents of U.S. policy toward the bomb, uncertainties that had not been resolved by NSC-30. What it had broadly termed America's "political responsibility" in a war was left, for example, unexplained and undefined. To one administration planner this responsibility was limited to warning the Russian people that the United States would use the bomb in a war.[34]

Perhaps the most important issue left unresolved by NSC-30 was not whether atomic bombs would be used, but—as the State Department critique observed—"rather when and how such weapons should be used." The circumstances under which the United States might actually initiate a nuclear war and the types of targets then to be destroyed were purposely left for military planners to resolve. But they were also questions at the heart of U.S. policy toward the bomb, the State Department objected. "Should we, for example, in the event of war, begin by bombing major centers of population in enemy territory or start with smaller centers important for transportation or specific industries?" The bomb and the nature of modern war had blurred other distinctions as well. "Depending upon conditions in the enemy country, the bombing of

major population centers or centers having special sentimental significance might mobilize popular sentiment for resistance in a manner to
prolong the war"—the consideration that had prompted Stimson to
strike Kyoto from Groves' target list of Japanese cities.

After Intermezzo, there could obviously be no serious consideration
of a U.S. policy renouncing the use of nuclear weapons in a war. Even
the author of the State Department critique of NSC-30 conceded that
the questions the policy raised "should be answered not so much on the
basis of humanitarian principles as from a practical weighing of the
long-run advantage to this country." But there was also, as that critique
pointed out, no recognition of the fact that an unsettled ethical dilemma
lay at the heart of NSC-30 and of America's increasing reliance upon
the bomb. What the authors of the "Policy on Atomic Warfare" recognized as the need for a "blending" of strategic with moral and political
considerations in wartime was not resolved there. Nor was any solution
evident to the critics of NSC-30. The State Department analyst could
only observe somewhat wistfully about the ethical dilemma of NSC-30:
"I wonder if it would not be helpful to our National Military Establishment if this thought were more fully developed and guide lines—if any
are possible—laid out for aid in strategic planning?"

Lacking any more definite guidance from civilian authority, American
military leaders had already begun to supplant the amorphous "political
responsibility" alluded to in NSC-30 with more narrow and pragmatic
considerations in their planning. The "Policy on Atomic Warfare" did
not resolve—but may actually have exacerbated—armed services compe-
tition over the budget, custody of the bomb, and the definition of
wartime roles. An air force paper at the end of the year on the "doctrine
of atomic air warfare" showed that confusion persisted in U.S. military
thought on the place of nuclear deterrence in American strategy: "The
objective of United States military forces in being is to prevent the
initiation of warfare by an aggressor, or failing in that, to win the war."[35]

Notably, the prospect that the United States might initiate a nuclear war with an attack upon Russian cities—an idea encompassed by
the planning of the joint chiefs as early as summer 1947—was in no way
proscribed by the policy on atomic warfare. To be sure, such an attack
was never envisioned as preventive war *per se*. Thus the joint chiefs
acknowledged the need for prior approval from the President and Congress. And Truman himself was convinced, as he told Leahy, that the

American people would never tolerate the use of the bomb for "aggressive purposes."[36] But the fact that striking the first blow was never specifically ruled out shows the disparity between actual military planning and the "blending" of strategic with moral and political considerations called for by NSC-30.

The details of contemporary U.S. war plans, as well, point up this gap between policy and planning. The air force component of Fleetwood, readied by fall 1948, proposed that virtually the entire U.S. arsenal of atomic bombs be dropped upon Russian cities in the first month of the war. Another option in the plan was an "atomic blitz," utilizing every American atomic bomb and bomber in a single cataclysmic attack. In such a blitz, Moscow alone would be the target of eight bombs meant to devastate forty square miles of that city; another seven bombs would be allocated to destroy Leningrad. If the war lasted as long as two years, approximately two hundred more atomic bombs would be directed against Russia, obliterating as much as 40 percent of Soviet industry and killing nearly 7 million people. The initial air-atomic offensive, air force planners expected, would stem the Russian advance in Europe and the Middle East, and "could well lead to Soviet capitulation."[37]

Remarkably, there seemed little appreciation in the air force's plan of the possibilities for deterring further Soviet military operations once the war had broken out, and even less of a belief that the war could be limited. Nor did the plan appear to see the illogic of foreclosing tacit negotiations with the enemy by bombing his major cities and governmental centers at the outset. Indeed, the avowed goal of the Strategic Air Command's Curtis LeMay—the capability "to deliver the entire stockpile of atomic bombs, if made available, in a single massive attack" —assumed that not only diplomacy but even strategy itself ended if (or when) deterrence failed.[38]

The willingness of U.S. military planners to consider attacking Russian cities at the initiation of a war may have been prompted in part by their knowledge that the Soviets would be unable to respond in kind until they too had the bomb—a consideration not mentioned, but almost certainly recognized by drafters of war plans. There is an ironic counterpoint to the air force plan and to NSC-30, therefore, in the conclusion of a separate State Department study that even with the atomic bomb the Russians would be unlikely to strike American cities at the outbreak of war. Presumably, another reason why air force planners intended to bomb cities first was the obvious vulnerability of such targets and the limited number of atomic bombs in the U.S. arsenal. The peculiar vulnerability of the Russians to a strategy aimed at destroying their cities was a point stressed by the State Department study: "Russia has few cities to lose. . . . Only Moscow and Leningrad could conceivably house the highly centralized administrative services of the Soviet Government for any length of time; and they, like all other Soviet cities, are desperately over-crowded."[39]

American policy and strategy on atomic warfare had evolved by increments throughout 1948. NSC-30 determined that the United States would use atomic weapons in the event of a war with Russia—even a war that the United States itself initiated. Fleetwood specified that the bombs would be used first to destroy cities and kill civilians in order to force Soviet capitulation. Since the evacuation of Europe by U.S. troops would be delayed or deferred altogether under Fleetwood—pending the outcome of the air-atomic offensive—there was now the evident hope, if not yet the expectation, that this blow alone might compel the Russians to surrender.[40]

Thus the bomb had at last become the "winning weapon" on which Allied victory would depend in the event of war—a weapon so important to military planning that even discussion of not using it in war was branded dangerous.

"A Situation Which Is Not War"

It was neither as a winning weapon nor as a determinant of foreign policy that the atomic bomb briefly became an issue in Truman's 1948 presidential campaign. During the tense summer of that year, while the Russian blockade and the answering American airlift continued in Berlin, the matter of Soviet espionage had once again dominated the headlines of U.S. newspapers, given impetus by the arrest of State Department employee Alger Hiss as an alleged Russian spy. The campaign of Republican Thomas Dewey had focused upon the domestic problems plaguing the Truman presidency—recurrent strikes, unemployment, and recession—until the Hiss case and espionage charges leveled against nuclear scientist Edward Condon revived popular concern for the safety of the "atomic secret."[41]

Truman's celebrated dismissal of the resurgent spy hysteria as a "red herring" became itself a major issue of that campaign. The actual paucity of evidence for the allegations of spying did not prevent such charges from gaining a wide currency among the public in the mounting atmosphere of crisis. Truman himself had unwittingly given credence to the secrecy mania when he established the President's Temporary Commission on Employee Loyalty shortly after the 1946 elections. His reason for creating the commission, he explained at the time, was "to take the ball away from Parnell Thomas," chairman of the House Un-American Activities Committee and the foremost congressional "red-baiter." However, the climate of suspicion had so spread in the country after the administration's adoption of the hard line toward Russia that Truman's "temporary" commission became permanent in March 1947.[42]

It was this climate that caused Groves to be again called before Congress in September to testify on spies. Blaming atomic espionage upon an unnamed foreign power "and its misguided and traitorous domestic sympathizers," Groves' testimony became a *cause célèbre.* Significantly, his assertion earlier in the year that the Russians would be unable to build atomic bombs in quantity "even with possession of the Manhattan project's blueprints" went virtually unremarked in the ensuing controversy.*

Behind renewed charges concerning Russian spying on the bomb was the House Committee on Un-American Activities. HUAC's fall 1948 report on Soviet espionage clearly had as its target not the supposed Russian agents named therein but the political future of the Truman administration—a fact which compelled the Justice Department to issue a rebuttal deploring the "political gymnastics" that had motivated the report.[44]

The "political gymnastics" of Groves, HUAC, and other would-be prosecutors of supposed Russian spies were, of course, insufficient to defeat Truman, whose victory over Dewey confounded pollsters and pundits alike. But the 1948 campaign made clear that no presidential honeymoon would follow the election, as it had Truman's original accession to the office. Indeed, Truman's entire second term would be

___

*Groves' crucial caveat—"in quantity"—suggests that he was still counting on what he assumed was the West's preclusive monopoly of atomic raw materials to ensure that the Russians, even with U.S. blueprints, would not be able to build a stockpile of bombs. In this same article, however, he deprecated Soviet achievements in science and technology and dismissed claims that the Russians were making progress toward building a bomb. The latter was a task, Groves asserted, for which the Russians were "technologically and even psychologically unequipped."[43]

haunted by so many allegations and disclosures concerning Soviet espionage—some of them genuine—that the 1948 campaign would appear in retrospect but a prelude to the later ordeal.

Conceivably one reason for Truman's upset of Dewey may have been the apparently diminishing prospect of war with Russia, which was widely perceived as a sign of the success of the administration's hard-line policy. Despite the continued wrangling of Soviet and American negotiators over the details of Western access to Berlin, that city by the end of 1948 had ceased to be the focus of a war scare. Symbolic of this easing of tension was a mid-November report by the National Security Council which urged that the dispute over Berlin be settled through the United Nations. The easing of tensions, of course, did not mean the end of the cold war. The air force showed it was not unmindful of this fact by its November assurance to the joint chiefs that, if necessary, it could simultaneously sustain Berlin with an airlift and launch the planned air-atomic offensive against the Soviet Union.[45]

Indicative, too, of the calm returning to the conduct of U.S. foreign policy after the tumultuous spring and summer was General Lucius Clay's curious admission to Forrestal on November 13 that "we were unduly apprehensive about the Russians," who Clay now believed could be held at the Rhine if they invaded western Europe. Since the Cassandra-like Clay had been the first to cry wolf in the war scare of the previous March, and had only been restrained by Forrestal and Truman over Berlin the following July, the confident self-assurance of his latest insight must have been particularly galling to Forrestal.[46]

Even Marshall—who throughout the year had been concerned that the United States not "provoke" the Russians into military action—now expressed optimism for the future. His change in attitude had been partly motivated, he confided to Forrestal, by his belief that "the Soviets are beginning to realize for the first time that the United States would really use the atomic bomb against them in the event of war."[47] Despite the upbeat attitude of Marshall and Clay, Forrestal—always the Jeremiah of the Truman administration—was characteristically unwilling to relax at the evidence that the year-long crisis in Soviet-American relations might be ending. His outlook remained essentially unchanged from the opinion he had expressed the previous October: "We are looking at a situation which is not war, but certainly is a lot grayer than it was last May."[48]

With the adoption of a policy on atomic warfare, and Truman's assurance that he would authorize the use of nuclear weapons in war, the ambiguity remaining in America's situation was primarily political, not military. The lack of clarity which still afflicted America's political strategy concerned the long-term solution to the threat posed by Russia. Responding at year's end to Forrestal's repeated entreaties for a "comprehensive statement of national policy," the National Security Council and George Kennan's Policy Planning Staff in the State Department independently drafted versions of a program which attempted to define containment in pragmatic terms. Unlike the strident call for mobilization of the nation's moral defenses represented by NSC-7, this statement was meant to put forward a specific program for American victory in the cold war.

In their version, the National Security Council posited a continuing—albeit uneasy—peace between the United States and Russia. But it made clear that this peace was to be only a prosecution of the cold war by nonmilitary means. The principal American objective remained to "reduce the power and influence of Moscow" so that Russia would no longer constitute a threat to U.S. interests. Preferably, this would be brought about by forcing a fundamental change in Soviet policies. The United States could encourage this change, the council believed, by encouraging "federalism" among the separate ethnic nationalities within Russia and independence among the communist regimes of eastern Europe. The result of this approach might be, it argued in a curious and unexplained phrase, to compel the Russian government "to recognize the practical undesirability of acting on the basis of its present concepts and the necessity of behaving, at least outwardly, as though it were the converse of those concepts that were true."[49]

This intended transformation of Russia was to be effected "by means short of war," and without necessarily resulting in the overthrow of the Russian government. On this last point, however, the members of the National Security Council were ambiguous. If Soviet communism collapsed as a result of American efforts, they wrote, "we would view this development without regret; but we would not assume responsibility for having sought or brought it about."

The changes in Russia to be brought about as a condition of American victory in a war would be correspondingly more ambitious. These would certainly include the "liberalization" of governments in eastern

Europe, the dismantling of Russia's military establishment, and the dissolution of the Communist Party as the unchallenged political authority in the Soviet state. But the peace settlement would not include any specific postwar border arrangements, the granting of independence to any national minority, or even necessarily the "decommunization" of liberated territory. In a lesson seemingly learned from the previous war, the council eschewed the "wartime emotionalism" that had ultimately resulted in disappointment following previous victories.

Most remarkable about this study was its authors' frank recognition of what America—even as the victor in a nuclear war—*"could not hope to achieve"* in the war's aftermath. Unlike Germany and Japan in the Second World War, Russia would not be required to surrender unconditionally: "We must recognize that whatever settlement we finally achieve must be a *political* settlement, *politically* negotiated." Significantly, the council thought unconditional surrender not only militarily unfeasible but politically unwise, insofar as there "is a strong possibility that if we were to take the utmost care, within limits of military feasibility, not to antagonize the Soviet people by military policies which would inflict inordinate hardship and cruelties upon them, there would be an extensive disintegration of Soviet power during the course of a war which progressed favorably from our standpoint."

This theme of limitations upon what America could hope to accomplish by military force was carried even further in the Policy Planning Staff's statement of national policy, which circulated within the State Department only a week after the National Security Council completed work on its own version. The State Department study—bearing Kennan's imprint—was more an alternative to than an elaboration of the council's effort, nonetheless. It deemphasized military confrontation with the Soviet Union and stressed instead the peculiarly ideological nature of the cold war. The vision of Russia it projected was thus at odds with that of the council and of most military analysts. "[P]hysical destruction was far more severe than is generally realized in the west . . . the war-weariness of the Soviet peoples is as great, if not greater, than in the case of any other of the major countries," Kennan wrote. This view also promoted the novel, even heretical, theory that the Russians with the bomb "may actually prove to be more tractable in negotiation . . . and no longer feel that they are negotiating at so great a disadvantage." Armed with the bomb, the Russians would be restrained by "political factors" from attacking American cities in a first strike, due to "a certain political reluctance on the Soviet side to resort without provocation to methods of mass destruction aimed against civilian elements in other countries."[50]

Kennan's study made its most notable departure from the common wisdom concerning Russia by concluding that the Russians had neither a timetable for conquest nor the expectation of inevitable war with capitalism. As before, his concern was with Russian intentions rather than capabilities. He recommended consequently that the United States put its energy behind preparations designed to deter the long-term danger of a deliberate Soviet attack. Specifically, Kennan's analysis rejected the "peak danger" argument promoted within military circles, which contended that war was likely to occur whenever Russia obtained a sufficient number of bombs to attack the United States with a reasonable chance of success. The notion of "peak danger" had been used by Forrestal and the joint chiefs to justify their requests for an increase in the military budget. Kennan's proposal urged that the emphasis of U.S. military planning be shifted from a sudden emergency buildup of forces to a gradual, moderate increase. He believed such long-term readiness would be the more assured means of deterring Soviet aggression by making plain to the Russians that security for the United States was more than a waiting game, and by thus encouraging western Europe to believe in America's lasting commitment to its defense.

The two major new ideas contained in these rival drafts for a "comprehensive statement of national policy"—the limitation upon military means for achieving America's political goals in the confrontation with Russia, and the necessity for long-term preparedness—were further developed by their authors during November 1948.[51] The easing of tensions over Berlin by this time seemed, indeed, to vindicate Kennan's judgment concerning the chronic nature of the Soviet-American confrontation. However, it was the council's concern with an acute Russian threat more than Kennan's long-range prognosis that won out in the final draft.

The official expression of national policy, dubbed NSC-20, reflected, not surprisingly, its complex origins. While the Russian threat to U.S. security was appraised there to be both "dangerous and immediate," the corrective proposed for U.S. policy was a state of military and psychological preparedness "which can be maintained as long as necessary as a deterrent to Soviet aggression." Perhaps in response to the extreme measures considered by NSC-7, added to NSC-20 was a warning of the dislocation that might occur with an overreaction to the external peril. Among new American objectives was "to avoid permanently impairing our economy and the fundamental values and institutions inherent in our way of life."[52]

Considering its importance, this exposition of containment strategy was a remarkably brief document, unburdened with the lengthy and sometimes tortuous arguments of its antecedents. Possibly for that reason it was read and approved by Truman with unusual rapidity—in the course of one day, November 24—and circulated to every high-level member of the administration during the Cabinet meeting on December 3. The President's concern with the cost of NSC-20 was indicated by the fact that copies were also sent to the budget director and to the chairman of the Council of Economic Advisers. By year's end, the document had officially become America's grand strategy for dealing with the Soviet Union and communism—a strategy purposefully directed at reducing Soviet power and influence by methods short of war, and at deterring a deliberate Russian attack upon the West for the unspecified duration of the cold war.

"The Only Balance We Have"

Despite the flurry of decision-making nearing the end of 1948 regarding the "Policy on Atomic Warfare," NSC-20, and Fleetwood, there were still significant questions concerning the atomic bomb and American security left unresolved. Chief among these as concerned Forrestal were the custody issue and the 1950 military budget. On the first question, he found Truman remained "rocklike" in favor of civilian control after the 1948 election. Undeterred by previous refusals, Forrestal again urged the President to increase the military budget from $15 billion to $17 billion in a letter of December 1. As before, however, Truman stayed firm on the lower figure—ironically citing NSC-20, the study which Forrestal's efforts had initiated, to justify his claim that a sudden increase in spending was not warranted. Curiously, Forrestal seemed to accept the President's verdict, writing of Truman on December 13: "He is a hard-money man if ever I saw one, and believing as I do that we can't afford to wreck our economy in the process of trying to fight the 'cold war,' there is much to be said for his thesis of holding down spending to the absolute minimum of necessity."[53]

However, this was a thesis Forrestal himself was still unwilling—or unable—to promote before the joint chiefs, where disagreement on budget allocations and other matters had seemingly become endemic. The individual services continued to be split, for example, on the earliest probable date for a Russian atomic bomb. But none was yet willing to share Kennan's view that the date was unimportant.[54]

Of more immediate significance was the military's continuing intramural dispute on the use of the atomic bomb in warfare. An Army General Staff study toward the end of the year had sided with Kennan in its assumption that a Soviet-American war would be fought primarily between the two opposing air forces, and hence that Soviet atomic attacks—at least initially—would not be directed "against the industry as a whole or the population of the Allies." The army urged that the "Allies should develop and demonstrate the themes that the Soviet Bloc cannot win militarily and that Allied weapons will be used humanely against vital targets of a military character."[55]

The air force's operational planning left little doubt that its conception of a war differed fundamentally from that of Kennan and the army. The Strategic Air Command's emergency war plan specifically stated that "the highest priority target system is that system constituted by the major Soviet urban-industrial concentrations."[56]

SAC's targeting plan was objected to by the navy on grounds that it overestimated air force capabilities and violated American moral principles. But the fact that the joint chiefs ultimately approved the plan at year's end signified the ascendancy that air-power doctrine had gained in American strategy because of the atomic bomb. Of course, the air force's ascendancy would not go unchallenged. Indeed, the wide disparity between the services over doctrine, budgets, and roles would become even more evident in the acrimonious debate on the military budget that reached a crescendo the following year.

Perhaps the most remarkable feature of American strategy was the disparity that remained uncorrected—and even unobserved—between America's avowed political aims in the event of a war with Russia and the military means of accomplishing them. Had war actually erupted toward the end of 1948, the nation's civilian leaders would presumedly have been surprised—if not horrified—to discover that the conditional "*political* settlement, *politically* negotiated" they expected to arrange at war's end had been foreclosed at its outset by the air force's obliteration of Moscow, Leningrad, and as many as sixty-eight other Russian cities.

Additionally, the prospect that the United States might initiate such an attack, and the certainty that American bombers would then kill millions of Russian civilians when the Soviet Union had neither the capability nor, according to the State Department and the army, the intention of responding in kind, could hardly have created the kind of conciliatory postwar environment envisioned by the civilian authors of NSC-20.

In retrospect, 1948 seemed anything but one of the "years of opportunity" for the United States that James Forrestal had once prophesied. Twice during that year the United States had thought itself on the verge of war, despite its monopoly of atomic bombs. When these crises had receded, contradictions remained in America's response to the Soviet threat—in the dichotomy between political goals and military means, for example; and in the conflict between the military's doctrine of deterrence and its actual planning to fight and win a nuclear war.

Fortunately, neither the spring war scare nor the Berlin crisis of the summer caused these contradictions to be manifested in a Soviet-American war. Nor did the atmosphere of crisis panic the Truman administration into adopting the draconian domestic measures proposed in NSC-7 under the expansive rubric of "national security"—though the 1948 campaign suggested that these ideas were not dead so much as merely dormant.

If it had still not created opportunities for the United States, the atomic bomb at least seemed to ensure against the outbreak of a real war, or a forfeit of the cold war to the Russians. Just because of the crises of 1948, the bomb had become firmly—and, it appeared, permanently—established as the centerpiece of American military strategy.

Upon his return that November from a brief visit to Europe, Forrestal made this point in a letter to Truman in which he professed to be "increasingly impressed by the fact that the only balance we have against the overwhelming manpower of the Russians, and therefore the chief deterrent to war, is the threat of . . . immediate retaliation with the atomic bomb."[57] But he expressed neither relief at nor approval of this state of affairs. A belated convert to air-atomic strategy, Forrestal had, in fact, already joined a minority in the military and the administration who now questioned the wisdom of this increasing trend toward reliance upon the atomic bomb. To these critics of the modern atomic blitz, this trend was viewed variously as dangerous, immoral, and potentially catastrophic for the nation.

14

The Monopoly Ends

"The fences are gone. And it was we, the civilized, who have pushed standardless conduct to its ultimate."
David Lilienthal, journal entry, December 1947

". . . I know that the Russians would use it on us if they had it."
President Truman to David Lilienthal, February 1949

"The Central Question"

Having weathered the crises of the previous year, and convinced by them of the necessity for long-range planning, the Joint Chiefs of Staff turned their attention early in 1949 to the drafting of a plan for a possible war with the Soviet Union occurring as late as 1957. Code-named Dropshot, the plan was the first to incorporate the conclusions of the recent "comprehensive statement of national policy," NSC-20, as well as the first effort to predict military and political developments well into the future. In some ways prescient and in others remarkably shortsighted, Dropshot's predictions were most notable for their assumption that America's atomic advantage over Russia would be enduring—a myth which would be exploded before year's end.

Even as the Pentagon was putting the finishing touches to Dropshot, the earliest assumptions of its previous war planning, particularly those concerning the air-atomic offensive and its effects, were increasingly being called into question in both secret and public forums. This attack upon current U.S. strategic doctrine was all the more important because it originated within the military establishment itself, and was based there on ethical as well as practical grounds. Indeed, not only Dropshot but all military planning in 1949 would be conducted under the growing shadow of two related doubts. The first of these was whether the air-atomic offensive acknowledged to be the foundation of U.S.

strategy could be undertaken in the way imagined and with the results envisioned by its peacetime planners. The second was whether such an attack, even if successful, would not contradict fundamental American values and forfeit the political settlement that was America's avowed wartime aim.

Forrestal had been among the earliest to express skepticism concerning the first point. "The central question," he wrote Truman in fall 1948, " . . . is whether or not our bombers can get in to deliver this attack." Privately, Forrestal already had come to a tentative conclusion on that question: "I do not believe that air power alone can win a war any more than an Army or naval power can win a war, and I do not believe in the theory that an atomic offensive will extinguish in a week the will to fight." Victory, he believed, would require both a longer time and the waging of a more conventional war on land and at sea. "Then, and only then, can the tremendous striking power of air be applied in a decisive—and I repeat decisive—manner."[1]

Forrestal's doubts were shared by Chief of Naval Operations Louis Denfeld. A futile effort by Denfeld in October 1948 to resolve the doctrinal differences of the navy and air force had prompted him to write a succinct account of his objections to air-atomic strategy: The "unpleasant fact remains that the Navy had honest and sincere misgivings as to the ability of the Air Force successfully to deliver the bomb by means of unescorted missions flown by present-day bombers, deep into enemy territory in the face of strong Soviet air defenses, and to drop it on targets whose locations are not accurately known."[2]

Private doubts concerning the morality of U.S. atomic strategy were expressed at this time by Atomic Energy Commission Chairman David Lilienthal in his journal: "Is not the worst fact about modern scientific weapons—notably the atomic bomb—the effect they have upon moral concepts, those patiently built, fragile steps out of the jungle from which man has emerged?" Like Forrestal, Lilienthal's question was rhetorical. But his answer in particular seemed rooted, uncharacteristically, in despair: "All ethical limitations of warfare are gone, not because the means of destruction are more cruel or painful or otherwise hideous in their effect upon combatants, but because there are no individual combatants."[3]

Although the events of 1949 would lend credence to the arguments against air-atomic strategy, neither the pragmatic objection of Forrestal and Denfeld to that strategy nor the moral qualm raised by Lilienthal was sufficient to force a reexamination of U.S. reliance upon the atomic bomb while the monopoly lasted. The complacency that the atomic monopoly engendered meant that few in the administration shared Lilienthal's view of the bomb as "an asset readily depreciating."[4] It was by necessity rather than conviction that the Truman administration had become wedded to the bomb. Its assumptions concerning the value of that weapon in peace or war henceforth remained unexamined, but no longer unchallenged.

"The Great Moral Issue Involved"

As a long-range war plan, Dropshot shared many of its short-range predecessors' presumptions—and flaws. The joint chiefs' early uncertainty as to whether the air-atomic offensive alone would prove decisive was reflected in their estimate that a war occurring as late as 1957 might be won in only two to four weeks of atomic raids, or could last three years and require a land invasion of Russia. There was also some confusion in Dropshot—the first war plan guided by NSC-20—about the real role of the forces required for victory. Its explicit aim was "to deter Soviet armed aggression." Yet the priority which the plan's air-atomic offensive assigned to the destruction of Russia's nuclear stockpile and atomic-bomb production plants seemed less suited to a deterrence strategy than to one aimed at delivering a preemptive, disabling blow.

Apparently never clear in their own minds whether a surprise Russian attack would begin with nuclear strikes upon Strategic Air Command bases, a non-nuclear invasion of western Europe, or a combination of the two, Dropshot's planners nevertheless committed the United States to an atomic attack upon Russian cities.* "Inseparable from the destruction of urban areas," the planners observed, "major destruction would be accomplished on industry itself."[5]

Like Fleetwood, Dropshot provided for a "strategic offensive" in western Europe and a "strategic defensive" in the Far East (although Mao Zedong's victory in China would invalidate the latter contingency

---

*As did the joint chiefs' only operational war plan, Fleetwood. One contradiction of earlier planning seems to have been resolved in Dropshot—the Soviets' governmental centers, Moscow and Leningrad, would not be destroyed until the beginning of the second week of war. Whether this change was a consequence of clearer strategic thinking or simply a reflection of technical limitations upon strategy is not clear from the plan, however.

within a matter of months). But it put an even greater reliance upon the atomic bomb—the immediate and widespread employment of which was deemed "essential" for victory by the plan's authors. It was believed that the Russians by 1957 would have some atomic bombs, but assumed too that the United States would have many more. Charioteer, the Air Force's nuclear annex to Dropshot, posited that the United States would have not only a qualitative advantage but numerical superiority "in the order of 10 to 1" over Russia with regard to atomic bombs by that date. Russia was expected to have a stockpile of 250 atomic bombs "at the most" by 1957, the limiting factor then as before being its presumedly scant resources of uranium ore.[6]

The virtual certainty that the Russians would have some atomic bombs eight years hence and a desire to preserve something of the Russian economy for postwar reconstruction prompted the authors of Dropshot to briefly consider a radical alternative to the plan: "[I]t may become advisable to abandon the concept of destruction of the enemy's physical *means* to wage war in favor of a concept involving destruction of his will through selective attack of limited complexes or mass attack of people with, in each instance, a minimum of damage to physical property." Attacks aimed solely at instilling psychological terror, and the wholesale use of chemical or biological agents as well as atomic bombs, were alternatives only to be considered after further study. The success of Dropshot depended not upon the psychological vulnerability of the enemy but upon the devastation wrought by the bomb. For that reason it was "necessary that weapons of mass destruction be applied as early as possible and to the extent estimated to be necessary for the destruction of the Soviet ability to resist without undue emphasis on their intangible effects."

Of course, Dropshot was as much a reflection as a creation of its time. Among its adjuncts was a plan drafted by the National Security Council at the request of the joint chiefs dealing with internal threats in the event of war. Subsumed under the category of a "fertile field" for Soviet espionage, subversion, and sabotage were European émigrés, ethnic minorities, "intelligent people . . . who . . . have a perennial weakness for 'causes,' " and "various youth and women's organizations." In an analysis that obviously borrowed from other contemporary appraisals of the Soviet threat—and anticipated subsequent ones—the council's report presented a scarifying vision of bacteriological agents introduced into U.S. reservoirs and atomic bombs smuggled in the cargo holds of

Russian ships to destroy American ports. Going even further than NSC-7, which concerned merely peacetime threats to internal security, the council confronted the danger of a wartime fifth column in Dropshot with provisions for the mass arrest of Americans suspected of disloyalty.[7]

Dropshot also mirrored the anxiety of its creators concerning the short-term future of the defense budget. The seventy-group air force and the proposed "new navy" had both been victims of Truman's $14.4 billion austerity budget, which went to Congress in early 1949. An appreciation of the necessity for selling Dropshot to the President and Congress was indeed evident in the argument, contained in an appendix to the plan, that the $22–23 billion annual cost of preparing for the war well over the horizon represented only 10 percent of the country's gross national product. Calculating that the total cost of a war to the United States might be $3 trillion, the drafters of Dropshot represented their program as an "insurance premium" amounting "to but 2 percent of the possible cost of the war."[8]

While American military planning naturally remained "top secret," the existence and even some of the operating assumptions behind Dropshot and its predecessors became known to the public in late 1948 and early 1949 through accounts appearing in newspapers and magazines. These accounts were inspired by those in the Pentagon eager either to promote their branch of armed service or to let them serve as a warning to the Russians. Imaginative renditions of a possible Soviet-American nuclear war published by *Fortune, Collier's,* and *The Saturday Evening Post,* as well as the *New York Herald Tribune* and the *New York Times,* prominently portrayed the air-atomic offensive envisioned by planners.[9]

Significantly, virtually all of these articles shared with actual U.S. war plans a common assumption: that American nuclear supremacy would be enduring. On more detailed questions—such as the extent of anticipated American casualties and the number of bombs currently in the U.S. atomic arsenal—these popular accounts were either silent or wildly optimistic. As late as fall 1951, for example, *Collier's* hypothesized "Operation Eggnog," an entirely fanciful war plan in which American marines parachuted behind the Urals to destroy Russia's atomic stockpile and preempt an attack upon the United States.[10]

The government was perhaps understandably reticent to answer sensitive questions concerning American nuclear strength or anticipated casualties in an atomic war. A February 1949 request by Senator Brian

McMahon that the AEC disclose the size of the stockpile to facilitate public discussion of defense issues was rejected outright by the President and Lilienthal.[11]

Enough clues existed, nonetheless, for the average citizen to receive a generally accurate picture of American strategy. *Aviation Week* reported in mid-March that the "nonstop flight around the world of a Boeing B-50A bomber had strong military and political repercussions" since it proved the feasibility of mid-air refueling for medium bombers —a necessary step for the air force to reach targets deep within Russia. The air force's subsequent announcement that it had 390 such bombers "on order" left no doubt of its commitment to the doctrine of air-atomic attack. Air force plan Trojan for a war beginning early in 1950 underscored that commitment. Trojan provided for a total of three hundred atomic bombs to be used in the initial attack upon Russia. Seventy more bombs were apportioned for a second attack immediately to follow the first, with an unspecified number to be kept in reserve. The fact that the number of bombs in the first two attack waves approximated the total expected to be in the stockpile by 1950 demonstrated the critical importance that the air force now attached to the initial effect of an air-atomic offensive.[12]

But even if vaguely aware of the new realities of warfare in the atomic age, the American public was still not privy to the political costs and implications of U.S. military strategy. The man in the street was oblivious, for example, to the severe strictures upon freedom that the National Security Council would ordain to counter the incipient threat of nuclear war. Unknown, too—indeed, unremarked apart from the secret reports of the air force—was the fact that the nation's civilian defense had been indefinitely deferred so that the air force could direct its resources and efforts to the air-atomic offensive.[13]

Few citizens, in any case, shared with internationalist Grenville Clark a concern with the "great *moral* issue involved in drifting into a war in which the *premeditated plan* of campaign calls for (or at least inevitably involves) the destruction of non-combatants (old men, women, and children) on a great scale. That this is the planned strategy is not in doubt," Clark complained in a letter to Lilienthal. "It is explicit in General Spaatz's articles in *Life* magazine, in [Air Force] General Kenney's frequent interviews, in [Air Force] Secretary Symington's speeches and the like. It is implicit in our steady building of bases almost surrounding the Soviet Union and in the development of longer and longer range bombers; also, of course, in the steady and, one must suppose, the increased production of atomic bombs." To Clark the fascination of the abomination was itself a danger: "Do you not think that some of our military people have gone quite beyond their proper function under our system in talking and writing so freely and constantly about war with Russia?"[14]

"A Strategy of Desperation and Weakness"

By spring 1949 a growing number of military men had begun to express private doubts about both the feasibility and the wisdom of the strategy of atomic blitz. Beyond the need for secrecy, one reason these critics did not speak out publicly was the absence of any clear alternative to such a strategy. Military opponents of the adopted doctrine recognized, with Forrestal, that an air-atomic attack aimed at destroying cities was perhaps all that current constraints of budget and technology would allow. The $14.4 billion defense budget would confine the United States, Forrestal told the joint chiefs the previous October, "only to the mounting of the atomic offensive from Britain." The strategic conundrum he had posed on that occasion—"whether you are going to try to do anything else"—was still unsolved by them.[15] Air force planners tacitly acknowledged limitations of a different sort in their decision to target Russian cities. "After due consideration of the number of atomic bombs available, the radii of action of Allied air forces, the estimated bombing accuracy, the available weight of attack and the time required for realization of [the bombing's] effects," they had concluded that cities presented the most promising targets in a nuclear war.[16]

Finally, there was an inescapable ambivalence to the protest of military leaders against an overreliance upon the atomic blitz, brought about simply because of the role they expected to play in the nation's defense. As one of the architects of the administration's decision to dispatch the B-29s to England, Forrestal himself was perhaps the best embodiment of this conflict. Believing that the public and his colleagues in the Pentagon held an inflated idea of the atomic bomb's destructiveness and importance in warfare, he also understood the need not to depreciate the effects of the bomb lest the Russians begin to doubt its efficacy. Forrestal shared Winston Churchill's conviction that the United States must be careful not to "write down" the bomb.[17]

An even greater danger than seeming to undermine the nation's defense by such criticism, however, would be to stake American security upon an unproved—and unworkable—strategy. Army Chief of Staff Omar Bradley branded the atomic blitz a plan to "put all your eggs in one basket." To Major General Alfred Gruenther, the chairman of the Joint Strategic Planning Committee, it was simply a "gamble."[18]

Intent upon assuring that the United States would not become any more committed to an air-atomic strategy until the air force proved its claim that the bomb "could be dropped where, how and when it was wanted," Forrestal awaited the findings of the two separate studies he had commissioned the previous fall. In mid-February, the interservice group assigned to study the feasibility of launching an atomic blitz against Russia, chaired by Lieutenant General John E. Hull, reported that they were still far from agreement on that vital question. A second attempt to answer the question would not begin until the following April. The deliberations of the group given the task of determining the probable effectiveness of a hypothetical blitz, headed by Air Force Lieutenant General Hubert Harmon, were apparently characterized by greater unanimity. But the Harmon Report would not be ready till the following spring.[19]

Until the Hull and the Harmon studies were completed, what Forrestal had earlier called the "central question" of U.S. strategic planning—"whether or not our bombers can get in to deliver this attack"—remained unanswered. A related question of equal significance —whether or not those bombers alone could win the war—remained as well a matter of purest speculation.

Perhaps understandably, the interim response of the joint chiefs to this uncertainty concerning the air-atomic offensive was to request an increase in the production of atomic bombs. Because of the successful Sandstone tests and of new fabrication techniques at Los Alamos, the Atomic Energy Commission by late 1948 was able to produce more bombs than had once been deemed "adequate" by the joint chiefs for the coming year. By January 1949, however, the strategic situation—and the definition of "adequate"—had changed. Reflecting the anxiety that had caused Forrestal to commission the Hull and Harmon studies, the joint chiefs informed Lilienthal "that the currently established military requirements for scheduling bomb production should be increased substantially and extended." Precisely how many more bombs would be necessary in the joint chiefs' estimation was withheld by them pending the conclusions of the two reports.[20]

The desire of the joint chiefs to err on the side of caution in forecasting the nation's military requirements was certainly explicable to Lilienthal. But he suspected that the latest request was founded less upon careful strategic analysis than upon a habit of demanding all the traffic would bear from the AEC's bomb factories.

In fact, Lilienthal's suspicion was correct.[21] Of more immediate and tangible concern, however, was the sort of uncritical thinking that he believed lay behind the request. Following Pentagon briefings on Sandstone, he had been disturbed by the evident enthusiasm of military leaders—and his fellow commissioners—regarding the prospects for bigger and more destructive bombs. There was in this enthusiasm nothing of the second thoughts that Lilienthal himself had begun to have concerning the prospective use of nuclear weapons against civilians, and which he had given vent to in his journal more than a year earlier.[22]

Yet there was a positive aspect to the joint chiefs' request as he saw it. Since stepped-up production of atomic bombs would require presidential authorization, Lilienthal was for the first time hopeful that the need to justify their request might cause the joint chiefs to reveal the assumptions behind the dark art of nuclear strategy. Those assumptions could then be opened both to criticism and rethinking not only as to feasibility, but as to their ethical implications.[23]

Lilienthal's initial efforts to bring his growing doubts to the President's attention had encountered frustration. Meeting with Truman in early February, he found the latter "weighed down" by the responsibilities of the office, and unreceptive to the argument that granting the joint chiefs' request without a challenge would weaken civilian control of the military. Above all, the President seemed in no mood to reconsider previous assumptions on the bomb. Lilienthal was also "caught off balance" by Truman's evident preoccupation with the weapon's growing importance: "[Truman] began by saying that the atomic bomb was the mainstay and all he had; that the Russians would have probably taken over Europe a long time ago if it were not for that. Therefore he had to guard it very carefully." There was already, the President felt, "too much talk about the bomb" as a result of the services' "continual squabbling," and particularly the air force's "raving" for seventy groups.[24]

While given no encouragement by Truman at this meeting, Lilienthal knew he was not alone in opposing the atomic blitz on moral grounds. It was a cause that enlisted odd allies. Two of the army's best-known generals, Eisenhower and Marshall, had each expressed revulsion at the idea of atomic warfare. But both were convinced of the need to prepare for that gruesome contingency.[25] Most vocal in opposition to an air-atomic strategy were high-ranking officers of the navy. Practical as well as ethical considerations had been behind the unsuccessful effort of Admiral Louis Denfeld to block the joint chiefs' approval of Fleetwood. Likewise, a well-publicized speech in January 1949 by Rear Admiral Daniel Gallery constituted a *post hoc* moral argument against air force strategy, since it came after congressional approval of the 1950 defense budget. Gallery complained that "many of our military planners" were "losing sight of the objectives for which a war should be fought by a democratic and 'civilized society' like the United States." Singling out "the prophets of the ten-day atomic blitz," he observed sarcastically that "levelling large cities has a tendency to alienate the affections of the inhabitants and does not create an atmosphere of international good will after the war." Gallery's final argument and conclusion were on fundamental grounds: "A strategy based on the sole object of preventing defeat in war is an unworthy one for a country of our strength. . . . It is a strategy of desperation and weakness. . . . I believe we should abandon the idea of destroying enemy cities one after another until he gives in and find some better way of gaining our objective."[26]

Neither Denfeld's criticisms of Fleetwood nor Gallery's belated broadside against the air force brought about the reexamination of U.S. strategy that each had hoped for. But only months later the two men would be given a forum for their views in Congress.

In the winter of 1949, there seemed little indication that Truman —who could most easily bring about that reexamination—was receptive to reappraisals on the bomb. Approaching the President a week after the meeting where Truman had complained about the air force's "raving," Lilienthal found him less concerned with the morality of dropping the bomb than with the danger of a nuclear-armed Soviet Union: "Dave, we will never use it again if we can possibly help it. But I know the Russians would use it on us if they had it."[27]

Unknown to Lilienthal at the time, Truman was not entirely insensitive to the need for reconsideration of the premises behind American strategy. The President's subsequent decision to defer approval of the joint chiefs' request for more bombs pending the conclusions of a special study he convened on the subject indicates that Truman was more concerned with the bomb's implications than his glib remarks to Lilienthal suggest. In fact, Truman's principal objection to the expanded weapons program was its cost.[28] But he could not have been unaware of additional reasons against taking such a step. In recent days other members of the administration had voiced criticism of the drift toward greater reliance upon the bomb.

On April 5, 1949, Truman's new budget director, Frank Pace, Jr., sent him a memorandum warning that approval of the military's air-atomic strategy would unwittingly commit him to the wholesale and virtually indiscriminate use of nuclear weapons in the event of war. Pace was equally concerned that the air force might become as wedded to the bomber as the navy had been to obsolete battleships after the First World War.[29] Truman's comment to Eben Ayers a few days later that the air force was "putting all its eggs in one basket" by building long-range bombers showed his sensitivity to the second of Pace's suggestions: "[Truman] said they are ordering more B-36s and new bombers and he feared that if he succeeds in getting the atomic bomb eliminated as a weapon that they will find a lack of proper coordination with the sea and land forces."[30]

The President's request at this time that he be briefed on air force plans for an attack upon Russia also revealed a gradual awakening to the first part of Pace's warning. Indeed, the briefing given Truman on air force war plan Trojan could only have confirmed what Pace had predicted—that political choices in a war would be excluded by the adopted strategy. Trojan provided for the all-out atomic bombing of Soviet cities and industries with European-based B-29s and B-50s, and B-36s based in the United States. The contemplated air-atomic offensive would kill between 3 million and 5 million Russians and leave up to 28 million homeless. But the air force admitted to a significant element of uncertainty in its estimates. Awaiting the Hull Report, Trojan's planners had based their estimates on the dubious assumption that all the bombers would get to their targets and all the atomic bombs would be delivered. These planners also left the impression—but did not state outright—that the initial air-atomic offensive alone would be enough to knock Russia out of the war.[31]

If Trojan left any doubt that the growing U.S. dependence on the bomb had the effect of diminishing or even eliminating choices in the event of war, that lesson should have been clear in the circumstances which surrounded creation of NATO.

The signing of the pact establishing the North Atlantic Treaty

Organization on April 4, 1949, acknowledged the responsibility of America's western European allies to assist in their own defense. The original rationale of NATO had been to provide a feeling of security for Europe until the Marshall Plan could restore economic and political stability. As this concept and talks on NATO progressed, however, the pact's emphasis had subtly shifted from psychological to physical security.

To some extent, the need to rely upon the bomb for the defense of Europe had been anticipated in the talks leading to the formation of NATO. A background paper prepared in September 1948 for American participants in those talks noted, therefore, that the "continued presence of U.S. forces in Western Europe is important since an attack upon them would bring the United States immediately and directly into war. Nevertheless, something more is needed to counteract the fear of the peoples of Western Europe that their countries might be overrun by the Soviet Army before effective help could arrive."[32] That "something more" would be the atomic bomb.

Even so, the fact that the atomic bomb was initially excluded from discussions on NATO seemed to promise that the pact would be an exception to the air-atomic emphasis in American military planning. The language of the pact made no mention of the bomb. U.S. war planning thus far had also pointedly rejected the idea that the bomb should be employed in Europe, even to halt a Soviet invasion. The joint chiefs feared not only the lasting damage that would be caused by the weapon's use, but the political and economic consequences to follow in its wake.[33]

Yet only three days after the signing of the pact—even as Truman was being briefed on Trojan—the thinking behind the strategy to defend Europe began to change. On April 7 the Pentagon committee detailed to study the implementation of NATO recommended that war plans for Europe be reconsidered with regard to the possible use of "new weapons." Abandoning the notion of a protracted land battle with the Russians in Europe, the committee held out the alternative of a "delaying action in which the possibilities offered by air forces and mass destruction weapons would be put to their full use." The earlier prohibition against the use of nuclear weapons on European soil was ignored. Significantly, the justification for this radical departure from the initial concept of NATO was undramatic, and represented not so much a new idea of strategy as a desire to reduce expenditures and manpower requirements in accordance with the administration's austerity budget.[34]

This last was a goal with which the public and many in Congress could sympathize. As had been the case with universal military training, the bomb was increasingly seen as a replacement for, rather than an adjunct to, NATO. An April article in *The Nation* concerning conservative opposition to NATO in the Senate singled out Republican William Jenner as typical of this way of thinking: "Jenner was in the last war and believes a land-war holding action against Russia would be futile . . . He counts up Russian divisions and the divisions available in Western Europe and insists that it all adds up to another Dunkirk. . . . He is against the [NATO] pact and for air power and the bomb."[35]

Ultimately, neither the warnings of Lilienthal and Pace nor Truman's briefing on Trojan changed the President's mind on the central importance of the bomb in American strategy. Truman himself made this clear when he assured a delegation of Democratic congressmen in early April that he "wouldn't hesitate" to use the bomb if circumstances required it. He and the National Security Council had already approved plans for the construction of airfields in the United States from which the "heavy punch" against Russia would be launched in the event of a war. Earlier, representatives of the Strategic Air Command and the Royal Air Force had finalized joint "pre-D-Day" plans for the air-atomic offensive from Great Britain.[36]

Of course, doubts about the role of that offensive in U.S. strategy remained. After his Air Force briefing, Truman reiterated that the findings of the Hull and Harmon committees were to be reported to him as soon as they became available. He also again deferred a decision on the joint chiefs' request for an expanded weapons program. To the disappointment of opponents of air-atomic strategy in the administration, these steps were taken not out of concern that current war planning was immoral or excluded political choices, but in reaction to a narrower consideration: whether the air-atomic offensive could be launched as contemplated, and if it would then succeed.

"Its Early Use Would Be Transcending"

When finally available in mid-May, the Harmon Report on the probable effectiveness of the air-atomic offensive did more to increase than assuage doubts about U.S. military strategy. It explicitly challenged a principal tenet of this strategy—that the atomic bomb would allow the United States to deter or, if necessary, to fight and win a war with Russia.

In assuming that all bombs would be delivered accurately in the attack —an assumption to be questioned subsequently in the Hull Report—the Harmon committee predicted that the physical destruction caused by America's atomic blitz would be substantially less than the air force's estimate, and that Russian losses in any case "could either be alleviated by Soviet recuperative action" or mitigated in their effect by post-attack adjustments in Russia's economy. The report thus gave little hope that the air-atomic offensive alone could compel a Soviet surrender.[37]

Equally disturbing in its implications was the committee's prediction concerning the psychological or "intangible" effects of the bomb upon Russia. Far from the collapse of the communist regime and the "revolt on every border" that Baruch had forecast for Russia in the wake of a nuclear attack, the Harmon committee thought "atomic bombing would validate Soviet propaganda . . . stimulate resentment against the United States, unify these people and increase their will to fight."

The report deprecated the idea advanced by NATO planners that the atomic bomb would be able to stop a Red Army advance into western Europe or the Middle East. Instead, Soviet capabilities in such an invasion "would not be seriously impaired" by atomic bombing at the outset; the eventual defeat of the Russian onslaught would be accomplished not by the bomb but by resurgent Allied armies. The report even predicted that use of the atomic bomb "will produce certain psychological and retaliatory reactions detrimental to the achievement of Allied war objectives and its destructive effects will complicate post-hostilities problems." A final ominous note was that first use of the atomic bomb by the United States would "open the field and set the pattern" for employment of "any weapons of mass destruction," and result in "maximum retaliatory measures" by the Russians.

While the Harmon Report was the first official account to draw attention to the evident contradictions of U.S. strategy—in the conflict between military means and political ends, for example, and in the effect of atomic bombing to unify rather than demoralize an enemy—its authors curiously endorsed the air-atomic emphasis of U.S. strategy in their conclusion. Having conceded that use of the bomb was likely to prove "detrimental" to U.S. interests in a war, the committee ultimately surrendered the logic of its own argument when it concluded lamely that the bomb *might* be decisive in a war—if used promptly and in sufficient numbers. Unwittingly presenting an implicit case for a preemptive attack with the bomb, the report's summary reasoned that "the advantages of its early use would be transcending."*

The Harmon Report drew fire from military leaders not for its tacit endorsement of preemptive attack, but for its disparagement of the bomb's utility in war. It was attacked on this basis by Air Force General Hoyt Vandenberg in particular. Certainly the report was not intended to prompt any fundamental rethinking of American strategy, since its conclusion finally succumbed to the current emphasis on the bomb. There was, it seemed to say, no alternative to dependence upon that weapon.

Any prospect of the Harmon Report's becoming a subject of controversy in the administration was obviated when, contrary to Truman's instructions, it did not reach the President's desk until much later, at which time its conclusions were no longer relevant.

The decision of Louis Johnson—secretary of defense since Forrestal's firing in March 1949—to withhold the Harmon Report from Truman and subsequently to misrepresent its findings to the President was probably motivated by his desire not to undermine the case for air power.[39] As the administration's new defender of budgetary austerity to the military, Johnson was not only sympathetic to arguments promoting air-atomic strategy, but wholeheartedly committed to the bomb. Thus he suffered none of the ambivalence that had characterized Forrestal's tenure in the office.

The argument against air-atomic strategy might have been strengthened had even the preliminary findings of the Hull committee become known at this time. That study cast serious doubt upon the ability of U.S. bombers to penetrate Soviet air defenses in sufficient numbers to deliver a stunning initial blow without incurring losses that would make a sustained air offensive impossible. Additional problems and oversights contained in existing air force war plans—a shortage of aviation fuel and aircraft parts, for example, and the unanticipated vulnerability of bases in Britain—made the success of current war plans still more problematic.† Largely because of the controversial and disturb-

---

*Typical of the paradoxes contained in the report was the testimony of Charles Thayer, a State Department expert on Russia. Thayer believed that use of the atomic bomb by the United States in a war with Russia "would set the Russian people solidly against the Americans at first and strengthen their will to resist." Yet he suggested that the United States in a war destroy Soviet cities "at once and completely in order to get the maximum effect."[38]

†A series of air force training exercises from 1947 to 1949 underscored the problems yet to be solved before the Strategic Air Command could launch its atomic blitz. In one mock raid on New York

ing nature of its conclusions, however, the Hull Report would not be completed and sent to the President until the following January. By then the time for a dispassionate review of U.S. strategy was well past.

With the Harmon Report suppressed and the Hull Report unavailable throughout the critical summer of 1949, some doubts about and objections to U.S. strategy surfaced nonetheless in reaction to the joint chiefs' draft of a new emergency war plan, code-named Offtackle.

The immediate successor to Fleetwood, Offtackle was more than seven months in preparation, reflecting the lessons learned and the interservice battles fought over the previous three years. It resolved once and for all the indecision of the joint chiefs concerning strategy in the Middle East. The vital oil fields would be held if militarily possible. Another contentious issue apparently settled by Offtackle concerned the navy's wartime role. Previous planning had specified that the navy's aircraft carriers would "supplement and support the air offensive" in the event of war. But Offtackle decreed that the navy's role would be severely limited by the small number of carriers allowed it in the austerity budget. As if to confirm the navy's diminished status, Defense Secretary Johnson promptly suspended construction on the first of its new "supercarriers," the U.S.S. *United States,* as an "economy measure."

While less than a decisive victory for the air force, Offtackle's emphasis upon the atomic blitz made it the first war plan to accept implicitly that the air-atomic offensive would be not only the principal focus but perhaps the sole extent of America's war effort.

Offtackle was also unique among war plans in the number and severity of disagreements between its drafters—differences spurred on as well, of course, by the controversy over the Harmon Report. At the center of this dispute was continued disagreement within the Pentagon over the effectiveness of the atomic blitz and the choice of cities as targets.[41] Offtackle settled these differences only by ignoring them. The plan as approved skirted the question of the air-atomic offensive's probable effectiveness, and specified merely that the

---

City during spring 1947 little more than half of SAC's bombing force—about 101 planes in all—was able to get airborne; the remainder were grounded because of poor maintenance or missing parts. Nor did the situation improve with the introduction of the B-36 and B-50 in 1948. In a nighttime mock raid that year upon Dayton, Ohio, not a single bomber completed its mission as planned—prompting SAC commander Curtis LeMay to call it "just about the darkest night in American military aviation history."[40]

atomic bomb be used both against Russia directly and to slow any Soviet advance into western Europe. The interservice differences mirrored in the Harmon Report and Offtackle delayed approval of the latter by the joint chiefs until the end of 1949—by which time many of its assumptions concerning war with Russia were already obsolete.[42]

Unto themselves, it is likely that neither the doctrinal controversy submerged in Offtackle, nor the disturbing findings of the Harmon and Hull committees (had they become known), nor the objections of critics in the administration would have been a sufficient impetus to force a fundamental rethinking of the nation's dependence upon the atomic bomb. The beginnings of such a reexamination seemed to exist in Truman's repeated deferral of the joint chiefs' request for more bombs and in the doubts he expressed about the direction of American strategy that spring. Against these, however, was the unstated assumption that, because of the budget and demobilization, reliance upon the bomb was unavoidable. For a serious critique of American strategy to have received a hearing at this time it would have required a more definite focus—upon either the practical or the moral failure inherent in the idea of the atomic blitz, for example—as well as a specific champion from among the disparate opponents of the new doctrine.

Such a champion might have been found in Lilienthal. But he was under public attack by Senator Bourke Hickenlooper for alleged "incredible mismanagement" of the Atomic Energy Commission—actually part of a continuing effort by conservative senators to remove the liberal chairman from office. Under these circumstances, it was impossible for Lilienthal to speak out against the air-atomic emphasis of U.S. strategy.[43]

Forrestal, perhaps a more likely figure in that role, was, fatefully, now gone from the administration. Caught in an impossible position between the budget demands of the joint chiefs and the fiscal conservativism of the administration, Forrestal had been fired from the post of defense secretary the previous spring. Feeling in no small part a failure for his inability to reconcile these two irreconcilable interests, and also sensitive to how the nation still seemed not to heed his warnings on the Russian threat, he had been under increasing mental and emotional strain. By April, when Truman first took even a cursory interest in U.S. strategy, Forrestal was hospitalized for exhaustion and depression. By

May, when the administration might have had the benefit of his counsel concerning Offtackle, the Harmon Report, and the preliminary findings of the Hull committee, he was dead—a suicide.*

Whether anyone in the administration could have retained Truman's confidence long enough and presented the case against sole reliance on the bomb persuasively enough to bring about a review of strategy is certainly questionable. By July, Truman's consideration of the joint chiefs' request for more bombs showed that he seemed less troubled by the military's air-atomic emphasis than by the cost of an alternative. Indeed, Truman was ultimately willing to support the cost of increased bomb production by further reducing expenditures outside "the atomic weapons area."[45]

Any alternative to complete reliance on the bomb, therefore, would first have had to resolve a dilemma created by the contradiction of strategy and budget—a dilemma that Forrestal had called attention to during the Berlin crisis, but that remained unresolved at the time of his death. Technical problems, for example, hindered the development of nuclear weapons meant for battlefield use. But a more serious obstacle continued to be the budget.[46] The 1950 budget made it impossible for the United States to carry on even the most limited conventional war envisioned by the joint chiefs' planning if the initial air-atomic attack alone did not compel Russia's surrender, and austerity would reduce the scale of that attack to raids launched only from Britain and Suez.[47] Offtackle, the latest product of the planning staff, thus remained both a dream and a fiction of its authors because of its tenuous assumption that an early and massive atomic attack might knock Russia out of the war. The Harmon Report's revelations of just how tenuous this assumption was—and the evidence as yet unremarked by the Hull committee that it amounted, in fact, to little more than a careless hope—should logically have prompted a review of the earliest

---

*Contained in a scrapbook among Forrestal's papers was a quote from Mark Twain in J. M. Gillis' *False Prophets*. Forrestal may have sympathized with its sentiment: "A myriad of men are born, they labor and sweat and struggle for bread. They squabble and scold and fight. They scramble for little mean advantages over one another. Age creeps upon them. Infirmities follow. Shames and humiliations bring down their prides and their vanities. Those they love are taken from them, and the joy of life is turned to aching grief. The burden of pain, care, misery, grows heavier year by year. At length, ambition is dead. Longing for release is in its place. It comes at last, the only unpoisoned gift earth ever had for them. They vanish from a world where they were of no consequence, where they have achieved nothing, where they were a mistake and a failure, and a foolishness, where they have left no sign that they ever existed, a world which will lament them a day, and forget them forever."[44]

assumptions behind American military strategy in the atomic age. Belatedly, that review would be forthcoming in the late summer and early fall of 1949. But it would have then neither a clear focus nor the sponsorship of a particular individual, and its recommendations were soon overtaken by events.

"Traveling Down the Atomic Road Rather Too Fast"

The particular vulnerability of a strategy entirely dependent on the atomic bomb had been raised the previous March by members of the National Security Council in their report to the President recommending extension of the Anglo-American *modus vivendi*. Seeking to put nuclear weapons into perspective against the background of international politics, the report acknowledged that atomic bombs were a "unique weapon" not only in their impact upon military affairs but "by the fact that as of the present the United States alone possesses them." Yet the danger inherent in America's atomic advantage was also thought to be obvious: "Once the Soviet Union has atomic bombs a critical reexamination of our war plans will probably be required." This vital caveat was ignored in the midst of administration efforts to obtain congressional sanction for a renewed *modus vivendi*.[48]

Representing an exception to the administration's complacency on the subject of the Russian bomb was, not surprisingly, George Kennan. Kennan feared the "psychological impact" at home and abroad of accelerated U.S. atomic-bomb production. This concern with the bomb "did not represent strong conviction but rather an uneasy feeling that we were traveling down the atomic road rather too fast," Kennan explained. Accordingly, he concluded "that it might be to the nation's advantage if it were decided that the bomb would never be used."[49]

Kennan's uneasiness evidently grew that summer, for in mid-August he guided the State Department's Policy Planning Staff in an assessment of the political implications of a Soviet atomic bomb. Kennan presented the purpose of this report as not so much to prepare for the eventuality of the monopoly's end as to confirm with some assurance that the monopoly still endured. His subterfuge may have been, in fact, the diplomat's solution to what Kennan recognized as likely to be a sensitive question, or simply a way of assuring that his views would be taken seriously. The subject of the atomic monopoly's end had already been briefly considered in an early draft of NSC-20, but it was deleted from the final version of that statement of national policy. Kennan also knew from personal experience that Dean Acheson—who replaced the ailing Marshall as secretary of state in January—viewed the notion of forswearing use of the weapon as heretical, even though Acheson shared Kennan's own feeling that the atomic bombing of civilians was immoral.[50]

Kennan's memorandum was the first to deal with a problem that had received scant attention or even acknowledgment in the administration—the inevitability of the monopoly's end. It argued that the end of U.S. atomic hegemony would bring with it a significant but not catastrophic change in the international situation. This might include a temporary shift toward more aggressive behavior on the part of the Soviet Union, and a greater inclination toward neutrality on the part of "third countries" caught between the United States and Russia. However, as before, Russian intentions and not capabilities were of preeminent importance in Kennan's analysis. Whatever Russia's efforts at atomic diplomacy, he recommended that the monopoly's end should prompt the United States to reevaluate its stand on international control of the bomb, with a view possibly to reopening negotiations at the UN.[51]

Another of Kennan's recommendations—that the United States develop the capability to detect a Soviet nuclear explosion—had been anticipated the previous year by AEC Commissioner Lewis Strauss. Partly because of Strauss' efforts, the AEC and the Pentagon had established such a program despite the opposition of many in the administration—and some in the commission—who believed that any detection program was at best premature and probably an unnecessary expense. Even earlier, the CIA initiated a broad series of intelligence-gathering operations aimed not only at ascertaining when the Russians might have an atomic bomb, but at predicting their rate of producing them.*

Members of the administration, military leaders, and atomic scientists were still far from unanimity on the question of when the

---

*Strauss wrote in his memoirs of official reaction to the monitoring program idea: "The experts for the most part believed the construction of an atomic bomb was simply beyond the immediate competence of Russian science or the capability of existing industrial organization in the Soviet Union. . . . The majority opinion set the time substantially further in the future, while not a few believed it beyond Soviet capacity in *any* time scale likely to be of concern to us."[52]

atomic monopoly would end. Instead, a wide spectrum of estimates
existed as late as fall 1949. Kennan's memorandum seemed to suggest
that the monopoly's end was imminent—if it had not already occurred, unknown to the administration. His view was in accord with
the opinion of perhaps a majority of scientists, and—curiously—a majority of citizens.[53] Acheson and Lilienthal had each predicted that the
Soviet atomic bomb might come in 1950 or 1951. The assumption of
Offtackle was that the Russians would not have a bomb during 1950
but might have one in 1951. This guess was a more conservative assessment than that of either the Finletter Report—which considered 1953
a likely date—or the CIA's December 1947 estimate, which thought it
"almost certain" that the Russians could not have a bomb before
1951. Presumably, this conservativism was engendered by better and
more complete intelligence in 1949 on Soviet progress toward an
atomic bomb.[54]

In the minority as concerned actual numbers—but not influence—
were those who contended that the Russians were from five to fifteen
years away from the ability to build atomic bombs "in quantity." Apparently still holding to this view, apart from the inevitable Groves, were
the U.S. embassy in Moscow, Truman himself, and former Secretary of
State James Byrnes—whose premature memoir asserted in 1947 that it
would be from seven to ten more years before the Russians had a
bomb.[55]

Nor did there seem to be any concern in the administration at
this time, apart from Kennan's memorandum, with either preparing
the American people for the monopoly's end or accommodating military plans to that eventuality. At the end of August the joint chiefs
were primarily concerned with integrating the bomb into NATO strategy for the defense of Europe. Approved two weeks later by the National Security Council as NSC-57, their plan sanctioned the first-use
of nuclear weapons by the United States. It was also the first to en-
compass the "umbrella" concept of NATO, in which U.S. atomic
hegemony would provide not only the principal deterrent against a
Russian attack on Europe but also the means for halting Soviet aggression if deterrence failed. While the usefulness of the bomb in America's European strategy had been seriously questioned by the Harmon
Report, there was no such doubt evident among the joint chiefs or the
members of the National Security Council. Nor was there yet any recognition by them of how the security of Europe—or that of the

United States—would be affected by the end of America's atomic hegemony.[56]

"We Are in a Straight Race with the Russians"

Sometime between the joint chiefs' completion of their NATO report and its approval by the National Security Council there occurred the event which that report had neglected to consider—an event that changed or even invalidated the premise on which it and virtually all of U.S. planning on the bomb had been founded. Indeed, at the very time that Kennan and the Policy Planning Staff were speculating on the implications of a Russian atomic bomb, the world was confronted by its reality.

Subsequent studies by the air force and navy placed the first Soviet nuclear test as sometime during the latter half of August in Asiatic Russia. In early September, U.S. analysts could only say that radioactivity from the blast was hardly more than one month old, "and was probably younger than one month." The AEC's monitoring program was the first to sound the alert, on September 9, that a Russian test might have taken place. Rainwater samples from contaminated clouds confirmed on September 14 that the explosion had been of an actual bomb and was not a laboratory accident. Later results showed that the bomb had utilized plutonium and was of an advanced design, akin to the weapon dropped on Nagasaki.[57]

Initial reaction in Washington was shocked disbelief. Even though navy reports by mid-September showed that the samples obtained from monitoring were "extremely hot" in terms of radioactive contamination, and well above the natural background count, there was a tendency to dismiss the results as a misreading or as evidence of an accident in the Soviet nuclear program. Among those persisting in doubts that the Russians had a bomb was Defense Secretary Johnson—who initially considered withholding evidence of the test from other members of the administration, as he had withheld the Harmon Report—and General Groves, who publicly subscribed to the nuclear-accident theory.[58] Incredibly, one skeptic in the administration reacted to the news with a suggestion that the monitoring program be disbanded. A few members of the congressional Joint Committee on Atomic Energy briefly discussed the possibility of an atomic strike on Soviet nuclear facilities.[59]

Informed on September 12 of the likelihood that the monopoly had ended, Truman, too, proved reluctant to accept the evidence and its implications. As much as a week later, Lilienthal found the President still resisting any public announcement of the Soviet test—partly for political reasons. The ever-present domestic anxiety about spies, the triumph of communism in China the previous month, and the pending devaluation of Britain's currency (whose Labour government advised Truman against announcing the test) all militated against immediate disclosure of the news. But Truman also confessed to Lilienthal that he remained unconvinced the Russians had an actual bomb.[60]

The President did not deem the time right for public announcement of the Soviet test until some days after Lilienthal's visit, when he informed the Cabinet and the public together of the news on September 23. Significantly, the wording of the White House press release mirrored his persistent doubts, pointedly referring only to a nuclear explosion in Russia and not specifically to a bomb.*

While calculated to reflect a mood of calm deliberation for the benefit of the public, Truman's announcement created no illusion within the administration as to the implications of a Russian bomb—whatever the term used to describe it. It "changed the situation drastically," Lilienthal wrote, "and . . . the talk about our having anticipated everything and following the same program we had before is the bunk." Air Force Secretary Stuart Symington, reflecting that the Finletter Report had predicted a Russian bomb for 1953, lamented to Louis Johnson "that even this gloomy hypothesis was too optimistic; and by a substantial period." It was not the past but the future that most concerned Budget Director James Webb, at the Cabinet meeting where Truman told of the news. "We are in a straight race with the Russians," he announced.[62]

---

*Before releasing the news of the Soviet test to the public, Truman required a signed statement from each member of the scientific committee assigned to review the radioactive samples, attesting to the existence of a Russian bomb. Even years later he expressed doubt that the Russians had nuclear weapons.[61]

15

The Race Begins

"This whole discussion makes me feel I was seeing the same film, and a punk one, for the second time."

James Conant to David Lilienthal, October 1949

"[Truman] went on to say that we had got to do it—make the bomb—though none wants to use it. But, he said, we have got to have it only for bargaining purposes with the Russians."

Eben Ayers, diary, January 1950

" 'We Have No Other Course' "

The Russian atomic test signaled not only the end of American nuclear hegemony but the start of the Soviet-American arms race. For many, the next logical step for the United States in that race was the expansion of atomic-bomb production that had been under consideration since the previous May. The committee that Truman had formed to study the joint chiefs' request—consisting of Johnson, Acheson, and Lilienthal—had yet to be informed of the rationale behind that expansion, or of the alternatives to such a step. Lilienthal feared that the Soviet bomb had made dispassionate consideration of the subject more difficult, if not impossible: "We keep saying, 'We have no other course'; what we should say is 'We are not bright enough to see any other course.' "[1] Reluctantly, he joined the other members of the committee in recommending the program, but privately regretted that their report to the President had not called for the reexamination of American strategy which he felt was needed more than ever with the atomic monopoly's end.

Lilienthal's grudging endorsement of the expanded weapons program seemed a tacit recognition, indeed, that there was no realistic alternative to traveling farther and faster down what Kennan had called the "atomic road." But he also hoped that by proceeding down this path an even more dangerous course under consideration by the administration might be avoided—the development of vastly more powerful weapons of mass destruction.

Truman waited only a week after this recommendation to approve the $319 million expansion program. Significantly, only after he had sanctioned the program did the President ask the joint chiefs for an account of the assumptions underlying it. Truman's decision had been prompted, therefore, by the need to confront the new dangers that suddenly seemed to threaten the country. The Russian bomb was obviously one such threat in the fall of 1949, as was the sensational uncovering of more alleged Soviet "atom spies," and the recent communist conquest of China.

It was not the actual explosion of the Russian bomb that stunned America's political and military strategists so much as it was the realization this event afforded that their earliest assumptions concerning Russia and the bomb had been wrong. The Russian bomb revealed nothing new about Soviet intentions. But in the wake of greatly increased estimates of Russian capabilities, Soviet intentions seemed more threatening.

The expanded atomic-weapons program was only one reaction to this perception of a larger threat. Truman's decision in January 1950 to proceed with development of the hydrogen super-bomb was also brought about in large part because of mounting political pressures to meet that threat, as was his endorsement at this time of a more aggressive strategy for fighting the cold war, now virtually regardless of costs. The H-bomb decision and the promulgation of a new cold war strategy ignored the reexamination of the administration's political and military assumptions sought by Lilienthal and Kennan. The effect of these decisions was not only to confirm but actually to increase American reliance upon nuclear weapons. The logic of depending upon bigger and better bombs to keep —and shape—the peace had thus become as ineluctable as the arms race itself. This same logic would dictate the standards under which the cold war at home and abroad would be fought henceforth.

"Some Cheap, Easy Way Out"

Ever since atomic scientists had recognized the military potential of atomic energy, some among them had looked to the even greater destructive potential of a thermonuclear bomb, or "Super." The possibility of such a weapon had been cited by Vannevar Bush and James Conant in 1944 as one reason why the United States should not attempt to follow a policy of monopoly concerning the atomic bomb, since the supply of the raw material necessary for this weapon—hydrogen—was essentially limitless.[2] In the anxious days following the collapse of the London Council of Foreign Ministers, Secretary of State Byrnes had urged that Manhattan Project scientists begin work on the "Super" immediately. Since then the technical exigencies of the atomic-weapons program and the tensions of the international situation had directed that the scientists' efforts be applied to building a nuclear arsenal. The notion of the "Super" had correspondingly faded.

With the unexpectedly early end of America's atomic advantage, however, prospects for the "Super" revived. Among those intent upon its development were Los Alamos physicists Edward Teller and Ernest Lawrence. Teller was perhaps the first scientist to actively promote the hydrogen bomb, but both he and Lawrence found ready converts in Senator Brian McMahon and Atomic Energy Commissioner Lewis Strauss. McMahon was already thinking beyond expanded atomic-bomb production, while Strauss was attracted to the hydrogen bomb as a "quantum jump" in weapons development—a means, in effect, of reestablishing America's nuclear hegemony.[3]

Lilienthal reacted to the argument for the "Super" with skepticism and even revulsion when Strauss promoted it at the commission's October meeting. "[It] would tend to confuse and, unwittingly . . . make it more difficult to find some other course," he wrote. There was also a note of exasperation on his part concerning the lessons as yet unlearned about the atomic bomb: "[D]id it provide a sense of security to us, or much elbow room? What happened to the 'deterrent'—hadn't we seen how thin these arguments had proved in the past; why would it be different in the future?" His was a "feeling," Lilienthal confessed, "that we are all giving far too high a value to atomic weapons, little, big, or biggest; and that just as the A-bomb obscured our view and gave a false sense of security, we are in danger of falling into the same error again in discussion of [the 'Super']—some cheap, easy way out."[4]

Another participant in the early debate on the atomic bomb, Robert Oppenheimer, was dismayed at what seemed an uncritical acceptance of the need for a super-bomb. For Oppenheimer there was no doubt that the sudden impetus for the "Super" had come from the Soviet atomic test. McMahon's committee, he wrote, "having tried to find something tangible to chew on ever since September 23rd, has at last found its answer. We must have a super, and we must have it fast."[5]

Convinced neither that the super-bomb was feasible nor that it would, if feasible, prove decisive in war, Oppenheimer marveled that "this thing appears to have caught the imagination, both of congressional and of military people, as *the answer* to the problem posed by the Russian advance." Privately admitting that "it would be folly to oppose exploration of this weapon"—a prediction his own career would tragically bear out—Oppenheimer refused to accept the super-bomb "as the way to save the country and the peace." Instead, the allure of the "Super" was "full of dangers," and represented to him a doomed effort to "return to a state of affairs approximating monopoly."[6]

The reservations of Lilienthal and Oppenheimer were generally shared by the scientists who composed the Atomic Energy Commission's General Advisory Committee, and who convened at the end of October to consider the "Super's" prospects and implications. As scientists, many of the committee's members objected to the hydrogen bomb on technical grounds, viewing any crash effort to develop the weapon as premature until more was understood about the mechanics of fusion. The super-bomb to them seemed equally unwarranted from the viewpoint of strategy, since "reprisals by our large stock of atomic bombs would be comparably effective to the use of a super."[7]

However, to these scientists, as well as to Lilienthal and Oppenheimer, the practical and strategic liabilities of the "Super" were all subordinate to a more fundamental concern. The majority of the committee's members rebelled at the very concept of the hydrogen bomb, whose immense destructive force made its effects necessarily indiscriminate, and hence capable of "exterminating civilian populations." The scientists' individual statements, appended to the committee's recommendation against development of the super-bomb, showed that their essential objection to the new weapon was ethical. The "Super" was branded by them "a weapon of genocide," and "necessarily an evil thing considered in any light."*

---

*The practical objection to the "Super"—that it would prove unworkable—was mistakenly overrated by Oppenheimer and some other scientists. Virtually all of these critics ceased to object to the super-bomb on pragmatic grounds once it was shown to be feasible. However, their moral objection to the weapon remained. Misestimates on the effects of nuclear weapons, even by atomic scientists, were not uncommon. AEC Commissioner Sumner Pike, initially a foe but later a reluctant proponent of the "Super," believed that radioactive fallout from nuclear tests posed no hazard to human health.[8]

To yet another early participant in the all-but-forgotten initial controversy over the atomic bomb, James Conant, there was an uncomfortable sense of *déjà vu* about the debate over the "Super" in fall 1949. "This whole discussion," he told Lilienthal, "makes me feel I was seeing the same film, and a punk one, for the second time."[9]

"A Billion-dollar Blunder"

The sudden bankruptcy of the policy of monopoly because of the Russian bomb was also a reason for navy critics of U.S. strategy to redouble their efforts at forcing a reexamination of its air-atomic emphasis. The forum for what would subsequently be termed the "admirals' revolt" was a week-long series of hearings conducted in mid-October by the House Armed Services Committee. Those hearings were convened to consider a specific navy allegation: that the air force's reliance upon the new B-36 bomber represented "a billion-dollar blunder." But they quickly expanded to cover the whole spectrum of interservice differences over the atomic blitz.

There was, of course, nothing new by this time in arguments against the air force's version of air-atomic strategy. Before he directed the Harmon and Hull committees to study those problems, Forrestal had even briefly considered staging a modern-day joust between air force bombers and navy interceptors as a means of testing—and possibly deflating—the claims of air-power proponents. Aviator Billy Mitchell had similarly debunked the myth of the battleship's invulnerability to air attack more than a generation before. Forrestal's own sense of diplomacy had restrained him from actually proposing such a bizarre contest, and he subsequently deplored the efforts of navy officers engaged in what he considered "destructive criticism of a sister Service" by denigrating "the capabilities of the bomber aircraft of the Air Force to penetrate enemy territory."[10]

Since Forrestal's departure, however, the navy had clearly been losing its propaganda war with the air force over the future direction of strategy. Chief of Naval Operations Louis Denfeld wrote in September 1949 that the situation in the Pentagon "has slowly gotten progressively worse" for the navy, since Defense Secretary Johnson "has surrounded himself by Army and Air Force officers and cannot help but listen to their advice."[11] No longer willing to suffer the loss of appropriations and prestige in silence, "new navy" advocates counterattacked in the House hearings, their charges given additional drama by the news of the Soviet bomb.

The first public criticism of the B-36 bomber had surfaced in an unlikely place—*Aviation Week* magazine. Suggesting that the new bomber was not the "super plane" that air force enthusiasts claimed, the editors called for a critical review of the decision to make the atomic-armed B-36 America's principal strategic weapon.[12] Yet the furor over the B-36 was really more a symbolic than a substantive issue in the House hearings. What appeared to the press, the public, and many congressmen as a single-minded effort to discredit the air force was, in fact, only the spearhead of an attack that the navy had hoped to make on a much broader front. However, it was forbidden from doing so on the grounds of security while the findings of the Harmon and Hull committees remained secret. The real target of that attack was to have been neither the B-36 nor the air force, but air-atomic strategy itself. Frustrated in their efforts at directing the hearings to an investigation of the feasibility of the atomic blitz, navy spokesmen tried another tack—the charge that American strategy, because of its reliance upon weapons of mass destruction, was inherently immoral.[13]

This shift in tactics gave the navy's argument a confused, even schizophrenic quality. Initially professing skepticism about the atomic bomb's effectiveness in war, the navy had subsequently appeared to embrace the bomb willingly in hopes that the geographical difficulties of intercontinental bombing would guarantee it a wartime role. With the scuttling of its first supercarrier, however, and its failure to shoot down the B-36 at the hearings, the navy retreated to an amended version of its former argument—that use of the bomb was not only militarily ineffective, but ethically insupportable. Hardly surprising was the sarcastic observation of one air force officer, who probably spoke for many at the hearings, that to the navy an immoral weapon was one it was unable to use.[14]

In fact, the navy's argument against the atomic blitz was complex but logically sound. It was based in part upon a comparison of atomic bombing with the conventional "saturation" bombing of the Second World War, which the Air Force's own *Strategic Bombing Survey* had determined was ineffective, if not inhumane. A less theoretical objection to air-atomic strategy was the navy's contention that strategic bombing would jeopardize the stability of any postwar peace by the bitterness it created in the homeless survivors, just as satura-tion bombing was believed to have prolonged the previous war.[15] The navy's argument on moral grounds, therefore, had pragmatism at its heart. As an alternative to the atomic blitz, navy representa-tives proposed that carrier-based bombers launch tactical atomic raids against the invading Soviet armies.[16] Curiously, the most compelling argument against an overreliance on the bomb—the fact that the monopoly's recent end put the future of deterrence in doubt—was not used by the navy, perhaps out of fear that this might undermine its own case. This argument was only once broached by navy officers in the course of the hearings, and then quickly abandoned.[17]

On the defensive at the start of these hearings, the air force went over to the attack on the question of morality. Indeed, the ap-parent indecisiveness of navy spokesmen left them open to the coun-tercharge that their sole motivation was the interests of their service; air-atomic advocates claimed that the end result of the navy's allega-tions would be to undermine American security. Air Force General Hoyt Vandenberg argued that the atomic blitz was moral insofar as it would save American lives: "A prime objective of this country must be to find a counterbalance to the potential enemy's masses of ground troops other than equal masses of American and Allied ground troops. . . . No such balancing factor exists other than strate-gic bombing."[18] The fact that the Harmon Report had already cast serious doubt upon the effectiveness of such bombing, and that the interim findings of the Hull committee suggested an air-atomic at-tack could not be carried out as planned in any case, could not be used by navy representatives at these sessions for reasons of secrecy. Instead, they were forced to retreat to the misunderstood moral ar-gument, which unwittingly took attention away from the questions they had wished to confront.

The navy's argument ultimately foreclosed the discussion of strat-egy it had meant to stimulate. Not only did navy representatives fail to discredit air-atomic strategy, therefore, but their failure even seemed to justify that strategy's emphasis upon the bomb. *Aviation Week* reported in late October that the air force's success in repulsing the navy's attack appeared to guarantee both the doctrinal and the budgetary ascendency of air power.[19]

"So Little Moral Protest"

It was hardly surprising that the navy's emphasis upon moral objections to American strategy elicited little sympathy from the pragmatic members of the House committee, the administration, or the public. The popular attitude toward the morality of atomic bombing was at best ambivalent. Grenville Clark had stressed the unique nature of the moral dilemma created by atomic weapons when he complained to Lilienthal in 1949 "that this deliberate, planned in advance destruction of non-combatant life is something that the American people has never before been asked to accept, and is inexpressibly shocking to the conscience."[20]

In reality, the bombing of Hiroshima had occasioned scant moral outrage among Americans at the time. "Not the least extraordinary fact about the postwar period is that mass extermination has awakened so little moral protest," philosopher Lewis Mumford observed in late 1945.[21] Public-opinion surveys bear out Mumford's observation. A Gallup poll taken only two weeks after the destruction of Hiroshima showed that 85 percent of Americans approved of the bombing. A *Fortune* survey two months after the Japanese surrender indicated that many citizens felt remorse over the act, but a majority —53.5 percent—still approved the atomic bombings "without reservation." The *Fortune* poll showed as well the dangers of what members of the National Security Council feared as "wartime emotionalism." Thus nearly a quarter of those questioned thought that the United States should have dropped many more atomic bombs "before Japan had a chance to surrender." Indeed, 13 percent of the respondents to a December 1944 Gallup poll favored the outright extermination of the Japanese.[22]

The passage of time and efforts to put the atomic bombings in perspective—such as the publication of John Hersey's *Hiroshima* in 1946—naturally changed attitudes toward the atomic bomb. A 1947 poll by the Social Science Research Council, for example, showed that a majority of citizens believed the bomb made war less likely. But a majority as well were willing to drop the bomb on an enemy, whether or not he used it against the United States first.[23]

. . .

Alternately bemused and disgusted by the spectacle of interservice rivalry in Congress, Truman put a prompt end to the "admirals' revolt" by dismissing Denfeld and other navy participants shortly after the inconclusive hearings were abandoned. But it was also Truman—apparently never aware of the substantive issues behind the abortive "revolt" —who on his own and a month later raised the question that the navy had wanted to answer at the hearings. Citing the "immediate need for the best conclusions that can be developed from the information now available," the President requested the findings of the Hull committee on the probable effectiveness of an air-atomic attack against Russia.[24]

The Hull Report, when finally available to the President on January 23, would substantially bear out the navy's allegations in the October hearings. By that date, however, the argument against the air force and the atomic blitz was already about to be made obsolete by the new and even more horrific vision of a war fought with "super-bombs."[25]

As the shock of the Russian bomb wore off, the Truman administration seemed outwardly unaffected by the atomic monopoly's end. The President's own repeated public assurances that the Soviet test had not taken the United States unawares even seemed an implicit argument against any steps to counter the Russians' achievement. But Truman's claim that the government had not been surprised was freely contradicted by a consensus of newspaper and magazine articles following announcement of the test.[26]

Actually, the administration's illusion of calm had begun to shatter, inwardly, only weeks—if not days—after the Russian bomb was confirmed, and the assumptions on which the policy of monopoly had been based were proved wrong. Only the previous June, a briefing paper prepared for the joint chiefs' appearance before a congressional appropriations committee had stressed that America's defense was at least adequate. The joint chiefs were instructed to testify that "our degree of military readiness is not the ultimate, nor even entirely satisfactory from the purely military standpoint, but we do consider that it does provide a reasonable degree of security and a basis from which ultimate success may be achieved in the event of hostilities." Even this qualified endorsement of military preparedness was lacking, however, in the aftermath of the Russian bomb.[27]

One cause of the turnabout in thinking following the monopoly's end was the soon-evident fallacy of Groves' confident reassurance, only a day after Truman's announcement of the Soviet test, that America's real concern should not be the Russian bomb *per se* "but how good that one is and how many they have, and can they catch up with us."[28] Groves' expectation was that America's supposed monopoly of atomic raw materials would either prevent the Russians from building many additional bombs or, at the minimum, keep the Soviets' nuclear stockpile to only a fraction of that of the United States. Yet the secret evidence of radioactive samples confirmed subsequent announcements by the Russians themselves that the weapon tested had been of an advanced design more sophisticated and efficient than the bomb that destroyed Hiroshima. By this single fact were America's vaunted "know-how" and the allegedly preclusive raw-materials monopoly together exposed as illusory. Conceivably, this was a much ruder shock to those initiates of Groves' work in the Manhattan Project and the Combined Development Trust than the unexpectedly early advent of the Russian bomb. It was also, fatefully, the origin of the myth that the atomic secret had been stolen by spies.*

Indicative, too, of the change in perceptions brought about by the monopoly's end was the Pentagon's mid-October reassessment of the Russian bomb's effect upon Western strategy. This study ascribed to the Russians the capability previously denied them "of producing an effective quantity of bombs in a relatively short period of time." The advanced nature of the Soviet bomb raised the even more disturbing prospect, U.S. planners warned, that "Russia has developed a simpler method of harnessing Atomic Energy than our own."[30]

This shift in the perception of the Russian threat led to a change in other assumptions concerning U.S. security. In the event of a nuclear war, the Pentagon now speculated, Russia could blunt the effect of America's atomic attacks by moving industry into a western Europe occupied by the Red Army. "This course would enable Russia to achieve dominance over all of the Eurasian land mass, and place her in position for an early conquest of Africa, and the isolation of the Western Hemisphere for later attack, before U.S. industry could recover."[31] The

---

*The uranium for the Russian atomic bomb evidently came from the Saxony region of eastern Germany. Groves, in fact, had been advised by the War Department as early as November 1946 that the Russians were utilizing German uranium; subsequent State Department and CIA reports confirmed the mammoth scale of Russian mining in Saxony. The claim of exclusive "know-how" rested in large part upon the shaped explosive "lens mold" of the implosion-type bomb—a technology in which the Russians were acknowledged by American scientists to have been the most advanced before the Second World War. The claim that they had transmitted information to Russia on lens-mold design was the essence of the case against Ethel and Julius Rosenberg.[29]

timing and character of the Russian atomic test also necessitated a considerable revision of U.S. estimates concerning the future size of the Soviet nuclear arsenal. While the most pessimistic of the joint chiefs' earlier predictions had foreseen only twenty bombs in the Russian stockpile by mid-1955, October estimates declared that the Soviets might have that number in just a few months, and could be expected to possess at least 110 bombs by mid-1953. It was thought that "A-day," the earliest date the Russians might be able to launch a decisive attack against the United States, should be moved up correspondingly—though how far was still a subject of dispute. "No agreed intelligence projecting enemy capabilities in 1954 and taking into consideration enemy possession of the atomic bomb in 1949 exists," the army noted. But the possibility of an "all-out war" between the United States and Russia by 1951–52 was not ruled out by the joint chiefs.[32]

For the perennial advocates of air power, the news of the Russian test was an opportunity as much as a threat. Arguing that the Soviets now had the ability to "Pearl Harborize" American defenses, air-power enthusiasts urged that the administration reconsider its rejection of the seventy-group Air Force.[33] While unwilling to sacrifice his austerity budget upon that particular altar, Truman tacitly acknowledged the seriousness of the situation by again requesting the Hull committee's findings as soon as they became available. The joint chiefs also ordered a revision of the short-range emergency war plan Offtackle. Significantly, Dropshot—the long-range war plan which had assumed continued U.S. nuclear superiority—was abandoned by them altogether.[34]

"And Hark What Discord Follows"

One of the major but unforeseen results of the Russian atomic test was the impetus that it gave to the debate in the administration over the super-bomb. In an effort to resolve that debate quickly, Truman had appointed the same members of the group that had advised him on increased atomic-bomb production—Lilienthal, Acheson, and Johnson —to a committee concerned with the future of the "Super." Dubbed the "Z Committee" by Lilienthal, this advisory body itself exemplified the conflicting emotions and thoughts in the government on the subject of the hydrogen bomb. As such, it also mirrored the larger disagreement over the direction of American strategy.

Observing that his opposition to that strategy had "not proven contagious the previous fall," Lilienthal continued to object to "the continuing reliance upon big bombs" which the "Super" represented. Such reliance, he wrote in his journal, was "a means of deception," not the least of which was self-deception: "If we keep saying we want the [international] control policy when we don't, we are perhaps fooling others, but we shouldn't commit a fraud upon ourselves."[35]

The AEC chairman found little support for his ideas in the Cabinet. Formerly allied with Lilienthal on most matters concerning the atomic bomb, Acheson was ambivalent on the "Super," believing that there was a need to balance the President's prior commitment to international control of nuclear weapons against the future requirements of U.S. security. Louis Johnson felt no such hesitation. Just as he had supported increased atomic-bomb production, Johnson was wholeheartedly in favor of the super-bomb.[36]

Reflecting similar disagreement within the State Department over the "Super" was the conflict between George Kennan, about to retire from the government, and Paul Nitze, Kennan's replacement as head of the Policy Planning Staff.[37] Like Johnson, Nitze was an early and unabashed proponent of the hydrogen bomb. Troubled that a positive decision on the "Super" might become a juggernaut taking America down the atomic road, Kennan had begun drafting in October an eighty-page statement against the super-bomb which, when completed the following January, he hoped to present to Truman as his parting act in the administration.

Like Lilienthal, Kennan rested his argument upon ethical objections to the "Super" and the strategy of atomic blitz. Together, he wrote, the two "reach backward beyond the frontiers of western civilization, to the concepts of warfare which were once familiar to the Asiatic hordes." History had shown that the utility of such weapons in diplomacy was doubtful, Kennan wrote. Their very power gave nuclear weapons "peculiar psychological overtones" and "a certain top-heaviness as instruments of our national policy" in peacetime; and only the "vague and highly dangerous promise of 'decisive' results" in the event of war. The super-bomb would also be a weapon out of all proportion to what the United States might wish to accomplish in war or peace. As fond as Truman of literary allusions, Kennan professed to see a "prophetic applicability" to the "Super" in the lines from *Troilus and*

Cressida: "Take but degree away—untune that string/ And hark what discord follows . . ."*

Going well beyond the moral critique of the super-bomb was Kennan's call for "a clean and straight beginning" in American policy toward nuclear weapons. Such a policy would include renouncing their first use, and reviving serious efforts toward achieving international control.[39]

Even as the debate over the "Super" raged among members of the Z Committee and in the State Department, the joint chiefs had yet to enter the controversy by the late fall of 1949. To Lilienthal, Kennan, and other foes of the super-bomb, the apparent indifference of military leaders was thought to be less a sign of disinterest than tacit confirmation of their argument that the hydrogen bomb was, by its very nature, not a military weapon but an instrument of indiscriminate destruction. Indeed, the military's own targeting studies lent credence to that contention. They concluded that, apart from a few hardened or especially large objectives in Russia, "the majority of targets do not require a more powerful bomb because of area limitations." Even one of the most vocal proponents of the "Super"—Senator Brian McMahon—conceded that "there are scarcely more than two or three urban targets in all Russia which measure up to the tremendous destructive power of [the super-bomb], and they could be thoroughly attacked with ordinary atomic bombs." Accordingly, the joint chiefs' report to Truman in late January 1950 on the strategic significance of increased atomic-bomb production neglected to include the super-bomb among future military requirements.[40]

Subsequent to prodding by civilian advocates of the "Super" such as Strauss and Lawrence, however, the joint chiefs and members of the Atomic Energy Commission's Military Liaison Committee suddenly professed to find a virtue in its necessarily indiscriminate nature. Revealingly, the principal argument for the "Super" made by joint chiefs chairman Omar Bradley had little or nothing to do with military advantage, but concerned only the bomb's psychological value *vis-à-vis* the Russians. "Possession of a thermonuclear weapon by the USSR without such possession by the United States would be intolerable," he claimed,

---

*Then everything includes in power—
Power into will, will into appetite,
And appetite, a universal wolf,
So doubly seconded with will and power,
Must make perforce a universal prey
And last eat up himself.[38]

both by its "profoundly demoralizing effect upon the American people" and by the "tremendous psychological boost" it would afford Soviet leaders.[41]

The intangible attraction of "psychological" superiority subsequently assumed a dominant place in the military's advocacy of the super-bomb. There was, indeed, a hauntingly familiar ring to the brief on the "Super" that the joint chiefs sent to Truman in mid-January. Arguing that a U.S. monopoly of the hydrogen bomb "might have a sobering effect in favor of peace" and "might be a decisive factor if properly used" in war, the joint chiefs wrote of its ability to "grossly alter the psychological balance between the United States and the USSR," adding that American possession of the "Super" might tilt "the balance . . . grossly in favor of the United States until such time as the USSR had developed a stockpile of super bombs."

The joint chiefs' memorandum revealed an argument for the "Super" that was at best logically inconsistent, and possibly disingenuous. It was not the intent of U.S. strategy, they averred, "to destroy large cities *per se,*" but "only to attack such targets as are necessary in war in order to impose the national objectives of the United States upon an enemy." It was "folly to argue whether one weapon is more immoral than another," for "in the larger sense, it is war itself which is immoral, and the stigma of such immorality must rest upon the nation which initiates hostilities." Pointedly, the joint chiefs did not rule out use of the "Super" as a preemptive rather than just a retaliatory weapon of war. In fact, their rationale as to why the United States should retain a right to use the "Super" first—"the best defense is a good offense"—was, by extension, a prima facie case for preventive war.

The possibility that use of a weapon as indiscriminate in its effects as the "Super" would actually make America's limited war objectives less attainable was nowhere mentioned by the joint chiefs. Neither was the prospect mentioned that the first nation to use weapons of mass destruction against civilians would most likely suffer humanity's moral stigma. Nor, finally, did their psychological claim for the super-bomb ultimately rest upon any firmer ground than the moral claim against it made by Lilienthal, Kennan, and the scientists of the Atomic Energy Commission. It was this supposed psychological benefit that Kennan thought gave nuclear weapons their "peculiar" overtones in foreign policy, and which Lilienthal had branded the previous October as the fundamental flaw of America's dependence upon the atomic bomb.

Public-opinion surveys also suggest that the joint chiefs were much more affected by the psychology of the "Super" than were the American people. In a November 1950 poll barely a quarter of those questioned believed the hydrogen bomb would "easily" assure victory in a war with Russia; 37 percent saw the super-bomb as playing a "significant" role in a war, whereas 20 percent believed the weapon would make "no difference at all."[42]

Either unaware of or unconvinced by this sentiment, the joint chiefs based their final plea for the "Super" upon the dubious premise that it would restore to the United States the elusive advantage lost since the Soviet atomic test, and that "the public expects the Department of Defense to take action necessary to regain the favorable balance previously held."

Despite their evident attachment to the ancient bromide that "the best defense is a good offense," the joint chiefs apparently never believed that the American public would expect—or sanction—an unprovoked, preemptive atomic attack upon the Soviet Union. It is perhaps surprising that the idea of preventive war was not more generally discussed during the years of America's atomic monopoly. One reason may be that a preemptive attack made before the Russians had an atomic bomb would come too soon, but one made once they had broken the atomic monopoly would be too late. Certainly the threat, at least, of preventive war was implicit in the atomic league proposed to the joint chiefs by Bernard Baruch and Fred Searls in May 1946. The joint chiefs themselves had once suggested that the President and Congress might want to consider undertaking something akin to preventive war when it became evident that Russia's version of the Manhattan Project was close to success—this development itself being considered a provocation—and U.S. war planning never excluded that possibility. By September 1949 the United States had clearly missed its opportunity, although some in Congress, the administration, and the press were reluctant to admit that the moment had passed. Members of the Joint Committee on Atomic Energy, for example, discussed the possibility of preventive war when they learned of the Soviet atomic test. The prospect was brought up once again by Nitze's Policy Planning Staff at a policy review of spring 1950 as one path the United States might take, and it was not readily abandoned by columnist Joseph Alsop even after 1950.

In the midst of the "Super" debate, Secretary of State Dean Acheson was surprised to discover that the idea was still not dead. Thus one member of a Senate delegation to his office urged that the administration consider Russia's refusal to accept international control "to be in itself an act of aggression which would provoke a declaration of war on our part." Another senator asked in evident exasperation: "[W]hy don't we get into this thing now and get it over with before the time is too late?" Later that fall, Navy Secretary Francis Matthews and War College director Orville Anderson apparently had similar thoughts in mind; Matthews suggested that Americans become the first "aggressors for peace." Although both men were subsequently dismissed by Truman— presumably for their outspokenness on the subject—the notion of preventive war survived elsewhere into the Eisenhower administration. Curtis LeMay has noted in his memoirs that it was discussed by senior air force officers while he was SAC commander in 1953.*

"There Actually Was No Decision to Make"

Truman evidently found the joint chiefs' argument for the "Super" persuasive, whatever its demerits in logic. In a telephone call on January 19, Truman told Sidney Souers, director of the National Security Council, that the joint chiefs' recommendation "made a lot of sense, and . . . he was inclined to think that was what we should do." Truman was more definite two days later in a comment to Eben Ayers: "The President indicated to us at a staff meeting this week, when the possibility of questions [about the super-bomb] coming up at a press conference was raised, that he has reached his decision. He did not disclose what it was, however."[44]

With Truman's mind apparently already made up on the subject, the culminating debate on the super-bomb in the Oval Office on the last day of January was anticlimactic. The pall left by the Soviet atomic test and the changed perception of the Russian threat made the prospect of abandoning the "Super" all but unthinkable. By this time not only the joint chiefs but the National Security Council and the Z Committee had

---

*The Russians were certainly not unmindful of American discussions concerning preventive war. In a recent book on Soviet-American relations by two Russian history professors, the section on the advent of the atomic bomb is dominated by provocative statements of prominent Americans urging a preventive or preemptive nuclear attack upon Russia. The Soviet historians contend that the American government silenced military leaders who doubted the omnipotent nature of the bomb, and knowingly provoked the nuclear arms race. They conclude that the "[m]onopoly of atomic arms did not nullify traditional foreign policy."[43]

endorsed a limited program to determine the feasibility of the weapon, though with varying degrees of enthusiasm. Defense Secretary Johnson, already shown to be as tireless and unscrupulous in promoting the hydrogen bomb as he had the strategy of atomic blitz, bypassed the Z Committee by forwarding the joint chiefs' report directly to the President. Johnson hoped by this expedient to ensure a quick, favorable decision.[45]

Acheson decided to withhold Kennan's eighty-page argument against the "Super" from the President—partly from conviction, but also as a matter of tactics. The moral claim against the weapon, he believed, had been vitiated by the debacle of the abortive "admirals' revolt," and was further undermined by the crisis atmosphere attending the advent of the Russian atomic bomb. Kennan himself did not participate in the debate; he had retired as head of the Policy Planning Staff at the beginning of the year. There is no evidence that Truman ever saw —or was even aware of—his elaborate opus on the super-bomb and American strategy.[46]

Also about to retire from the administration, Lilienthal alone was left to present the final and quixotic argument against the "Super." Like Acheson, he had bowed to the inevitability of the super-bomb. But he hoped to use the occasion of the Oval Office meeting to plead once again for the reexamination of American policy toward nuclear weapons that he, Forrestal, and Kennan had been urging upon the administration since the spring of 1948. Lilienthal's appeal was abruptly cut short, however, by Truman's brief announcement that the United States would proceed with a program to determine the feasibility of the hydrogen bomb. His dissent at the January 31 meeting, Lilienthal later wrote, was like saying "no to a steamroller." Disillusioned and depressed, he told an aide after Truman's decision that the AEC had become "nothing more than a major contractor to the Department of Defense."[47]

Ironically, Lilienthal's endorsement months earlier of increased atomic-bomb production—in the hope that this step would make the "Super" unnecessary—had apparently assured Truman's choice of the hydrogen bomb. Truman told Eben Ayers a week after the White House meeting that "there actually was no decision to make on the H-bomb. . . . The President said this really was a question that was settled in making up the budget for the AEC last fall when 300,000,000 dollars was allotted." There was a final—and familiar—impetus to his decision, Truman admitted: "He went on to say that we had got to do it—make the bomb—though none wants to use it. But, he said, we have got to have it only for bargaining purposes with the Russians."[48]

By his decision to proceed with the "Super," Truman confirmed the growing dependence of U.S. strategy upon nuclear weapons. The decision committed not only American strategy but also American security to what the Franck committee in 1945 had termed the "fragile hope" of staying ahead in the nuclear arms race. Indeed, the fact that the President chose to view the super-bomb decision as merely an extension of his previous decision to increase atomic-bomb production demonstrated how the arms race had already begun to create its own momentum.

It was also indicative of the ease with which most Americans had begun to adapt to the manifest terrors of the thermonuclear age that Truman's announcement of his decision to proceed with development of the "Super"—which many newspapers had come to call the "hell bomb"—occasioned little public excitement. Neither surprise nor disappointment greeted Truman's announcement to the Cabinet. Ayers wrote in his diary for the 31st: "The remainder of the day was fairly quiet. I went home by trolley for dinner. . . ."[49]

"The Cold War Is . . . a Real War"

After announcing his decision, Truman made one concession to his critics by acceding to their request that he begin a major review of American policies for fighting the cold war. This was hardly a major victory for such critics, however. In fact, a review of cold war strategy had been planned months earlier for the coming year. On January 5, 1950, the National Security Council began its own study, and two weeks later one was initiated under the direction of the State Department Policy Planning Staff's new director, Paul Nitze. Most important, Truman's decision on the "Super" seemed itself to foreclose any serious considerations of major changes in the administration's policies. Also militating against any thorough review were the death of Forrestal and the retirement of Lilienthal and Kennan—the three most vocal challengers of American policy concerning Russia and the bomb.

In the weeks that followed Truman's H-bomb decision, the review of cold war strategy begun with the new year seemed even less likely to result in the type of changes that critics had urged. The perjury conviction of alleged spy Alger Hiss on January 21 had not influenced Truman's decision, but it was undoubtedly taken by many Americans as additional evidence that the United States was losing the cold war to Russia.[50] Only three days after Truman's announcement of the 31st, the arrest of British physicist Klaus Fuchs on charges of spying for the Soviet Union appeared to confirm this direful judgment. Fuchs had worked on the atomic bomb project during the war at both Los Alamos and Harwell, and was widely—but mistakenly—thought to have taken part in early research on the "Super."

While neither Hiss' conviction nor the arrest and subsequent confession of Fuchs affected the decision on the super-bomb, both together clouded the atmosphere in which the review of American cold war strategy would be conducted. A 1951 congressional report on Russian spying concluded that Fuchs did more damage "than any other spy, not only in the history of the United States, but in the history of nations. . . . the extent of the espionage damage known to have been inflicted upon the atomic energy position of the United States [by him] is indisputably severe." Yet the findings of that report cast doubt upon this very allegation, noting that Fuchs' treachery may only have advanced the Soviet atomic bomb project by a period of eighteen months—hardly the breakthrough or quantum leap claimed in the report's conclusion.[51]

Recently released Justice Department documents on what the FBI called the "Foocase" support Oppenheimer's claim at the time that Fuchs' efforts were probably of little or no use to the Russians. Fuchs' knowledge of the Manhattan Project primarily concerned uranium enrichment, not the chemistry of plutonium—with which the Russians made their first atomic bombs. Also, the allegation made in FBI reports that Fuchs "knew as much about the hydrogen bomb as any American scientist" in the Manhattan Project during the 1940s is less damaging than it might seem, since until 1950 that "knowledge" consisted mostly of serious doubts that the "Super" was feasible.[52]

The effort of former Manhattan Project scientists to put Fuchs' treason in perspective, however, only caused the FBI to investigate them in turn, and subsequently to impugn their loyalty without evidence. One such example of harassment was the memorandum sent by J. Edgar Hoover to FBI offices around the country relating the "off record" comment of physicist Hans Bethe to a newsman "that he could understand why [Fuchs] did what he did and he sympathized with [Fuchs'] attitude because a scientist is of the world and works for the world." Hoover ordered that Bethe be put under surveillance.[53]

The administration's immediate but little-noticed disclaimer when announcing the Russian bomb—that it had been developed without "anything stolen or copied from us"—was apparently accurate, Fuchs notwithstanding.* One definite result of Fuchs' espionage, however, was a new and final crisis in the beleaguered course of Anglo-American cooperation on atomic energy. Having already agreed to a renewal of the *modus vivendi* on sharing atomic raw materials, U.S. and British negotiators concerned with broadening such cooperation were compelled to abandon their efforts following Fuchs' arrest and the subsequent disclosure of lax security at Harwell. Henceforth, the British would be forced to rely entirely upon their own efforts in the commercial and military development of atomic energy. The United States would turn in its search for uranium to newly discovered sources in South Africa, and its own as-yet-untapped domestic resources.[55]

With Hiss and Fuchs as the most recent reminders of Russian treachery, it was no longer Soviet intentions but Soviet capabilities that most concerned the members of the joint chiefs, the National Security Council, and the State Department in their collective task of gauging the threat to American security.

The joint chiefs' January 1950 review of U.S. military requirements characterized this threat as of a seriousness previously unappreciated and growing, despite what they had hoped would be "the sobering effect" of America's decision to proceed with the super-bomb. Foremost among their concerns was the newly acknowledged possibility of a Russian nuclear attack upon the United States. The previous November, the air force's chief of staff had warned his colleagues that "almost any number of Soviet bombers could cross our borders and fly to most targets in the

---

*Another irony of the Fuchs case is that the studious physicist hardly fit the congressional committee's vision of a communist agent: "[A] lack of moral standards combined with an overweening and childlike arrogance—all induced by exposure to Communist recruiting techniques during early manhood—characterizes the Soviet spy." In fact, Fuchs proved that secrecy could be as much a weapon as a foil. At a secret Anglo-American conference on declassification procedures in October 1947, he broke with other scientists by protesting the early release of information on the bomb. Joining Fuchs in this objection at the conference was British diplomat Donald Maclean, who defected to Russia in 1951. The information that Maclean, as British representative on the Combined Development Agency, could have supplied concerning the West's stockpile of atomic raw materials and Western efforts to keep uranium out of Russian hands would certainly have been of greater value to the Soviets than anything known by Fuchs. America abandoned its membership in the Combined Development Agency after the revelation of Fuchs' spying.[54] Concerning the effect of Soviet espionage, see also the Epilogue.

United States without a shot being fired at them." But it was not until late January 1950 that the army, assigned responsibility for the air defense of North America, began to consider the problem.[56]

A spate of planning and intelligence studies by the joint chiefs in mid- and late February echoed the theme of a burgeoning Soviet threat. In response to Russia's nascent nuclear capability, one report recommended that in a war the air force launch its initial atomic raids upon Soviet atomic stockpiles and laboratories, rather than against Russian cities. A separate preview of a possible Russian attack upon the United States foresaw the immediate destruction of U.S. military bases with atomic bombs, Soviet paratroop landings in Alaska and Labrador, and the use of chemical and bacteriological warfare by the Russians in Europe and America—but not, curiously, attacks against U.S. cities themselves. A report concerned with the future of NATO asserted that Russia's nuclear capability might deter the United States from using atomic bombs in the defense of Europe—this despite the fact that the joint chiefs' only operational emergency war plan, Offtackle, had concluded that the bomb was necessary in Europe's defense.[57]

Indeed, far from the rapid collapse of Soviet resistance upon the initiation of an atomic blitz which the Air Force had predicted the previous summer, revised estimates by the joint chiefs attributed to Russia the ability to wage a protracted—and even victorious—war. They credited the Soviets, for example, with the capacity to "simultaneously" bomb Great Britain, invade and conquer Europe—including Norway, Sweden, the Iberian Peninsula, and the Strait of Gibraltar "if necessary" —as well as the Near and Middle East, and attain "limited objectives" in the Far East. The Russians, it was feared, would be able to achieve these objectives on the ground even as they maintained an extensive air and sea offensive against Allied communications, sabotaged and subverted "Allied interests around the world," and attacked military bases "within range" by air. "It is believed that the Soviet Union would have sufficient armed forces to undertake all the campaigns listed above and still have adequate reserves," this dire scenario concluded.[58]

None of the cataclysmic visions now entertained by the nation's military leaders was as distressing, however, as the report given Defense Secretary Johnson on February 20 by the AEC's Military Liaison Committee concerning its estimate of "maximum Soviet capabilities for atomic warfare." This study's premise was that, partly because of espionage,

"Soviet A-Bomb and H-Bomb capabilities are much higher" than any previous estimate, including that made earlier the same month by the Central Intelligence Agency.[59]

The CIA study had concluded that, as a dictatorship, the Soviet Union was "probably peculiarly vulnerable to atomic attack"; Russia would in any case be unable to threaten the United States with a "decisive" attack until mid-1954 at the earliest. Like Kennan, the CIA's analysts believed that possession of nuclear weapons by Russia would probably not cause any dramatic change in Soviet policy or tactics.

Given the climate of anxiety in Washington by the winter of 1950, however, the CIA's relatively optimistic assessment was fated to be either dismissed or considered as representing only Russia's "minimum" nuclear capability.

A particularly controversial feature of the CIA report was its assessment of Soviet intentions: "It has been asserted that only the existence of the U.S. atomic bomb prevented the USSR from carrying out an intention to continue its military advance to the Atlantic in 1945. There can be no doubt that the U.S. atomic bomb had a sobering and deterrent effect on the USSR. There is no reason to suppose, however, that the USSR had any such intention in 1945 or subsequently."

A State Department critique of this study retorted "that *lack* of evidence of a Soviet intention to use military force on the United States [cannot] be taken as *evidence* of the *absence* of such a Soviet intention." The objection of the army's analysts was much stronger, arguing that even "dissemination of the [CIA] paper and its use for planning purposes could seriously affect the security of the United States." The CIA assessment was branded "dangerous" by the air force, which contended in a curious rebuttal that "the Soviets made a major contribution to the outbreak of World War II," doing "nothing to prevent that war, and everything to make it a reality."[60]

Conceding that their calculations might "appear to be of a fantastic order," the members of the Military Liaison Committee meant to show "the other end of the bracket" regarding Soviet capabilities. In fact, one alarming hypothesis of their study had been anticipated in an earlier joint chiefs' estimate of the Soviet test's importance; the implications of the AEC committee's fearful conjecture were equally "of a fantastic order." Thus the same analysts who had formerly predicted that Russia's shortage of atomic raw materials would be a decisive disadvantage in the Soviets' efforts to build a bomb now professed to see an unexpected bonus for them in that supposed handicap. Indeed, the Russians whom Groves had dismissed in 1948 as "unequipped" to build a bomb were considered by Military Liaison Committee members to be possibly well ahead of the United States in the atomic arms race by early 1950.*

The Russians might have achieved this turnabout, committee members Kenneth Nichols, Herbert Loper, and Robert LeBaron argued, "by the adoption of alternative methods which we, unimpelled by necessity, have not conceived, or if conceived, have eliminated as less promising." More worrisome still was the prospect that, because of this initial frustration, the Russians would have put an early and fortuitous emphasis upon development of more efficient weapons—such as the "Super." The specter raised by the conclusion of the committee's top-secret report—that Russia's atomic "stockpile and current production capacity are equal or actually superior to our own, both as to yields and numbers" and that a Soviet hydrogen bomb "may be in actual production" already —showed that America's policy of monopoly was not only bankrupt, but had now been turned upside down by the Russian bomb.[62]

First to admit the failure of previous assumptions underpinning their planning were the joint chiefs. Just the year before they had confidently assumed that the United States would retain a tenfold atomic advantage over Russia until at least 1957. Now, in 1950, it was feared that this ratio might have already been reversed. Consequently, they "most urgently" advised Truman at the end of February to undertake the very course of action they had refrained from recommending in January[63]—a "crash" effort to develop the super-bomb.

The departure of Lilienthal and Kennan from the government removed any serious obstacle to such an effort. The belated conversion of Defense Secretary Johnson to the cause of increased military spending also assured that the austerity budget would no longer be a barrier. Johnson admitted in the course of post-monopoly congressional hearings into U.S. defense policy, therefore, that having erred on the estimate of the atomic monopoly's duration he had subsequently undergone a change of heart on the need to severely limit military spending.[64] His

---

*One of the authors of this report was Major General Kenneth Nichols. Nichols was Groves' former deputy and a key figure in the wartime work of the Manhattan Project's Murray Hill Area. Groves had also wanted Nichols as his replacement on the Military Liaison Committee. David Lilienthal rejected Groves' request, however, believing that Nichols was too "mercurial" for the job. When Admiral Lewis Strauss replaced Lilienthal as AEC chairman in January, he appointed Nichols to the committee.[61]

abandonment of the austerity budget was perhaps only symptomatic of the more fundamental concern that now gripped the administration regarding Russia. Truman, too, seemed to share that concern. Although the Atomic Energy Commission informed him that an "all-out" effort to develop the super-bomb would cost at least $100 million over previous estimates, the program was approved without hesitation by the President in early March.[65]

The changed perception of Soviet military capabilities in the wake of the Russian atomic test and the dire hypothesis of the Nichols-LeBaron memorandum assigned a new importance to the administration's pending review of American cold war strategy. As Kennan had predicted, the escalation in what was now understood as Soviet capabilities led inexorably to an escalation as well in what was thought to be the Soviet threat. In the matter of reassessing intentions as well as capabilities, moreover, the very conditions of fear and uncertainty which brought this reassessment into being precluded its producing any new understanding of Russia, or any dramatic turnabout in American policy.

By the end of March 1950, the joint chiefs and Nitze's Policy Planning Staff had outlined four new alternative approaches for American foreign policy in response to the Russian threat. Of the four, the two extremes were to return to an isolationist foreign policy, on the one hand, or to launch a preventive nuclear war against Russia, on the other. Both were only briefly considered and then dismissed as impractical and politically unacceptable. Given longer consideration was the alternative of a renewed effort at international control of the bomb, or vaguely defined "affirmative measures [meant] to foment and support unrest and revolution in eastern Europe and Russia"—the "current Soviet cold war technique used against the Soviet," one analyst observed.[66]

What would otherwise have been a fifth possibility—that of continuing the current policy—was deemed not only to be likely to result in failure, but to contain a certain political risk as well. A State Department survey of American public opinion in early March assessed, therefore, that most citizens would support "adoption of stronger U.S. foreign policy measures." Indeed, unless such measures were forthcoming, this survey concluded, there might be "increasing public pressure, which could become dangerous, for some sort of bold action."[67]

A return to international control had been part of the "clean and straight beginning" that Kennan had hoped to urge upon the administration in the period of soul-searching after the Russian atomic test. Even the joint chiefs—belatedly recognizing that "the existence of two large opposing atomic capabilities may be a greater incitement to war than a deterrent to war"—had become the unlikely advocates of international control at that time, motivated by the worry that her closed society gave Russia a decisive advantage in planning a surprise atomic attack. But the joint chiefs, too, had ultimately abandoned international control as a practical course for a second time when they acknowledged it "impossible to hope that an effective plan . . . can be negotiated unless and until the Kremlin design has been frustrated to a point at which genuine and drastic change in Soviet policies has taken place."

Truman himself had perhaps had the last word on this subject in summer 1949 when he told a gathering of administration advisers at Blair House: "I am of the opinion we'll never obtain international control. Since we can't obtain international control we must be strongest in atomic weapons."[68]

It was thus in the belief that every other alternative was likely to be either politically unacceptable or doomed to failure that this collective review of American strategy and policy put forward its recommendation that the United States "confront [Russia] by means of a rapid build-up, sufficiently advanced by mid-1954, and by means of action intended to wrest the initiative from the Soviet Union."[69]

While recognizing that the Russian challenge to the United States was "of the same character" as that depicted by NSC-20, the joint Pentagon–State Department study argued that recent developments showed this challenge to be both more serious and "more immediate than had previously been estimated." Specifically, Russia's actual possession of atomic bombs and the looming prospect of a Soviet "Super" "have greatly intensified the Soviet threat to the security of the United States." Russia's capabilities, not intentions, were the principal concern in this study, since the latter were no longer believed to be in doubt: "The Soviet Union, unlike previous aspirants to hegemony, is animated by a new fanatic faith, antithetical to our own, and seeks to impose its absolute authority over the rest of the world." What was termed the "fundamental design of the Kremlin" did not exclude the prospect that Russia would initiate a nuclear war—"swiftly and with stealth"—as early as 1954.[70]

Significantly, the Pentagon–State Department study did not contain estimates as to what the recommended rapid buildup of U.S. military strength would cost. Nor were such estimates forthcoming before the study was submitted to Truman in mid-April, though he had requested them. In his memoirs, Acheson explained this omission as resulting from disagreements over such estimates among the drafters. Documents appended to the study suggest that the increases envisioned might necessitate a doubling or even tripling of 1950's $14.4 billion defense budget for many years. They would certainly require, in any case, major public sacrifice as well as "domestic financial and economic adjustments."*

Designated NSC-68, this culminating product of the policy review requested by the President the previous January was not immediately approved by Truman—in part because of its still-unspecified costs. But its importance in laying the groundwork for the permanent mobilization of the United States in the cold war was almost immediately recognized in the administration. Ultimately, NSC-68 provided the funds and the rationale not only for the "all-out" effort to build the super-bomb but for the conventional rearming of America as well.

Truman's approval of NSC-68 some months later as the seminal expression of American foreign policy—in circumstances which themselves appeared to underscore the validity of its analysis—seemed to accept as inevitable the increasing militarization of the cold war. It also announced a principle which would be guiding throughout the remainder of his administration and, indeed, well into the next generation— "that the cold war is in fact a real war in which the survival of the free world is at stake."

"A Situation of Great Danger"

Insofar as they were each given impetus by the sudden end of America's nuclear monopoly, Truman's decisions to proceed with the "Super" and with NSC-68 were properly the culminating events of the policy on the atomic bomb that had begun with the destruction of Hiroshima. In peacetime, that policy had neither guaranteed American security nor

---

*According to a December 1950 cost accounting of NSC-68, the necessary transformation of the home front would be stark. It was anticipated that the mobilization of industry, for example, would cause automobile production to decline by 60 percent or more from its 1950 level. Housing construction would be cut by one-third; production of televisions and radios by "much more than this, if not eliminated entirely, in order to meet military demands for electronics."[71]

perceptibly advanced American interests; instead, it may have spurred parallel Soviet developments in weaponry. Had war with Russia occurred, the joint chiefs' own reappraisals in the aftermath of the Soviet bomb left little doubt that the "winning weapon" would have been militarily indecisive—and almost certainly would have forfeited the negotiated peace that the United States sought. Indeed, the very existence of NSC-68 seemed a tacit admission on the administration's part that not even its decision for the super-bomb was sufficient to guarantee American security, once the atomic monopoly had ended and the policy of monopoly lay in ruins.

Certainly any new illusion of security that the super-bomb and NSC-68 may have given the Truman administration was shattered within months by the communist invasion of South Korea. From its outset, the June 1950 invasion was branded by the CIA as "undoubtedly undertaken at Soviet direction." Concurring in this view at emergency meetings on the crisis, the National Security Council believed that the Korean attack signaled a new readiness on the part of the Kremlin to provoke local conflicts where Russian interests were at little risk, but not necessarily a radical departure in Soviet strategy. The implications of the attack were ominous nonetheless. The council anxiously forecast similar eruptions throughout a virtual galaxy of world trouble spots—in Yugoslavia, Germany, Austria, Hong Kong, Tibet, Burma, and Iran.[72]

As with the 1948 crisis over Berlin, the reaction of the nation's military leaders to the Korean invasion was to stress America's relative weakness. Were the Soviets to compound the Korean invasion with another blockade of Berlin, for example, the joint chiefs decided that a reprise of the 1948 airlift would be both "militarily unsound and impractical under present conditions." They also warned in late August that the United States "should not permit itself to become engaged in a general war with China" if Chinese troops entered the fighting—a distant concern at the time, but reality only three months later. If the Russians entered the war directly, the United States should immediately evacuate Korea, begin full-scale mobilization, and "prepare to execute war plans." One indication of the seriousness with which the joint chiefs viewed the situation in Korea was their request for a specific statement of American and Allied objectives in the event of global war. This detail, they felt, was still lacking in the nation's cold war strategy.[73]

Truman's initial reaction to the Korean invasion was surprisingly subdued—even optimistic. At a July 8 Cabinet meeting he seemed to find reassuring an observation concerning Soviet tactics that the Lutheran bishop of Berlin had made the day before. The President, appointment secretary Matthew Connelly noted, agreed with the bishop that "70% of the Russian attitude is bluff."[74]

With the summer's battlefield reverses, however, this early hopefulness gave way increasingly to despair, as the joint chiefs' hurried preparations for war indicated.[75] The unexpected entry of the Chinese into the war the following November eliminated the last lingering traces of optimism, bringing about a reassessment of American strategy in Korea and in the cold war generally.

This reassessment concerned in particular the implementation of NSC-68. By early fall, the initial hesitancy prompted by that program's cost had been overcome by the seemingly urgent need for action. Consequently, NSC-68 was approved by Truman "as a statement of policy to be followed over the next four or five years." When General Douglas MacArthur's home-by-Christmas offensive became a debacle by early December, however, the National Security Council concluded that the desperate situation in Korea "imparted a new urgency to the appraisal of the nature, timing, and scope of programs" in NSC-68. The Chinese military intervention, specifically, had "created a new crisis and a situation of great danger." Under these changed circumstances, the council no longer believed that the period of maximum danger would begin in 1954, but was rather "directly before us." The buildup of U.S. forces over a four-year period was now "unacceptable" and must be accomplished, instead, "as rapidly as possible."[76] Less than a week after this disturbing report—as American marines were in retreat from the Chosin Reservoir near the border with China—National Security Council director James Lay reminded its members and the President of the need to accelerate the implementation of NSC-68 "in light of the present critical situation."[77]

For some concerned with the course of communist aggression, not even emergency implementation of NSC-68 was thought to be a sufficient response. Indeed, the mood of tension and fear in the wake of the Chinese intervention was not unlike that created by news of the Soviet atomic bomb the year before. As with that earlier event, too, the attention of government and public alike in the winter of

1950–51 turned to what was still America's principal military asset—
her atomic bomb.*

Significantly, even at the peak of the Chinese onslaught of late
November 1950—the nadir of American fortunes of war in Korea—the
joint chiefs never recommended the use of the bomb in that conflict.
A November 29 report by the chiefs' Joint Strategic Survey Committee
advised that employment of nuclear weapons would be inappropriate
except "under the most compelling military circumstances": a forced
evacuation of Korea or an impending military disaster. One week later
a study by the joint chiefs' Strategic Plans Committee contemplated the
tactical use of nuclear weapons if Russia entered the war. Neither report
was acted upon by the joint chiefs themselves, however, and both were
withdrawn from circulation in the Pentagon some weeks later, when the
military crisis eased.†

The fact that American intentions concerning use of the bomb in
the Far East were not known outside the innermost circle of the administration may have prompted a hope on Truman's part that this very
uncertainty could be used to advantage in Korea. In a November 30 press
conference the President, responding to a reporter's question, declared
that the United States would employ "every weapon we have" to end the
conflict in Korea. Although Truman subsequently dodged the question of
whether that included the atomic bomb, he added that the decision to use
a particular weapon might be left to the field commanders.[80]

---

*The shock of the Korean invasion finally unsettled the equanimity of CIA analysts concerning
Soviet capabilities. A July 4, 1950, assessment by the agency's Joint Atomic Energy Intelligence
Committee on the "Status of the Soviet Atomic Energy Program" revised the CIA estimate of the
previous February regarding the number and sophistication of Russia's nuclear weapons. What
before had been considered the likely maximum number of atomic bombs in the Soviet arsenal was
now deemed "a reasonable estimate"; the analysts thought that the hydrogen bomb "could be
available to Soviets today." The revised CIA report also accepted the worst-case analysis of AEC
experts by conceding that the Russians' refining techniques using very low-grade uranium ore "were
employed extensively and were unexpectedly successful. . . . Thus, the Soviets are now in a position
where the supply of uranium ore is no longer critical."[78]

†One reason for military leaders' reluctance to recommend use of the bomb in Korea was its obvious
unsuitability for that kind of war. Major General Kenneth Nichols, chairman of the AEC's Military
Liaison Committee in 1950 and an outspoken proponent of military custody of nuclear weapons,
reluctantly acknowledged that there were no useful targets in Korea for the bomb. Nichols also
worried that an unimpressive show of the weapon in Korea might reduce the effectiveness of
America's nuclear arsenal by 75 percent in the eyes of the Russians—who were still, of course, the
principal enemy. General Omar Bradley, chairman of the joint chiefs, reacted strongly to the idea
of using nuclear weapons in Korea. "I've never heard anything so preposterous in my life," he told
a meeting of military leaders. Nonetheless, not all in the Pentagon shared this view. By fall 1951
the U.S. Air Force was conducting simulated atomic raids against targets in South Korea using
conventional bombs.[79]

What may have been a deliberate effort to create doubt in the minds of Russian or Chinese leaders concerning U.S. intentions did not materially affect the war—but it did worry the British sufficiently for them to seek assurances from Truman that the bomb would not be used without consultation. The President the following week promised Prime Minister Attlee that he would be informed before a bomb was dropped, but the British received no promise that they would be consulted on the decision itself. For the fourth and final time during the Truman administration, Britain's request for a veto over any American decision to use the atomic bomb was perfunctorily refused.[81]

Despite his ambiguous press-conference remarks on the bomb, Truman had consistently refused to be stampeded by the bad news from Korea into a precipitous decision on its use in the Far East. Like the joint chiefs, he saw the bomb only as a weapon of last resort. Even when the military situation in Korea worsened, Truman rejected any steps that would have increased U.S. preparedness at a cost of diminishing his control over the nation's nuclear arsenal. Not until early July 1950, shortly after the North Korean invasion, did the President approve the stockpiling of the bomb's non-nuclear components at forward bases in England—the first time that even this incomplete portion of the nation's principal deterrent had crossed the Atlantic. On December 6, 1950, after the Chinese had crossed the Yalu in force, Truman endorsed the joint chiefs' request that non-nuclear components of the bomb be stocked on board the aircraft carrier USS *Franklin Roosevelt,* stationed in the Mediterranean.

Two years later, when the military situation in Korea was stalemated on the ground, Truman told aides that he would consider use of the bomb if the North Koreans and Chinese refused to agree to an armistice, or violated an armistice that all had agreed upon. In an entry of January 27, 1952, in the private journal he kept intermittently from 1945 to 1953, Truman detailed the type of action he was considering: "It seems to me that the proper approach now would be an ultimatum with a ten day expiration limit, informing Moscow that we intend to blockade the China coast from the Korean border to Indo-China, and that we intend to destroy every military base in Manchuria, including submarine bases, by means now in our control and if there is further interference we shall eliminate any ports or cities necessary to accomplish our peaceful purposes." In this note to himself, the President was under no illusion as to the possible consequences of such a move. "This means all out war," Truman wrote. "It means that Moscow, St. Petersburg [Leningrad], Mukden, Vladivostock, Pekin, Shanghai, Port Arthur, Dairen, Odessa, Stalingrad and every manufacturing plant in China and the Soviet Union will be eliminated. This is the final chance for the Soviet Government to decide whether it desires to survive or not."

Truman's comment to his aides and his intemperate private note were obviously a result of the President's frustration over the deadlocked armistice talks—"Dealing with Communist Governments is like an honest man trying to deal with a numbers racket king or the head of a dope ring," he remarked as preface to his "ultimatum"—and hence were more an expression of pique than of policy. Even when contemplating the dread prospect of using the bomb, therefore, Truman proved unwilling to dilute civilian authority over it. He rejected a request from the joint chiefs the following November that they be given automatic permission to transfer the non-nuclear components of atomic bombs to "areas of danger" in a time of crisis.[82]

While resolved not to use the atomic bomb in Korea except *in extremis*, Truman and the joint chiefs were under mounting pressure from critics of the administration's strategy in the war to exploit what all now recognized as a wasting asset in the confrontation with Russia and China. Dropping nuclear weapons in the Yalu River to irradiate China and sowing radioactive waste to impede the Chinese advance down the Korean peninsula were two suggestions for exploiting that asset from the administration's best-known critic, Douglas MacArthur.[83] As their actions would show, it was not as the "winning weapon"—a guarantor of victory in Korea—but as a means of avoiding defeat there that the nation's highest civilian and military leaders considered use of the atomic bomb.

Among the most drastic proposals to come out of the reassessment brought about by the Korean War was NSC-100, "Recommended Politics and Actions in Light of the Grave World Situation." Submitted to the National Security Council and the President in January 1951 as an alternative to NSC-68, NSC-100 was sponsored by Stuart Symington, chairman of the National Security Resources Board and former secretary of the air force. Symington recommended that the United States take the offensive in the cold war with the atomic bomb, its "prime power advantage . . . which every week from here on will steadily decline." He urged specifically that the United States evacuate Korea and begin a combined air-and-sea campaign against China using nuclear weapons.

Symington suggested, further, that America announce by NSC-100 that any further acts of Soviet aggression "in areas to be spelled out" would result in an immediate nuclear attack upon Russia itself.

Essentially an ultimatum to Russia and a prescription for a preventive war with China, NSC-100 was defended by Symington as establishing a "moral justification" for use of the atomic bomb. It provided as well, he argued, "a measure of moral freedom" for the United States, since America would not henceforth be limited to using the bomb only in retaliation against a Russian atomic attack.[84] Acknowledged by its author as a strategy of "political showdown" with the Soviet Union, NSC-100 was offered as the preferred alternative to the containment strategy of NSC-68. Like the post-Korea version of the latter, it saw the period of maximum danger from Russia as approaching sooner than originally expected. Unlike even the revised version of NSC-68, however, Symington assumed that the Russians would deliberately begin a war in the near future. In the aftermath of the communist invasion of Korea, he warned, "who doubts any longer that the Soviets will attack when ready?"

As an intended replacement for NSC-68, NSC-100 challenged American cold war strategy on two broad fronts. Just as the Soviet atomic bomb had proved the flaw in earlier assessments of Russian capabilities, so the Korean invasion had shown the error of earlier assumptions concerning Russian intentions: "[T]he nature—as well as the degree—of our current defense build-up is inconsistent with the problem of survival that we face, because it is related to a basic strategic plan which has now become out-dated by recent reverses, and by a new assumption as to the critical date." NSC-68 was thus declared obsolete, and hence unsound.

Though Truman's secret journal confirms that he gave at least momentary consideration to one provision of NSC-100—the nuclear ultimatum to Russia—Symington's drastic alternative to containment was ultimately rejected outright by the administration. Truman privately entertained the notion that the atomic bomb could still be America's "winning weapon" as late as spring 1952, but he resisted the attempt to force a showdown with Russia over what was by then plainly a wasting asset.*

---

*On May 18, 1952, when the Korean armistice talks were again stalled over the issue of repatriating prisoners of war, Truman returned in his journal to the theme he had introduced the previous January—an ultimatum to Russia. In this entry, the President posed the ultimatum as a series of

The Korean War, of course, was not the last occasion when it was urged that the United States exploit the supposed diplomatic or military potential of the bomb. While it preceded President Dwight Eisenhower's inauguration by almost exactly two years, NSC-100 anticipated the "massive retaliation" and "immaculate war" doctrines of that administration. In fact, Symington's emphasis upon regaining the initiative in the cold war, his stress upon building up sea and air power at the expense of ground forces, and his consideration of preemptive atomic attack all reflected the reliance upon nuclear weapons that had become a legacy of the Truman administration, and that would characterize as well the Eisenhower-Dulles years.

Shortly after assuming office, President Eisenhower ordered a reconsideration of the use of nuclear weapons in Korea as part of his administration's "New Look" military policy. While the subsequent study urged no radical departure from the policy of containment, the joint chiefs in May 1953 recommended that the National Security Council consider the "extensive" use of strategic and tactical nuclear weapons against both China and North Korea if the armistice negotiations broke down and the administration decided to risk a world war for the sake of victory in Korea. The council concurred in the joint chiefs' recommendation. The signing of the Korean armistice two months later, however, rendered further consideration of this option moot.[86]

There was another sense in which NSC-100 was prophetic. As Symington had predicted, the steady erosion of America's atomic advantage inevitably undermined the credibility of a policy based upon nuclear supremacy. This erosion occurred despite the rhetoric of "liberation" and "brinkmanship" that attended the foreign-policy pronouncements of Secretary of State John Foster Dulles in the Eisenhower administration. Yet so fixed had that policy become that not even Dulles' recognition of its failure toward the end of his career (and life) was sufficient to change it.[87]

Indeed, neither Khrushchev's "rocket rattling" over Suez in 1956

---

rhetorical questions to Soviet leaders: "Now do you want an end to hostilities in Korea or do you want China and Siberia destroyed? You may have one or the other which ever you want. . . . You either accept our fair and just proposal or you will be completely destroyed." A further entry suggests that Truman wished to read "Confucius on morals" to the Russians, along with "Buddah's code," the Declaration of Independence, the French Declaration on Liberty and Fraternity, the Bill of Rights, the fifth, sixth, and seventh chapters of St. Matthew, and St. John's prophecy on the Antichrist. Truman's anger is obvious from the fact that he signed this entry "The C. in C. [Commander in Chief]."[85]

nor the trauma created by Russia's launching of *Sputnik* the following year was enough to overcome the dominance of inherited assumptions concerning the supposed political and military utility of the bomb, even when the policy of supremacy—like the earlier policy of monopoly— seemed suddenly to be turned upside down. Although *Sputnik* in particular briefly convinced Americans that the Soviets might have a "winning weapon" in the intercontinental ballistic missile, its larger effect was to spur an acceleration of the arms race, the consequences of which are all too visible today.

It would only be after the world had gone to the brink of nuclear war over Cuba in 1962 that the signing of the Partial Nuclear Test-Ban Treaty signaled the tentative willingness of the United States and Russia to put some limits upon their quest for unilateral military advantage. Despite that willingness, however, peace today remains dependent upon what, since 1945, has been the "fragile hope" of avoiding a nuclear catastrophe.

EPILOGUE

During fall 1945, at the peak of public controversy over American policy on the atomic bomb, columnist Walter Lippmann wrote of the dangers posed by an irrational attachment to an atomic secret. "[I]f the secret cannot be kept," Lippmann warned, "it is unnecessary to argue whether it ought to be kept. . . . Moreover, it would be in the highest degree dangerous to suppose we were keeping the secret if in fact we were not. . . . For that could only give us, as it has already given many, a false sense of security and a false sense of our own power. . . ."[1]

Nearly five years later, when that warning seemed prophetic and Truman's pending decision on the hydrogen bomb had reopened the debate on American power and security, Lippmann returned to the theme he had first raised in the shadow of Hiroshima. Writing to physicist Chester Barnard, he reflected upon the extent to which American policy on the atomic bomb had been influenced—or even determined—by the mistaken assumption that the nation's nuclear supremacy would be enduring: "[I]f we had known in 1948 how far advanced the Soviet Union was toward the production of bombs . . . would [we] not have then changed our tactics and attitudes?"[2]

Barnard, then completing a *Scientific American* article opposing the "Super," concurred strongly in his reply:

> The fallacy which governed the tactics and attitudes of that time was in the minds of the people and in the country and of the representatives in Congress, particularly in the Senate. There there was a belief, a most deadly illusion, that we could retain a monopoly of the facilities and the knowledge for the production of fissionable materials. . . . Hence if you should say of the tactics of the negotiations and the attitude about them that [they were based] upon a popular fallacy as to the indefinite continuance of the monopoly, I should agree.[3]

. . .

That expectation of continuing nuclear supremacy which Barnard termed "a popular fallacy" and "a most deadly illusion" was, in fact, a cause of the false sense of security and power which had been so suddenly and dramatically undermined by 1950. There can be no question of the attraction that the prospect of a lasting atomic advantage had for many Americans. It was this allure which blinded such initial critics of the policy of monopoly as James Conant and Vannevar Bush to the fatal flaw in that policy. It later caused others, such as Secretary of State James Byrnes, Bernard Baruch, and General Leslie Groves, to ignore evidence that the atomic monopoly was not preclusive and was rapidly slipping away. Ultimately, it locked the Truman administration into a policy of trying to outrace the Russians in the development of new and more terrible means of destruction.[4]

Seeking a cause many years after Hiroshima for the fundamental miscalculation in American estimates concerning the Russian atomic bomb, Leo Szilard—the scientist to whom Byrnes had given Groves' assurance that the Russians were without uranium—mused: "If you are an expert, you believe that you are in possession of the truth, and since you know so much, you are unwilling to make allowances for unforeseen developments."[5] Of course, the peculiar insularity that the monopoly fostered was common not only to civilian and military planners in the Truman administration, but to the public as well. Wishful thinking as much as unforeseen events contributed to the error. Even those citizens who had accustomed themselves to the idea that American nuclear supremacy would be short-lived, one pollster discovered, "continued to talk entirely in terms of the monopoly" when discussing the future.[6]

There was still another "deadly illusion" that was not dispelled with the collapse of the policy of monopoly in 1949, as shown by Truman's decision on the super-bomb and by the evolution of NSC-68. This was the fallacious assumption concerning the utility of nuclear weapons: their supposed efficaciousness in diplomacy, and their alleged capacity to avert military confrontations. It survives as myth to the present day, although the experience of American foreign policy since 1950 has only tended to confirm that more nearly the opposite of this tenet is true.* Nuclear weapons some thirty-five years after the destruction of Hiro-

---

*Psychiatrist Robert Lifton has recently written of this attitude as "nuclearism": "a secular religion, a total ideology in which . . . the mastery of death and evil . . . are achieved through the power of a new technological deity." Lifton argues that the "nuclear believer or 'nuclearist' allies himself with that power and feels compelled to expound on the virtues of the deity. He may come to depend on the weapons to keep the world going."[7]

shima have yet to convincingly prove themselves an asset to diplomacy —even though the United States has variously held superiority, supremacy, and a monopoly in such weapons during that time.

This is not to argue that an altogether different policy on the bomb than that adopted by the Truman administration would have avoided the cold war or could have lessened subsequent Soviet-American enmity. Apart from a shared interest in survival, Russia and the West have certainly not bridged their differences; nor does the gap between them seem to have perceptibly narrowed. But simply because a more cooperative attempt was never attempted, its possible results cannot be known. It would be facile to claim, moreover, that the policy of monopoly has been vindicated in the light of subsequent events. Rather, by straining relations with traditional allies like Britain and by giving impetus to the nuclear arms race, that policy had the effect of intensifying the cold war —just as the lingering hope for a "winning weapon" threatens the current tenuous stability of Soviet-American relations.

The deadly illusion of enduring nuclear supremacy also had its price at home. Indeed, it may be that the more serious and lasting impact of America's brief period of nuclear hegemony was not upon foreign policy, but at home, by creating an atmosphere of failed expectations and anxiety. The atomic secret's effect upon the domestic cold war was to give credibility to the bogus espionage scare that began in 1946 and that was revived—on equally dubious grounds—during the 1948 election campaign. The documented evidence of spying in the cases of Klaus Fuchs and Donald Maclean,* the conviction for perjury of Alger Hiss, and the 1950 espionage trial of Ethel and Julius Rosenberg all lent a seeming credence to what has become a persistent myth of the nuclear era: that the atomic secret was a tangible commodity stolen by spies, rather than a product of arrogance and misconception.

The actual damage done to American security by Soviet atomic

---

*Maclean's spying—like that of Fuchs—was publicly portrayed as much more damaging to American interests than classified official accounts of the time indicated. Hence a top-secret "damage assessment" concerning Maclean, sent to the FBI by the Atomic Energy Commission shortly after his defection, concluded that "only a rough order-of-magnitude estimate of fissionable material could be derived from [his] information." Maclean's knowledge might actually have served to deceive the Russians, the authors of the report noted, for "we do not believe that the information available to Maclean in 1947–8 would now be of any appreciable aid to the Soviet Union because of the changes in the rate and scale of the U.S. program which have taken place in the intervening years. . . . the results would be widely misleading as to our present or prospective position in fissionable materials. . . ."[8]

espionage cannot be accurately assessed even today. But probably of far greater value to the Russians than any technical data they may have gained by spying was their certain knowledge that Western assumptions concerning "primitive" Soviet technology and the preclusive nature of the West's atomic raw materials monopoly were false. The harm done by Soviet spies was certainly far less significant than the hysteria induced by the fear of such spying.

Conducted against the backdrop of the Korean War and in the midst of resurgent "atom spy" allegations, the Rosenbergs' trial for the theft of the atomic secret—still branded the "crime of the century" by the FBI—represents perhaps the culminating domestic event of the era begun with Truman's announcement of the atomic bomb dropped upon Hiroshima. But it was hardly the last episode to show the political fallout of the unexpectedly early Soviet atomic test.

One of the compounded ironies of this era is that the myth of the atomic secret would be exposed some months after the Rosenbergs' execution by the man most responsible for creating and promoting that myth—General Leslie Groves. Testifying at the 1954 AEC investigation into Robert Oppenheimer, whose loyalty was declared suspect for his earlier opposition to the "Super" and to air-atomic strategy, Groves acknowledged that "reliance on what the Russians could or could not do was based on primarily the supplies of materials which I felt would be available to them." He had overlooked, Groves admitted, Soviet access to uranium ore in Russian-occupied eastern Germany after the war.[9] That Groves' belated and unrepentant admission of error went unnoticed in the three-week and thousand-page testimony of the security hearings is perhaps no more remarkable, given the climate of opinion in 1954, than that the charge of disloyalty against Oppenheimer would be upheld.

Oppenheimer—as much as Hiss, the Rosenbergs, and the other victims or villains of the cold war—became a symbol of the political era created by the atomic bomb. Truman, at various times either a defender or a detractor of the scientist, seemed to recognize this in a 1952 letter to Atomic Energy Commissioner Gordon Dean. "I feel as you do that Dr. Oppenheimer is an honest man," the President wrote. "In this day of character assassination and unjustified smear tactics it seems that good men are made to suffer unnecessarily. . . . I hope we will live through the smear age without destroying our Bill of Rights."[10]

The fact that what Truman aptly dubbed "the smear age" began with the end of American nuclear hegemony was hardly coincidental. That unfortunate era was in substantial part the inevitable result of the false sense of security and power which Lippmann cautioned against in the aftermath of Hiroshima, but that misplaced faith in a winning weapon had brought about. As Lippmann was aware in 1950, American policy on the atomic bomb in the cold war had come full circle. Reliance upon a winning weapon had not only been the inspiration for that policy, but was its ironic legacy as well—the legacy of an arms race now renewed with even greater intensity; and of a frantic search for traitors at home and new allies abroad. In these alone, where security itself would prove elusive, the illusion of security remained.

NOTES

ABBREVIATIONS USED IN THE NOTES

AEC U.S. Atomic Energy Commission
FR: Foreign Relations of the United States (Government Printing
Office, Washington, D.C.), 1945–1950
HSTL Harry S Truman Library Institute, Independence, Missouri
MEDR Manhattan Engineer District Records, Modern Military Section,
National Archives, Washington, D.C.
NSC National Security Council
OSRD Office of Scientific Research and Development
PPOP Public Papers of the Presidents (Government Printing Office,
Washington, D.C.), 1945–1950
PSF President's Secretary's File, Harry S Truman Library Institute
RG Record Group
UNAEC United Nations Atomic Energy Commission
USJCS United States Joint Chiefs of Staff Records, Modern Military
Section, National Archives, Washington, D.C.

Prologue

1. Concerning the effect of the atomic bombs upon Hiroshima and Nagasaki, see, for example, Pacific War Research Society, *The Day Man Lost Hiroshima* (Palo Alto, Calif., 1968), 236–8; J. C. Marx, *Seven Hours to Zero* (New York, 1967), 178–84; F. Knebel and C. W. Bailey, *No High Ground* (New York, 1960), 179–85; and Gordon Thomas and Max M. Witts, *Enola Gay* (New York, 1977), 311–25.
2. The charge of "atomic diplomacy" was first made in 1948 by a British scientist, P. M. S. Blackett, who claimed that the bombing of Hiroshima was "not so much the last military act of the second World War, as the first major operation of the cold diplomatic war with Russia now in progress." Cf. P. M. S. Blackett, *Military and Political Consequences of Atomic Energy* (London, 1948). On the "atomic diplomacy" debate, see also Gar Alperovitz, *Atomic Diplomacy: Hiroshima and Potsdam* (New York, 1965), and Barton J. Bernstein, "The Atomic Bomb and American Foreign Policy, 1941–1945: An Historiographical Controversy," *Peace and Change*, Spring 1974.
3. See Bernstein, "The Atomic Bomb"; and Gregg Herken, "An Unfinished History of the Atomic Age," in Michael Hamilton, ed., *Anticipating Catastrophe* (Grand Rapids, Mich., 1977).

4. Byrnes is quoted in the interview with Edward Weintal, Dulles Oral History Project, John Foster Dulles MSS, Princeton University.
5. The phrase is used by scientist Chester Barnard in a letter of February 8, 1950, to Walter Lippmann, Correspondence File, J. Robert Oppenheimer MSS, Library of Congress.

Chapter 1

1. Interview with Walter Brown, November 1979, Columbia S.C. Eben Ayers diary, August 6–8, 1945, HSTL.
2. Ayers' account of the Hiroshima decision is in the "Atomic Bomb" folder, Box 227, PSF, HSTL.
3. Concerning atomic-energy policy during the Roosevelt years, see the excellent account by Martin J. Sherwin, *A World Destroyed, The Atomic Bomb and the Grand Alliance* (New York, 1975). Sherwin writes (p. 63): "Even during the early stages of the war, it is clear the policies governing the development of the atomic bomb were being formulated with an eye toward potential postwar implications."
4. "Effect of Foreseeable New Developments . . . ," August 24, 1945, "Air Force" Series, (7-18-45), Sec. 1, USJCS.
5. To what extent and in how much detail the raw-materials situation was discussed at this meeting remains a matter of conjecture, however. Groves' own diary indicates he took along a series of "colored diagrams and charts" to the briefing. The existence of these at the briefing is confirmed by former AEC commissioner Lewis Strauss. In 1948, Groves told Congress that he gave Truman an account of Soviet espionage in the Manhattan Project at this meeting. Diary, Box 24, Commanding General's File, MEDR; Lewis Strauss, *Men and Decisions* (New York, 1962), 185. See also U.S. Congress, "Report on Soviet Espionage Activities in Connection with the Atom Bomb," House Un-American Activities Committee, 80th Congress, 2nd Session (Washington, D.C., 1948), 163–5. Unfortunately, no copy either of the 24-page memorandum or of the charts and diagrams could be found in Groves' papers or among the MED Records at the National Archives.
6. Henry Stimson diary, December 31, 1944, Henry L. Stimson MSS, Yale University. See also Henry L. Stimson and McGeorge Bundy, *On Active Service in Peace and War* (New York, 1947), 616.
7. Truman is cited in Daniel Yergin, *Shattered Peace: The Origins of the Cold War and the National Security State* (Boston, 1977), 86. Wallace's comment is in John Morton Blum, ed., *The Price of Vision: The Diary of Henry A. Wallace* (Boston, 1973), 45.
8. Harry S. Truman, *Memoirs: Year of Decisions* (New York, 1955), 104. Other members of the Interim Committee were James Conant and Vannevar Bush of the President's Office of Scientific Research and Development, scientist Karl T. Compton, Navy Undersecretary Ralph Bard, Assistant Secretary of State William Clayton, and Truman's secretary of state-designate, James F. Byrnes.
9. Stimson diary, June 6, 1945; "Memo of Conference with President," June 6, 1945, Correspondence File, Stimson MSS.
10. Stimson diary, June 19, 1945.
11. Stimson diary, May 15, 1945.
12. Truman is quoted in Charles Bohlen, *Witness to History, 1929–69* (New York, 1973), 216; and in Robert Donovan, *Conflict and Crisis: The Presidency of Harry S Truman,*

1945–48 (New York, 1977), 34. Truman's recently discovered "journal"—a series of notes he wrote to himself between April 1945 and January 1953—confirms that the President hoped the atomic bomb might make a difference at Potsdam. On July 17, the day after the successful atomic test in New Mexico, Truman met Stalin for the first time. According to the journal, the President asked the Soviet leader if he had any questions he wished to bring up outside the agenda for the meeting. "He did," Truman wrote, "and it is dynamite—but I have some dynamite too which I'm not exploding now." Truman journal, July 17, 1945, HSTL.

13. Concerning the advice to Truman on the eve of the Potsdam meeting, see the excellent official history of the AEC by Richard G. Hewlett and Oscar G. Anderson, Jr., *The New World, 1939/1946: A History of the United States Atomic Energy Commission,* I (University Park, Pa., 1962), 382–92; Sherwin, *A World Destroyed,* 221–8; and "W.B.'s book," July 16–18, 1945, James F. Byrnes MSS, Clemson University, South Carolina.

14. Stimson and Bundy, *On Active Service,* 637. Stimson diary, June 19, 1945.

15. According to his journal, Truman thought that the atomic bomb would make Russian entry into the war unnecessary: "Believe Japs will fold up before Russia comes in. I am sure they will when Manhattan appears over their homeland." Truman journal, July 18, 1945, HSTL.

16. Stimson and Bundy, *On Active Service,* 638–9.

17. Truman, *Year of Decisions,* 458. Truman journal, July 25, 1945, HSTL.

18. Georgei K. Zhukov, *Memoirs of Marshal Zhukov* (New York, 1971), 675. Strobe Talbott, ed. and trans., *Khrushchev Remembers* (Boston, 1970), 58–60.

19. Truman, *Year of Decisions,* 460–4.

20. Ibid., 462. Truman to R. Bohnen, undated, "General File" folder, Box 112, PSF, HSTL. Truman's underlining of the passage from Hamlet is noted in Merle Miller, *Plain Speaking: An Oral Biography of Harry S Truman* (New York, 1973), 248. Secretary of War Stimson agreed with the President's decision to remove Kyoto from the list of targets submitted by Manhattan Project director Leslie Groves. Stimson's reason was perhaps more pragmatic than humanitarian, however—he feared that destruction of this great cultural shrine by the United States might drive the Japanese into the arms of the Russians after the war. Truman journal, July 25, 1945, HSTL.

21. Ayers diary, August 8, 1945, HSTL. Many American Catholics opposed the atomic bombings, just as they opposed the saturation bombing of cities in Europe and Japan. See Social Science Research Council, *Public Reaction to the Atomic Bomb and World Affairs* (Ithaca, 1947), 9–10.

22. Truman is quoted in Blum, ed., *The Price of Vision,* 474–5. On the matter of the third atomic bomb, see Harrison to Stimson, July 23, 1945, folder 64, Box 151, Harrison-Bundy File, MEDR. Concerning the likelihood of its use, see Barton J. Bernstein, "The Perils and Politics of Surrender: Ending the War with Japan and Avoiding the Third Atomic Bomb," *Pacific Historical Review,* February 1977; and Sherwin, *A World Destroyed,* 234–7. Truman wrote in his journal on July 25 that he had instructed Stimson to use the bomb "so that military objectives and soldiers and sailors are the target and not women and children. . . . The target will be a purely military one and we will issue a warning statement asking the Japs to surrender and save lives." A Japanese army headquarters was in fact located outside Hiroshima, but most of those killed in the bombing—as Truman subsequently learned—were civilians. The warning statement referred to in the journal was actually the Potsdam ultimatum, which included nothing about the bomb *per se* but simply directed that

the Japanese should surrender or face "the destruction which threatens them." Truman journal, HSTL.

23. See R. J. C. Butow, *Japan's Decision to Surrender* (Stanford, Calif., 1954), 153–4; and Bernstein, "Perils and Politics of Surrender." Truman journal, July 25, 1945, HSTL.

24. Truman, *PPOP,* 1945, I, 97–9. "Memo Discussed with the President," April 25, 1945, folder 60, Harrison-Bundy File, MEDR. The text of Stimson's memo, and a memorandum by Groves on the briefing of Truman, written after the meeting, are in Sherwin, *A World Destroyed,* 291–4.

Chapter 2

1. Stimson diary, March 5 and August 9, 1945, Stimson MSS. Interview with Gordon Arneson, October 19, 1979, Washington, D.C. In spring 1946, Stimson reflected on the missed opportunity of a direct approach to Russia. "No other problem has been so constantly in my thoughts as this one," he wrote. Although he subsequently came to believe that cooperation would have been precluded anyway by the attitude of the Russians, Stimson did not change his mind about the real obstacle: "The focus of the problem does not lie in the atom; it resides in the hearts of men." See "The Bomb and the Opportunity," *Harper's,* March 1946, 204–10.

2. Text of Stimson's speech in *New York Times,* August 10, 1945.

3. Concerning this phase of Stimson's career, see Elting E. Morison, *Turmoil and Tradition: A Study of the Life and Times of Henry L. Stimson* (Boston, 1960), Part III.

4. Morison, *Turmoil and Tradition,* 639.

5. Stimson diary, September 4, 1945.

6. An early version of Stimson's memorandum, dated August 29, 1945, is in folder 20, Harrison-Bundy File, MEDR. The final memo, with an accompanying explanation of Stimson's change of mind, is also in Stimson and Bundy, *On Active Service,* 642–6; and in U.S. Department of State, *Foreign Relations of the United States* (henceforth *FR*): 1945, II (Washington D.C., 1971), 40–4.

7. Stimson diary, September 12, 1945.

8. *New York Times,* September 12, 1945.

9. Joseph E. Davies journal, September 18, 1945, Joseph E. Davies MSS, Library of Congress.

10. Minutes of the September 7, 1945, Cabinet meeting, "Appointment Calendar," Matthew J. Connelly MSS, HSTL.

11. Eben Ayers diary, October 5, 1945, HSTL.

12. Attlee's letters to the President are in the "President–Prime Minister Attlee" folder, Box 97, William Leahy MSS, HSTL. Excerpts from the Attlee-Truman correspondence are also in *FR:* 1945, II, 36–7; 40; 58–9. Concerning Attlee's side of this correspondence, see Francis Williams, *A Prime Minister Remembers: The War and Post-War Memoirs of the Rt. Hon. Earl Attlee* (London, 1962), 101–2.

13. Blum, ed., *Price of Vision,* 481.

14. This account of Stimson's last Cabinet meeting is from notes in the "Appointment Calendar," Connelly MSS, HSTL; and from the Stimson diary, December 11, 1945. Because of a heart attack shortly after leaving the government, Stimson did not write his account of the meeting until December 1945. Other—often conflicting—versions of that meeting are: Vannevar Bush, *Pieces of the Action* (New York, 1970), 295;

William A. Reuben, *The Atom Spy Hoax* (New York, 1955), 106; Truman, *Year of Decisions*, 525–7; Forrestal diary, September 21, 1945, James V. Forrestal MSS, Princeton University.

15. Part of Forrestal's account is also printed in Walter Millis, ed., *The Forrestal Diaries* (New York, 1951), 94–6. In his entry on the meeting, Forrestal charged that Wallace was "completely, everlastingly and wholeheartedly in favor of giving [the bomb] to the Russians." Wallace, naturally, has a different version. Blum, ed., *Price of Vision*, 482–3.

16. Blum, *Price of Vision*, 482–5.

17. Dean Acheson, *Present at the Creation: My Years in the State Department* (New York, 1969), 124–5.

18. Stimson diary, December 11, 1945.

19. Stimson and Bundy, *On Active Service*, 646. Concerning Stimson's attraction to Roosevelt's style of diplomacy, see "Note of a Telephone Conversation with John J. McCloy," May 19, 1945, "1945 Correspondence" folder, Stimson MSS.

20. Truman, *Year of Decisions*, 579.

21. On public opinion concerning the atomic bomb, see H. G. Erskine, "The Polls: Atomic Weapons and Nuclear Energy," *Public Opinion Quarterly*, Summer 1963, 172–3; U.S. Department of State, *The International Control of Atomic Energy: Growth of a Policy* (Washington, D.C., 1946), 13; and Social Science Research Council, *Public Reaction to the Atomic Bomb and World Affairs*, 1–12. Concerning congressional opinion, see *New York Times* for September 28, 30, and October 2, 1945.

22. *New York Times*, September 30, 1945.

23. Acheson to Truman, September 25, *FR:* 1945, II, 48–50.

24. Vannevar Bush to Truman, "Scientific Interchange on Atomic Energy," September 25, 1945, Doc. 217, "Selected AEC Documents," U.S. Dept. of Energy, Washington, D.C. Excerpts from this memorandum are also in Truman, *Year of Decisions*, 579.

25. Ayers diary, September 24, 1945, HSTL.

26. Ibid., September 23, 1945.

27. Attlee to Truman, September 28, 1945, Box 97, William Leahy MSS, HSTL.

28. Text of Truman's speech in *New York Times*, October 4, 1945; and in Truman, *Year of Decisions*, 581–4. Concerning the origins of the speech, see Hewlett and Anderson, *New World*, 424–7; Acheson, *Present at the Creation*, 124–5; and Lisle A. Rose, *After Yalta: America and the Origins of the Cold War* (New York, 1973), 139.

29. This was the passage excised from the State Department draft: "Scientific opinion appears to be practically unanimous that the essential theoretical knowledge upon which the discovery is based is already widely known. There is also substantial agreement that foreign research can come abreast of our present theoretical knowledge in a comparatively short time. Science holds out little prospect of developing effective defensive measures. Our power to destroy has now far outstripped our capacity for defense." Draft of Truman's speech is in Harrison to Patterson, October 3, 1945, folder 66, Harrison-Bundy File, MEDR.

30. A transcript of the President's press conference is in Truman, *PPOP*, 1945, I, 381–8. Excerpts are also in Truman, *Year of Decisions*, 585.

31. Bush to Truman, "Scientific Interchange on Atomic Energy." A year later Bush would be out of favor with Truman. The President twice refused to grant Henry Stimson's request that Bush be given the Distinguished Service Medal for his work in the government. Among other things, Truman was miffed that Bush had not

attended a previous ceremony awarding him the Legion of Honor Medal. See Stimson
to Truman, July 15, and Robert Patterson to Stimson, July 25, 1946, "1946 Correspondence" folder, Stimson MSS.
32. "Notes," undated, folder 13, Commanding General's File, MEDR.
33. *New York Times,* October 9, 1945.
34. Blum, ed., *Price of Vision,* 504.
35. Truman, *PPOP,* 1945, I, 402.
36. "Memorandum of Conversation at the White House," "Control of Atomic Energy"
file, J. Robert Oppenheimer MSS, Library of Congress, Washington, D.C. Despite
his pessimistic appraisal on this occasion, world government had been a pet cause of
the young, idealistic Truman. Since 1910, Truman once bragged to an aide, he had
carried a piece of paper in his wallet with these words from Tennyson's "Locksley
Hall": "Till the war-drum throbb'd no longer, and the battle flags were furled/ In the
Parliament of man, the Federation of the world." Donovan, *Conflict and Crisis,*
49–50.
37. "W. B.'s book," September 17, 1945, Byrnes MSS.
38. Truman's foreign policy statement is printed in Truman, *PPOP,* 1945, I, 431–8;
excerpts also appear in Truman, *Year of Decisions,* 589–90.
39. Stimson diary, September 5, 1945.
40. Truman, *Year of Decisions,* 481. On Truman's concern with domestic problems at
this time, see also Jonathan Daniels, *Man of Independence* (New York, 1950), 295–7;
Alfred Steinberg, *The Man from Missouri* (New York, 1962), 125–9; Truman, *Year
of Decisions,* 481–5; and Donovan, *Conflict and Crisis,* 107–15.

Chapter 3

1. By Byrnes' own account, he was informed of the bomb by President Roosevelt one
"hot summer afternoon" in 1943 "for no apparent reason" other than that FDR
wished "to watch my amazed reaction." Truman, still a senator, learned of the
Manhattan Project's existence by accident (and then was not told of its purpose) when
he questioned the immense sums being spent on the secret project. Stimson inter-
vened on that occasion to dissuade Truman from pressing a threatened investigation.
James F. Byrnes, *Speaking Frankly* (New York, 1947), 257.
2. Truman, *Year of Decisions,* 87.
3. Leo Szilard, "Reminiscences," in Donald Fleming and Bernard Bailyn, eds., *Perspectives in American History,* II (Boston, 1963), 126–41.
4. Byrnes is cited in Truman, *Year of Decisions,* 20.
5. "W. B.'s book," July 20, 1945, James F. Byrnes MSS, Clemson Univ.
6. "W. B.'s book," July 24, 1945, Byrnes MSS.
7. Concerning Byrnes' changing attitude toward the bomb at Potsdam, see "Interview
with James F. Byrnes," undated, Herbert Feis MSS, Library of Congress; and Thomas
G. Paterson, "Potsdam, the Atomic Bomb, and the Cold War: A Discussion with
James F. Byrnes," *Pacific Historical Review,* May 1972.
8. Davies diary, July 29, 1945, Joseph E. Davies MSS.
9. "Memo for the Record," August 18, 1945, folder 98, Harrison-Bundy File, MEDR.
This document is also in Sherwin, *World Destroyed,* 314–15. J. Robert Oppenheimer
complained to Henry Wallace in October 1945 that "Byrnes . . . felt . . . we could
use the bomb as a pistol to get what we wanted in international diplomacy." Blum,
ed., *Price of Vision,* 497.

10. Concerning Byrnes' background and personality, see Robert Messer, "The Making of a Cold Warrior: James F. Byrnes and American-Soviet Relations, 1945–46" (unpublished doctoral dissertation, Univ. of California, Berkeley, 1975). Roosevelt is quoted in Yergin, *Shattered Peace,* 111.

11. Byrnes, *Speaking Frankly,* 70.

12. On resentment of Byrnes within the American delegation at Potsdam, see Yergin, *Shattered Peace,* 122.

13. See, for example, Byrnes' instruction to Stettinius, *FR:* 1945, II, 56.

14. Minutes of the London Council of Foreign Ministers may be found in *FR:* 1945, II, 99–559.

15. "W. B.'s book," September 24, 1945, Byrnes MSS.

16. Calvert to Groves, November 13, 1945, folder 20, Commanding General's File, MEDR.

17. Concerning the antecedents to the African trusteeship issue, see *FR:* 1945, II, 61 ff., 288, 297; and Byrnes, *Speaking Frankly,* 96.

18. "W. B.'s book," September 24, 1945, Byrnes MSS.

19. Molotov is cited in Hugh Dalton's diary, October 5, 1945. The author is indebted to Professor James Gormly for permission to quote from the Dalton diary. On Molotov's comment to Bevin, see also Herbert Feis, *From Trust to Terror: The Onset of the Cold War, 1945–1950* (New York, 1970), 98.

20. Concerning acrimony at the conference over the Balkan peace treaties, see *FR:* 1945, II, 114–15, 182–5, 194–201, 243–7; Byrnes, *Speaking Frankly,* 100–1; Rose, *After Yalta,* 46–8; Lloyd C. Gardner, *Architects of Illusion: Men and Ideas in American Foreign Policy, 1941–1949* (Chicago, 1970), 90–3; Lynn E. Davis, *The Cold War Begins: Soviet-American Conflict over Eastern Europe* (Princeton, 1974); and Patricia Dawson Ward, *The Threat of Peace* (Kent State, 1979).

21. "Minutes . . ." October 16, *FR:* 1945, II, 59–61.

22. Davies diary, September 10, 1945, Davies MSS. On the origins of the "Big Four" security treaty proposal, see Gardner, *Architects of Illusion,* 93–4.

23. Edward Weintal transcript, Dulles Oral History Project, Dulles MSS.

24. Stalin and Truman are quoted by Wallace in Blum, ed., *Price of Vision,* 475, 489. Truman wrote in his private Potsdam journal: "I can deal with Stalin. He is honest —but smart as hell." In a later entry, the President's impression of Molotov was less favorable. He thought the Soviet foreign minister "lacks sincerity." Truman journal, July 17 and 25, 1945, HSTL.

25. Near the end of the conference, Byrnes told Brown "that he had to talk with Stalin and have an understanding whether Russia was preparing for war or peace." Brown also wrote of this conversation: "We agreed on winding this conference up the best we could and then work [at having] the next meeting in Moscow where we would be close to Stalin and JFB could work on him. Otherwise, none of us saw any chance." "W.B.'s book," September 17, 1945, Byrnes MSS.

26. Bohlen's is a personal view of Byrnes at the conference. Bohlen, *Witness to History, 1929–1969* (New York, 1973), 244–7.

27. "Memo of Conversation . . . ," November 7, 1945, "London Council of Foreign Ministers" folder, Dulles MSS. See also Weintal transcript and James F. Byrnes transcript, Dulles Oral History Project, Dulles MSS.

28. Truman's comment to Stettinius is cited in John Lewis Gaddis, *The United States and the Origins of the Cold War, 1941–47* (New York, 1972), 275. Davies diary, September 18, 1945, Davies MSS.

29. The term is Daniel Yergin's. In *Shattered Peace,* Yergin's excellent narrative history

of the cold war, he notes that the term applies not only to the historic struggle of the superpowers but to the contending views of "orthodox" and "revisionist" historians (pp. 6–7).

30. Blum, ed., *Price of Vision*, 501–2; Davies diary, October 9, 1945, Davies MSS.
31. "Memorandum of conversation . . .," December 11, 1945, "Council of Foreign Ministers: London, 1945" folder, Byrnes MSS.
32. Byrnes, *Speaking Frankly*, 108.
33. "Notes," undated, folder 629, Byrnes MSS. The text of Truman's speech on Japan is in Truman, *PPOP*, 1945, I, 152–5.
34. Davies diary, October 9, 1945, Davies MSS. Concerning Byrnes' instructions to his staff, see text of untitled speech, "London Council of Foreign Ministers" folder, Dulles MSS.
35. "American Relations with the Belgian Congo," Byrnes to Truman, October 23, 1945, U.S. Department of State, "Selected File on Atomic Energy," National Archives.
36. "Minutes of a Meeting of the Secretaries of State, War, and Navy," October 23, *FR:* 1945, II, 59–61.
37. Harold Smith diary, October 5, 1945, Harold Smith MSS, HSTL.
38. Concerning correspondence between Truman and Attlee, see the "Joint Chiefs of Staff" folder, Box 97, William Leahy Diary, National Archives; or Leahy MSS, HSTL. Attlee's letters were also prompted by the considerable pressure upon him from within the Labour Party to gain Truman's assurances that Britain would have a role in the postwar development of atomic energy. On this point, see Williams, *A Prime Minister Remembers*, 108–10.
39. Text of Byrnes' speech in *New York Times*, November 6, 1945.
40. Forrestal diary, November 6, 1945, Forrestal MSS.
41. "Memo by Bush to the Secretary of State," November 5, *FR:* 1945, II, 69–73. Concerning Bush's declining role in the government after Roosevelt's death, see Bush to Conant, November 7, 1945, Vannevar Bush MSS, Library of Congress; Rose, *After Yalta*, 139–40; and Vannevar Bush, *Pieces of the Action* (New York, 1970), 296.
42. Bush to Conant, November 8, 1945, Bush MSS.
43. Details on the British loan and Keynes' comment are in F. W. F. Smith, *Halifax: The Life of Lord Halifax* (London, 1966), 552–5.
44. Concerning the Quebec and Hyde Park agreements, see Sherwin, *World Destroyed*, 85–8; 109–10.
45. Attlee's comment is cited in Williams, ed., *A Prime Minister Remembers*, 108. On the "Attlee plan" furor, see Ian Jacob diary, November 12–14, 1945, Public Records Office, London; and *New York Times*, November 11–13, 1945.
46. Groves' instructions to War Department aide Gordon Arneson concerning the British were "to hold the fort and give nothing, but be amiable about it." Interview with Gordon Arneson, October 1979, Washington, D.C. Groves' efforts to avoid cooperating with the British sometimes went to extraordinary lengths. In contravention of an order from FDR, he tried—unsuccessfully—to prevent a British scientist from visiting the Hanford atomic plant in the fall of 1944. His response to a British request for information on construction of an atomic pile was that they simply not try to build one. Perhaps the best example of this anglophobia, however, was the "diplomatic history" which Groves himself wrote for the Manhattan Project. In it, he complained of the Washington conference that the British "seemed to have a viewpoint not of how can we enter into a secret agreement without violating the [UN] charter—but how can we do it without getting caught. . . . They did not appear to be concerned

as to whether it would violate the charter in spirit although they wished to be in a safe position so that if any trouble arose the blame would fall on the U.S." Groves apparently thought better of his next line, for he deleted it from the official "history": "They would be in there [sic] usual saintly position." Concerning Groves and the British, see Margaret Gowing, *Britain and Atomic Energy, 1939–1945* (London, 1964), 341; and Margaret Gowing, *Independence and Deterrence, 1945–1952* (London, 1974), 91. See also "Diplomatic History of the Manhattan Engineer District," undated, folder 103, Commanding General's File, MEDR; and Leahy to Groves, September 27, 1944, folder 11, ibid.

47. At Truman's order, no verbatim account of the meetings on board the *Sequoia* was kept. A chronology of Anglo-American negotiations for this period, however, is the "Memorandum by Captain R. Gordon Arneson to the Secretary of War," April 17, *FR:* 1945, II, 63–9. Truman drafted an account of his meeting with Attlee and King the day following their meeting. See this untitled memo of November 12, 1945, in the "National Security Council—Atomic" folder, Box 200, PSF, HSTL. Other accounts of the meetings and of the internal rivalries there are Bush to Conant, November 10, 1945, Bush MSS; "Memo of a Conversation Between Secretary of State Byrnes and British Ambassador Halifax," November 9, 1945, U.S. State Department, "Selected File on Atomic Energy," National Archives; and Hewlett and Anderson, *New World,* 462–3.

48. Truman's account of the meeting on board the *Sequoia* glosses over the clash of personalities at the summit. Bush had already threatened to "step out" of the conference if the President's speechwriter and occasional adviser, Samuel Rosenman, appeared on the yacht. As it developed, neither man was invited aboard. Groves hinted darkly in his memoirs that he had been purposely excluded from the meetings upon the advice of "someone in the State Department." He suspected Acheson. Leahy's presence on the boat is a mystery too, since his past record as an adviser on the bomb was hardly impressive. In the course of a briefing on the Manhattan Project prior to the first atomic test, he had blurted out: "This is the biggest fool thing we have ever done. The bomb will never go off, and I speak as an expert in explosives." Bush to Conant, November 10, 1945, Bush MSS. Leslie Groves, *Now It Can Be Told* (New York, 1962), 237. Leahy is cited in Yergin, *Shattered Peace,* 135.

49. A draft of the communiqué from the *Sequoia* ended with the following line, deleted from the final version: ". . . there should be consultation at the earliest possible date with the other permanent members of the Security Council." Untitled document, November 12, 1945, "National Security Council—Atomic" folder, Box 200, PSF, HSTL. Bush to Conant, November 10, 1945, Bush MSS.

50. Bush to Conant, November 10, 1945, Bush MSS.

51. Groves undertook the revision of the Quebec Agreement, he wrote in his memoirs, because "I was familiar enough with the subject to know what those decisions should have been, regardless of who arrived at them, or what they actually were." Groves, *Now It Can Be Told,* 403. Concerning Groves' role at the summit, see also David E. Lilienthal, *The Journals of David E. Lilienthal: The Atomic Energy Years, 1945–1950* (New York, 1964), 25–6.

52. Text of the Agreed Declaration in *New York Times,* November 16, 1945. Text of the two secret records in *FR:* 1945, II, 68; 75.

53. Ian Jacob diary, November 12–15, 1945, Public Records Office, London. The author is indebted to Professor James Gormly for permission to cite from the Jacob diary.

54. "Atomic Energy," undated, "Atomic Energy" folder, Byrnes MSS. The British would

later be of one mind as to responsibility for the misunderstanding. Dwight Eisenhower reported after a visit to England in the summer of 1947: "The British blame Groves. . . . he led them to believe that 'cooperation' . . . meant exchange of engineering data on the construction of facilities." Shortly after the Washington conference adjourned, in fact, Groves had written Patterson explaining that "the words 'full and effective' . . . to the British mean more than they do to me." "You will note that . . . the memo does not recommend 'full and effective cooperation' beyond the field of basic scientific research." Byrnes remarked upon this press criticism in his 1947 memoir, *Speaking Frankly,* 257–68. James F. Byrnes, *All in One Lifetime* (New York, 1958), 326–7. Concerning the pressures then upon Byrnes from Congress and others in the administration worried by the administration's exclusion of Russia, see Rose, *After Yalta,* 128; and Hewlett and Anderson, *New World,* 470. On the press, see also *Nation,* November 17 and 24, 1945.

55. On Russian accusations at this time, see *New York Times,* November 12 and 19, 1945.
56. *New York Times,* November 17 and 21, 1945.
57. Byrnes claimed in his second volume of memoirs that the idea of a Moscow summit came to him one day "the week before Thanksgiving, a day which I spent quietly, clearing my desk of accumulated papers . . . with only the ticking of an old grandfather clock for company. . . ." If, indeed, the ticking of the grandfather clock was an inspiration for Byrnes' effort at politically defusing the atomic bomb in relations with Russia, it is also true that he was not unmindful of increasing criticism in the press of the fact that the Washington conference had ignored Russia completely. See, for example, *New York Times,* November 14 and 18, 1945.
58. Forrestal diary, December 4, 1945, Forrestal MSS.
59. Stimson diary, September 21, 1945, Stimson MSS.

Chapter 4

1. Concerning Byrnes' mood upon leaving for the Moscow conference, see Bohlen, *Witness to History,* 247.
2. Truman wrote Stalin that Soviet-American "difficulties are assuming exaggerated proportions in the minds of our respective peoples and are delaying in many ways the progress, which we both desire to expedite, towards peace and reconstruction." He assured the Soviet leader that their differences—on the Far Eastern Commission, the Balkan peace treaties, and the atomic bomb—were not great, and might be resolved by "a full and frank talk" with Byrnes. Untitled document, December 12, 1945, "Atomic Energy Control Commission, UN" folder, Box 112, PSF, HSTL.
3. "Memorandum of conversation," December 11, 1945, Davies File, Byrnes MSS.
4. The "scientist's" quote is in Alice Kimball Smith, *A Peril and a Hope: The Scientists' Movement in America, 1945–1947* (Chicago, 1965), 112. Smith's excellent book is a history of the "reluctant lobby" of scientists and its role in the atomic policy debate.
5. Other members of the State Department committee were Carroll Wilson, aide to Bush; Herbert Marks, aide to Acheson; Joseph E. Johnson of the State Department (a later architect of the Marshall Plan); Henry Smyth, a Princeton physicist; and J. Robert Oppenheimer, a principal scientist in the Manhattan Project and outspoken proponent of international control. The internal notes and minutes of the committee can be found in folder 63, Harrison-Bundy File, MEDR. For the end result of the committee's efforts, see "Draft Proposals on Atomic Energy for Submission to the Soviet Government," December 10, *FR: 1945,* II, 92–6.

6. Benjamin Cohen felt that the final proposal was not definite or generous enough in its offer to cooperate with the Russians. "I had a fear," Cohen told the author on this point, "that it would become too obvious to the Soviets that they would get things only as they [might] be able to work it out on their own." Interview with Benjamin V. Cohen, May 18, 1973, Washington, D.C. An account of the deliberations of the committee is also in Hewlett and Anderson, *New World*, 471–3.

7. Bohlen, *Witness to History*, 250.

8. Halifax to Byrnes, December 6, *FR:* 1945, II, 597–8.

9. "W. B.'s book," November 23, 1945, Byrnes MSS. Davies diary, December 11, 1945, Davies MSS.

10. "Record of Trans-Atlantic Teletype Conference . . . ," November 26, *FR:* 1945, II, 582–5. Byrnes also made a vain effort to mollify the French for their exclusion from the conference; see *FR:* 1945, II, 601–2. Concerning Byrnes' withdrawn concession to the British, see Byrnes to Bevin, December 6, *FR:* 1945, II, 596–7; and *New York Times*, December 8, 1945.

11. Molotov to Harriman, December 8, *FR:* 1945, II, 605. Byrnes, *Speaking Frankly*, 116–17.

12. Bohlen, *Witness to History*, 248. George F. Kennan, *Memoirs, 1925–1950* (New York, 1967), 286–8.

13. Forrestal to Byrnes; and Patterson to Byrnes, December 11, *FR:* 1945, II, 96–8. Bowing to pressure from Groves and the War Department, the State Department committee later sent a memorandum to Byrnes at Moscow advising him that, "based on military as well as other security considerations, the subject of sources of raw materials must be left to a later period." See "Exchange of Information concerning Natural Resources and Raw Materials of Fissionable Substances," undated, folder 63, Harrison-Bundy File, MEDR. Groves' sensitivity to the raw materials situation is understandable. On this point, see Chapter 5.

14. Arthur H. Vandenberg, Jr., ed., *The Private Papers of Senator Vandenberg* (Boston, 1952), 225; 227.

15. Vandenberg believed that the bipartisanship to which he had mortgaged his political career entitled him to some political favors from the Truman administration. During fall 1946, he wrote the President asking for the latter's support in the upcoming elections. There is no evidence that Truman honored this request or played any other role in Vandenberg's reelection, however. Arthur Vandenberg to Robert Hannegan, undated, Vandenberg Correspondence File, Byrnes MSS.

16. Byrnes had chosen Dulles, he wrote, because "Dulles had not been active in partisan politics." James F. Byrnes transcript, Dulles Oral History Project, Dulles MSS.

17. Untitled document, November 19, 1945, "Council of Foreign Ministers, 1945" folder, 1971 Supplement, Dulles MSS.

18. On the committee's instructions to Byrnes for that briefing, see "Supplemental Notes of 6 December, 1945," "State Department Working Committee" Box, Oppenheimer MSS. The comments by Vandenberg and Connally are cited in Vandenberg, ed., *Private Papers*, 228.

19. Davies diary, December 8, 11, 1945, Davies MSS. A more extensive account by Davies of this episode is included in the Byrnes MSS. Significantly, Byrnes made no mention of the incident in either volume of his memoirs. See "Trouble Threatens Behind Byrnes' Back," December 11, 1945, Davies File, Byrnes MSS. Truman's private journal shows that he had mixed feelings about Byrnes—and the State Department—as early as the Potsdam conference. He wrote on July 7, 1945: "Had a long talk with my able and conniving Secretary of State. My but he has a keen mind! And

he is an honest man. But all country politicians are circuitous in their dealings. When they are told the straight truth, unvarnished it is never believed—an asset sometimes. . . . The smart boys in the State Department, as usual, are against the best interests of the U.S. . . . But they are stymied this time. Byrnes and I shall expect our interests to come first." Truman journal, HSTL.

20. Davies to Byrnes, December 11, 1945, Davies File, Byrnes MSS.

21. Concerning Conant's role at Moscow, see James B. Conant, *My Several Lives* (New York, 1970), 484–7. Vandenberg's suspicions are ironic, since part of the task assigned to Conant at Moscow was gathering what information he could upon Russian progress toward an atomic bomb.

22. Vandenberg, ed., *Private Papers*, 229–30. State Department Working Committee to Byrnes, December 19 and 21, 1945, folder 63, Harrison-Bundy File, MEDR.

23. Vandenberg, ed., *Private Papers*, 229–30. The "directive" Truman spoke of was apparently just the State Department's draft proposal, which he had received from Byrnes. That Truman read the proposal—and understood its implications—is doubtful from the evidence of this incident. See the untitled document of December 12, 1945, "Atomic Energy Control Commission, UN" folder, Box 112, PSF, HSTL.

24. Blum, ed., *Price of Vision*, 516; 530.

25. Truman reflected of Potsdam, Ayers recounts, that "it would go down in history as a bad conference. Yet, [Truman] said nothing more could have been done because they were confronted with so many accomplished facts before they started. He had in mind the *faits accomplis* of the Russians." Ayers diary, January 24, 1946, HSTL. In a letter Truman wrote to Dean Acheson in March 1957 but never sent, he portrayed himself at Potsdam as "an innocent idealist" and Stalin as "the unconscionable Russian Dictator"—though he went on to remark, ruefully, anent Stalin: "And I liked the little son of a bitch." Truman to Acheson, March 13, 1957, Truman journal, HSTL.

26. Ayers diary, December 16 and 19, 1945.

27. Ayers diary, December 12, 1945.

28. Tom Connally, *My Name Is Tom Connally* (New York, 1954), 290.

29. Acheson to Byrnes, December 15, *FR:* 1945, II, 609–10.

30. Byrnes to Acheson, December 17, ibid., 611. Concerning the extent of the change between the original "Draft Proposals on Atomic Energy for Submission to the Soviet Government" and the final "United States Proposals on Atomic Energy," see ibid., 92–6; 663–6.

31. Some of these proposals went further than the original State Department plan. One urged Byrnes to announce to the Russians that the United States "is willing to proceed with the USSR on the basis of bilateral discussions . . . either concurrently with or prior to any discussions within the proposed [UN] commission." Attached to this proposal was a suggested "Declaration of Principles re Scientific Freedom" that would have established "free foreign interchange of scientists and free publications," an international scientific agency, and an exchange of experimental nuclear reactors. See "Provision of Nuclear Reactors for Research Purposes," folder 20, Harrison-Bundy File, MEDR.

32. Acheson to Byrnes, December 20, *FR:* 1945, II, 707–8. Concerning the belated inclusion of the stages provision by Byrnes, see ibid., 698.

33. Conant to Bush, December 31, 1945, Correspondence File, Bush MSS. Byrnes was perhaps as surprised as Conant. See Byrnes, *All in One Lifetime*, 337.

34. "Memorandum of Conversation Between [Stalin] and [Byrnes]," December 23, *FR:* 1945, II, 756.

35. Bohlen, *Witness to History*, 250.

36. Byrnes was not so confident, however, as to risk reviving domestic criticism of him for bringing Conant along. When the latter earnestly proposed on the last day of the conference that Soviet-American interchange on atomic energy begin immediately, he was quietly ignored. Byrnes, *All in One Lifetime*, 336–7. Bohlen, too, interpreted Stalin's rebuff of Molotov as signifying a change in Russian attitudes toward the bomb. Bohlen, *Witness to History*, 250.

37. On the dispute at Moscow over control of the UNAEC, see *FR:* 1945, II, 735, 740–1; and the "Communiqué on the Moscow Conference of the Three Foreign Ministers," December 27, ibid., 815–24.

38. Vandenberg, *Private Papers*, 232–4.

39. Davies diary, December 18, 1945, Davies MSS.

40. It is true, as Byrnes later claimed, that telegraph and telephone communications were poor throughout the duration of the conference. But it is also likely that Byrnes used technical difficulties as an excuse for not keeping Truman informed of actions he would almost certainly have disapproved. Bohlen recounts that when he reminded Byrnes at Moscow of his obligation to send reports to Truman, the former responded "sharply" that he knew when that was necessary and when it was not. It was also during the Moscow conference that Byrnes told Harriman: "I'm not going to send any daily reports [to Truman]. I don't trust the White House. It leaks. And I don't want any of this coming out in the papers until I get home." Bohlen, *Witness to History*, 250. Byrnes' comment to Harriman is quoted in Rose, *After Yalta*, 158.

41. Acheson, *Present at the Creation*, 136. Byrnes, *All in One Lifetime*, 343. Text of Byrnes' speech in *New York Times*, December 31, 1945.

42. Ayers diary, January 2, 1946, HSTL. Byrnes gives an account of how the communiqué came to be broadcast before his report reached Truman in *All in One Lifetime*, 342–3.

43. Most accounts of this incident agree that Truman did not—as he later claimed in his memoirs—read the letter verbatim to Byrnes, but merely used it as a framework for more moderate criticism. Byrnes, probably for reasons of pride, chose to ignore the whole episode in his memoirs. The text of this letter is in the President's memoirs. Truman, *Year of Decisions*, 604–6. The Ethridge Report, and its role in the Moscow conference, are considered in Davis, *Cold War Begins*. See also Yergin, *Shattered Peace*, 143–6, 160. Concerning the Truman-Byrnes feud, see Acheson, *Present at the Creation*, 136; and Messer, "James F. Byrnes." Byrnes' account of the meeting with Truman is substantially different from that of the President; see *All in One Lifetime*, 343–5.

44. "Official Files Held Here for Secrecy," folder 620, Byrnes MSS.

45. The comments by Leahy and Rosenman are cited in Rose, *After Yalta*, 159.

46. Davies diary, January 7, 1946, Davies MSS.

47. One participant at the UN meeting in London, Edward Weintal, confirms the important role that Vandenberg and Dulles played there and at Moscow in forcing Byrnes to retreat on his initiative to the Russians. Weintal argues that Byrnes was "quite prepared to go very far in accommodating the Soviets on atomic cooperation with the United States," and "it was really the two Republicans who stood very firm and finally persuaded Byrnes to be very strict with the Russians on atomic energy." Weintal transcript, Dulles Oral History Project, Dulles MSS. Vandenberg, ed., *Private Papers*, 245. Concerning the compromise at the London UN meeting, see also *FR:* 1946, I, 725–7; and Yergin, *Shattered Peace*, 184.

48. In both volumes of his memoirs, Byrnes would cite his discovery of a heart ailment

in early 1946 as the reason for his leaving the administration. In fact, the initially pessimistic medical report was later found to be in error, but it nonetheless provided a convenient justification for Byrnes' retirement. Concerning Byrnes' decision to resign, see Messer, "James F. Byrnes."

49. Byrnes is quoted in Yergin, *Shattered Peace,* 192. Davies concluded of Byrnes' retirement: "Evidently deciding that he faced hopeless odds, he struck out on a new path of 'patience and firmness' which proved too patient to satisfy critics in this country or to command confidence with the Russians." Davies diary, January 7, 1947, Davies MSS.

50. Byrnes, *All in One Lifetime,* 348. Concerning subsequent cooperation between Byrnes and Vandenberg, see Chapter 7.

51. In his memoirs, Acheson wrote of Vandenberg: "One of Vandenberg's stratagems was to enact publicly his conversion to a proposal, his change of attitude, a kind of political transubstantiation. The method was to go through a period of public doubt and skepticism; then find a comparatively minor flaw in the proposal, pounce on it, and make much of it; in due course propose a change, always the Vandenberg amendment. Then, and only then, could it be given to his followers as true doctrine worthy of all men to be received. . . . Its strength lay in the genuineness of his belief in each step." Acheson, *Present at the Creation,* 223. In fairness, it might be noted that Vandenberg privately characterized Acheson as "the kind of lawyer I'd like to have if I were guilty as hell." Vandenberg is cited in the Edward Weintal transcript, Dulles Oral History Project, Dulles MSS.

Chapter 5

1. Lilienthal, *Atomic Energy Years,* 9–10.

2. Stimson diary, April 24, 1945, Stimson MSS.

3. Concerning the Interim Committee meeting, see Hewlett and Anderson, *New World,* 354. The "striking discrepancy" is noted in Leslie Groves diary, Dec. 12, 1945, Box 24, Commanding General's File, MEDR.

4. *New York Times,* August 10, 1945.

5. Concerning Groves' advice to Truman, see "Notes," undated, folder 13, Commanding General's File, MEDR. In the course of a meeting with Truman during the spring of 1946, J. Robert Oppenheimer also got the impression that the President believed the Russians would not get the bomb. Nuell Pharr Davis, *Lawrence and Oppenheimer* (New York, 1968), 260. Groves apparently shared Truman's view that the Russians might be incapable of building the hydrogen bomb. On this point, see J. R. Oppenheimer, *The Open Mind* (New York, 1955), 70.

6. Originally, Szilard asked to see Truman but was refused an interview with the President. Szilard's memorandum is in the "Atomic" folder, Byrnes MSS; and in Morton Grodzins and Eugene Rabinowitch, eds., *The Atomic Age: Scientists in National and World Affairs* (New York, 1963), 13–18. He also gave Byrnes a remarkably prescient vision of the future Soviet-American arms race, entitled "Atomic Bombs and the Postwar Position of the United States in the World." Szilard's version of the meeting is in "Reminiscences," Fleming and Bailyn, eds., *Perspectives in American History,* II, 126–41. Byrnes gives a very different version of the meeting with Szilard; see *All in One Lifetime,* 284. Byrnes had probably been told by Groves of the raw-materials monopoly and the Combined Development Trust early in April 1945. He was, in any

case, certainly convinced of its importance after the bombing of Hiroshima. Groves' diary thus has the following entry for August 18, 1945: "[George] Harrison said Byrnes wants trust to go ahead full tilt." Groves diary, August 18, 1945, Box 24, MEDR.

7. Concerning this meeting, see Hewlett and Anderson, *New World,* 359–60. Another historian has commented on the fact that Byrnes listened to Groves and ignored the atomic scientists. See Gardner, *Architects of Illusion,* 90–3.

8. Groves, *Now It Can Be Told* (New York, 1962), xii.

9. Ibid., 285–6.

10. Concerning Groves' program for the purchase of uranium after 1942, see Vannevar Bush to General Styer, September 11, 1942, AEC Doc. 146, U.S. Dept. of Energy. See also Groves to Patterson, December 3, 1945, folder 40, Harrison-Bundy File, MEDR.

11. According to Manhattan Project records, the Murray Hill Area was "finally established" on June 15, 1943, "as an exploration and development program to determine and evaluate the entire world's resources of uranium ore [and] to make recommendations for the acquisition of the strongest possible control of the production and disposal of such resources as might be accessible." See the "Draft Historical Report for Project S-37," December 1, 1944, Box 22, MEDR. This document is also in Anthony C. Brown and Charles B. MacDonald, eds., *The Secret History of the Atomic Bomb* (New York, 1977), 192–9. An aide to Groves testified in 1949 that "efforts were made to buy up all sources of uranium" shortly after June 1942, when the army took over the Manhattan Project. See *New York Times,* December 4, 1949. Groves, *Now It Can Be Told,* 101, 176.

12. Groves, *Now It Can Be Told,* 176.

13. Hewlett and Anderson, *New World,* 288.

14. Upon Groves' recommendation that Sengier was "vastly important to the Allied cause" the Belgian was awarded America's highest civilian honor, the Medal of Merit, after the war. On Sengier's service to the Manhattan Project, see Groves, *Now It Can Be Told,* 33–7, 125–8; and Hewlett and Anderson, *New World,* 85–6.

15. Concerning the Belgian negotiations and Sengier's role in them, see Major Traynor's "Notes," April–May 1944, folder 16, Commanding General's File, MEDR.

16. Concerning the effect of this discovery upon the Murray Hill Area's master plan, see the October 1944 "Survey of the World's Sources of Uranium and Thorium," Box 22, MEDR; and Hewlett and Anderson, *New World,* 33–4.

17. Major Traynor's "Notes," April–May 1944, folder 16, Commanding General's File, MEDR.

18. Groves to Bundy, February 6, 1945, folder 34, Harrison-Bundy File, MEDR.

19. Groves, *Now It Can Be Told,* 17; Hewlett and Anderson, *New World,* 285–6.

20. Groves is cited in Robert Jungk, *Brighter Than a Thousand Suns* (New York, 1956), 182.

21. Documents concerning the work of the Murray Hill Area are in *FR:* 1945, II, 317–18. Regarding the role of the British in this work see ibid., 8–9, and Gowing, *Britain and Atomic Energy,* 137–42.

22. Concerning the Manhattan Engineer District Scientific Intelligence Mission (Alsos), see Groves, *Now It Can Be Told,* 185–249; Samuel A. Goudsmit, *Alsos* (London, 1947); and "Supplement to Manhattan District History," Box 9, MEDR. See also Brown and MacDonald, eds., *Secret History of the Atomic Bomb,* 210–33.

23. Concerning Paperclip and Project 63, see Bradley to Johnson, "Denial of German Scientists to the USSR," May 9, 1951; and "General Allocation Policy on Secret

Weapons—Exploitation of German Scientists," Sec. 20, Box 172, "Atomic" Series, (5-1-45), USJCS Records.

24. In his memoirs, Groves wrote that he and the Alsos staff "seemed to be almost alone in our appreciation of the potential value of German scientists to the Russians." His francophobia may have been inspired by the belief that a French scientist in the Manhattan Project was passing secrets to the Russians. Groves, *Now It Can Be Told*, 244.

25. Groves' remarks were made in testimony at the 1954 security hearing for physicist J. Robert Oppenheimer. See U.S. Atomic Energy Commission, *In the Matter of J. Robert Oppenheimer* (Washington, D.C., 1954), 173. Concerning Groves' early perception of the Russian threat, see Groves, *Now It Can Be Told*, 139–41.

26. U.S. AEC, *In the Matter of J. Robert Oppenheimer*, 173.

27. Concerning the controversial uranium shipment, see U.S. Congress, "Hearings Regarding the Shipment of Atomic Material to the Soviet Union During World War II," House Un-American Activities Committee, 81st Congress, Second Session (Washington, D.C., 1950), esp. 935–50; Bernard Newman, *Soviet Atomic Spies* (London, 1952), 43–6; and *New York Times*, Dec. 4, 1949. Said one Groves aide of the uranium metal at issue in the hearings: "We would like to see the Russians when they try to use *that* in a pile."

28. Concerning the American scientist in Moscow, see "Memorandum . . .," June 19, 1945, folder 20, Commanding General's File, MEDR. Conant's impressions are cited in "Memorandum of Conversation," April 19, 1946, "Toward the 14 June Proposal," Bernard M. Baruch MSS, Princeton University.

29. David Lilienthal told the author in February 1979: "We did send covert operations into Russia and they came back and said there isn't any [uranium]." The only part of the Manhattan Engineer District files still classified is the "Foreign Intelligence Supplement," which includes covert operations in other countries. Concerning those operations in Germany and Japan, see "Foreign Intelligence Supplement Nos. 1–3," "Supplement to Manhattan District History," Box 9, MEDR. See also "World Index Map," February 28, 1945, "Draft Historical Report of Project S-37," December 1, 1944, Box 22, MEDR; or Brown and MacDonald, *Secret History of the Atomic Bomb*, 191–9. The uncompleted survey of Germany was perhaps the crucial oversight of the Murray Hill Area's staff. On this point, see also the Epilogue.

30. Stimson to Truman, June 18, 1945, folder 34, Harrison-Bundy File, MEDR. Groves to Bundy, February 6, 1945, folder 34, Harrison-Bundy File, MEDR. Though he at one time expressed the view that "thorium will be the ultimate means of producing what we are after," Groves changed his mind by December 1945. The day before his briefing to the Combined Policy Committee on the raw-materials monopoly he informed Patterson that further research had indicated "a substantial amount of uranium" was first necessary for thorium to be usable in a nuclear reaction. Since Groves did not believe the Russians had uranium, thorium no longer seemed important and was ignored in his report. Groves to Patterson, December 3, *FR:* 1945, II, 84–5.

31. Details of these last-minute negotiations, including those with the Swedish government, are included in *FR:* 1945, II, 24–40; 45–7. The thoroughness with which the Murray Hill Area staff approached their task is indicated by the estimate that Swedish uranium deposits contained only 1 percent usable ore.

32. The British negotiators for the trust had better luck, signing contracts with both the Dutch and the Indian governments before August 6, 1945. The Manhattan Project representatives in Sweden at least achieved their main goal of keeping the ore out of

the hands of the Russians. Thus the Swedes agreed not to sell their uranium to any bidder. The frantic nature of the Swedish negotiations is evident in *FR:* 1945, II, 45–7.

33. Groves' report on the raw-materials monopoly is in Groves to Patterson, December 3, 1945, folder 40, Harrison-Bundy File, MEDR; and in *FR:* 1945, II, 84–9.

34. See, for example, Szilard's letter of August 15, 1939, to President Roosevelt, Appendix I, "Reminiscences," Fleming and Bailyn, eds., *Perspectives in American History,* 142–8.

35. One reason why Bush and Conant dismissed the idea of a raw-materials monopoly as impractical was the prospect they foresaw that the atomic bomb would give way to the hydrogen bomb—"for the supply of heavy hydrogen is essentially unlimited and the rarer materials such as uranium and thorium would be used only as detonators." Bush and Conant to Stimson, September 30, 1944, folder 77, Harrison-Bundy File, MEDR. Their memo is also in Sherwin, *World Destroyed,* 286–8.

36. The Franck Report is in A. K. Smith, *Peril and a Hope,* 371–83; and in Barton J. Bernstein, ed., *The Atomic Bomb: The Critical Issues* (Boston, 1976), 25–8.

37. Perhaps the greatest barrier to the scientists was Groves himself, since all appeals to the President went through him first. In late July 1945, Szilard forwarded a petition with the signatures of seventy scientists urging that Truman not drop the bomb "unless the terms which will be imposed upon Japan have been made public and Japan knowing these terms has refused to surrender." Groves deliberately withheld the petition for a week, so that Truman did not receive it until after the bomb had been dropped on Hiroshima. See Leo Szilard, "The Story of a Petition," Fleming and Bailyn, eds., *Perspectives in American History,* II, 154–65. Groves commented in his memoirs on the workings of "need-to-know" within the Manhattan Project: "We made certain that each member of the project thoroughly understood his part in our total effort—that, and nothing more." Groves, *Now It Can Be Told,* 179. He was distrustful of the scientists in part because he believed that science and not the nation was their higher loyalty. Groves created his own classification of "ultra-secret"—above the government's "top secret"—for material he considered especially sensitive.

38. Text of Groves' speech in *New York Times,* September 22, 1945.

39. Concerning the basis of Groves' estimate for a Soviet atomic bomb, see "Minutes for the Files," September 28, 1945, folder 68, Harrison-Bundy File, MEDR.

40. This memorandum in *FR:* 1946, I, 1197–1203.

41. "Effect of Foreseeable New Developments . . .," August 24, 1945, "Air Force" Series (7-18-45), Sec. 1, USJCS Records.

Chapter 6

1. Connally, *My Name Is Tom Connally,* 288.

2. "The President," Dulles wrote, "said that he thought the question resolved itself down to the matter of whether or not the people and Congress were prepared to trust the President. However, he had not actually studied the pending legislation. . . ." "Memorandum of Conversation," March 16, 1946, "1971 Supplement," Dulles MSS.

3. Concerning the drafting of the Royall-Marbury bill and the early struggle over domestic control, see Hewlett and Anderson, *New World,* 412–15.

4. It was for this reason that Stimson had emphasized the urgent need to resolve the domestic-control issue in the same meeting he proposed the direct approach to Russia. Stimson diary, September 12, 1945, Stimson MSS.

5. Acheson, *Present at the Creation,* 124.

6. Groves and Patterson had scheduled a meeting of the Interim Committee for September 28 to discuss ways of getting the bill around the State Department. See Groves, *Now It Can Be Told,* 390.

7. Alice K. Smith, an historian of the scientist movement, notes that during September–October 1945 the concern of most politically aware scientists shifted from international control to domestic control, largely because of the immediate threat seen in the May–Johnson bill. A. K. Smith, *Peril and a Hope,* 128–52; 211–19. On this point, see also Hewlett and Anderson, *New World,* 432; and "Secrecy and Censorship Seen as Fatal to Progress in Atomic Research," *New York Times,* October 14, 1945. For a political scientist's view of the sharp division between the "realist" and the "control" school of scientists, see Robert Gilpin, *American Scientists and Nuclear Weapons Policy* (Princeton, 1962).

8. Oppenheimer is quoted in A. K. Smith, *Peril and a Hope,* 148. Patterson to Compton, November 9, 1945, folder 68, Harrison-Bundy File, MEDR.

9. Patterson to Byrnes, November 1, 1945, folder 50, Harrison-Bundy File, MEDR.

10. Groves underscored his distrust of the approach suggested by Bush and Conant at the bottom of this memo: "Told to GLH [George Harrison, a War Department aide] many times—Gr." Groves to Harrison, July 25, 1945, folder 9A, Commanding General's File, MEDR.

11. Groves to Byrnes, February 13, *FR:* 1946, I, 1206.

12. Urey is cited in Walter Millis, *Arms and the State* (New York, 1958), 162.

13. The magazine's editorial writer wrote of the bill: "It discusses the issue of atomic power in such narrow terms of national security that we have very strong suspicions the bill came straight from the War Department to the desks of Senator Johnson and Representative May." *Nation,* October 20, 1945.

14. Hewlett and Anderson, *New World,* 429–35.

15. Groves, Patterson, Bush, and Conant were May's principal witnesses in the hearings. *New York Times,* October 10, 1945. Hewlett and Anderson, *New World,* 437–8.

16. Smith's comment is cited in Rose, *After Yalta,* 139. The disclosure that the Manhattan Project budget was hidden in other appropriations is in Groves, *Now It Can Be Told,* 360.

17. One—perhaps not entirely serious—proposal by Urey was that the United States drop all fissionable material (presumably denatured) into the Mississippi River. During Groves' testimony, the subject of Russia also came up, though obliquely. Asked what other countries would be able to manufacture atomic bombs, the Manhattan Project director mentioned only Britain and Sweden. Amid "general laughter," one senator commented to Groves that "because you left out some countries by elimination you can tell what country is being talked about." *New York Times,* November 30, 1945. Some members of the McMahon committee wanted the central focus of domestic control legislation to be upon the peacetime application of atomic energy to industry and medicine. Groves, however, opposed "any agency which concerns itself primarily with possible peacetime uses of atomic energy." "Any commission such as that proposed in the May–Johnson bill," he wrote in January 1946, "must have as its primary concern the military security of the United States." See Groves diary, December 12, 1945, Commanding General's File, MEDR.

18. The authors of the bill wrote a book about the drafting of that measure and its fate, in which their motivations are explained. Cf. James R. Newman and Brian S. Miller, *The Control of Atomic Energy* (New York, 1948).

19. The committee that Byrnes had entrusted with drafting an American proposal for international control of the bomb was also encountering resistance from Groves at this time. On this point, see Chapter 7.
20. Truman is quoted by Wallace in Blum, ed., *Price of Vision*, 527.
21. Ibid., 530–2. In this same entry, Wallace records Patterson as saying that if he was asked how many bombs the United States then had, he would answer "None." Patterson's remarkable admission was apparently technically correct, since the weapons themselves remained unassembled at this time. Concerning the bomb and United States military preparedness, see Chapter 10.
22. One "essential" amendment included replacement of the original part-time nine-member commission with one that had three full-time members appointed by the President. Another stated that the commission "should establish principles and policies with the approval of the President for carrying on its work, consistent with the purposes of the Act." Truman to Patterson and Forrestal, November 28, 1945, folder 67, Harrison-Bundy File, MEDR. An accompanying letter to Patterson from Royall showed the latter's opposition to Truman's idea of dropping military representation. Thus Royall had written on Truman's memo next to this provision an emphatic *"no."* Royall to Patterson, undated; and Patterson to Truman, December 12, 1945, folder 67, Harrison-Bundy File, MEDR. Concerning the early recognition by some of the perils of atomic energy's "peaceful uses," see Richard Hewlett and Francis Duncan, *The Atomic Shield, 1947/1952: A History of the United States Atomic Energy Commission*, II (University Park, Pa., 1969), 202–4.
23. Text of that letter in *New York Times*, March 1, 1946; and in Harry S Truman, *Memoirs: Years of Trial and Hope* (New York, 1956), 4–5.
24. *New York Times*, November 8, 1945.
25. Untitled memorandum by Groves, January 2, *FR:* 1946, I, 1197–1207.
26. Blum, ed., *Price of Vision*, 508. Wallace—obviously not an admirer of Groves—collected anecdotes about the Manhattan Project director in his diary. For example, in mid-December 1945 Wallace related to Truman a story about Groves that he had heard from Condon. He informed the President that Groves was "a Roosevelt hater and a Mrs. Roosevelt scorner. I told the President that Groves felt that Roosevelt had made some blunders with regard to the international handling of atomic energy and that he, General Groves, would straighten the matter out on his own." Ibid., 472, 500, 506, and 508.
27. Concerning early knowledge of Russian spying, see U.S. Congress, House Un-American Activities Committee, "Hearings Regarding the Shipment of Atomic Material to the Soviet Union During World War II" (Washington, D.C., 1950), 935–9, and "Report on Soviet Espionage Activities in Connection with the Atom Bomb" (Washington, D.C., 1948), 163–5; U.S. Congress, Joint Committee on Atomic Energy, *Soviet Atomic Espionage* (Washington, D.C., 1951), 2–25; Groves, *Now It Can Be Told*, 138–41. Stimson diary, September 9, 1943, Stimson MSS. Truman and King are quoted on Soviet espionage in J. W. Pickersgill and D. F. Forster, *The Mackenzie King Record, 1944–1946*, IV (Toronto, 1968), 40–1. Truman was given further details on the Canadian spy case at the November 1945 Washington conference, which King had assumed was called to discuss the espionage investigation. Historian Lisle Rose argues that Truman's "exceptionally casual response" to King's news on both occasions indicates that the President had already been informed of the slight danger actually posed by "atom-spies." Rose, *After Yalta*, 138.
28. "The Atom-General Answers His Critics," *Saturday Evening Post*, June 19, 1948.

29. "Intelligence and Security," MED History, Book I, v. 14, Box 8, MEDR.

30. Ibid. This section is also reprinted in Brown and MacDonald, eds., *Secret History of the Atomic Bomb*, 200–10. Concerning the case of the servicemen and their souvenir photos, see U.S. Congress, Joint Committee on Atomic Energy, *Soviet Atomic Espionage*, 195–205.

31. Cf. Henry D. Smyth, *Atomic Energy for Military Purposes* (Princeton, N.J., 1945). Stimson diary, August 1, 1945, Stimson MSS. At a secret military conference on atomic energy in September 1946, Groves acknowledged that "the Smyth Report disclosed nothing we felt was of any value to another nation. . . . [T]here wasn't a nation, with which we were concerned, where a group of the leading scientists in our opinion couldn't produce the Smyth Report themselves—with a few exceptions—and we felt that in the course of the development of the atomic bomb . . . requiring from 5 to 7 years if a nation had a great deal of help from us, and up to 15 to 20 if they tried to get it without secrecy from us, in [sic] the Smyth Report would have saved the other nation about two weeks time in the overall period of time in a period of years." See untitled transcript, September 23–26, 1946, Box 3, Series 1946–337, Records of the U.S. Air Force, Record Group 341, Modern Military Section, National Archives.

32. Groves, *Now It Can Be Told*, 349. Groves would later blame Robert Oppenheimer for forcing the "premature" release of the Smyth Report. Stimson diary, August 1, 1945, Stimson MSS.

33. *New York Times*, September 30, 1945. Concerning public opinion on the bomb, see Social Science Research Council, *Public Reaction to the Atomic Bomb and World Affairs*, 2–16.

34. Truman's remark to Stettinius is cited in Gaddis, *United States and the Origins of the Cold War*, 253. Bush is quoted in Yergin, *Shattered Peace*, 135. Barnard to Lippmann, February 10, 1950, Chester Barnard File, Oppenheimer MSS.

35. J. Edgar Hoover to Harry Vaughan, October 11, 1946, "FBI—Atomic Bomb" folder, Box 167, PSF, HSTL. Steinhardt to Byrnes, November 19, 1945, folder 20, Harrison-Bundy File, MEDR. Groves' lack of concern regarding Czech uranium is noted in U.S. AEC, *In the Matter of J. Robert Oppenheimer*, 175–6. Concerning Russian statements on their progress toward an atomic bomb, see *FR:* 1949, V (Washington, D.C., 1976), 656–7.

36. *New York Times*, February 24, 1946.

37. Erskine, "The Polls . . .," *Public Opinion Quarterly*, Summer 1963, 175–83.

38. See Drew Pearson's column in the *Washington Post*, February 4–8, 1946. Pearson's own diary and collected papers, unfortunately, shed little light upon the source or sources for his spy stories.

39. Pickersgill and Forster, *Mackenzie King Record*, IV, 135. King would later write in his diary that subsequent stories by Pearson confirmed his opinion that the original spy disclosures "had all been done to cause USSR feeling to be diverted from [the] State Department and to have it appear . . . that Canada and not the U.S. had taken the initiative in the matter. . . ." Ibid., 142.

40. Concerning McNaughton's scoop and its source, see "February" folder, Box 9, McNaughton MSS, HSTL. The impact of McNaughton's exclusive is also detailed by Rose, *After Yalta*, 169.

41. Concerning the Canadian spy case, see Canadian Government, *The Report of the Royal Commission to Investigate Disclosures of Secret and Confidential Information to Unauthorized Persons* (Ottawa, 1946), esp. 447–57, 615–16; U.S. Congress, *Soviet Atomic Espionage*, 121–3; and Igor Gouzenko, *This Was My Choice* (New York,

1947). On the Russians' admission of spying, see *New York Times,* February 17, 1946.

42. Concerning Groves' opinion that the spies should be tried in a closed court, see Groves diary, April 3, 1946, v. II, MEDR. The final result of the investigation into the Canadian spy ring is noted in Reuben, *Atom-Spy Hoax.*

43. Fuchs, a British scientist, spied for the Russians until his arrest in 1950. Maclean was Britain's representative on the Combined Policy Committee, and defected to the Soviet Union in May 1951. Concerning the value of Maclean and Fuchs to the Russians, see Epilogue.

44. Reuben, *Atom-Spy Hoax,* 23–46.

45. A. K. Smith, *Peril and Hope,* 101. Perhaps typical of the scientists' viewpoint was this editorial of mid-March 1946 in a trade journal: "The spy scare, the most recent testimony of military officials before the Special Senate Committee on Atomic Energy and a growing mistrust or suspicion of Russia are three of the more pertinent reasons why the McMahon Bill providing for civilian control of atomic energy at the national level appears momentarily at least to be losing ground to the discredited May–Johnson proposal which would give the military dictatorial power in the field of nuclear energy." *Chemical and Engineering News,* March 18, 1946.

46. Hewlett and Anderson, *New World,* 501–2.

47. See "February" folder, Box 9, McNaughton MSS, HSTL.

48. Urey quoted in *New York Times,* March 3, 1946.

49. Groves' letter to Hickenlooper, *New York Times,* March 21, 1946.

50. Hewlett and Anderson, *New World,* 504–8.

51. The AEC historians argue that the passage of the Vandenberg amendment proved "the McMahon group could keep a rein on the scientists." Ibid., 510. More to the point, however, is Smith's observation on the demoralization of the scientists: "indeed there are no signs that they were disposed even to take the bit in their teeth." A. K. Smith, *Peril and Hope,* 414.

52. McMahon to Truman, March 28, 1946, "Atomic Energy Safe File 2," Patterson File, MEDR. Blum, ed., *Price of Vision,* 569.

53. Ayers diary, March 4, 1946, HSTL.

54. Truman's letter is quoted in Yergin, *Shattered Peace,* 154.

55. Concerning Truman's retreat from earlier support of the McMahon bill, see *PPOP,* 1946, I, 155–7; A. K. Smith, *Peril and Hope,* 343–82; and Hewlett and Anderson, *New World,* 509–10.

56. *New York Times,* November 27, 1945.

57. *New York Times,* June 14, 1946.

Chapter 7

1. Harriman's telegrams of April 6 and 11, 1945, may be found in the "Russia" File, Forrestal MSS.

2. For what became known as the "Bohlen Report," see "The Capabilities and Intentions of the Soviet Union as Affected by American Policy," December 10, 1945, U.S. Department of State Records, National Archives.

3. "Naval Intelligence Memorandum of Information," January 21, 1946, "Russia" File, Forrestal MSS.

4. "Capabilities and Intentions of the USSR in the Postwar Period," February 12, 1946, "USSR" Series, (3-27-45), Sec. 3, USJCS Records.

5. Concerning Stalin's announcement of the five-year plan and reaction to it, see

Millis, ed., *Forrestal Diaries*, 134–5; and *New York Times*, February 10, 1945.

6. Truman's comment to Leahy is noted in Gaddis, *United States and the Origins of the Cold War*, 304.

7. Although the Michigan senator would later claim that he personally had inspired Byrnes' turnaround on Russia, Vandenberg actually learned of the upcoming hard-line speech planned by Byrnes and decided to anticipate it by one day. Ayers diary, February 28, 1946, HSTL. On the motivation behind Vandenberg's speech, see Vandenberg, ed., *Private Papers*, 246. Texts of Vandenberg's and Byrnes' speeches in *New York Times*, February 28 and March 1, 1946. On the timing of Vandenberg's speech, see Gaddis, *United States and the Origins of the Cold War*, 306 ff.

8. So sensitive had Byrnes become to criticism of his relationship with Truman that in April 1946 he would claim that he and the President "have never had any difference in views that was not quickly reconciled." Byrnes to Baruch, April 19, *FR:* 1946, I, 777–8.

9. Sending a navy task force to accompany the *Missouri* had been Forrestal's idea, but it was rejected by the President. The *Missouri* eventually sailed alone. Ayers diary, February 28, 1946, HSTL.

10. For the view that Kennan was well aware of the favorable reception that his "long telegram" would have in Washington, see Gardner, *Architects of Illusion*, 270–300. Concerning Forrestal's role in the "long telegram," see also Admiral Sherman to Forrestal, March 17, 1945, "Russia" File, Forrestal MSS.

11. The text of Kennan's "long telegram" is reprinted in Kennan, *Memoirs, 1925–1950*, 547–59.

12. Ibid., 281.

13. Ayers diary, June 13, 1946, HSTL.

14. The aide is quoted in Yergin, *Shattered Peace*, 224.

15. According to Vandenberg, he told Molotov at Paris that "the United States was not going to give up the bomb; not going to compromise or trade; not going to give up our immortal souls." Vandenberg to Dulles, May 13, 1946, Correspondence File, Dulles MSS.

16. Byrnes, *Speaking Frankly*, 255–6. Davies diary, May 25, 1946, Davies MSS. Byrnes is quoted on U.S. nuclear testing in Yergin, *Shattered Peace*, 218. King is cited in Pickersgill and Forster, *Mackenzie King Record*, 150.

17. Acheson, *Present at the Creation*, 151.

18. The entire text of Churchill's speech is in J. P. Morray, *From Yalta to Disarmament* (New York, 1961), 43–52; excerpts are in *New York Times*, March 6, 1946.

19. On Russian reaction to the speech, see Yergin, *Shattered Peace*, 175–9.

20. Wallace and Bevin are quoted in ibid., 176, 233. Concerning Truman's prior knowledge of the speech, see Byrnes, *All in One Lifetime*, 349. On public reaction to the speech in the United States, see Gaddis, *United States and the Origins of the Cold War*, 289–315.

21. Groves' assessment of the value of British aid to the Manhattan Project was equally blunt: "Certainly it is true that without any contribution at all from the British, the date of our final success need not have been delayed by a single day." "Diplomatic History of the Manhattan Engineer District," undated, folder 103, Harrison-Bundy File, MEDR.

22. Acheson is quoted in Lilienthal, *Atomic Energy Years*, 25–6.

23. Acheson, *Present at the Creation*, 166.

24. Concerning Groves' obstructionism, see Groves to Byrnes, February 13, *FR:* 1946,

I, 1204–7; and "Draft Report to the Combined Policy Committee by a Sub-Committee," February 15, ibid., 1207–13.

25. Lilienthal, *Atomic Energy Years*, 25–6.
26. Attlee to Truman, April 16, *FR:* 1946, I, 1231–2; Truman, *Years of Trial and Hope*, 12–13. Truman to Attlee, April 20, *FR:* 1946, I, 1235–7.
27. On the Canadian government's unwillingness to support the British in their claim, see Stone to Acheson, April 29; and Acheson to Truman, May 6, *FR:* 1946, I, 1244–5.
28. Concerning the details of this settlement, see the memorandum from Acheson, Bush, and Groves to U.S. members of the Combined Policy Committee, May 7; and "Memorandum by a Sub-Committee . . . ," May 13, *FR:* 1946, I, 1245–7.
29. Acheson, *Present at the Creation*, 166. Interview with Gordon Arneson, October 1979, Washington, D.C.
30. The aide is quoted in Hewlett and Anderson, *New World*, 510.
31. Ibid., 505–6.
32. The Dulles-Muste correspondence, consisting of two letters from the pacifist and one from the future secretary of state, may be found in the "Communism" folder, Dulles MSS.

Chapter 8

1. Lilienthal, *Atomic Energy Years*, 9–10. Untitled note, June 3, 1946, "Toward the 14 June Proposal," Bernard M. Baruch MSS, Princeton University.
2. Lilienthal was apparently surprised to discover from Acheson that Groves had "entered into contracts involving other countries . . . without even the knowledge of the Department of State." Lilienthal, *Atomic Energy Years*, 9–10.
3. Acheson, *Present at the Creation*, 152.
4. Groves, *Now It Can Be Told*, 411.
5. Hewlett and Anderson, *New World*, 533–7.
6. Lilienthal, *Atomic Energy Years*, 26.
7. Ibid., 14. The most comprehensive account of the Board of Consultants meetings, based upon Acheson's minutes, is Hewlett and Anderson, *New World*, 534–54. See also Daniel Lang, "Seven Men on a Problem," *New Yorker*, August 17, 1946, 49–60.
8. The description of nuclear power plants as a "harmless" use of atomic energy would, of course, be disputed today. Some of the dangers inherent in the domestic application of atomic energy were recognized as early as the outset of the atomic age. See, for example, Hewlett and Duncan, *Atomic Shield*, 204–5.
9. Chester Barnard to Walter Lippmann, June 20, 1946, Correspondence File, Lilienthal MSS.
10. "It wasn't that we can persuade the Russians, but that the Russians will persuade themselves," Lilienthal has said on this point. According to Lilienthal, Herbert Marks was the board member most skeptical of their success, but even he showed the confidence—or arrogance—created by the bomb. In a meeting at which it was suggested that the Russians might not accept the American plan, Marks exclaimed, "Then we'll just destroy them." Interview with David E. Lilienthal, February 24, 1979, Princeton, N.J.
11. Ibid.
12. "Report on the International Control of Atomic Energy," p. 79, Box 66, Baruch MSS.
13. Hewlett and Anderson, *New World*, 540–5.

14. Bush, *Pieces of the Action*, 298.
15. Hewlett and Anderson, *New World*, 552–4.
16. Concerning early enthusiasm for the Acheson-Lilienthal Report, see Bush, *Pieces of the Action*, 298; Conant, *My Several Lives*, 492–3; Acheson, *Present at the Creation*, 152. By 1954, his loyalty in question, Oppenheimer had become more guarded about the prospects for international control: "My own view is that only a profound change in the whole orientation of Soviet policy, and a corresponding reorientation of our own, even in matters far from atomic energy, would give substance to the initial high hopes." See U.S. AEC, *In the Matter* of *J. Robert Oppenheimer*, 578.
17. *New York Times*, March 27, 1946. Groves to Patterson and Forrestal, March 27, 1946, folder 10, Commanding General's File, MEDR.
18. An investigation into the source of the leak by an aide to Bernard Baruch cited McCloy in its conclusion "that Byrnes favored publication [of the report]." Byrnes and Baruch to Truman, March 26, *FR:* 1946, I, 767. Concerning the leak of the Acheson-Lilienthal Report, see also Groves, *Now It Can Be Told*, 412; Acheson, *Present at the Creation*, 154. Eberstadt to Baruch, March 28, 1946, Box 62, Baruch MSS.
19. The *Tribune* is cited in Yergin, *Shattered Peace*, 237. Concerning Baruch, see Margaret Coit, *Mr. Baruch* (Boston, 1947).
20. Lilienthal, *Atomic Energy Years*, 30.
21. At least two Presidents to whom Baruch claimed he was an "adviser" were unpersuaded by the charm of the "park-bench statesman." FDR dismissed Baruch as "that old Pooh-bah"; Truman's private view of his politically useful appointee was no more charitable. Byrnes, too, would eventually join in this deprecating view of Baruch. Roosevelt is cited in Yergin, *Shattered Peace*, 79. Truman, *Years of Trial and Hope*, 20–25. Byrnes, *All in One Lifetime*, 385. Concerning Baruch's appointment, see also Truman, *Years of Trial and Hope*, 9–10; Bernard M. Baruch, *Baruch: The Public Years* (New York, 1960), 362; Baruch to Byrnes, March 31, 1946, "Correspondence on Atomic Energy," Baruch MSS; and Byrnes to Baruch, April 19, *FR:* 1946, I, 777–8. The "internationalist" was Herbert Marks. See "Memo . . . ," May 1, *FR:* 1946, I, 780–83.
22. Lilienthal, *Atomic Energy Years*, 30–1. One writer has suggested that there was an economic motive behind Baruch's choice of advisers, since all together hoped to gain a dominant position in the new industry of atomic energy "from raw materials to the finished product." See James S. Allen, *Atomic Imperialism* (New York, 1952), 108. While this seems rather farfetched, it is true that Baruch, Byrnes, and Searls were all officers and investors in the Newmont Mining Corporation, a company that specialized in uranium mining. When both were out of the administration, Searls requested of Byrnes that he use his connections to protect the threatened tax status of Newmont. Searls to Byrnes, January 17, 1948, Searls folder, Byrnes MSS.
23. Concerning Bush's views, see Bush to Byrnes, April 16, 1946, Correspondence File, Bush MSS.
24. *New York Times*, March 19, 1946.
25. Baruch to Swope, June 16, 1947, Correspondence File; and "Notes on Bernard Baruch," Baruch MSS. See also Lilienthal, *Atomic Energy Years*, 32.
26. Lilienthal, *Atomic Energy Years*, 41–2.
27. A transcript of Oppenheimer's telephone call is in Hoover to Byrnes, May 23, 1946, "Atomic" folder, Byrnes MSS. One of Oppenheimer's close associates notes that FBI surveillance of the scientist began in late 1942. Interview with Gordon Arneson,

October 1979, Washington, D.C. Oppenheimer's prediction on the Baruch plan, confided to Lilienthal, was remarkably prescient: "The American disposition (if negotiations in UN fail) will be to take plenty of time and not force the issue in a hurry; that then a 10–2 report will go to the [Security Council] and Russia will exercise her veto and decline to go along. This will be construed by us as a demonstration of Russia's warlike intentions. And this will fit perfectly into the plans of that growing number who want to put the country on a war footing, first psychologically, then actually. . . . The Army directing the country's research; Red-baiting; treating all labor organizations, CIO first, as Communist and therefore traitorous, etc. . . ." Lilienthal, *Atomic Energy Years,* 70.

28. In a June 1946 article for the *Bulletin of the Atomic Scientists,* Oppenheimer intimated that his major reason for keeping a distance from the Baruch delegation was so that he could remain independent to advocate the Acheson-Lilienthal Report. A subsequent interview with his biographer, however, shows that his private views concerning the prospect of international control changed when Baruch became head of the U.S. delegation to the UN Atomic Energy Commission: "That was the day I gave up hope, but that was not the day for me to say so publicly." Davis, *Lawrence and Oppenheimer,* 260.

29. Lilienthal, *Atomic Energy Years,* 42–3. On the amendments proposed, see Searls to Baruch, March 31, 1946, "Correspondence on Atomic Energy," Baruch MSS.

30. Coit, *Mr. Baruch,* 571.

31. Lilienthal, *Atomic Energy Years,* 42–3.

32. "Notes of a Conversation," June 1, 1946, "Toward the 14 June Proposal," Baruch MSS.

33. Hoover to Byrnes, May 27, 1946, "Atomic" folder, Byrnes MSS.

34. Lilienthal, *Atomic Energy Years,* 49–50. Notes made by members of the Baruch delegation upon a copy of the Acheson-Lilienthal Report reveal their early skepticism about the prospects for international control. One staffer wrote: "How can this plan be handled within our free enterprise structure without nationalization—which would endanger our whole way of life?" International cooperation was branded there "an adventure in human nature that has never succeeded." But the most candid admission of all concerned the report's conclusion: "Is [the] premise right—should there be international control?" "A Report on the International Control of Atomic Energy," pp. 68, 77–8, Box 66, Baruch MSS.

35. Acheson, *Present at the Creation,* 155.

36. Peterson to Patterson, May 29, 1946, "Atomic Energy Safe File 2," Patterson File, MEDR.

37. "Memo . . . ," May 22, 1946, "Atomic" Series, (8-15-45), Sec. 2, USJCS Records. Concerning Arnold's contribution to Searls' proposal, see Barton J. Bernstein, "The Quest for Security: American Foreign Policy and International Control of Atomic Energy, 1942–1946," *Journal of American History,* March 1974, 1035. In a 1947 letter to Winston Churchill, Baruch gave a preview of his conception of "condign punishment" under the terms of the atomic league: "If war ever comes between Russia and a first-class power or combination of powers, there will be a revolt on every border. . . . No one in his senses would invade Russia. All one need do would be to bombard her from every direction from the air, destroying her cities and crops. Then those on the borders or a small mobile force could move in any direction they wished. No war against Russia now would be conducted like Napoleon or Hitler did." Baruch to Churchill, July 22, 1947, "1947 Correspondence" File, Baruch MSS.

38. "Memo . . . ," June 7, 1946, "Atomic" Series, (8-15-45), Sec. 3, USJCS Records. This document is in *FR:* 1946, I, 843–6. See also "Enclosure 'B'," July 20, 1946, "Atomic" Series, (8-15-45), Sec. 3, USJCS Records.
39. JCS to Baruch, June 5, 1946, "Atomic" Series, (8-15-45), Sec. 3, USJCS Records.
40. See Baruch to Eisenhower et al., May 24, 1946, "Toward the 14 June Proposal," Baruch MSS. Their replies are in "Toward the 14 June Proposal," Baruch MSS. The letters of Eisenhower and Nimitz are also in *FR:* 1946, I, 853–6.
41. "Summary . . . ," June 15, 1946, "Toward the 14 June Proposal," Baruch MSS.
42. "Memo . . . ," June 1, *FR:* 1946, I, 824–6.
43. Hoover to Byrnes, May 23, 1946, "Atomic" folder, Byrnes MSS.
44. "Notes . . . ," April 4, 1946, "Correspondence on Atomic Energy," Baruch MSS. "Memorandum . . . ," April 19, 1946, "Toward the 14 June Proposal," Baruch MSS.
45. An early and constant critic of the Baruch plan, British scientist P. M. S. Blackett, pointed out that "immediate and certain" punishment was actually a prescription for preventive war since the nature of the violation that would prompt such a penalty was not spelled out. Truman required that the original wording be reinstated before approving the Baruch plan. P. M. S. Blackett, *Fear, War, and the Bomb* (New York, 1949), 149.
46. Patterson and Acheson felt "the British have a just claim." "Memo . . . ," May 1, *FR:* 1946, I, 1242–3.
47. "Memo . . . ," June 6, 1946, "Correspondence on Atomic Energy," Baruch MSS. Baruch to Truman, June 6, *FR:* 1946, I, 838–9. The State Department's suggested revisions are in Acheson to Byrnes, June 6, ibid., 836–7.
48. Swope is quoted in Coit, *Mr. Baruch,* 571. Stimson to Baruch, undated, 1946 Correspondence, Stimson MSS.
49. Byrnes is cited in Lilienthal, *Atomic Energy Years,* 58–9.

Chapter 9

1. The text of Baruch's speech is in U.S. Department of State, *The International Control of Atomic Energy: Growth of a Policy* (Washington, D.C., 1946), 138–47. Portions of the speech are also in *New York Times,* June 15, 1946.
2. "Summary . . . ," July 20, 1946, "Atomic" Series, (8-15-45), Sec. 3, USJCS Records.
3. Concerning the generally favorable press reaction to the Baruch plan, see the June 15, 1946, *Washington Post, Chicago Tribune,* and *Los Angeles Times.*
4. See "Press Reaction" folder, "Correspondence on Atomic Energy," Baruch MSS.
5. Lippmann's column, entitled "Mr. Baruch and the Veto," appeared in the June 20, 1946, *Washington Post.* See also his column there two days later. A memorandum of the Lippmann-Barnard conversation of June 25, 1946, may be found in the Barnard folder, Oppenheimer MSS.
6. *New York Times,* June 20, 1946.
7. Fleming to Baruch, July 2, 1946; and reply of July 10, "Correspondence on Atomic Energy," Baruch MSS.
8. Truman to Baruch, July 10, 1946, "Correspondence on Atomic Energy," Baruch MSS. Patterson is cited in the Groves diary, March 19, 1946, Box 24, MEDR.
9. Memorandum, May 29, 1946, "Toward the 14 June Proposal," Baruch MSS.
10. Blum, ed., *Price of Vision,* 565–6. Concerning other reasons for the postponement, see Dewey to Forrestal, June 10, 1946, "Atomic Energy Safe File 2," Patterson File, MEDR.

11. Blum, ed., *Price of Vision,* 566.

12. *Pravda* is cited in Joseph Nogee, *Soviet Policy Toward International Control of Atomic Energy* (Notre Dame, 1961), 62.

13. Hancock to Searls, July 16, 1946, Box 56, Baruch MSS.

14. Baruch evidently did change his mind on the veto later on. In 1961 he told Gordon Arneson that a particular critic of his veto stand had probably been right. Baruch's principal regret on the veto, however, was that it had given the Russians a propaganda advantage. Interview with Gordon Arneson, October 1979, Washington, D.C. Barnard to Lippmann, January 20, 1947, Correspondence File, Lilienthal MSS.

15. Lilienthal, *Atomic Energy Years,* 74–7.

16. "Notes . . . ," August 1, *FR:* 1946, I, 869–73.

17. Coit, *Mr. Baruch,* 595. Hancock to Swope, August 8, 1946, "Toward the 14 June Proposal," Baruch MSS.

18. Hancock to Acheson, August 15, 1946, "Toward the 14 June Proposal," Baruch MSS. "Notes . . . ," August 1, *FR:* 1946, I, 869–73.

19. "Notes . . . ," August 15, 1946, "Toward the 14 June Proposal," Baruch MSS.

20. Gromyko is quoted in a JCS memorandum on the meeting with Baruch. At a conference with the representatives of the joint chiefs on August 22, Baruch decided not to propose the atomic-league idea he had considered the previous June. The joint chiefs' account of that meeting noted: "Mr. Baruch will stick to the original plan and will not risk incurring the onus of setting up an anti-Soviet alliance by broaching any other plan that excludes the Soviets. . . . There is no other plan in case of the failure of Mr. Baruch to achieve a success along the lines of the original U.S. proposal. . . . The question of what to do in case of failure will devolve upon the Joint Chiefs of Staff and the government." Untitled document, August 26, 1946, "Atomic" Series, (8-15-45), Sec. 4, USJCS.

21. Farrell to Hancock, August 15, 1946, "Toward the 14 June Proposal," Baruch MSS.

22. "Stages . . . ," August 16, *FR:* 1946, I, 877–81. Baruch to Ickes, August 29, 1946, "Toward the 14 June Proposal," Baruch MSS. In a separate memo to Baruch, however, Hancock reflected that the plan might "rationally" appear to other nations as an attempt by the United States to retain the atomic monopoly. Hancock to Baruch, undated, Box 52, Baruch MSS.

23. "Notes . . . ," August 22, *FR:* 1946, I, 885–92; and "Notes . . . ," August 23, 1946, Box 52, Baruch MSS.

24. "Notes . . . ," September 10, *FR:* 1946, I, 906–11.

25. Lawrence Cottrell and Sylvia Eberhardt, *American Opinion on World Affairs in the Atomic Age* (Princeton, N.J., 1948), 113. On popular support in the United States at this time for international control, see Cottrell and Eberhardt; and H. G. Erskine, "The Polls: Atomic Weapons and Nuclear Energy," *Public Opinion Quarterly,* Summer 1963, 168–9. Concerning the emotional effect of the "atomic secret" upon public opinion, see Cottrell and Eberhardt, 33, 58; and Erskine, 168.

26. Mimeographed copy of lecture and discussion, undated, "Correspondence on Atomic Energy," Baruch MSS.

27. "Notes . . . ," September 9, *FR:* 1946, I, 904.

28. Baruch to Truman, September 17, *FR:* 1946, I, 919–29.

29. "Memo . . . ," September 19, *FR:* 1946, I, 932–5.

30. Wallace's July letter is reprinted in Blum, ed., *Price of Vision,* 589–601.

31. Ibid., 603, 612–3. This hard-line approach was confirmed during the Wallace incident by a report entitled "American Relations with the Soviet Union," prepared by Truman aides Clark Clifford and George Elsey. The Clifford-Elsey Report, submitted to

the President in early September, essentially followed the advice of Kennan's "long telegram" in its prescription that America should use her power "to restrain the Soviet Union and to confine Soviet influence to its present area." On the report, see Donovan, *Conflict and Crisis,* 221–2.

32. Concerning Byrnes' reaction to the Wallace affair, see Donald Russell to Byrnes, September 16, 1946, and Byrnes to Truman, September 18 and 19, 1946, in "Paris Council of Foreign Ministers, 1946" folder, Byrnes MSS; and Byrnes, *All in One Lifetime,* 374–6.

33. Memorandum, September 19, *FR:* 1946, I, 934.

34. Groves to Hancock, August 16, *FR:* 1946, I, 877–81. See also Groves diary, August 1, 1946, Box 24, MEDR.

35. Concerning Maclean's subsequent defection and his value to the Russians, see Epilogue. During spring 1946 Groves requested of Byrnes that the activities of the Trust not be brought up in the coming UN talks. See Groves to Byrnes, April 2, *FR:* 1946, I, 1223–4.

36. The "hidden veto" of the Baruch plan is noted in Gardner, *Architects of Illusion,* 193; Joseph I. Lieberman, *The Scorpion and the Tarantula* (Boston, 1970), 328; and Yergin, *Shattered Peace,* 238. The argument that the Baruch plan in effect provided for a preventive war against Russia is in George Quester, *Nuclear Diplomacy: The First Twenty-five Years* (Boston, 1970), 37–8. "Memo . . . ," August 27, *FR:* 1946, I, 887.

37. The "rebuttal" and other documents related to the Wallace incident were published in the *New York Times,* October 3, 1946. Wallace revealed only that his source of information on the Baruch plan had been "a man from UNRRA who is now abroad." Lieberman, *Scorpion and the Tarantula,* 357. The third stage provided for establishing international control over world uranium and thorium sources; the fourth, over those plants processing these materials; and on up to the ninth and final stage—abolition of America's nuclear monopoly. Baruch and his associates would never decide, however, whether in the last stage the U.S. atomic arsenal should be destroyed or simply surrendered to the UN. Since Gromyko had rejected the Baruch plan within two weeks of its introduction, they undoubtedly considered the question moot.

38. "Memorandum . . . ," September 27, *FR:* 1946, I, 939–44.

39. It was not Wallace's efforts to draw attention to the Baruch plan's "fatal flaw," but his call for a temporary moratorium on bomb production, that attracted support at home. Editorializing in Wallace's defense, the *Washington Post* cautioned that the real danger of the incident had been that "it may tend to harden and crystallize the official American attitude in a situation where flexibility is essential to the successful conduct of negotiations." If, as a result, Baruch were to become "so zealous for self-vindication that he cannot yield on any aspect of the plan which he has sponsored, then the prospect for an atomic development agreement is very slim indeed," the editorial concluded. *Washington Post,* October 3, 1946.

40. A survey conducted by the delegation revealed that only 4 percent of newspaper editorials at the end of October had sided with Wallace during the feud, whereas eleven editorials remained "factually neutral." Thus, the report concluded, some 90 percent of magazine, newspaper, and radio coverage championed Baruch in the controversy. Erskine, "The Polls: Atomic Weapons and Nuclear Energy," *Public Opinion Quarterly,* Summer 1963, 113. The delegation's study of public reaction to the Wallace incident is in Hancock to Baruch, October 28, 1946, Box 57, Baruch MSS. Concerning Baruch's response to his critics, see "Baruch and Hancock Defend the American Plan," *Bulletin of the Atomic Scientists,* November 1, 1946.

41. Bush to Conant, October 21, 1946, Correspondence File, Bush MSS.

42. "Notes . . . ," October 1, *FR:* 1946, I, 944–9. See also *New York PM,* September 26, 1946.

43. Concerning the abortive meeting between Molotov and Byrnes, see Lindsay to Baruch, October 21, *FR:* 1946, I, 955–60; and "Notes . . . ," September 25, 1946, "Correspondence on Atomic Energy," Baruch MSS.

44. "Transcript . . .," October 28, 1946, "Correspondence on Atomic Energy," Baruch MSS.

45. "Memo . . .," November 21, *FR:* 1946, I, 1024–30. Vandenberg, ed., *Private Papers,* 291. On the Paris Council of Foreign Ministers and Vandenberg's role there, see Byrnes, *Speaking Frankly,* 239–43. Before the conference Truman had had the Joint Chiefs of Staff prepare a study of previous diplomatic agreements violated by the Russians. See "Presidential Request . . . ," July 25, 1946, folder 1, Box 1, "Recently Declassified Documents," USJCS Records.

46. Baruch to Acheson, November 2, *FR:* 1946, I, 982–3. A conversation later that month between Acheson and Baruch showed that the latter's views on abolishing the veto had not changed. "Transcript . . . ," November 26, 1946, "Correspondence on Atomic Energy," Baruch MSS. Text of Molotov's proposal in *New York Times,* October 30, 1946.

47. Searls to Byrnes, October 24, *FR:* 1946, I, 963–6. See also Searls to Byrnes, November 10, 1946, Searls folder, Byrnes MSS. More recently, David Lilienthal commented on Searls' importance to the furtherance of the belief that a preclusive monopoly of atomic raw materials was possible: "The most significant thing, one that was quite a shocker . . . related to the availability of uranium. . . . How that happened God only knows. . . . But I have a very sharp recollection: Searls was persuaded that there was a very limited amount of uranium in any case; [he] didn't know how much uranium there was even in the United States. . . ." Interview with David Lilienthal, February 1979, Princeton, N.J.

48. Groves to Byrnes, October 24, *FR:* 1946, I, 1258.

49. Truman to Bush, August 2, 1946, "Atomic Energy Control Commission, UN" folder, Box 112, PSF, HSTL. Concerning Truman's selection of Lilienthal, see also Hewlett and Anderson, *New World,* 622.

50. Searls to Lindsay, July 19, 1946, Box 64, Baruch MSS. Lindsay to Baruch, October 21, *FR:* 1946, I, 960. Lindsay to Captain Alvaro Alberto, September 10, 1946, Box 63, Baruch MSS.

51. Eberstadt's comment is in "Notes . . . ," August 15, 1946, "Toward the 14 June Proposal," Baruch MSS. James Conant was also speaking at this time of "an atomic league or nuclear union." See his speech before the National War College, "The Atomic Age," October 1946, "Atomic Energy Safe File 2," Patterson File, MEDR.

52. "Memo . . . ," November 21, *FR:* 1946, I, 1033–6.

53. A young member of Baruch's staff would later write of this second rebuff to Molotov: "We perhaps made a great mistake in not accepting." He was apparently alone in the delegation with this opinion. J. R. Burton to Hancock, December 15, 1946, "Toward the 14 June Proposal," Baruch MSS.

54. Gromyko is cited in Lieberman, *Scorpion and the Tarantula,* 377.

55. Hewlett and Anderson, *New World,* 615–16.

56. Vandenberg to Baruch, December 28, 1946, "Correspondence on Atomic Energy," Baruch MSS.

57. Johnson to Byrnes, December 31, *FR:* 1946, I, 1106–7. Baruch, *Public Years,* 379.

58. Baruch's suspicion was correct. Britain's sensibilities had been further wounded by Truman's response to a mid-December letter from Prime Minister Attlee prodding the President on the year-old Anglo-American agreement for "full and effective cooperation" on atomic energy. Truman's cheery wishes for the coming year, and his assurance to Attlee that he was "giving your messages the most careful consideration with my advisers," could not disguise the obvious fact that he had no intention of cooperation with the British. Britain's belated show of defiance at the UN as well as her embargo of Indian thorium to the United States may have been intended as pressure tactics. The results surely confirmed to the British the weakness of their bargaining position. Attlee to Truman, December 17; and reply, December 28, *FR:* 1946, I, 1259.

59. Lilienthal, *Atomic Energy Years*, 123.

60. "Proposals Regarding Atomic Energy Policies," August 14, 1947, Records of the UNAEC, OPR/RSC Lot 57D–688, U.S. Department of State. Benjamin Cohen has noted that Baruch's replacement at the UN, Fredrick Osborn, appreciated "a need to keep the effort going," but he did not regard further negotiations as promising and thought a U.S. initiative to push them would be "counterproductive." Interview, January 1972, Washington, D.C. At a meeting in late March 1947, Osborn also confessed to a luncheon gathering of atomic scientists: "I never had, for a moment, expected to reach any sort of agreement with the Russians." See Fredrick Osborn diary, March 29, 1947, "UNAEC Diary" folder, Box 2, Fredrick Osborn MSS, HSTL.

61. The agreement concerning the transfer of authority from Groves and the War Department to Lilienthal and the AEC was worked out on the day after Christmas, only four days before the commission was to begin its work. Whether Truman played a role in breaking the deadlock between the army and the commission is unclear, but the White House appointment file notes that Groves met with the President on New Year's Eve. Concerning the transfer, see Hewlett and Anderson, *New World*, 654–5. December 31, 1946, "Appointment File," Matthew Connelly MSS, HSTL.

Chapter 10

1. The visionary, Army Air Force General Henry H. ("Hap") Arnold, is cited in Michael Sherry's excellent book *Preparing for the Next War: American Plans for Postwar Defense, 1941–1945* (New Haven, Conn., 1977), 195.

2. Interview with David E. Lilienthal, February 1979, Princeton, N.J. During a 1949 congressional hearing Lilienthal characterized the United States as "unarmed" at the time he took over the AEC. *New York Times*, May 26, 1949. Concerning this unpreparedness, see also the essay by David Rosenberg, "American Atomic Strategy and the Hydrogen Bomb Decision," *Journal of American History*, May 1979, 62–6.

3. Lilienthal's report is in the "NSC Atomic Energy—Annual Reports" folder, Box 200, PSF, HSTL.

4. Truman, *Years of Trial and Hope*, 339.

5. Lilienthal is cited in Hewlett and Duncan, *Atomic Shield*, 47–8.

6. Ayers diary, October 14, 1946, HSTL.

7. Interview with David E. Lilienthal; Rosenberg, "American Atomic Strategy and the Hydrogen Bomb Decision," 65; Hewlett and Anderson, *New World*, 624–33.

8. Leahy's report and supporting documents from the Atomic Energy Commission may be found in "Atomic" Series, (8-15-45), Secs. 4–7, Box 166, USJCS Records. The number of atomic bombs in the U.S. arsenal in 1945 was still classified as of 1980.

A graph released by the Department of Energy in 1977, however, shows not only that the number was extremely low, but that it did not increase substantially from 1945 to early 1948. Estimates for this period of the bombs stockpiled range from less than six to about two dozen. A shortage of critical parts, difficulties in the bomb-fabrication process, and a severe shortage of raw materials probably further reduced the number of operationally ready bombs from this number and held their production rate to as low as five a year. Concerning speculation on the number of bombs in the U.S. arsenal, see JCS 2081/1 "U.S." Series, (5-23-46), Sec. 4, USJCS Records; Rosenberg, "American Atomic Strategy and the Hydrogen Bomb Decision," 65, 68–9; Vincent Davis, *Postwar Defense Policy and the U.S. Navy, 1943–1946* (Chapel Hill, N.C., 1966), 250; and Yergin, *Shattered Peace,* 265–6.

9. "Memorandum," LeMay to L. C. Craigie, August 23, 1946, File 1946/1/471.6, Air Force Record Group 341, Modern Military Section, National Archives. Concerning other AAF complaints of exclusion from vital information on the bomb, see L. C. Craigie to LeMay, August 23, 1946, same file; and LeMay's testimony before the War Department's Equipment Board, January 8, 1946, File 1946/4/452.1, Air Force Record Group 341.

10. *Newsweek,* September 12, 1945. Stimson, "The Decision to Use the Atomic Bomb," *Harper's,* February 1947. Documents from the Manhattan Project indicate that Groves wished Tokyo to be the target for the third atomic bomb, although that city had already been virtually destroyed by the incendiary raids of March 1945. "Report on Overseas Operations—Atomic Bomb," September 27, 1945, Part VII, MED History, MEDR.

11. Problems of the navy's atomic bomber are noted in Davis, *Postwar Defense Policy,* 42.

12. October 25, 1945, "USSR" Series, (3-27-45), Sec. 2, USJCS Records.

13. The threat of a Soviet bomber attack would long precede the advent of intercontinental-range ballistic missiles. Initial optimism on the part of military planners concerning the ICBM had been generated partly by the development of the German V-2 near the end of the war. Feasibility studies conducted by the air force from 1945 to 1947, however, dampened this early enthusiasm and ultimately caused strategic planners to err on the side of caution by a margin of some years. Concerning predictions of the ICBM, see JCS to LeMay, November 26, 1945, File 322/1945, Box 2, Air Force Record Group 341, National Archives; "Effects of Foreseeable New Developments . . .," August 24, 1945, "Air Force" Series, (7-18-45), Sec. 1, USJCS Records. See also Quester, *Nuclear Diplomacy,* 3; and *New York Times,* March 2 and April 10, 1947. Concerning the effects of new weapons and doctrines upon military planning for the postwar period before the bomb, see Sherry, *Preparing for the Next War,* 27–52, 120.

14. David Rosenberg has noted, for example, that the air force by January 1946 had a total of only twenty-seven bombers capable of carrying atomic bombs. Rosenberg, "American Atomic Strategy and the Hydrogen Bomb Decision," 65.

15. Concerning early air force planning, see Perry M. Smith, *The Air Force Plans for Peace, 1943–1945* (Baltimore, 1970); and the author's review of this book in "L'Aviation américaine et l'après-guerre," *Revue d'histoire de la deuxième guerre mondiale,* No. 98, April 1975, 96–8.

16. P. M. Smith, *Air Force Plans for Peace,* 1–23.

17. The AAF report is cited in Yergin, *Shattered Peace,* 210. Regarding the changing nature of air force estimates, see also Sherry, *Preparing for the Next War,* 219.

18. See Sherry, *Preparing for the Next War,* 205–8; P. M. Smith, *Air Force Plans for Peace,* 3–8; and Walter Millis, *Arms and Men* (New York, 1956), 309.

19. The quotations are from Sherry, *Preparing for the Next War,* 35; and Forrestal diary, May 15, 1946, Forrestal MSS.

20. Willett's conclusion—after consulting government experts on Russia and a Jesuit scholar—was that Stalin, though intent upon world conquest, had no exact timetable. Concerning Forrestal's other efforts to answer that question, and his role in Kennan's article, see "Russia" File, Forrestal MSS; Millis, ed., *Forrestal Diaries,* 97, 107, 127–9; and Gardner, *Architects of Illusion,* 270–300.

21. Forrestal's "no prospective enemy" quotation is cited in Davis, *Postwar Defense Policy,* 186. The navy view that Soviet intentions were defensive did not prevent Forrestal from engaging in a show of gunboat diplomacy plainly meant to impress the Russians. Such was the intent of his request that the United States send a naval task force to the Mediterranean during the fall 1945 crisis in Iran—a force subsequently scaled down by Truman to the battleship *Missouri*—and of Operation Frostbite, a March 1946 navy maneuver that sent a carrier task force into the Arctic Ocean. Concerning the navy's postwar planning and Forrestal's role in it, see "Naval Intelligence Memorandum . . . ," January 21, 1946, "Russia" File, Forrestal MSS; Robert G. Albion and Robert H. Connery, *Forrestal and the Navy* (New York, 1962), esp. 183–5; and Sherry, *Preparing for the Next War,* 20, 32–4, 92–4.

22. Forrestal's comments are from the "1945" folder, "Cabinet Meetings" Box, Matthew Connelly MSS, HSTL; and Sherry, *Preparing for the Next War,* 208.

23. Kenneth W. Condit, "The History of the Joint Chiefs of Staff: The Joint Chiefs of Staff and National Policy, 1947–1949" [JCS History], vol. II, 179, USJCS Records. Concerning other expressions of the "new navy" idea, see *New York Times,* February 6, 1948; Davis, *Postwar Defense Policy,* 191–208; and P. M. Smith, *Air Force Plans for Peace,* 246–8.

24. In this case, army planning would seem a revision of the old bromide about generals learning the lessons of past battles only in future wars—since here the lessons afforded by Pearl Harbor were ignored. Concerning early army planning for the postwar period, see Sherry, *Preparing for the Next War,* 35–8.

25. Eisenhower is cited in Yergin, *Shattered Peace,* 212; Patton in Sherry, *Preparing for the Next War,* 189.

26. Sherry, *Preparing for the Next War,* 208.

27. Concerning the "preparedness ideology" and its effect upon postwar planning, see ibid., 133, 208, 233–8.

28. "Revision of Policy . . . ," undated, folder 1, Box 1, "Recently Declassified Documents," National Archives. "Estimate of Soviet Post-War Capabilities and Intentions," February 5, 1945, Joint Intelligence Committee, folder 2, ibid. "United States Post-War Military Policy," August 20, 1945, Joint Staff Planners, "U.S." Series, (5-13-45), Sec. 1, USJCS Records.

29. Concerning UMT and unification, see Sherry, *Preparing for the Next War,* 58–90.

30. On Forrestal's early doubts about unification, see "History of Attempted Suppression of Naval Aviation by the Army," "Unification" File, Forrestal MSS; and Yergin, *Shattered Peace,* 201. For a sample of the controversy that surrounded the Eberstadt Report, see, for example, the letter sent by Stuart Symington to Eberstadt, October 25, 1948, "F. Eberstadt" folder, Box 216, Hanson Baldwin MSS, Yale University; Millis, *Arms and the State,* 150–5; and Yergin, *Shattered Peace,* 213. Concerning the congressional hearings, see U.S. Congress, "Hearings Before the House Committee on Military Affairs on HR 515," 79th Congress, 1st Session (Washington, D.C., 1945); and Demetrious Caraley, *The Politics of Military Unification* (New York, 1966), 302–10.

31. "Report of the Joint Strategic Survey Committee . . . ," October 30, 1945, "Atomic" Series, Sec. 1, Box 165, USJCS Records.

32. "Statement of the Effect of Atomic Weapons on National Security and Organization," January 12, 1946, "Atomic" Series, Sec. 1, Box 165, USJCS Records.

33. Ibid.

34. "Military Position of the United States in the Light of Russian Policy," October 9, 1945, folder 2, Box 1, "Recently Declassified Documents," National Archives.

35. The AAF officer was Curtis LeMay. See "Memorandum . . . ," LeMay to Chief of Air Staff, December 21, 1945, File 1945/2/322, Air Force Record Group 341, National Archives. The rewritten JCS report is noted in a letter from Admiral Leahy to Truman, October 23, 1945, "Atomic" Series, Sec. 1, Box 165, USJCS Records.

36. Concerning early and modern theories of air power, see Bernard Brodie, *Strategy in the Missile Age* (Princeton, N.J., 1959), 3–107; Edward M. Earle, ed., *Makers of Modern Strategy* (Princeton, N.J., 1943); and Alexander de Seversky, *Victory Through Air Power* (New York, 1942).

37. U.S. Air Force, *United States Strategic Bombing Survey* (Washington, D.C., 1946). See also David MacIssac, "The United States Strategic Bombing Survey, 1944–47" (unpublished Ph.D. dissertation, Duke University, 1969).

38. The original draft version of the army's account of the atomic bombing argued that the Japanese government had decided to surrender by June 26, 1945. Patterson objected that this unnecessarily deprecated the role of the bomb. He insisted the account claim instead that the Japanese were looking for a way to surrender as early as May and had seized upon the destruction of Hiroshima as a convenient way out of their dilemma. There was little ambivalence in Groves' assessment of the bomb's role in the war: "The atomic bomb did not alone win the war against Japan, but it most certainly ended it, saving the thousands of Allied lives that would have been lost in any combat invasion of Japan." Groves released the Manhattan Project's account of the damage at Hiroshima, which he wrote, upon the publication of the *Survey* in order to counter the latter's conclusions about Japan's surrender and its account of radiation-induced deaths at Hiroshima. See A. de Seversky to Dewitt Wallace, June 18, 1946, "Atomic Energy Safe File 2," Patterson File, MEDR; Patterson to Army Chief of Staff, June 24, 1946, ibid., and "Report of the Manhattan Project Atomic-Bomb Investigating Group," MED History, MEDR.

39. Sherry, *Preparing for the Next War*, 231–2.

40. The "Spaatz Board Report" is in "Air Force" folder, Box 2, "Recently Declassified Documents," National Archives. The AAF briefing paper is cited in Yergin, *Shattered Peace*, 201.

41. Arnold is quoted in Sherry, *Preparing for the Next War*, 195.

42. Arnold was, in fact, the author of the atomic-league idea of worldwide bases that Searls and Baruch proposed to the Military Staff Committee of the U.S. delegation to the UNAEC in May 1946. Concerning the "Four Policeman" concept and the air force, see Sherry, *Preparing for the Next War*, 43–5.

43. Untitled document, T.S. 1388, November 1945, U.S. Air Force Historical Archives, Maxwell Air Force Base, Alabama.

44. LeMay to Chief of Air Staff, December 21, 1945, File 1945/2/322, Air Force Record Group 341, Modern Military Section, National Archives.

45. Concerning LeMay's opposition to the prevailing air force viewpoint, see also Joint Chiefs of Staff to LeMay, November 26, 1945, File 1945/2/322, AF RG 341, National Archives; "Discussion of the Effect of the Use of Atomic Energy on Air Forces in the Future," January 8, 1946, File 1946/4/452.1, AF RG 341, Na-

tional Archives; and Henry H. Arnold, *Global Mission* (New York, 1949), 612.
46. Concerning the creation of SAC, see Arnold, *Global Mission;* and David A. Anderson, *Strategic Air Command* (New York, 1976), 32–6.
47. "Memorandum by the Chief of Staff, U.S. Army," JCS 1477/6, January 21, 1946, "Atomic" Series, (8-15-45), Sec. 2, USJCS Records.
48. Groves' memorandum is reprinted in *FR:* 1946, I, 1197–1203.
49. Forrestal is cited in Sherry, *Preparing for the Next War,* 35. Forrestal personally discovered how far demobilization had gone when the navy was unable to assemble a crew in spring 1946 for Operation Deep Freeze, a naval task force to be sent to Alaska from San Francisco. Interview with Paul Nitze, October 1979, Washington, D.C.
50. "Military Position of the United States . . .," October 9, 1945, Joint Strategic Survey Committee, folder 2, Box 1, "Recently Declassified Documents," National Archives.
51. Concerning demobilization and the home front, see Sherry, *Preparing for the Next War,* 191–4; and John Morton Blum, *V Was for Victory: Politics and American Culture During World War II* (New York, 1976).
52. U.S. Department of Defense, *Selected Manpower Statistics* (Washington, D.C., 1971), 11–19.
53. "The Atomic Frame of Reference or Else," *Aviation News,* September 1945, 107.
54. "Atomic Bomb Hysteria," *Reader's Digest,* February 1946, 82–97. Concerning popular attitudes toward atomic energy, see also "Getting Used to the Bomb," *St. Louis Star-Times,* September 8, 1945. Lilienthal wrote to scientist Harry Winne of this editorial, "I very much fear that this is just what a large percentage of our people are doing. . . ." Lilienthal to Winne, September 18, 1945, Correspondence File, Lilienthal MSS. See also Lilienthal to Clark Clifford, December 14, 1948, ibid.
55. Concerning UMT and its fate, see Sherry, *Preparing for the Next War,* 54–90, 211, 220–6.
56. "Statement of the Effect of Atomic Weapons on National Security and Organization," March 31, 1946, "Atomic" Series, (8-15-45), Sec. 2, USJCS.
57. "Study of Certain Military Problems Deriving from Concept of Operations for *Pincher,*" April 13, 1946, "USSR" Series, (3-2-46), Sec. 1, USJCS Records. Concerning the joint chiefs and their changing view of Russia, see also Yergin, *Shattered Peace,* 270; Sherry, *Preparing for the Next War,* 165; and "Military Position of the United States . . .," October 9, 1945, Joint Strategic Survey Committee, folder 2, Box 1, "Recently Declassified Documents," National Archives.
58. Army Chief of Staff to Truman, October 23, 1945, "Atomic" Series, (8-15-45), Sec. 1, Box 165, USJCS Records.

Chapter 11

1. Untitled document, JCS to Baruch, June 5, 1946, "Atomic" Series, (8-15-45), Sec. 3, USJCS Records.
2. "Tentative Over-all Strategic Concept and Estimate of Initial Operations, Short Title: *Pincher,*" and "Enclosure B, Estimate of Initial Operations," June 18, 1946, "USSR" Series, (3-2-46), Sec. 2, USJCS Records. See also JCS History, II, 283, USJCS Records. In March 1946 began the first coordinated planning by all the services together, represented by the Joint War Plans Committee (later retitled the Joint Strategic Plans Group). The AAF's nuclear annex to Pincher, entitled Harrow, was prepared under the direction of Major General Curtis LeMay in fall 1946. See

Rosenberg, "American Atomic Strategy and the Hydrogen Bomb Decision," 64–5; and untitled document concerning "unilateral Air Force plan *Harrow,*" undated, "Air Force" folder, Box 2, "Recently Declassified Documents," National Archives. A spring 1946 summary by the Joint Intelligence Committee concluded: "The USSR . . . will not pursue its objective to a point which its leaders calculate would involve a genuine risk of war with the United States and Britain in the next five years." "Capabilities and Intentions of the USSR in the Post-War Period," February 7, 1946, folder 2, Box 1, "Recently Declassified Documents," National Archives. Compare this analysis of Soviet motives to the report by the same committee the previous year cited earlier and also in this folder.

3. See map in "Enclosure B, Estimate of Initial Operations," June 18, 1946, "USSR" Series, (3-2-46), Sec. 2, USJCS Records; and Rosenberg, "American Atomic Strategy and the Hydrogen Bomb Decision," 64–8.

4. JCS History, II, 304–10, USJCS Records. For details of a similar but later plan, see Thomas H. Etzold and John Lewis Gaddis, eds., *Containment: Documents on American Policy and Strategy, 1945–1950* (New York, 1978), 302–11.

5. Military authorities in the United States apparently overestimated the size of the Russian army, just as they miscalculated the size of America's nuclear stockpile. On misestimates of the strength of the Red Army, see, for example, Yergin, *Shattered Peace*, 270; and JCS History, II, 22, USJCS Records.

6. Untitled document, Joint Chiefs of Staff to Baruch, June 5, 1946, "Atomic" Series, (8-15-45), Sec. 3, USJCS Records.

7. Ibid.

8. Bush is quoted in "Effect of Foreseeable New Developments . . . ," August 24, 1945, "Air Force" Series, (7-18-45), Sec. 1, USJCS Records. The Jeffries Report is in A. K. Smith, *Peril and a Hope.* Bernard Brodie, ed., *The Absolute Weapon: Atomic Power and World Order* (New York, 1946). The book grew out of a Yale symposium.

9. Wolfers, "The Atomic Bomb in Soviet-American Relations," Brodie, ed., *Absolute Weapon*, 135–43. Brodie's role with regard to the atomic bomb did not end with the book. In 1947 he headed and was chief contributor to a symposium sponsored by the Library of Congress entitled "The Atomic Bomb and the Armed Services." Papers from that symposium may be found in the "1947 Subject File," Samuel Rosenman MSS, HSTL. Concerning deterrence before the atomic age, see George Quester, *Deterrence Before Hiroshima* (Boston, 1968); Alexander L. George and Richard Smoke, *Deterrence in American Foreign Policy: Theory and Practice* (New York, 1974); and Samuel Huntington, *The Common Defense* (New York, 1961), 451 ff. Wolfers' essay concerned another paradox of the atomic age which had just come to the attention of the joint chiefs—the self-deterring nature of nuclear weapons: "One need . . . only imagine the impression it would make on our urban population if a serious crisis in Soviet-American relations should be accompanied by the sudden realization that an atomic surprise attack was not beyond the realm of possibility."

10. *New York Times,* September 29, 1945. Concerning opinion at the unification hearings, see Davis, *Postwar Defense Policy*, 242.

11. Sherry, *Preparing for the Next War*, 201–2.

12. Ibid., 201, 213.

13. The need for smaller, tactical nuclear weapons to destroy such targets had been recognized by American military planners as early as two weeks after the bombing of Hiroshima. However, Groves had pointed out then "that research necessary to develop smaller bombs would have to be taken away from research now going on to perfect

the efficiency of the present size." Since research time and raw materials were already severely limited, the decision to develop tactical nuclear weapons would be deferred until late 1948. Such weapons would not be truly operational, moreover, until the time of the Korean War. See "Effect of Foreseeable New Developments . . .," August 24, 1945, "Air Force" Series, (7-15-45), Sec. 1, USJCS Records; untitled document, December 15, 1950, "Air Force" folder, Box 2, "Recently Declassified Documents," USJCS Records; and Rosenberg, "American Atomic Strategy and the Hydrogen Bomb Decision," 74.

14. Subsequently, army, navy, and AAF representatives would each take credit for inspiring Operation Crossroads. For various and conflicting accounts of the origin of the tests, see Sherry, *Preparing for the Next War,* 207; Davis, *Postwar Defense Policy,* 244–5; Caraley, *Politics of Military Unification,* 303–4; and Albion and Connery, *Forrestal and the Navy,* 180. On Manhattan Project plans for the test, see Chapter 7, "Ordnance Division," Manhattan Project History, MEDR. Concerning early consideration of targets for the first bomb, see "Effect of Foreseeable Developments . . . ," August 24, 1945, "Air Force" Series, (7-18-45), Sec. 1, USJCS Records.

15. Concerning Forrestal's efforts to anticipate criticism of the navy in the tests, see Bradley Dewey to Forrestal, June 10, 1946, "Atomic Energy Safe File 2," Patterson File, MEDR. Groves' instructions regarding Oppenheimer are in the memorandum from Colonel Exton to Patterson, February 15, 1946, in the same file.

16. Concerning the tests and the ambiguity of their results, see Davis, *Postwar Defense Policy,* 246–6; and William A. Shurcliff, *Bombs at Bikini: The Official Report of Operation Crossroads* (New York, 1947). The now-declassified official reports on Crossroads may be found in "Atomic" Series, Secs. 6–9, Boxes 169 and 170, USJCS Records.

17. Forrestal to Truman, August 30, 1946, "NSC Atomic Test—Misc." folder, Box 201, PSF, HSTL. Patterson and Groves joined with Forrestal in recommending against a third atomic test. See Patterson to Eisenhower, August 21, 1946, "Atomic Energy Safe File 2," Patterson File, MEDR.

18. Strauss, *Men and Decisions,* 210.

19. While no military expert could miss the essential caveat—"in numbers"—contained in the joint chiefs' report, there were also signs that this limitation was diminishing in importance. A later version of the same study read ". . . in numbers conceded to be available in the foreseeable future." See Rosenberg, "American Atomic Strategy and the Hydrogen Bomb Decision," 67; "Evaluation of the Atomic Bomb as a Military Weapon" and "Atomic Warfare Policy," June 30, 1947, Box 170, Sec. 9, USJCS Records.

20. Patterson to Eisenhower, March 10, 1947, "Atomic Energy Safe File 3," Patterson File, MEDR. The granting of the clearance did not give custody of the bomb to the military, however. Concerning the struggle over custody, see Hewlett and Duncan, *Atomic Shield,* 65–6, 169–70, 354–5; and Chapter 12.

21. Lilienthal, *Atomic Energy Years,* 217.

22. In order to accommodate Broiler, the following month the joint chiefs informed the War Department of their estimate that the "present strategic situation" required American military bases to be established in Iceland, Greenland, Labrador, the Azores, and the Japanese islands. "Memorandum by the Joint Chiefs of Staff . . . ," September 9, *FR:* 1947, I (Washington, D.C., 1973), 766–7. "Joint Outline War Plan, Short Title: *Broiler,";* and "Outline Plan of an Air Campaign, Primarily Strategic, Against Vital Elements of Soviet War-Making Capacity," "USSR" Series, (3-2-46), Sec. 8, USJCS Records.

23. "Outline Plan of an Air Campaign . . . ," "USSR" Series, (3-2-46), Sec. 8, USJCS Records.
24. "Strategic Implications of the Atomic Bomb," August 29, 1947, "USSR" Series, (3-2-46), Sec. 8, USJCS Records.
25. Ibid.
26. Forrestal is cited in JCS History, II, 283, USJCS Records.
27. Untitled document, October 29, 1947, "Atomic" Series (8-15-45), Sec. 7, USJCS Records.
28. Lovett to Admiral Leahy, October 22, 1945, "Atomic" Series, Sec. 1, Box 165, USJCS Records.
29. "Estimate of Initial Operations for *Pincher,*" June 18, 1946, "USSR" Series, (3-2-46), Sec. 2, USJCS Records.
30. Untitled memorandum, November 21, 1946, "Atomic" Series, Sec. 4, Box 166, USJCS Records.
31. "The Capabilities of the USSR in Regard to Atomic Weapons," July 8, 1947, "Atomic" Series, (8-15-45), Sec. 5, USJCS Records.
32. "Memorandum . . . ," November 13, *FR:* 1947, I, 861–3.
33. "Estimate of Probable Developments in World Political Situation up to 1956," November 17, 1947, "USSR" Series, (2-27-45), Sec. 27, USJCS Records. Concerning the views of the joint chiefs at this time, see also Etzold and Gaddis, eds., *Containment,* 285–97; and Yergin, *Shattered Peace,* 465.
34. "Memorandum . . . ," December 15, *FR:* 1947, I, 903–5. The CIA's 1947 estimate was more optimistic about the Russian bomb than its study of the previous year, which put the first Soviet test between 1950 and 1953. See "Soviet Capabilities for the Development and Production of Certain Types of Weapons and Equipment," ORE 3/1, October 31, 1946, "CIA Reports" Box, "Recently Declassified Documents," National Archives.
35. Concerning the polls and public opinion, see Cottrell and Eberhardt, *American Opinion on World Affairs in the Atomic Age,* 103; Erskine, "The Polls: Atomic Weapons and Nuclear Energy," *Public Opinion Quarterly,* 175; and Social Science Research Council, *Public Reaction to the Atomic Bomb and World Affairs,* 1–12.
36. The amended text of Baruch's June 13, 1947, speech before the War College may be found in the "1947" folder, Correspondence File, Baruch MSS.
37. Groves is cited in *New York Times,* October 31, 1947.
38. "Review . . . ," January 13, 1948, "USSR" Series, (3-27-45), Sec. 27, USJCS Records. The army's dissenting opinion is appended to this document. Another joint chiefs' study of this time, dealing with defense of the United States from Soviet attack, concluded that the great danger from Russia "until about 1952" would be "small-scale, sporadic one-way air attacks with current weapons (excluding mass destruction weapons)" and possibly also attacks by offshore Soviet submarines using missiles armed with high-explosive warheads. "Report by the Joint Strategic Plans Committee to the Joint Chiefs of Staff on Command Structure for the Defense of the United States," January 23, 1948, "U.S." Series, (5-23-46), Sec. 4, USJCS Records.

Chapter 12

1. "Résumé of World Situation," November 7, *FR:* 1947, I, 772–7. This document is also in Etzold and Gaddis, eds., *Containment,* 90–7.
2. The CIA was formed from the Central Intelligence Group, which in turn had its roots

in the wartime Office of Strategic Services. On the Truman administration and the CIA, see, for example, "National Security Directive on Special Projects," NSC-10/2, June 18, 1948, "NSC" Box, USJCS Records, also in Etzold and Gaddis, *Containment*, 125–8; and "Minutes . . . ," for May 20 and July 1, 1948, Box 200, "National Security Council" File, PSF, HSTL.

3. Concerning the origins of and the congressional battles over the Truman Doctrine and the Marshall Plan, see, for example, Joseph Jones, *The Fifteen Weeks* (New York, 1964); Walter LaFeber, *America, Russia and the Cold War* (New York, 1976); and Truman, *Years of Trial and Hope*, 128–9, 134–44.

4. Marshall is cited in Millis, ed., *Forrestal Diaries*, 340.

5. Ayers diary, September 30 and October 18, 1947, HSTL.

6. *New York Times*, February 3, 1948.

7. Forrestal to Baldwin, January 2, 1948, Correspondence File, Hanson Baldwin MSS, Yale University. The text of the letter to the Senate is in Millis, ed., *Forrestal Diaries*, 350–1.

8. Molotov is cited in Millis, ed., *Forrestal Diaries*, 340 ff.

9. Interview with David E. Lilienthal, February 1979, Princeton, N.J. "Combined Strategic Offense and Defense Warheads," undated, U.S. Department of Energy, Washington, D.C.

10. The importance of the Congo's uranium to the United States atomic-bomb project is revealed in an incident recollected by Lilienthal. In 1946, Carroll Wilson, secretary to Lilienthal's board of consultants, came to the latter in "despair." "We're out of business," Wilson announced. "There's a strike in Katanga and the uranium mine of the Belgians is flooded and it will take two or three years to get it back." Wilson obviously overestimated the effect of both the strike and the flood. The U.S. ambassador in Belgium warned the State Department in early 1947 that French communists, presumed to be under the direction of the Kremlin, were attempting to undermine the West's preclusive claim to the Congo's uranium ore. See *FR:* 1947, I, 783–4.

11. As of early 1948, the Anglo-American Combined Development Agency was negotiating with the governments of India, South Africa, Norway, and New Zealand for the uranium and thorium ore in their possession. On these negotiations, see *FR:* 1948, I, Pt. 2, 691–4.

12. Concerning domestic sources of atomic raw materials, see Hewlett and Duncan, *Atomic Shield*, 147–9, 172–4.

13. Millis, ed., *Forrestal Diaries*, 339.

14. This hope that the *modus vivendi* might be the means for undoing earlier Anglo-American cooperation on atomic energy was, of course, also the reason why other notorious anglophobes, like Senators Vandenberg and Hickenlooper, supported the negotiations. Forrestal, as Groves before him, expected that a virtual U.S. monopoly of atomic raw materials would allow America to control—or even forestall—the development of atomic energy in Britain. Truman believed wrongly that this was a specific provision of the *modus vivendi*. On this point and the origins of the *modus vivendi*, see Hewlett and Duncan, *Atomic Shield*, 275–83.

15. The terms of the *modus vivendi* provided that the unequal division of uranium ore between the United States and Britain would end at the beginning of 1950 and henceforth that sharing be on a 50-50 basis. In the mid-1950s, however, the British were persuaded to return to an 80-20 split of the ore by the United States, which claimed heightened cold war tensions and pleaded use on the basis of need. Concerning these agreements from the British side, see Gowing, *Independence and Deterrence*,

42–4, 138–40. Another historian writes of Britain's role in the "junior partnership": "In retrospect, it is difficult to understand her forbearance." However, England's own military planning and continuing postwar economic crisis had tied her to American strategic concepts by early 1948. See Richard N. Rosecrance, *Defense of the Realm* (New York, 1976), 85–92, 118.

16. Concerning Acheson's support for the atomic-league idea, see Hewlett and Duncan, *Atomic Shield*, 270 ff.

17. On the importance of Maclean and Fuchs to Soviet atomic espionage, see Epilogue; and Gowing, *Independence and Deterrence*, 45–8, 244, 303 ff.

18. Hewlett and Duncan, *Atomic Shield*, 172–84.

19. "The Production of Fissionable Material," January 21, 1948, Box 167, "Atomic" Series, (8-15-45), Sec. 8, USJCS Records. "Combined Strategic Offense and Defense Warheads," undated, U.S. Department of Energy. Concerning the increased production of atomic bombs after spring 1948, see also Rosenberg, "American Atomic Strategy and the Hydrogen Bomb Decision," 65–8; York, *Advisors*, 13–28; and JCS History, II, USJCS Records, 530. Other obstacles remained to an air-atomic strategy, however. A fall 1948 JCS memorandum noted that there were not yet enough teams to assemble a hundred atomic bombs for use in a single attack. See "Decision on JCS 1745/15," September 2, 1948, folder 1, Box 1, "Recently Declassified Documents," USJCS Records.

20. Groves was "deeply disappointed," according to Lilienthal, when he was not chosen to head the new AEC. Groves' effort to replace himself on the Military Liaison Committee with a close aide, Kenneth Nichols, was also frustrated by Lilienthal. Groves "took this all very personally," Lilienthal noted. Interview with David E. Lilienthal, February 1979, Princeton, N.J. Nichols later took an interest in Russian nuclear capability. On this point, see Chapter 15. The summer spy "scandal" actually concerned the relatively innocuous—and ultimately unsuccessful—attempt by some former army officers to sell photographs of early atomic bombs to the *Baltimore News Post.* The paper contacted the FBI, and the individuals were arrested. The incident occurred while Groves, as head of the Manhattan Project, was responsible for security regarding the bomb. Concerning this case of supposed espionage, see Hoover to Vaughan, October 11, 1946, Box 167, "A—Communist" folder, PSF, HSTL; "Breach of Security" folder, Box 81, 380.01 file, (7-19-45), USJCS Records, MED History, vol. 14, Box 8, "Leakage of Information Cases," MEDR; and Chapter 6.

21. Concerning attacks upon the McMahon Act in Congress, see Hewlett and Duncan, *Atomic Shield*, 331–3.

22. Concerning this meeting and Groves' resignation, see ibid., 151–2.

23. Knowland to Truman, July 28, 1947, "Groves" folder, Box 917, HSTL.

24. *New York Times*, February 2, 1948.

25. Since the Air Policy Commission was composed largely of representatives from the air force and from aircraft manufacturers, its recommendation of an expanded air force occasioned no surprise. Forrestal thought it a means for the administration to direct the air-power dispute and to take the latter away from the Congress' rival Aviation Policy Board. Concerning the commission and its bias, see Millis, ed., *Forrestal Diaries*, 388; and Yergin, *Shattered Peace*, 342–3.

26. Royall is quoted in Lilienthal, *Atomic Energy Years*, 391.

27. President's Air Policy Commission, *Survival in the Air Age: A Report by the President's Air Policy Commission* (Washington, D.C., 1948). The Finletter Report was, of course, not the first forum for the expanded air force. For arguments similar to those

contained in the report, see "Air Power—the Key to Peace and Prosperity," *Aviation,* October 1945; "Bigger Air Force Is Prime Need for U.S. Survival—Policy Report," *Aviation Week,* January 1948; and "Peace Through Realism," *Aviation Week,* October 1946.

28. Concerning these studies, see JCS History, II, 525, USJCS Records.

29. The air force officer is cited in Yergin, *Shattered Peace,* 337.

30. Truman is quoted in ibid., 350.

31. Clay's telegram is in Millis, ed., *Forrestal Diaries,* 387. Curiously, no record of this message has been found in the files of the Joint Chiefs of Staff. Clay's excitable nature was evident as early as the previous April in this outburst during a telephone conference with army leaders in Washington: "Why are we in Europe? . . . We have lost Czechoslovakia. . . . We have lost Finland. . . . Norway is threatened. . . . We retreat from Berlin. . . ." Transcript of conversation, April 10, 1948, "Berlin Crisis Book" 3, Plans and Operations of Army General Staff, USJCS Records, National Archives. This transcript is also in Jean Edward Smith, ed., *The Papers of General Lucius D. Clay: Germany 1945–49* (Bloomington, Ind., 1974), vol. 2, 622–3.

32. Concerning the pragmatic considerations behind Clay's psychic inspiration, see, for example, Gardner, *Architects of Illusion,* 165–73.

33. Gruenther's briefing is noted in Millis, ed., *Forrestal Diaries,* 374–7. For the joint chiefs' interest in basing rights and the State Department's response, see *FR:* 1947, I, 766–7. Forrestal is cited in Millis, ed., *Forrestal Diaries,* 373. On Marshall and his views, see JCS History, II, 18–24, USJCS Records.

34. Millis, ed., *Forrestal Diaries,* 388.

35. Ibid., 395. Popular opinion was less assured. A broadcast by Walter Winchell at this time, in which the radio commentator stressed both America's desire for peace and her willingness to fight even a nuclear war, prompted a positive and emotional response from listeners. See, for example, *New York Times,* March 10, 1948.

36. Grover to Gruenther, March 13, 1948, "USSR" Series, (3-2-46), Sec. 12, USJCS Records.

37. Reflecting uncertainty about the prospects for retaining the Middle East—a doubt that surfaced in every U.S. war plan up to 1949—Grabber rejected a possible air base at Cairo-Suez in favor of one at Karachi. "Brief of Short-Range Emergency Plan, Short Title: *Grabber,*" March 17, 1948, "USSR" Series, (3-2-46), Sec. 12, USJCS Records.

38. Millis, ed., *Forrestal Diaries,* 464.

39. On Kennan's recommendation, see *FR:* 1948, I, 2, 523–6.

40. "The Position of the United States with Respect to Soviet-Directed World Communism," March 30, 1948, "NSC Meetings," Box 203, PSF, HSTL. NSC-7 is also in *FR:* 1948, I, 2, 546–50; and Etzold and Gaddis, eds., *Containment,* 164–9.

41. Merle Miller, *Plain Speaking,* 97. Truman is quoted in the "Cabinet Minutes" folder, November 17, 1950, Matthew Connelly MSS, HSTL. Some weeks earlier, however, Truman, according to Connelly, "warned cabinet officers that he is opposed to wire tapping and asked [the] cabinet to watch this activity carefully." September 15, 1950, Matthew Connelly MSS. Concerning Truman and the CIA, see also Donovan, *Conflict and Crisis,* 309–11; Etzold and Gaddis, eds., *Containment,* 125–8; and "Minutes . . . ," May 20 and July 1, 1948, "National Security Council" File, Box 200, PSF, HSTL.

42. Clay's telegram and the response to it are cited in JCS History, II, 125, USJCS Records. Millis, ed., *Forrestal Diaries,* 408.

43. Concerning CIA and U.S. embassy reports on Berlin at this time, see Millis, ed.,

Forrestal Diaries, 409; and *FR:* 1948, I, 2, 550–7. Truman is quoted by Forrestal in Millis, ed., 398.

44. JCS History, II, 120–2, USJCS Records.
45. Concerning Sandstone and security precautions regarding the nuclear arsenal, see Hewlett and Duncan, *Atomic Shield,* 158–60; and Rosenberg, "American Atomic Strategy and the Hydrogen Bomb Decision," 70–1.
46. Interview with David E. Lilienthal, February 1979, Princeton, N.J.
47. Hewlett and Duncan, *Atomic Shield,* 159, 175–6.
48. On the Key West meetings, see JCS History, II, 179–84, USJCS Records. The Key West Agreement was printed in *Army and Navy Journal,* April 3, 1948, 807 ff.
49. Concerning Pearson's article, see, for example, the *Philadelphia Bulletin* of April 10, 1948. On the navy memo and the origins of the air force–navy feud, see also Paul Hammond, "Super Carriers and B-36 Bombers: Appropriations, Strategy and Politics," in Harold Stein, ed., *American Civil-Military Decisions* (Tuscaloosa, Ala., 1963), 479–81. Some navy proponents charged that the editorial policy of the *Reader's Digest* favored the air force over their service, and that the controversial articles had even been written in the air force's public information office. See Caraley, *The Politics of Military Unification,* 262. Concerning the bias of those articles in favor of air-atomic strategy see, for example, "A Navy—or An Air Force?" and "Peace Through Air Power," in the December 1948 and February 1949 *Reader's Digest.*
50. JCS History, II, 286–8, USJCS Records. Denfeld to JCS, April 6, 1948, "USSR" Series, (3-2-46), Sec. 13, USJCS Records.
51. The comment is contained in an untitled and undated memorandum in the "Unification" folder, Forrestal MSS.
52. Ayers diary, April 21, 1948, HSTL.
53. Truman to Forrestal, May 13 and June 3, 1948, "U.S." Series, Sec. 7, Box 35, USJCS Records.
54. *New York Herald Tribune,* April 23, 1948. JCS History, II, 241, USJCS Records.
55. "Brief of Short-Range Emergency War Plan, Short Title: *Doublestar,*" June 8, 1948, "USSR" Series, (3-2-46), Sec. 16, USJCS Records. Ironically, Denfeld's usual opponent among the joint chiefs, Air Force General Spaatz, joined with the navy in urging that Grabber be rejected as an inadequate basis on which to plan for a war with Russia. Spaatz' objection to Grabber, however, was that it was predicated on a fifty-five-group, rather than a seventy-group, air force. JCS History, II, 234–7, USJCS Records.

Chapter 13

1. Webb is quoted by Lilienthal, *Atomic Energy Years,* 350–1. Pacifist A. J. Muste thought that the very nature of nuclear weapons threatened civilian control of the military. He wrote to David Lilienthal: "It has always seemed to me that as long as the United States continues to produce atomic weapons, and as long as war remains in the picture, civilian control of atomic projects is likely to be extremely limited. As soon as a war scare develops, it seems certain that control—on the grounds of military secrecy—will be turned over again completely to the military. It is distressing to think that in reality the military may not get their hands off the thing at all." Muste to Lilienthal, February 20, 1947, Correspondence File, Lilienthal MSS.
2. Various other individuals, including General Clay, have taken responsibility for the idea of sending the bombers across the Atlantic. Forrestal would seem to have the best

claim, however, since he had already advocated sending B-29s to Greece as a show of force. In any case, one bomber group was deployed in Germany before the crisis broke, and details for the transfer of B-29s to England had been worked out as part of "joint emergency war plan" Halfmoon (later Fleetwood) just before Forrestal made his suggestion. On this point see Millis, ed., *Forrestal Diaries,* 456–7; and JCS History, II, 288–9, USJCS Records.

3. W. Phillips Davison, *The Berlin Blockade* (Princeton, N.J., 1958), 157; Millis, ed., *Forrestal Diaries,* 456.

4. Concerning Clay's proposals for actions in the crisis, see Millis, ed., *Forrestal Diaries,* 459–60; and Berlin "Hot File," Plans and Operations of Army General Staff, USJCS Records. LeMay's plan to bomb the Russians is noted in his interview for the Dulles Oral History Project, Dulles MSS, Princeton University. The fate of the two trains is noted in Donovan, *Conflict and Crisis,* 365–6.

5. Documents concerning the June 28, 1948, meeting at the Pentagon and an account of the decisions made there may be found in the Berlin "Hot File," Plans and Operations of Army General Staff, USJCS Records.

6. "U.S. Air Power Flowing Back to Europe," *Aviation Week,* August 2, 1948. Concerning the air force's preparations for war in Europe, see also *Aviation Week,* August 9, 1948. On Truman's reaction to the Pearson story, see Ayers diary, October 14, 1946, HSTL. On the transfer of the bombers to Europe, see Webb to Truman, July 22, 1948, "NSC Atomic Energy—Budget" folder, Box 200, PSF, HSTL; and JCS History, II, 139, USJCS Records. The two B-29 squadrons sent to Germany were placed on three-hour alert, as was the B-29 group sent to England. Another bomber group assigned to France was kept on forty-eight-hour alert in the United States. See "Estimate of Berlin Situation," June 29, 1948, and "Urgent Message," Bradley to Clay, undated, "Hot File," Plans and Operations of Army General Staff, USJCS Records.

7. Truman and Royall are quoted in Lilienthal, *Atomic Energy Years,* 391.

8. Royall to Forrestal, July 19, 1948, "Berlin Crisis Book" 3, Plans and Operations of Army General Staff, USJCS Records.

9. Concerning National Security Council instructions during the Berlin crisis, see NSC "Action Memorandum" 77 and 84 of July 1948 in "NSC" Box, USJCS Records. The army's report on the crisis is the "Estimate of Berlin Situation," June 29, 1948, Berlin "Hot File," Plans and Operations of Army General Staff, USJCS Records.

10. Dulles to Baruch, June 23, 1948, Correspondence File, "1971 Supplement," Dulles MSS.

11. The joint chiefs as a group were not consulted on Berlin until the following October, well after the initial crisis had passed, and then only after they had taken deliberate steps to end their isolation. One cause of this isolation may have been disagreements among themselves. The previous January an army contingency plan for dealing with a crisis over Berlin had specifically rejected consultation with the other services. Concerning the role of the joint chiefs in the Berlin crisis, see L. C. Korb, *The Joint Chiefs of Staff* (New York, 1978), 15; and JCS History, II, 160–4, USJCS Records.

12. "List of Military and Quasi-Military Measures Which Could Be Applied Against the USSR," July 23, 1948, "U.S." Series, (8-20-43), Sec. 17, USJCS Records. Concerning the deliberations of the National Security Council at this time, see NSC-24, "U.S. Military Courses of Action with Respect to the Situation in Berlin," July 28, 1948, "NSC" Box, USJCS Records.

13. On the importance of the bombers-to-Britain move in the evolution of deterrence

theory, as seen by some strategic analysts and historians, see, for example, Anderson, *Strategic Air Command*, 39–41; Millis, *Arms and Men*, 323–5; George and Smoke, *Deterrence in American Foreign Policy*, 107–39; and Davison, *Berlin Blockade*, 157.

14. Millis, ed., *Forrestal Diaries*, 488–9. "Memorandum . . . ," September 15, *FR:* 1948, I, vol. 2, 630. Interview with Gordon Arneson, October 1979, Washington, D.C.

15. Truman is quoted in Millis, ed., *Forrestal Diaries*, 458.

16. Truman is cited in Lilienthal, *Atomic Energy Years*, 377. Concerning the transfer of custody and arrangements for authorizing use of the atomic bombs, see Hewlett and Duncan, *Atomic Shield*, 537–9; and Gordon Dean to James Lay, June 24, 1952, "NSC—Atomic" folder, Box 202, PSF, HSTL. Truman's orders authorizing the shipment of non-nuclear components for atomic bombs overseas are in the "Atomic Weapons" folder, "NSC" Box, USJCS Records.

17. Rosenberg, "American Atomic Strategy and the Hydrogen Bomb Decision," 65–6. Interview with David E. Lilienthal, February 1979, Princeton, N.J.

18. Concerning the National Security Council's deferral of the policy on atomic warfare, see "Memorandum for the President," May 21 and July 2, 1948; "Minutes," May 20 and July 1, 1948, "NSC—Atomic" folder, Box 202, PSF, HSTL.

19. "Joint Outline Alternative War Plan, Short Title: *Intermezzo,*" July 15, 1948, "USSR" Series, (3-2-46), Sec. 18, USJCS Records. Concerning the origins of Intermezzo, see also the untitled memorandum, April 6, 1948, same series, Sec. 13.

20. Concerning the ideas put forward by Bohr and Einstein, see *FR:* 1947, I, 487–8; and *FR:* 1948, I, vol. 1, 388–99.

21. Hewlett and Duncan, *Atomic Shield*, 265.

22. Ibid., 266–70.

23. "Guidance on Military Aspects . . . ," July 14, 1947, "Atomic" Series, (8-15-45), Sec. 5, USJCS Records.

24. Hewlett and Duncan, *Atomic Shield*, 271–3. Concerning the suspension of the UNAEC, see also *FR:* 1947, I, 671–3.

25. "Joint Outline Alternative War Plan, Short Title: *Intermezzo,*" July 15, 1948, "USSR" Series, (3-2-46), Sec. 18, USJCS Records.

26. Concerning Fleetwood and its origins, see JCS History, II, 290–2, USJCS Records. A later version of this plan is in Etzold and Gaddis, eds., *Containment*, 315–23.

27. "Memorandum," September 13, 1948, "USSR" Series, (3-2-46), Sec. 20, USJCS Records. Concerning Cogwheel, see JCS History, II, 304–11, USJCS Records. See also on war planning, Rosenberg, "American Atomic Strategy and the Hydrogen Bomb Decision," 68–71.

28. "Guidance for U.S. Military Representatives . . . ," NSC-9/4, July 20, 1948, "NSC" Box, USJCS Records. Concerning the origins of NATO, see also Etzold and Gaddis, eds., *Containment*, 144–60.

29. Baruch to Dulles, October 5, 1948, "1971 Supplement," Dulles MSS. Baruch to Marshall, October 6, 1948, and Hancock to J. P. Davis, May 14, 1948, "Correspondence on Atomic Energy," Baruch MSS.

30. The Newport Agreement was meant to settle the outstanding disputes remaining from the Key West Agreement of the previous March. Like the earlier agreement, however, this new accord was destined to be only a temporary truce, soon overturned by continuing interservice rivalry and by the pressure of events. Concerning the Newport Agreement, see JCS History, II, 184–9, USJCS Records; and *Army and Navy Journal*, August 28, 1948, 1435.

31. "United States Policy on Atomic Warfare," September 10, *FR:* 1948, I, vol. 2, 624–8.

The text of NSC-30 is also in Etzold and Gaddis, eds., *Containment,* 339–43.

32. "Memorandum . . . ," September 15, *FR:* 1948, I, vol. 2, 630–1. Concerning reaction within the government to NSC-30, see also ibid., 629–30.

33. Truman is quoted in Millis, ed., *Forrestal Diaries,* 487.

34. "Memorandum . . . ," *FR:* 1948, I, vol. 2, 629.

35. "Doctrine of Atomic Air Warfare," December 30, 1948, U.S. Air Force Field Office for Atomic Energy, "Air Force" folder, Box 2, "Recently Declassified Documents," USJCS Records.

36. Truman's comment to Leahy is cited in Rosenberg, "American Atomic Strategy and the Hydrogen Bomb Decision," 67.

37. "Joint Emergency Outline War Plan for Period 1 July 1949–1 July 1950, Short Title: *Sizzle,*" September 13, 1948, "USSR" Series, (3-2-46), Sec. 20, USJCS Records.

38. A JCS memorandum indicates that LeMay's goal was still short of fulfillment. The number of atomic bombs that could be used in a single attack was one hundred, but the government as of fall 1948 still lacked sufficient bomb-assembly teams to prepare that entire number at one time. "Decision on JCS 1745/15," September 2, 1948, folder 1, Box 1, "Recently Declassified Documents," USJCS Records.

39. "Report to the National Security Council . . . ," August 25, *FR:* 1948, I, vol. 2, 615–24.

40. That military planners were not entirely oblivious to non-strategic concerns is evident in the conclusion of a May 1947 joint chiefs' report, which argued that Allied air attacks upon Soviet forces "in periphery areas" during a war would probably not be decisive and "must be qualified by the political considerations involved." See Etzold and Gaddis, eds., *Containment,* 302–11.

41. Concerning the 1948 revival of the spy scare, see Reuben, *Atom Spy Hoax,* 137–47; and *New York Times,* September 1–11, 1948. On the Hiss case and its impact upon the election, see Allen Weinstein, *Perjury: The Hiss-Chambers Case* (New York, 1978), 58, 357. Regarding Condon and the charges against him, see Reuben, 129–36.

42. Concerning the loyalty program, see Donovan, *Conflict and Crisis,* 292–3; Truman, *Years of Trial and Hope,* 309–35; and Richard M. Freeland, *The Truman Doctrine and the Origins of McCarthyism* (New York, 1972). On Parnell Thomas and HUAC, see Walter Goodman, *The Committee: The Extraordinary Career of the House Committee on Un-American Activities* (New York, 1968). The term "red herring" as applied to the spy scare was first used by a reporter, not Truman. See *PPOP,* 1948, 432.

43. Groves' testimony cited in *New York Times,* September 21, 1948. His prediction concerning the Russian bomb is in "The Atom-General Answers His Critics," *Saturday Evening Post,* June 19, 1948.

44. U.S. Congress, *Report on Soviet Espionage Activities in Connection with the Atom Bomb,* HUAC, 80th Congress/Second Session (Washington, D.C., 1948). The Justice Department statement is cited in Reuben, *Atom-Spy Hoax,* 137.

45. "Future Course of Action with Respect to Berlin," NSC-24/1, November 17, 1948, "NSC" Box, USJCS Records.

46. Clay is cited in Millis, ed., *Forrestal Diaries,* 526.

47. Ibid., 502.

48. Ibid., 506.

49. "U.S. Objectives with Respect to Russia," NSC-20/1, August 18, 1948, "NSC" Box, USJCS Records. This document is also in Etzold and Gaddis, eds., *Containment,* 173–203. Concerning the origins of NSC-20 in Forrestal's request, see *FR:* 1948, I, vol. 2, 589–93.

50. "Factors Affecting . . . ," NSC-20/2, August 25, *FR:* 1948, I, vol. 2, 615–24. Portions of this document are also in Etzold and Gaddis, eds., *Containment,* 297–301. One example of how NSC planners hoped to profit from the experience of the Second World War is that they intended in any future conflict to recruit Russian prisoners of war for anticommunist agitation.
51. "U.S. Objectives . . . ," NSC-20/3, November 2, 1948, "NSC" Box, USJCS Records.
52. "Report to the President by the National Security Council," NSC-20/4, November 23, *FR:* 1948, I, vol. 2, 662–9; also in Etzold and Gaddis, eds., *Containment,* 203–10.
53. Truman's comment on custody is in Donovan, *Conflict and Crisis,* 143. Forrestal to Truman, December 1, *FR:* 1948, I, vol. 2, 669–72. Millis, ed., *Forrestal Diaries,* 536.
54. An intelligence estimate prepared for the joint chiefs in December moved that date ahead to mid-1950, with the "greatest possible number of bombs in the Soviet stockpile in mid-1955" put at fifty. If the Russian bomb was delayed until mid-1953, however, this maximum number for 1955 was correspondingly lowered to twenty. "In both cases the most important limiting factor is the supply of uranium ore." There was one final, significant caveat: "If fresh resources are opened up in the near future [in Russia], the above estimates would have to be increased. . . . This cannot be predicted." Untitled memorandum, December 30, 1948, Joint Intelligence Group, "USSR" Series, (3-27-45), Sec. 34, USJCS Records.
55. The army study of December 16, 1948, is in Etzold and Gaddis, eds., *Containment,* 343–57.
56. "Evaluation of Current Strategic Air Offensive Plans," December 21, 1948, "USSR" Series, (10-23-48), Sec. 1, USJCS Records; also in Etzold and Gaddis, eds., *Containment,* 357–60.
57. Millis, ed., *Forrestal Diaries,* 538.

Chapter 14

1. Millis, ed., *Forrestal Diaries,* 537–8.
2. JCS History, II, 239, USJCS Records.
3. Lilienthal, *Atomic Energy Years,* 270.
4. Lilienthal is quoted in York, *Advisors,* 57.
5. "Joint Outline Plan . . . , Short Title: *Dropshot,*" January 31, 1949, "USSR" Series, (3-2-46), Sec. 28, USJCS Records. The plan, related documents, and commentary are also in Anthony C. Brown, ed., *Dropshot: The American Plan for World War III with Russia in 1957* (New York, 1978).
6. Contingency plans for a war beginning in 1955–56, code-named Charioteer, contained in "USSR" Series, (3-2-46), Sec. 6, USJCS Records. Another miscalculation by U.S. planners concerned the introduction of the intercontinental ballistic missile. Air force analysts had predicted in 1945 that ICBMs would soon make their appearance, but the joint chiefs doubted that they would be a threat before 1977. The air force estimate was more nearly correct. The date picked by Dropshot—1957— was the year that Russia launched the first earth satellite, inspiring fears of a "missile gap."
7. "Measures Required to Achieve U.S. Objectives . . . ," March 30, *FR:* 1949, I, vol. 2, 271–7. Among the measures to be taken in defense of "internal security" under this plan were "scrutinizing, curtailing, and counteracting, to the maximum extent possible, the open and clandestine activities of communists and other subversive groups, whether party members or not." In conditions of "war-related emergency,"

this program would be expanded to include the arrest and detention of U.S. citizens and aliens deemed a threat.

8. Brown, ed., *Dropshot,* 326.

9. See, for example, Spaatz' article "Strategic Thinking and Western Civilization," *Newsweek,* October 18, 1948; and "Peace Through Air Power," *Reader's Digest,* February 1949. Other accounts concerning the popular conception of nuclear war are noted in Warner Schilling, Paul Y. Hammond, and Glenn H. Snyder, *Strategy, Politics, and Defense Budgets* (New York, 1962), 48–51.

10. "Operation Eggnog," *Collier's,* October 1951. A year before, the joint chiefs had estimated that there might be 10 million U.S. civilian casualties in a nuclear war with Russia. "Implications of Soviet Possession of Atomic Weapons," January 31, 1950, "USSR" Series, (11-8-49), Sec. 1, USJCS Records.

11. Concerning McMahon's proposal and its fate, see Hewlett and Duncan, *Atomic Shield,* 352–3.

12. "Globe Hop Sets B-50's New Role," *Aviation Week,* March 14, 1949. On air force planning relating to Dropshot, see "Atomic" Series, (8-15-45), Sec. 15, USJCS Records; and Rosenberg, "American Atomic Strategy and the Hydrogen Bomb Decision," 71–3.

13. Concerning early defense planning, see JCS History, II, 536–42, USJCS Records.

14. Grenville Clark to Lilienthal, October 14, 1948, Correspondence File, Lilienthal MSS.

15. Millis, ed., *Forrestal Diaries,* 503.

16. Air force targeting studies are in "U.S." Series, (10-23-48), Sec. 1, USJCS Records. Concerning these plans, see also Etzold and Gaddis, eds., *Containment,* 357–60.

17. Churchill is quoted in Millis, ed., *Forrestal Diaries,* 523–4, 537.

18. The joint chiefs are quoted in ibid., 504–5.

19. Concerning the origins of the Harmon and Hull committees, see JCS History, II, 312; and Rosenberg, "American Atomic Strategy and the Hydrogen Bomb Decision," 71–2.

20. The joint chiefs' January estimate of military requirements was the first based upon an air force war plan rather than on the maximum production capacity of the AEC's atomic laboratories. Another reason for the increased estimate was the development of specialized nuclear weapons for use against small or hardened targets. JCS History, II, 531–4, USJCS Records. On the joint chiefs' request, see also Lilienthal, *Atomic Energy Years,* 377. War plan Trojan is in "Recently Declassified Documents," Box 3, USJCS Records.

21. In a memorandum sent to the President the following December, the joint chiefs admitted that the expanded atomic-weapons program would have no effect upon current U.S. military strategy but was justified as a hedge against future, unforeseen developments in nuclear weaponry. JCS History, II, 535–6, USJCS Records. On this point, see also Hewlett and Duncan, *Atomic Shield,* 178–81.

22. Lilienthal, *Atomic Energy Years,* 270.

23. Ibid., 460–3.

24. Ibid., 464.

25. Ibid., 363.

26. Concerning Denfeld and Fleetwood, see JCS History, II, 343–5. Gallery's speech is quoted at length in Rosenberg, "American Atomic Strategy and the Hydrogen Bomb Decision," 70.

27. Lilienthal, *Atomic Energy Years,* 474.

28. See the President's letter to the National Security Council, July 26, *FR:* 1949, 501–3.
29. Untitled letter, April 5, 1949, "NSC Atomic Energy—Budget" folder, Box 200, PSF, HSTL.
30. Ayers diary, April 8, 1949, HSTL.
31. Concerning the air force's April 20, 1949, briefing of the President, see "National Security Council—Atomic" folder, Box 199, PSF, HSTL; and *FR:* 1948, I, vol. 2, 625 ff. Estimates of casualties and damage are from the Harmon Report, details of which are printed in Etzold and Gaddis, eds., *Containment,* 360–4.
32. *FR:* 1948, III, 237–45; also in Etzold and Gaddis, eds., *Containment,* 144–53.
33. Concerning the origins of NATO, see *FR:* 1948, III, 237–45, 284–8; *FR:* 1949, IV, 240–41; and Etzold and Gaddis, eds., *Containment,* 144–60.
34. Concerning the rethinking of NATO strategy, see "Reconsideration of Organization . . . ," August 22, 1949, "Western Europe" Series, Secs. 26–29, Box 44, USJCS Records. For a comparison with early NATO planning, see "Guidance for U.S. Military Representatives . . . ," July 20, 1948, NSC 9/4, "NSC" Box, USJCS Records.
35. Thomas Sancton, "The Atlantic Pact: Trouble in the Senate," *Nation,* April 9, 1949.
36. Truman is quoted in *FR:* 1949, I, 463. Concerning preparations at this time for the air-atomic offensive, see NSC 45/1, "Airfield Construction in the United Kingdom and the Cairo-Suez Area," April 15, 1949; and untitled memorandum, Forrestal to Souers, March 17, 1949, "NSC" Box, USJCS Records. The above are also in *FR:* 1949, I, 285–7.
37. Concerning the Harmon Report and its reception in the Pentagon, see JCS History, II, 313–18; and Rosenberg, "American Atomic Strategy and the Hydrogen Bomb Decision," 71–5. The Harmon Report itself is in "U.S." Series, (10-23-48), Sec. 2. Excerpts are also in Etzold and Gaddis, eds., *Containment,* 360–4. Minutes of the Harmon committee are in Box 3, "Recently Declassified Documents," USJCS Records.
38. "Minutes . . . ," February–March, 1949, Box 3, "Recently Declassified Documents," USJCS Records.
39. Concerning Johnson's withholding of the Harmon Report, see Rosenberg, "American Atomic Strategy and the Hydrogen Bomb Decision," 76–7.
40. On the problems of the Strategic Air Command and the air force, see Curtis LeMay and MacKinlay Kantor, *Mission with LeMay* (New York, 1965), especially 429–33; and Anderson, *Strategic Air Command,* especially 32–60. Air force documents indicate that as late as April 1950 an insufficiency of fuel, overseas bases, and spare parts made it impossible to sustain an air-atomic offensive for a period longer than three months. One such report concluded, in essence, that the air force would be able to launch the atomic blitz but unable to attack Russia with conventional bombs in a protracted war. See, for example, untitled memorandum, Anderson to Symington, April 11, 1950, folder 1, Box 2, "Recently Declassified Documents," USJCS Records.
41. The subject of this debate, naturally, concerned the air-atomic offensive itself. In an unusual compromise of their differences, the authors of Offtackle appended to early drafts of the plan two different—and conflicting—interpretations of its effects. It was asserted in the air force's version that atomic bombing would "determine" the rapidity of victory and so "will be sustained until decisive results are attained" or until Soviet capabilities were sufficiently reduced for the allies to mount a successful offensive with conventional forces. The navy's opposing viewpoint—printed alongside the air force analysis in the plan—joined with some dissenters in the army to argue that the air-atomic offensive would only "influence" subsequent Allied action and would proba-

bly be indecisive unless accompanied by sustained ground and sea attacks against Russia. There was also disagreement within the plan as to whether the atomic blitz should be directed exclusively against urban industrial targets in the Soviet Union, as the air force intended, or against cities and "other elements of the Soviet offensive military power," the choice of the army and navy. An early version of Offtackle is included in the "USSR" Series, (3-2-46), Sec. 32; and in Etzold and Gaddis, eds., *Containment,* 324–34. Another tentative war plan—Bushwhacker—was intended to fill the gap existing between short-term and long-term planning. However, partly because of the pressure of events in 1949, Bushwhacker was never completed. Another effort at medium-range planning would not be made by the joint chiefs until 1950. Offtackle itself was not approved by the joint chiefs until almost the end of 1949. Concerning U.S. war planning at this time, especially as it affected the navy–air force rivalry, see JCS History, II, 296–311, USJCS Records.

42. On the revised air force component, see "Brief of Joint Outline Emergency War Plan, Short Title: *Offtackle,*" August 2, 1949, "USSR" Series, (3-2-46), Sec. 36, USJCS Records.

43. Concerning Hickenlooper's attack and its motivation, see Hewlett and Duncan, *Atomic Shield,* 358–61. On public understanding of the dispute, see *New York Times,* May 25–26, 1949.

44. Scrapbook, Box 4, Forrestal MSS.

45. Untitled memorandum, Truman to Souers, July 26, *FR:* 1949, I, 501–2.

46. Concerning the brief consideration given the idea of tactical nuclear warfare at this time, see untitled document, December 15, 1950, "Air Force" folder, Box 2, "Recently Declassified Documents," USJCS Records; and Rosenberg, "American Atomic Strategy and the Hydrogen Bomb Decision," 74.

47. The Strategic Air Command's Emergency War Plan 1-49 noted that the staging points for atomic raids against Russia might be limited to Britain and the United States "principally because of the lack of suitable operational air bases in the Cairo-Suez area." JCS 1844/32, August 23, 1949, folder 3, Box 1, "Recently Declassified Documents," USJCS Records.

48. Renewal of the Anglo-American *modus vivendi* was a comment upon the preeminent role of the atomic bomb in U.S. strategy. Initially opposed by anglophobes in the Senate, the renewal agreement was backed by Truman as "an arrangement in which we would certainly get much more than we gave." Failure to renew the *modus vivendi,* General Dwight Eisenhower explained to the senators, would mean a reversion to equal sharing of uranium ore—a situation that would soon lead to a slowdown of production at U.S. industries making bombs and even to the laying off of workers at those plants. "And who would take responsibility for explaining that to the American people?" Eisenhower asked. The renewed *modus vivendi* was approved by Congress and by Truman. On renewal, see Hewlett and Duncan, *Atomic Shield,* 299–302; Gowing, *Independence and Deterrence,* 241–6; and *FR:* 1949, I, 464–500. Eisenhower and Truman are quoted in "Record of the Meeting . . . ," July 14, *FR:* 1949, I, 476–81. The NSC study is "A Report to the President . . . ," March 2, 1949, *FR:* 1949, *FR:* 1949, I, 443–61.

49. "Memorandum . . . ," August 2, *FR:* 1949, I, 506–7.

50. A concern with how his ideas might be received was probably the reason why Kennan first sent his memorandum to Gordon Arneson, Acheson's aide, rather than to Acheson himself. "Political Implications of Detonation of Atomic Bomb by the U.S.S.R.," August 16, 1949, *FR:* 1949, I, 514–16. This document is also in Etzold and Gaddis, eds., *Containment,* 364–6.

51. A Central Intelligence Group–Central Intelligence Agency study of fall 1946 predicted that the first Soviet atomic bomb would be tested between 1950 and 1953, and that the Russians would have "a quantity of such bombs . . . by 1956." "Soviet Capability for the Development and Production of Certain Types of Weapons and Equipment," ORE 3/1, October 31, 1946, "CIA" Box, USJCS Records. See also Strauss, *Men and Decisions* (New York, 1962), especially 201–6. However, Strauss would later change his mind about telling the public of Russian progress. As AEC chairman in the mid-1950s, he opposed announcing that the Russians had a hydrogen bomb. Interview with Paul Nitze, October 1979, Washington, D.C.

52. Strauss, *Men and Decisions,* 202.

53. On the views of the scientists, see, for example, Grodzins and Rabinowitch, eds., *Atomic Age.* Concerning the predictions of Lilienthal and Acheson, see Hewlett and Duncan, *Atomic Shield,* 300 ff.; and "Memorandum . . . ," July 6, *FR:* 1949, I, 471–4. On public opinion, see Social Science Research Council, *Public Reaction to the Atomic Bomb and World Affairs,* 1–12.

54. As air force chief of staff, General Hoyt S. Vandenberg was in charge of the air force's foreign intelligence section, a job he inherited from the Armed Forces Special Weapons Project. David Lilienthal's impression of Vandenberg's performance in that role was hardly flattering: "Vandenberg was a very handsome fellow, but. . . ." Interview with David E. Lilienthal, February 1979, Princeton, N.J.

55. Byrnes, *Speaking Frankly,* 101–2.

56. "Reconsideration of Organization . . . ," August 22, 1949, "Western Europe" Series, Secs. 26–29, USJCS Records. See also NSC-57, "NSC" Box, USJCS Records.

57. "Identification of Radioactivity in Special Samples," October 4, 1949; and "Collection and Identification of Fission Products," September 26, 1949, in "NSC Atomic Bomb—Reports" folder, Box 199, PSF, HSTL. Some confusion still exists as to the actual date and location of the Soviet test. Oppenheimer put it at August 29 in Soviet Asia. Truman, in announcing the event to the Cabinet, said the test occurred between August 19 and 21 somewhere in central Siberia. In his memoirs, Nikita Khrushchev wrote that the test took place in the Ast-Art desert between the Caspian and Aral seas during July 1949. On the detection of the blast and the controversy it stirred in the United States, see JCS History, II, 527–9, USJCS Records; Hewlett and Duncan, *Atomic Shield,* 366; Strauss, *Men and Decisions,* 202–6; and Strobe Talbott, ed. and trans., *Khrushchev Remembers: The Last Testament* (Boston, 1970), 58–60.

58. *New York Times,* September 25, 1949.

59. Strauss, *Men and Decisions,* 206.

60. Lilienthal, *Atomic Energy Years,* 571–5; Hewlett and Duncan, *Atomic Shield,* 366–9.

61. York, *Advisors,* 34. *New York Times,* September 24, 1949. In 1955 Robert Oppenheimer criticized a statement made by Truman two years before in which the latter suggested that the Russians were still without either an atomic or a hydrogen bomb. Oppenheimer, *Open Mind,* 70. A biographer of Oppenheimer recounts a meeting of the scientist and Truman during spring 1946 in which the President cast doubt upon the Russians' ability to build an atomic bomb. Truman—according to Oppenheimer —seemed "serene, lit by mystic inner confidence" when he asked the scientist's opinion as to when the Russians would have a bomb. To Oppenheimer's frank admission of uncertainty, Truman responded that *he* knew. "When?" his guest asked. "Never" was the President's reply. Truman's doubts in 1949 about a Russian bomb may have been correct, even if ill-founded in a mistaken notion of superior U.S. know-how and preclusive control of atomic raw materials. Khrushchev's memoirs assert that the Soviet Union didn't have a deliverable nuclear weapon until 1950, and

even then had severe problems in producing atomic bombs—problems it was able to hide from the West. Strobe Talbott, ed. and trans., *Khrushchev Remembers*, 60, 66. Concerning the Russians' admission of the difficulties caused for them by the Combined Development Trust, see A. A. Santalov, *The Imperialist Struggle for Raw Materials Resources* (title in Russian; Moscow, 1955). The account of the meeting between Oppenheimer and Truman is in Davis, *Lawrence and Oppenheimer*, 260.

62. Lilienthal, *Atomic Energy Years*, 580. Letter, Symington to Johnson, November 8, 1949, "NSC Atomic Energy—Russia" folder, Box 201, PSF, HSTL. Webb is quoted in 1949 "Cabinet Minutes," Matthew Connelly MSS, HSTL.

Chapter 15

1. Lilienthal, *Atomic Energy Years*, 577.
2. Bush and Conant to Stimson, September 30, 1944, folder 77, Harrison-Bundy File, MEDR.
3. Concerning the genesis of the "Super," see Hewlett and Duncan, *Atomic Shield*, 30–1, 43, 59, 133; and Strauss, *Men and Decisions*, 216–17.
4. Lilienthal, *Atomic Energy Years*, 581, 591.
5. Oppenheimer is cited in Hewlett and Duncan, *Atomic Shield*, 378–9.
6. Oppenheimer is quoted in the transcript of a 1957 interview with Warner Schilling, Robert Oppenheimer MSS, Library of Congress. According to Paul Nitze, Oppenheimer's objections to the hydrogen bomb—in order of importance—were that it wouldn't work, that the test of its feasibility would divert too much nuclear material, that it would be too big to carry on a bomber if it did work, and that testing of the "Super" would make it easier for the Russians to develop one. Nitze believes that Oppenheimer's moral objections to the super-bomb developed only after Edward Teller proved the weapon's feasibility. Interview with Paul Nitze, October 1979, Washington, D.C.
7. The views of the scientists are contained in "Statement Appended to the Report . . . ," October 30, *FR: 1949*, I, 570–3.
8. On this point, see Hewlett and Duncan, *Atomic Shield*, 383–4; and York, *Advisors*, 41–74. Letter, Pike to Truman, December 7, 1949, "NSC Atomic Energy—Super Bomb Data" folder, Box 201, PSF, HSTL.
9. Lilienthal, *Atomic Energy Years*, 581.
10. Concerning the navy's feud with the air force as it appeared in print at this time, see *New York Times*, esp. March 3, 6–7, 13, 20, and April 19, 24, 1949. See also "The Struggle for American Air Power," *Reader's Digest*, April 1949; and "The Case for the Aircraft Carrier," *Reader's Digest*, May 1949. Forrestal's warning against navy criticism of the air force was in an October 1948 letter to Navy Secretary John Sullivan. However, the letter was never sent. Millis, ed., *Forrestal Diaries*, 514.
11. Letter, Denfeld to Hanson Baldwin, September 7, 1949, folder 190, Box 4, Hanson Baldwin MSS, Yale University.
12. "Kill the B-36 Rumors," *Aviation Week*, March 14, 1949. Concerning the B-36 controversy, see also *New York Times*, March 13, 1949; and *Saturday Evening Post*, June 26, 1949. Although the navy would ultimately lose to the air force in the matter of the B-36, its arguments in the case were later vindicated. Because of the faults identified by the navy at the hearings, the bomber would not become fully operational in the Strategic Air Command until 1951. See Anderson, *Strategic Air Command*, 73.

13. Concerning the hearings, see Stein, ed., *American Civil-Military Relations*, 505, 514–24; JCS History, II, 330–43, USJCS Records; and *New York Times*, October 8 and 11–13, 1949. Chief of Naval Operations Louis Denfeld was unjustly accused of inspiring an "anonymous" letter attacking the air force prior to the hearings. In a letter to *New York Times* military correspondent Hanson Baldwin, Denfeld disassociated himself from the letter, actually written by an overzealous proponent of the "new navy." It had "so little basis of truth it is inconceivable that anybody would put out a document of that kind," Denfeld wrote. See Denfeld to Baldwin, September 7, 1949, folder 190, Box 4, Hanson Baldwin MSS.

14. Stein, ed., *American Civil-Military Relations*, 524–36.

15. JCS History, II, 340–1, USJCS Records.

16. Ibid., 341; *New York Times*, October 11–13, 1949.

17. Stein, ed., *American Civil-Military Relations*, 520.

18. JCS History, II, 345–6, USJCS Records.

19. "Hopes Brighten for Bigger USAF Budget," *Aviation Week*, October 10, 1949.

20. Clark to Lilienthal, October 18, 1949, Correspondence File, Lilienthal MSS.

21. Lewis Mumford, "Gentlemen, You Are Mad!" *Saturday Review of Literature*, March 2, 1946. See also Mumford's "Miracle or Catastrophe," *Air Affairs*, July 1948.

22. Concerning the polls and moral reaction to Hiroshima, see, for example, *Public Opinion Quarterly*, Fall 1945, 385–530; and *Fortune*, December 1945. Religious leaders' reaction to the atomic bombing was mixed. Typically, Catholics tended to look upon it as a variant of saturation bombing and condemned it as inhuman; but liberal churchmen did not necessarily condemn the bombing, nor conservatives approve it. Liberal newspapers and journals like *PM, Nation*, and *New Republic* generally approved the bombing as the lesser evil. Socialists such as Lewis Mumford, Dwight Macdonald, and Norman Thomas, however, condemned it. Concerning church opinion, see S. J. Smothers, "An Opinion on Hiroshima," *America*, July 5, 1947, 379; James M. Gillis, "The Atom Bomb," *Catholic World*, September 1945, 451; "America's Atomic Atrocity," *Christian Century*, August 29, 1945, 974–6; and "He Could Not Thank God for the Atomic Bomb Victory," *Missions*, October 1945, 424. Concerning liberal political views on the bombings, see Lewis Mumford, *Values for Survival* (New York, 1946), esp. 78–9, 83, 94; "Atomic Anxieties," *New Republic*, August 20, 1945; "The Last War Front," *Nation*, August 25, 1945; and the editorial in *PM* for August 7, 1945.

23. Concerning public reaction to Hersey's *Hiroshima*, see George E. Hopkins, "Bombing and the American Conscience during World War II," *Historian*, May 1966, 451–73; John Latt and W. M. Wheeler, "Reaction to John Hersey's *Hiroshima*," *Journal of Social Psychology*, August 1948, 135–40; and Michael Yavendetti, "John Hersey and the American Conscience: The Reception of *Hiroshima*," *Pacific Historical Review*, October 1972, 24–49. Social Science Research Council, *Public Reaction to the Atomic Bomb and World Affairs*, 83–5.

24. Letter, Truman to Johnson, November 17, 1949, "National Security Council— Atomic" folder, Box 199, PSF, HSTL. On the reexamination of U.S. military strategy at this time, see also Truman to Johnson, April 21; and Johnson to Truman, April 27, 1949, same folder.

25. The Hull Report, also known as the "Weapons Systems Evaluation Group"—WSEG —Report, of February 10, 1950, is in the "U.S." Series, (10-23-48), Sec. 6, USJCS Records. Concerning the report and its fate, see also JCS History, II, 351–4. Truman was "noticeably surprised and disturbed by the report." Rosenberg, "American Atomic Strategy and the Hydrogen Bomb Decision," 84. One participant in the

meeting at which General Hull read the report noted that Johnson remarked to Truman at its conclusion: "There, I told you they'd say the B-36 is a good plane." The President, "looking disgusted," snapped back: "No, dammit, they said just the opposite." Philip Morse, *In at the Beginning* (London, 1978), 258–9.

26. Concerning various estimates of the monopoly's end, see "Did the Soviet Bomb Come Sooner Than Expected?" *Bulletin of the Atomic Scientists,* October 1949; and *New York Times,* September 24, 1949. The Joint Committee on Atomic Energy contradicted Truman's assurance. Its report of October 13, 1949, noted "Russia's ownership of the bomb, years ahead of the anticipated date." This claim was also made by the committee in a 1951 report on Russian spying. See Joint Committee on Atomic Energy, *Soviet Atomic Espionage,* 174–5.

27. "Questions Submitted to the Secretary of Defense . . . ," June 20, 1949, folder 2, Box 1, "Recently Declassified Documents," USJCS Records. Another setback for the Truman administration in 1949, the "loss" of China, apparently occasioned little concern among military planners. Because China was not expected to be a military threat for years to come—the Korean War was obviously not foreseen—the only change in short-range war plans was a revision of the antisubmarine campaign of Offtackle. See JCS 877/72, September 14, 1949, folder 2, Box 1, "Recently Declassified Documents," USJCS Records.

28. *New York Times,* September 25, 1949.

29. Concerning early knowledge of Russia's atomic-bomb project, see untitled memorandum, Patterson to Groves, November 1, 1946, "Atomic Energy Safe File 3," Patterson File, MEDR. This memorandum reads in part: "You will note that according to information uranium ore was discovered by the Russians in July along the border between Russian-occupied Germany and Czechoslovakia. . . . Please see that this information is conveyed to General [Hoyt] Vandenberg." Regarding Vandenberg's performance as head of foreign intelligence in the Manhattan Project, see Chapter 5. On intelligence estimates, see also untitled memorandum, December 15, *FR:* 1947, I, 904–5. Concerning the Russians' use of German uranium in their first bombs, see Arnold Kramish, *Atomic Energy in the Soviet Union* (Stanford, Calif., 1959), 26–9; U.S. Atomic Energy Commission, *In the Matter of J. Robert Oppenheimer,* 175–6; and Santalov, *Imperialist Struggle for Raw Materials Resources.* Even an article in the July 21, 1947, *New York Times* reported that the Russians were engaged in large-scale mining for uranium in German Saxony. A Soviet defector, Nikolai Grishin, revealed in 1953 that Project "Vismut," the Russian mining of uranium in Saxony, began just after the German surrender in May 1945. The high priority given the project was evident, Grishin noted, from the fact that the Red Army troops used as miners were given front-line rations. The soldier-miners were also told that Stalin personally followed daily reports on the output of the mines. See "The Saxony Uranium Mining Operation," in Robert Slusser, ed., *Soviet Economic Policy in Postwar Germany* (New York, 1953). On the importance of the lens-mold controversy to the Rosenberg case, see Roger M. Anders, "The Rosenberg Case Revisited: The Greenglass Testimony and the Protection of Atomic Secrets," *American Historical Review,* April 1978, 388–400. Concerning the estimated size, efficiency, and nature of the first Soviet atomic explosion, see "Estimates of the Effects of the Soviet Possession . . . ," April 6, 1950, ORE 91-49, "CIA" Box, National Archives.

30. "Effect of Russian Possession of an Atomic Bomb on Western Union Strategy and Defense Planning," October 17, 1949, "Western Europe" Series, (3-12-48), Sec. 32, USJCS Records.

31. Ibid. An addendum to SAC's "Emergency War Plan 1–49" after the Soviet atomic

test noted that the air force would have the additional mission of "retardation of Soviet advances in Western Eurasia." Untitled memorandum, November 4, 1949, folder 3, Box 1, "Recently Declassified Documents," USJCS Records.

32. The report by the army chief of staff to the joint chiefs concluded ". . . no over all U.S. intelligence estimate based on these conditions has been prepared. . . . No agreed U.S. concept of defense against atomic attack exists." "Estimates of Military Requirements . . . ," January 5, 1950, "Western Europe" Series, (3-12-48), Sec. 39, USJCS Records. Concerning the rethinking of U.S. defense plans by the joint chiefs in the wake of the Soviet bomb, see JCS History, II, 526.

33. The Russian bomb brought about the first detailed consideration of a Russian surprise nuclear attack upon the United States. See "Estimate of Soviet Union Capability for Surprise Attack," December 16, 1949, "U.S." Series, (12-14-48), Sec. 1, USJCS Records.

34. The updated version of Offtackle, dated December 19, 1949, is in "USSR" Series, (3-2-46), Sec. 28, USJCS Records. On changes in the plan, see also JCS History, II, 303; and "Estimate of Soviet Intentions and Capabilities—1950," January 10, 1950, "USSR" Series, (3-2-46), Sec. 45, USJCS Records.

35. Lilienthal, *Atomic Energy Years*, 615.

36. Concerning Acheson's position on the "Super," see "Memorandum . . . ," December 3, *FR:* 1949, I, 599–600. On other opinions in Washington regarding the hydrogen bomb, see *FR:* 1949, I, 569–617.

37. "Memorandum . . . ," December 19, *FR:* 1949, I, 610–11.

38. Concerning reaction in the administration to Kennan's January memorandum, see *FR:* 1950, I, 1–17.

39. "Memorandum . . . ," January 20, *FR:* 1950, I, 22–44. In a subsequent letter, Kennan pointed out a contradiction of American strategy when he wrote of the "unclarity in the councils of our Government as to the reasons why we were cultivating and holding these weapons. . . . The unclarity revolved around this question. Were we holding them only as a means of deterring other people from using them against us and retaliating against any such use of these weapons against us, or were we building them into our military establishment in such a way that we would indicate that we were going to be dependent upon them in any future war, and would have to use them, regardless of whether they were used against us first?" Kennan is cited in York, *Advisors*, 112. On his thinking at the time, see also Kennan, *Memoirs: 1925–1950*, 472–3; and *FR:* 1949, I, 585–6.

40. Letter, McMahon to Truman, November 21, *FR:* 1949, I, 588–95. The joint chiefs thought there were only four targets in the Soviet Union large enough to justify use of a hydrogen bomb. See Rosenberg, "American Atomic Strategy and the Hydrogen Bomb Decision," 83; and JCS History, II, 555, USJCS Records. One reason given by the joint chiefs for the need to increase atomic-bomb production was for "counter atomic offensive purposes, [since] the United States can well afford to expend several times the number of bombs in the Soviet stockpile to counter atomic attacks against the United States if such targets present themselves." See "Implications of the Accelerated Atomic Energy Program," October 28, 1949, folder 3, Box 1, "Recently Declassified Documents," USJCS Records.

41. On the viewpoint of the joint chiefs, see "The United States Military Position . . . ," November 23, *FR:* 1949, I, 595–6; Lilienthal, *Atomic Energy Years*, 580–1; Hewlett and Duncan, *Atomic Shield*, 393–9; and "Memorandum . . . ," January 13, *FR:* 1950, I, 503–11.

42. Erskine, "The Polls . . . ," *Public Opinion Quarterly*, 177. The super-bomb became

a topic of public discussion after Colorado Senator Edwin Johnson inadvertently revealed the secret administration debate on the weapon in a television broadcast of *Meet the Press.* Concerning the furor generated by Johnson's slip, see *Washington Post,* November 19, 1949.

43. When Acheson expressed "violent opposition" to the senators' suggestion, an aide asked the latter if they "honestly believed" the American public would sanction an unprovoked attack upon Russia: "I was greeted with the retort that they both felt strongly that as far as their own constituency were concerned, that they would back any such move to the hilt." "Memorandum . . . ," January 26, *FR:* 1950, I, 140–1. Matthews' speech is cited in Alfred Vagts, *Defense and Diplomacy* (New York, 1956), 329–33. Concerning the consideration of preventive war in the policy review, see "Study of War in the Atomic Age," February 15, 1950, "Atomic" Series, (8-15-45), Sec. 18, USJCS Records. The sentiments of Alsop and Anderson were noted by Paul Nitze. Interview, October 1979, Washington, D.C. LeMay, *Mission with LeMay,* 481. The Soviet history text is *Russia and the United States: U.S.-Soviet Relations from the Soviet Point of View* (Chicago, 1979), by Nikolai V. Sivachev and Nikolai N. Yakovlev.

44. "Memorandum . . . ," January 19, *FR:* 1950, I, 511–12. Ayers diary, January 21, 1950, HSTL.

45. Among the scientists' arguments against the "Super" was that the Russians might also soon develop a hydrogen bomb through espionage and the monitoring of U.S. super-bomb tests. Concerning this argument as it was made during the administration debate, see JCS History, II, 552–3. Physicist Herbert York suggests that the scientists' concern with disclosure by testing was justified. See York, *Advisors,* 94–109.

46. Concerning the January 31 meeting, see Acheson, *Present at the Creation,* 346–7; and Hewlett and Duncan, *Atomic Shield,* 406–9. Some in the administration besides Kennan urged that a negotiated settlement be offered the Russians in an effort to stop the nuclear arms race before the United States proceeded with the hydrogen bomb. Several of these new proponents of a direct approach, however, had in mind an ultimatum to the Soviet Union to forswear super-bombs or be attacked by the United States. Acheson in particular feared that a direct approach would now be used as a "blind." See JCS History, II, 542–4, USJCS Records. Lilienthal was either unaware or unapproving of Kennan's lengthy treatise calling for a review of strategy and policy concerning the bomb: "Kennan's method of presenting his ideas was not mine." Interview with David Lilienthal, February 1979, Princeton, N.J.

47. Lilienthal, *Atomic Energy Years,* 633. The Z Committee's report to the President is in *FR:* 1950, I, 513–23. Interview with Gordon Arneson, October 1979, Washington, D.C. Many years later Lilienthal explained that he had wanted to impress upon Truman the irreversible nature of a decision for the "Super": "I was holding over the possible verdict of history." He also thought that "if it hadn't been for Strauss," Truman might have listened to the arguments against the super-bomb. Interview, February 1979, Princeton, N.J.

48. Ayers diary, January 31, 1949, HSTL. The President's announcement of his decision on the super-bomb is in *FR:* 1950, I, 141–2.

49. Ayers diary, January 31, 1949, HSTL.

50. Concerning the Hiss case, see *New York Times,* January 28, February 22, and March 6–11, 1949; Allen Weinstein, *Perjury: The Hiss-Chambers Case* (New York, 1978); John C. Smith, *Alger Hiss: The True Story* (New York, 1976); and Victor Navasky, "The Case Not Proved Against Alger Hiss," *Nation,* April 8, 1978.

51. Joint Committee on Atomic Energy, *Soviet Atomic Espionage*, 14, 173–4.
52. See "Foocase," HQ 65–58805, (16-2-50), Files 4 and 6, Federal Bureau of Investigation. Concerning doubts that Fuchs contributed much of value to the Russian atomic-bomb project, see "Record of the Meeting . . . ," February 27, *FR:* 1950, I, 168–75; and York, *Advisors,* 37.
53. "Foocase," File 4, "1975 Series."
54. Untitled memorandum, September 23, *FR:* 1949, I, 537–8. Joint Committee on Atomic Energy, *Soviet Atomic Espionage,* 12. Concerning Fuchs and Maclean at the 1947 conference, see Philby, Burgess, and Maclean case, Bufile 100-374183, Secs. 3, 4, "Referrals," Federal Bureau of Investigation. Contrary to the claim made in Allen Weinstein's detailed and intriguing study of the Hiss case, Hiss had no access to substantive information on atomic energy.
55. Upon learning of the Fuchs case, Defense Secretary Louis Johnson tried to force the administration into abrogating the *modus vivendi* with the British. While unsuccessful in this, he did manage to end U.S. participation in the work of the Combined Development Agency. The Soviet atomic bomb had shown, in any case, that the agency had failed to maintain a preclusive monopoly of atomic raw materials. Concerning the end of Anglo-American cooperation and the impact of the Fuchs case, see Hewlett and Duncan, *Atomic Shield,* 312–14; and Gowing, *Independence and Deterrence,* 138–40. Even a year later Truman felt the issue of Anglo-American cooperation on atomic energy to be still so sensitive that he refused Prime Minister Winston Churchill's request to make the agreements public. See letter, Churchill to Truman, February 12, 1951, and Truman's reply of February 16, in "NSC Atomic Weapons Stockpile" folder, Box 202, PSF, HSTL.
56. JCS History, II, 537, USJCS Records.
57. Untitled Joint Intelligence Committee study, February 16, 1950, "Western Europe" Series, (3-12-48), Sec. 42. Concerning other reassessments of U.S. military strategy at this time, see "A Study of War in the Atomic Age," February 15, 1950, "Atomic" Series, (8-15-45), Sec. 18, USJCS Records; and "Implications of Soviet Possession of Atomic Weapons," February 21, 1950, "U.S." Series, (5-23-46), Sec. 4, USJCS Records. In the course of this rethinking, several contradictions of U.S. strategy became evident. The notion that the atomic bomb would no longer be a deterrent or an effective means of defense in Europe was contrary to the assumptions of a NATO report completed the year before. See "Strategic Concept for the Defense of the North Atlantic Area," December 1, *FR:* 1949, IV, 352–6. This document is also in Etzold and Gaddis, eds., *Containment,* 335–9.
58. Untitled Joint Intelligence Committee study, February 16, 1950.
59. "Basis for Estimating Maximum Soviet Capabilities for Atomic Warfare," February 20, 1950, "NSC Atomic Energy—Russia" folder, Box 201, PSF, HSTL.
60. "Estimate of the Effects of the Soviet Possession . . . ," April 6, 1950, ORE 91-49, Appendices A–D, Central Intelligence Agency.
61. The memorandum was written by MLC members Major General Kenneth Nichols and Brigadier General H. B. Loper. A civilian, Robert LeBaron, was appointed by Lilienthal in 1947 to head the committee. Interview with David Lilienthal, February 1979, Princeton, N.J.
62. Truman implied that the Russians might already have a hydrogen bomb in his announcement of the first Soviet atomic test. See *New York Times,* September 24, 1949.
63. Indicative of the turnabout in the joint chiefs' thinking is the fact that the earlier

debate concerning the likely effectiveness of an American atomic attack upon Russia was now replaced by a dispute over the damage that would be done by a Soviet nuclear attack upon the United States. "Implications of Soviet Possession of Atomic Weapons," February 21, 1950, "U.S." Series, (5-23-46), Sec. 4, USJCS Records.

64. On the change in Johnson's thinking at this time, see *FR:* 1950, I, 538–9, 541–2.

65. Concerning the "all-out" effort for the super-bomb, see "NSC Atomic Weapons—Thermonuclear" folder, Box 202, PSF, HSTL.

66. Concerning the origins of NSC-68, see the untitled State Department–Defense Department study and "A Report to the President," both of March 29, 1950, in "NSC-68" folder, "NSC" File, PSF, HSTL. On the review of U.S. policy at this time, see also *FR:* 1950, I, 126–234. There is substantial—and increasing—evidence that one result of this review was substantially to increase the CIA's covert operations in Russia and eastern Europe. See, for example, Thomas Powers, *The Man Who Kept the Secrets* (New York, 1979), 39–47.

67. "Memorandum . . . ," March 6, *FR:* 1950, I, 185–6.

68. Untitled memorandum, Johnson to Truman, April 5, 1950; and "Memorandum . . . ," Acheson to Truman, April 10, 1950, "NSC-68" folder, "NSC" file, PSF, HSTL. The approach of what would later be called the balance of terror was a point recognized in the CIA's February report on the implications of the Soviet bomb. Both this report and the joint chiefs' study, in fact, anticipated the "disengagement" argument that Kennan would put forward in the late 1950s as a solution to Soviet-American confrontation in Europe.

69. "A Report to the National Security Council . . . ," NSC-68, April 14, *FR:* 1950, I, 234–92. Excerpts of NSC-68 are also in Etzold and Gaddis, eds., *Containment*, 385–442.

70. "A Report to the National Security Council . . . ," NSC-68.

71. Acheson, *Present at the Creation*, 373–81. Concerning the anticipated costs of the plan, see also "NSC-68" folder, "NSC" File, PSF, HSTL; and JCS 2101/27, December 12, 1950, folder 1, Box 1, "Recently Declassified Documents," USJCS Records.

72. "The USSR and the Korean Invasion," June 28, 1950, Intelligence Memo 300, "CIA Reports" Box, USJCS Records. Concerning the National Security Council's reaction to the Korean invasion, see, for example, NSC-73, "The Position and Actions of the U.S. . . . ," July 1, 1950, "NSC" Box, USJCS Records.

73. Concerning the views of the joint chiefs on Korea, see NSC-76, "U.S. Courses of Action in the Event Soviet Forces Enter Korean Hostilities," July 21, 1950; and NSC-79, "U.S. and Allied War Objectives in the Event of Global War," August 25, 1950, in "NSC" Box, USJCS Records. On this point, see also JCS 2101/27, December 12, 1950, folder 1, Box 1, "Recently Declassified Documents," USJCS Records.

74. Truman is cited in Connelly's minutes on this meeting. See "1950" folder, Matthew Connelly MSS, HSTL.

75. The joint chiefs' latest emergency war plan, code-named Shakedown, assigned first priority in its targeting list to the Soviet Union's nuclear stockpile and atomic-bomb production facilities. Shakedown is included in "USSR" Series, (3-2-46), Sec. 18, USJCS Records.

76. NSC-68 was adopted at the sixty-eighth meeting of the National Security Council, on September 30, 1950. See NSC-68/4 of this date, "NSC" Box, USJCS Records. The influence of the Korean invasion upon U.S. military planning may be seen in NSC-68/3, December 8, 1950; and NSC-68/4, above.

77. Memorandum, Lay to National Security Council, December 15, 1950, "NSC" Box, USJCS Records.

78. "Status of the Soviet Atomic Energy Program," "Atomic Weapons" folder, "NSC" Box, USJCS Records.
79. Concerning consideration of the bomb's use, see Memorandum, Army Chief of Staff to Joint Strategic Survey Committee, December 3, 1950, folder 2, Box 1, "Recently Declassified Documents," and JCS History, III, Pt. 1, 372, USJCS Records. The military's reluctance to use the bomb in Korea is from JCS History, III, Pt. 2, v; and interview with Paul Nitze, October 1979, Washington, D.C. Regarding the military crisis caused by the Chinese intervention, see Hewlett and Duncan, *Atomic Shield*, 533–4; Gowing, *Independence and Deterrence*, 175–6, and Allen Whiting, *China Crosses the Yalu* (New York, 1960).
80. Hewlett and Duncan, *Atomic Shield*, 533. JCS History, III, Pt. 1, 349.
81. Concerning Attlee's meeting with Truman, see *Atomic Shield*, 532–3, and JCS History, III, Pt. 1, 376. At this conference Truman seemed on the verge of reestablishing close ties with the British on atomic energy. He proposed issuing a press statement, therefore, which told of his hope that the bomb would not be used again and "his promise to keep the Prime Minister informed of developments which might bring about any change in the situation." After the urgent importunings of advisers Arneson and Harriman, however, Truman changed the wording to read "desire" rather than "promise," while "any change" became simply "a change." Truman was similarly reminded by aides during a January 1952 meeting with British Prime Minister Churchill that the terms of the McMahon Act forbade the sort of renewed cooperation that Churchill had suggested and the President had then tentatively approved. It is likely that Truman in 1951–52, as earlier, simply didn't understand the implications of the commitment he almost made to the British. Interview with Gordon Arneson, October 1979, Washington, D.C.
82. Concerning Truman's decision to stockpile non-nuclear components of atomic bombs overseas and his consideration of the bomb's use in 1952, see Hewlett and Duncan, *Atomic Shield*, 522, 574; memoranda in "Atomic Weapons" folder, "NSC" Box, USJCS Records; and Truman journal, January 27, 1952, HSTL.
83. MacArthur's suggestions are noted in William Manchester's *American Caesar: Douglas MacArthur, 1880–1964* (Boston, 1978), 627.
84. NSC-100, "Recommended Policies and Actions in Light of the Grave World Situation," January 11, 1951, "NSC" Box, USJCS Records.
85. A comprehensive updating of NSC-68 was drafted at the end of the Truman administration, but never received the President's approval and was abandoned by the incoming Eisenhower administration. See NSC-141, "Reexamination of United States Programs for National Security," January 19, 1953, "NSC" Box, USJCS Records; and Truman journal, HSTL.
86. In summer 1953 a special advisory group of the new administration conducted its own survey of American cold war strategy—the so-called Solarium study—and recommended that the containment strategy of NSC-68 be continued. Concerning the origins of the Solarium study and its result, see the interviews with George F. Kennan and Robert C. Sprague, Dulles Oral History Project, Dulles MSS. On the joint chiefs' renewed thinking about use of the bomb, see JCS History, III, Pt. 2, v–vi, USJCS Records. Regarding the "New Look," see, for example, Huntington, *Common Defense*, 64–87.
87. Concerning Dulles' early thinking about military policy, see untitled memos, July 1 and November 30, 1950, "Notes and Memos" file, Box 2, Dulles MSS. On Dulles' change of heart concerning the strategy of massive retaliation and the "New Look," see George Kennan and Maxwell Taylor interviews, Dulles Oral History Project,

Dulles MSS. Regarding the original notion of "liberation," see "Interview . . . ," "1949" folder, "Speeches and Articles" File, Dulles MSS. The Eisenhower administration proved to be no keener than Truman's on the idea of reviving Anglo-American cooperation on atomic energy. When Foreign Minister Anthony Eden in 1953 once again importuned the United States for a veto on the use of the bomb, he was curtly told by Dulles that such a concession was impossible, since if it became known it would lead to Eisenhower's impeachment. Interview with Gordon Arneson, October 1979, Washington, D.C.

Epilogue

1. *New York Herald Tribune,* October 2, 1945.
2. Lippmann to Barnard, February 8, 1950, Chester Barnard File, Oppenheimer MSS.
3. Barnard to Lippmann, February 10, 1950, ibid.
4. Although Bush and Conant had each predicted in 1944 that it would take the Russians only from three to five years to build an atomic bomb, by 1946 both had come to endorse Groves' twenty-year estimate, Conant on the grounds that Russia lacked the uranium and technological base, and Bush on the grounds that a Soviet "crash effort" on the bomb would be "uneconomic." Bush's conversion to the longer estimate is noted in his testimony before the Senate, excerpts from which are in *New York Times,* December 12, 1945. Conant's second thoughts are in his October 1946 speech before the National War College. See "The Age of the Superblitz," "Atomic Energy Safe File 2," Patterson File, MEDR. Just the year before, Conant had dismissed the idea of controlling the spread of the atomic bomb by a monopoly of atomic raw materials. See Conant to Grenville Clark, October 8, 1945, Vannevar Bush MSS.
5. Leo Szilard, "Reminiscences," Fleming and Bailyn, eds., *Perspectives in American History,* II, 140–1.
6. Erskine, "The Polls . . . ," *Public Opinion Quarterly,* Summer 1963, 5.
7. Robert Jay Lifton, *The Broken Connection* (New York, 1979).
8. A recent and controversial book on Russian espionage by British journalist Andrew Boyle contends that Maclean and another, as-yet-unnamed Soviet spy had access to an "impressive array of detailed and carefully selected material on the nuclear thinking, planning and stockpiling of the Americans and their allies," including the number of bombs in the U.S. atomic arsenal. There is little evidence for Boyle's claim. An FBI report made one month after Maclean's defection in May 1951 noted that from January 1947 to August 1948 "he had knowledge of the transaction of the Combined Development Agency and of arrangements for securing raw materials and estimates of future production which were made at that time." But the AEC's damage assessment of the following month concluded that such an estimate would have been rendered meaningless by the rapid increase in the size of the American atomic arsenal after the spring of 1948. See untitled documents of June 19 and July 10, 1951 in Bufile 100-374183, Secs. 3 and 4, Serial 1-175, "Philby, Burgess, and Maclean Case," Federal Bureau of Investigation; and Andrew Boyle, *The Fourth Man* (New York, 1979), 295.
9. U.S. Atomic Energy Commission, *In the Matter of J. Robert Oppenheimer,* 175–6. Concerning the Russian atomic-bomb project, see also Chapter 15, fn. 29. On suspicion of Oppenheimer for failing to "enthuse" over the super-bomb, see the untitled

memorandum, Lieutenant Colonel Edwin Black to Vannevar Bush, November 29, 1949, "Atomic" Series, (8-15-45), Sec. 18, USJCS Records. Former War Department and AEC staffer Gordon Arneson has noted that Oppenheimer was placed under FBI surveillance, at Groves' request, in late 1942 or early 1943. Interview, October 1979, Washington, D.C.

10. Letter, Truman to Dean, August 26, 1952, "AEC—Gordon Dean" folder, Box 112, PSF, HSTL. Truman once told Bush that he liked Oppenheimer "very much," but in 1946 he characterized the latter as a "crybaby scientist," and he never publicly went to Oppenheimer's defense. Truman's remark to Bush is in a letter of August 2, 1946, "Atomic Energy Control Commission, UN" folder, Box 112, PSF, HSTL. See also Truman to Acheson, May 3, 1946, Box 201, PSF, HSTL. Concerning Oppenheimer as a symbol, see Allen Weinstein, "The Symbolism of Subversion: Notes on Some Cold War Icons," *American Studies*, October 1972, 165–79.

BIBLIOGRAPHY

The bibliography contains the major published and unpublished sources that were useful in the writing of this book. Some additional sources, such as articles in periodicals and newspaper accounts, are not listed here but are to be found in notes to the text.

MANUSCRIPT COLLECTIONS

Clemson University, Clemson, S.C.
Walter Brown
James F. Byrnes

Federal Bureau of Investigation, Washington, D.C.
"Foocase" Bufile HQ 65-58805, 1975 Series, Files 4–6
"Philby, Burgess, and Maclean Case" Bufile HQ 100-374183, "Referrals" and
    Serial 1–175, Secs. 3 and 4

Library of Congress, Washington, D.C.
Vannevar Bush
Tom Connally
Joseph E. Davies
Herbert Feis
William Leahy
J. Robert Oppenheimer
Robert Patterson

Modern Military Branch, National Archives, Washington, D.C.
Central Intelligence Agency Memoranda and Reports
Diaries of General Leslie Groves
Diaries of William Leahy
Manhattan Engineer District History
Manhattan Engineer District Records
National Security Council Minutes and Reports
Plans and Operations of the Army General Staff
Record Group 341, Records of the U.S. Air Force
Record Group 374, Records of the Armed Forces Special Weapons Project
U.S. Joint Chiefs of Staff History
U.S. Joint Chiefs of Staff Records

Princeton University, Princeton, N.J.
Bernard M. Baruch
John Foster Dulles
Ferdinand Eberstadt
James V. Forrestal
David E. Lilienthal

Public Records Office, London, England
Hugh Dalton Diary
Ian Jacob Diary
(I am grateful to Professor James Gormly for permission to quote from the
    Dalton and Jacob diaries.)

Harry S Truman Library Institute, Independence, Mo.
Eben Ayers
James F. Byrnes
Matthew Connelly
Leslie Groves
William Leahy
Frank McNaughton
"Official File"
Fredrick Osborn
President's Secretary's File
Samuel Rosenman
Harold Smith
Harry S Truman, Private Journal

U.S. Department of Energy, Washington, D.C.
Chart, "Combined Strategic Offense and Defense Warheads"
"Selected Atomic Energy Commission Documents"

U.S. Department of State, Washington, D.C.
Records of the United Nations Atomic Energy Commission
"Selected File on Atomic Energy, 1945–1947"

Yale University, New Haven, Conn.
Hanson Baldwin
Henry L. Stimson

INTERVIEWS

Gordon Arneson, Washington, D.C., October 1979
Walter Brown, Columbia, S.C., November 1979
Benjamin Cohen, Washington, D.C., May 1972
David Lilienthal, Princeton, N.J., February 1979
Paul Nitze, Washington, D.C., October 1979

BOOKS, ARTICLES, DOCUMENTS, AND DISSERTATIONS

Acheson, Dean. *Present at the Creation: My Years in the State Department.* New York, 1969.
————. *Sketches from Life of Men I Have Known.* New York, 1961.
Albion, Robert G., and Robert H. Connery. *Forrestal and the Navy.* New York, 1962.
Allen, James S. *Atomic Imperialism.* New York, 1952.
Alperovitz, Gar. *Atomic Diplomacy: Hiroshima and Potsdam.* New York, 1965.
————. *Cold War Essays.* New York, 1970.
Anders, Roger M. "The Rosenberg Case Revisited: The Greenglass Testimony and the Protection of Atomic Secrets," *American Historical Review,* April 1978.
Anderson, David A. *Strategic Air Command.* New York, 1976.
Arnold, Henry H. *Global Mission.* New York, 1949.
Attlee, Clement. *As It Happened.* London, 1954.
Barnet, Richard. *Who Wants Disarmament?* Boston, 1960.
Baruch, Bernard M. *Baruch: The Public Years.* New York, 1960.
Batchelder, Robert C. *The Irreversible Decision.* New York, 1962.
Bechhoefer, Bernard. *Postwar Negotiations for Arms Control.* Washington, D.C., 1961.
Berding, Arthur H. *Dulles on Diplomacy.* New York, 1965.
Bernstein, Barton J. "The Atomic Bomb and American Foreign Policy, 1941–1945: An Historiographical Controversy," *Peace and Change,* Spring 1974.
————. "The Perils and Politics of Surrender: Ending the War with Japan and Avoiding the Third Atomic Bomb," *Pacific Historical Review,* February 1977.
————, ed. *The Atomic Bomb: The Critical Issues.* Boston, 1976.
————, ed. *Politics and Policies of the Truman Administration.* New York, 1970.
————, and Allen Matusow, eds. *The Truman Administration: A Documentary History.* New York, 1966.
Bertin, Leonard. *Atom Harvest: A British View of Atomic Energy.* London, 1955.
Biörklund, Edward. *International Atomic Policy During a Decade.* London, 1955.
Blackett, P. M. S. *Atomic Weapons and East-West Relations.* London, 1956.
————. *Fear, War and the Bomb.* New York, 1949 (originally published as *Military and Political Consequences of Atomic Energy.* London, 1948).
Blum, John Morton. *The Price of Vision: The Diary of Henry A. Wallace.* Boston, 1973.
————. *V Was for Victory: Politics and American Culture During World War II.* New York, 1976.
Bohlen, Charles. *Promises to Keep: My Years in Public Life, 1941–1969.* New York, 1971.

————. *Witness to History.* New York, 1973.

Boyle, Andrew. *The Fourth Man.* New York, 1979.

Brodie, Bernard. "Atom Bomb as Policy Maker," *Foreign Affairs,* October 1949.

————. "The Development of Nuclear Strategy," ACIS Working Paper No. 11, UCLA, February 1978.

————. *Strategy in the Missile Age.* Princeton, N.J., 1959.

————, ed. *The Absolute Weapon: Atomic Power and World Order.* New York, 1946.

Brown, Anthony C., ed. *Dropshot: The American Plan for World War III with Russia in 1957.* New York, 1978.

————, and Charles B. MacDonald, eds. *The Secret History of the Atomic Bomb.* New York, 1977.

Bush, Vannevar. *Endless Horizons.* New York, 1946.

————. *Modern Arms and Free Men.* New York, 1949.

————. *Pieces of the Action.* New York, 1970.

Butow, R. J. C. *Japan's Decision to Surrender.* Stanford, Calif., 1954.

Byrnes, James F. *All in One Lifetime.* New York, 1958.

————. *Speaking Frankly.* New York, 1947.

Canadian Government. *The Report of the Royal Commission to Investigate Disclosures of Secret and Confidential Information to Unauthorized Persons.* Ottawa, 1946.

Cantril, Harley. *Public Opinion, 1935–1946.* Princeton, N.J., 1951.

Caraley, Demetrious. *The Politics of Military Unification.* New York, 1966.

Churchill, Winston. *The Hinge of Fate.* New York, 1950.

Clemens, Diane S. *Yalta.* New York, 1970.

Coit, Margaret. *Mr. Baruch.* Boston, 1947.

Compton, Arthur H. *Atomic Quest.* New York, 1956.

Conant, James B. *My Several Lives.* New York, 1970.

Condit, Kenneth W. *The History of the Joint Chiefs of Staff: The Joint Chiefs of Staff and National Policy.* Vols. I–II. Wilmingon, Del., 1979.

Connally, Tom, with Alfred Steinberg. *My Name Is Tom Connally.* New York, 1954.

Cottrell, Lawrence, and Sylvia Eberhardt. *American Opinion on World Affairs in the Atomic Age.* Princeton, N.J., 1948.

Curry, George. *American Secretaries of State: James F. Byrnes.* New York, 1965.

Dalton, Hugh. *High Tide and After: Memoirs.* New York, 1962.

Daniels, Jonathan. *Man of Independence.* New York, 1950.

Davis, Lynn E. *The Cold War Begins: Soviet-American Conflict over Eastern Europe.* Princeton, N.J., 1974.

Davis, Nuell Pharr. *Lawrence and Oppenheimer.* New York, 1968.

Davis, Vincent. *Postwar Defense Policy and the U.S. Navy, 1943–1946.* Chapel Hill, N.C., 1966.

Davison, W. Phillips. *The Berlin Blockade.* Princeton, N.J., 1958.

de Seversky, Alexander. *Victory Through Air Power.* New York, 1942.

Donovan, Robert. *Conflict and Crisis: The Presidency of Harry S Truman, 1945–48.* New York, 1977.

Druks, Herbert. *Harry S. Truman and the Russians, 1945–1953.* New York, 1966.

Dulles, John Foster. "Thoughts on Soviet Foreign Policy and What to Do About It," *Life,* June 3, 10, 1946.

Earle, Edward M., ed. *Makers of Modern Strategy.* Princeton, N.J., 1943.

Erskine, Helen G. "The Polls: Atomic Weapons and Nuclear Energy," *Public Opinion Quarterly,* Summer 1963.

Etzold, Thomas H., and John Lewis Gaddis, eds. *Containment: Documents on American Policy and Strategy, 1945–1950.* New York, 1978.

Feis, Herbert. *The Atomic Bomb and the End of World War II.* Princeton, N.J., 1966.

———. *Between War and Peace: The Potsdam Conference.* Princeton, N.J., 1960.

———. *From Trust to Terror: The Onset of the Cold War, 1945–1950.* New York, 1970.

Fleming, Donald, and Bernard Bailyn, eds. *Perspectives in American History,* II, 1963.

Freeland, Richard M. *The Truman Doctrine and the Origins of McCarthyism.* New York, 1972.

Gaddis, John Lewis. *The United States and the Origins of the Cold War, 1941–47.* New York, 1972.

Gardner, Lloyd C. *Architects of Illusion: Men and Ideas in American Foreign Policy, 1941–1949.* Chicago, 1970.

George, Alexander, and Richard Smoke. *Deterrence in American Foreign Policy: Theory and Practice.* New York, 1974.

Gilpin, Robert. *American Scientists and Nuclear Weapons Policy.* Princeton, N.J., 1962.

Goldman, Eric. *The Crucial Decade and After.* New York, 1960.

Goldschmidt, Bertrand. *The Atomic Adventure. New York, 1964.*

Goodman, Walter. *The Committee: The Extraordinary Career of the House Committee on Un-American Activities.* New York, 1968.

Goudsmit, Samuel A. *Alsos.* London, 1947.

Gouzenko, Igor. *This Was My Choice.* New York, 1947.

Gowing, Margaret. *Britain and Atomic Energy, 1939–1945.* London, 1964.

———. *Independence and Deterrence, 1945–1952.* London, 1974.

Graebner, Norman A., ed. *An Uncertain Tradition: American Secretaries of State.* New York, 1961.

Grodzins, M., and E. Rabinowitch, eds. *The Atomic Age: Scientists in National and World Affairs.* New York, 1963.

Groueff, Stephane. *Manhattan Project: The Untold Story of the Making of the Atom Bomb.* New York, 1967.

Groves, Leslie. "The Atom-General Answers His Critics," *Saturday Evening Post,* June 19, 1948.

———. *Now It Can Be Told.* New York, 1962.

Hamby, Alonzo L. *Beyond the New Deal: Harry S. Truman and American Liberalism.* New York, 1973.

Hamilton, Michael, ed. *Anticipating Catastrophe: A Study in Future Nuclear Weapons Policy.* Grand Rapids, Mich., 1977.

Haskins, C. P. "Atomic Energy and American Foreign Policy," *Foreign Affairs,* July 1947.

Hentoff, Nathan, ed. *The Essays of A. J. Muste.* New York, 1967.

Herken, Gregg F. "American Diplomacy and the Atomic Bomb, 1945–1947." Ph.D. dissertation, Princeton University, 1974.

————. " 'A Most Deadly Illusion': The Atomic Secret and American Nuclear Weapons Policy, 1945–1950," *Pacific Historical Review,* February 1980.

Hersey, John. *Hiroshima.* New York, 1946.

Hewlett, Richard G., and Oscar G. Anderson. *The New World: A History of the United States Atomic Energy Commission,* I, 1939/1946. University Park, Pa., 1962.

————, and Francis Duncan. *Atomic Shield: A History of the United States Atomic Energy Commission,* II, 1947/1952. University Park, Pa., 1969.

Huntington, Samuel. *The Common Defense: Strategic Programs in National Politics.* New York, 1961.

Jones, Joseph. *The Fifteen Weeks.* New York, 1964.

Jungk, Robert. *Brighter Than a Thousand Suns.* New York, 1956.

Kennan, George F. *Memoirs, 1925–1950.* New York, 1967.

————. *Memoirs, 1950–1963.* Boston, 1972.

————. *Russia, the Atom, and the West.* New York, 1958.

Kirkendal, Richard, ed. *The Truman Period as a Research Field: A Reappraisal, 1972.* Columbia, Mo., 1978.

Knebel, Fletcher, and Charles W. Bailey. *No High Ground.* New York, 1960.

Kolko, Gabriel. *The Politics of War.* New York, 1968.

————, and Joyce Kolko. *The Limits of Power.* New York, 1972.

Korb, L. C. *The Joint Chiefs of Staff.* New York, 1978.

Kramish, Arnold. *Atomic Energy in the Soviet Union.* Stanford, Calif., 1959.

————. Review of I. N. Golovin's *I. V. Kurchatov, Science,* August 25, 1967.

Krock, Arthur. *Memoirs: Sixty Years on the Firing Line.* New York, 1968.

LaFeber, Walter. *America, Russia and the Cold War.* New York, 1976.

Lang, Daniel. "Seven Men on a Problem," *New Yorker,* August 17, 1946.

Leahy, William D. *I Was There.* New York, 1950.

LeMay, Curtis, with MacKinlay Kantor. *Mission with LeMay.* New York, 1965.

Lieberman, Joseph I. *The Scorpion and the Tarantula: The Struggle to Control Atomic Weapons, 1945–9.* Boston, 1970.

Lilienthal, David E. *The Journals of David E. Lilienthal: The Atomic Energy Years, 1945–1950.* New York, 1964.

Lippmann, Walter. *The Cold War.* New York, 1947.

MacIssac, David. "The United States Strategic Bombing Survey," Ph.D. dissertation, Duke University, 1969.

Maddox, Richard. *The New Left and the Origins of the Cold War.* Princeton, N.J., 1973.

Manchester, William. *American Caesar: Douglas MacArthur, 1880–1964.* Boston, 1978.

Marx, J. C. *Seven Hours to Zero.* New York, 1967.

Messer, Robert. "The Making of a Cold Warrior: James F. Byrnes and American-Soviet Relations, 1945–46," Ph.D. dissertation, University of California, Berkeley, 1975.

Miller, Merle. *Plain Speaking: An Oral Biography of Harry S Truman.* New York, 1973.

Millis, Walter. *Arms and Men.* New York, 1956.

———. *Arms and the State.* New York, 1958.

———, ed. *The Forrestal Diaries.* New York, 1951.

Morison, Elting E. *Turmoil and Tradition: A Study of the Life and Times of Henry L. Stimson.* Boston, 1960.

Morray, James P. *From Yalta to Disarmament.* New York, 1961.

Morse, Philip. *In at the Beginning.* London, 1978.

Mumford, Lewis. *Values for Survival.* New York, 1946.

Navasky, Victor. "The Case Not Proved Against Alger Hiss," *Nation,* April 8, 1978.

Newman, Bernard. *Soviet Atomic Spies.* London, 1952.

Newman, James R., and Brian Miller. *The Control of Atomic Energy.* New York, 1948.

Nicolson, Harold. *Diaries and Letters, 1945–62.* London, 1971.

Nogee, Joseph. *Soviet Policy Toward International Control of Atomic Energy.* South Bend, Ind., 1961.

Oppenheimer, J. Robert. *The Open Mind.* New York, 1955.

Pacific War Research Society. *The Day Man Lost Hiroshima.* Palo Alto, Calif., 1968.

Paterson, Thomas G. "Potsdam, the Atomic Bomb, and the Cold War: A Discussion with James F. Byrnes," *Pacific Historical Review,* May 1972.

———. *Soviet-American Confrontation.* Baltimore, Md., 1973.

———, ed. *Cold War Critics.* Chicago, 1971.

Phillips, Cabell. *The Truman Presidency.* New York, 1966.

Pickersgill, J. W., and D. F. Forster. *The Mackenzie King Record: 1944–1946.* 2 vols. Toronto, 1968, 1970.

Powers, Thomas. *The Man Who Kept the Secrets.* New York, 1979.

President's Air Policy Commission. *Survival in the Air Age.* Washington, D.C., 1948.

Public Papers of the President: Harry S Truman, 1945–1953. Washington, D.C., 1961, 1963.

Quester, George. *Deterrence Before Hiroshima.* Boston, 1968.

———. *Nuclear Diplomacy: The First Twenty-five Years.* Boston, 1970.

Reuben, William A. *The Atom Spy Hoax.* New York, 1955.

Rogow, Arnold. *James Forrestal: A Study of Personality, Politics, and Policy.* New York, 1963.

Rose, Lisle A. *After Yalta: America and the Origins of the Cold War.* New York, 1973.

Rosecrance, Richard N. *Defense of the Realm.* New York, 1976.

Rosenberg, David. "American Atomic Strategy and the Hydrogen Bomb Decision," *Journal of American History,* May 1979.

Rosenbloom, Morris V. *Peace Through Strength.* New York, 1953.

Santalov, A. A. *The Imperialist Struggle for Raw Materials Resources* (title in Russian). Moscow, 1955.

Schapsmeier, Edward and Frederick. *Prophet in Politics.* Iowa City, Iowa, 1970.

Schilling, Warner; Paul Y. Hammond; and Glenn H. Snyder. *Strategy, Politics, and Defense Budgets.* New York, 1962.

Schnabel, James F., and Robert J. Watson. *The History of the Joint Chiefs of*

Staff: The Joint Chiefs of Staff and National Policy. Vol. III, Pts. 1–2. Wilmington, Del., 1979.

Shepley, James R., and Clay Blair, Jr. *The Hydrogen Bomb*. New York, 1954.

Sherry, Michael. *Preparing for the Next War: American Plans for Postwar Defense, 1941–1945*. New Haven, Conn., 1977.

Sherwin, Martin J. "The Atomic Bomb and the Origins of the Cold War: U.S. Atomic-Energy Policy and Diplomacy, 1941–45," *American Historical Review*, October 1973.

———. "The Atomic Bomb, Scientists, and American Diplomacy During the Second World War," Ph.D. dissertation, UCLA, 1971.

———. *A World Destroyed: The Atomic Bomb and the Grand Alliance*. New York, 1975.

Shurcliff, William A. *Bombs at Bikini: The Official Report of Operations Crossroads*. New York, 1947.

Sivachev, Nikolai V., and Nikolai N. Yakovlev. *Russia and the United States: U.S.-Soviet Relations from the Soviet Point of View*. Chicago, 1979.

Smith, Alice Kimball. *A Peril and a Hope: The Scientists' Movement in America, 1945–1947*. Chicago, 1965.

Smith, F. W. F. *Halifax: The Life of Lord Halifax*. Boston, 1966.

Smith, Jean Edward, ed. *The Papers of General Lucius D. Clay: Germany 1945–49*. Bloomington, Ind., 1974.

Smith, Perry M. *The Air Force Plans for Peace, 1943–1945*. Baltimore, Md., 1970.

Smyth, Henry D. *Atomic Energy for Military Purposes: The Official Report on the Development of the Atomic Bomb*. Princeton, N.J., 1945.

Social Science Research Council. *Public Reaction to the Atomic Bomb and World Affairs*. Ithaca, N.Y., 1947.

Spanier, John W., and Joseph Nogee. *The Politics of Disarmament*. New York, 1962.

Stein, Harold, ed. *American Civil-Military Decisions*. Tuscaloosa, Ala., 1963.

Steinberg, Alfred. *The Man from Missouri*. New York, 1962.

Stimson, Henry L. "The Bomb and the Opportunity," *Harper's*, March 1946.

———. "The Decision to Use the Atomic Bomb," *Harper's*, February 1947.

———, and McGeorge Bundy. *On Active Service in Peace and War*. New York, 1947.

Strauss, Lewis. *Men and Decisions*. New York, 1962.

Talbott, Strobe, ed. and trans. *Khrushchev Remembers*. Boston, 1970.

———, ed. and trans. *Khrushchev Remembers: The Last Testament*. New York, 1976.

Theoharis, Athan. *Seeds of Repression*. Chicago, 1971.

Thomas, Gordon, and Max M. Witts. *Enola Gay*. New York, 1977.

Truman, Harry S. *Year of Decisions: Memoirs*. New York, 1955.

———. *Years of Trial and Hope: Memoirs*. New York, 1956.

Ulam, Adam B. *The Rivals: America and Russia After World War II*. New York, 1971.

U.S. Atomic Energy Commission. *In the Matter of J. Robert Oppenheimer*. Washington, D.C., 1954.

U.S. Congress. House Committee on Foreign Affairs. *The Baruch Plan: U.S. Diplomacy Enters the Nuclear Age*. Washington, D.C., 1972.

———. House Committee on Military Affairs. *Hearings Before the House*

Committee on Military Affairs on HR 515. 79th Congress, 1st Session. Washington, D.C., 1945.

———. House Un-American Activities Committee. *Hearings and Reports of the House Un-American Activities Committee.* Washington, D.C., 1945–51.

———. HUAC. *Report on Soviet Espionage Activities in Connection with the Atom Bomb.* 80th Congress, 2nd Session. Washington, D.C., 1948.

———. Joint Committee on Atomic Energy. *Hearings and Reports of the Joint Committee on Atomic Energy.* Washington, D.C., 1945–51.

———. JCAE. *Soviet Atomic Espionage.* 82nd Congress, 1st Session. Washington, D.C., 1951.

U.S. Department of Defense. *Selected Manpower Statistics.* Washington, D.C., 1971.

U.S. Department of State. *Documents on Disarmament, 1945–59.* Washington, D.C., 1960.

———. *Foreign Relations of the United States, 1945–1950.* Washington, D.C., 1967–78.

———. *International Control of Atomic Energy: Growth of a Policy.* Washington, D.C., 1946.

———. *International Control of Atomic Energy: Policy at the Crossroads.* Washington, D.C., 1948.

U.S. Strategic Bombing Survey. *The Effects of Strategic Bombing.* Washington, D.C., 1946.

Vagts, Alfred. *Defense and Diplomacy.* New York, 1956.

Vandenberg, Arthur H., Jr., ed. *The Private Papers of Senator Vandenberg.* Boston, 1952.

Walton, Richard J. *Henry Wallace, Harry Truman, and the Cold War.* New York, 1976.

Ward, Patricia Dawson. *The Threat of Peace.* Kent, Ohio, 1979.

Weinstein, Allen. "The Symbolism of Subversion: Notes on Some Cold War Icons," *American Studies,* October 1972.

———. *Perjury: The Hiss-Chambers Case.* New York, 1978.

Welch, William. *American Images of Soviet Foreign Policy.* New Haven, Conn., 1970.

Wheeler-Bennett, John W. *John Anderson, Viscount Waverly.* New York, 1962.

Whiting, Allen. *China Crosses the Yalu.* New York, 1960.

Williams, Francis, with Clement Attlee. *A Prime Minister Remembers: The War and Post-War Memoirs of the Rt. Hon. Earl Attlee.* London, 1962.

Williams, William A. *The Tragedy of American Diplomacy.* New York, 1962.

Yavendetti, Michael. "John Hersey and the American Conscience: The Reception of *Hiroshima,*" *Pacific Historical Review,* October 1972.

Yergin, Daniel. "The Rise of the National Security State: Anti-Communism and the Origins of the Cold War," Ph.D. dissertation, Cambridge University, 1974.

———. *Shattered Peace: The Origins of the Cold War and the National Security State.* Boston, 1977.

York, Herbert. *The Advisors: Oppenheimer, Teller, and the Superbomb.* San Francisco, Calif., 1976.

Zhukov, Georgei K. *Memoirs of Marshal Zhukov.* New York, 1971.

INDEX

Absolute Weapon, The* (Brodie), 222
Acheson, Dean, 30–35, 39, 62n., 70,
86, 87, 97, 300, 318–19, 329, 351;
and Baruch plan, 168–70, 174, 177,
186, 264, *see also* Acheson-Lilienthal
Report; as chairman of Secretary of
State's Committee, 153–61, 162n.,
163, 165; and hydrogen bomb, 320,
396; and Kennan's paper on
H-bomb, 320; memorandum of, to
Byrnes in Moscow, 80–81, 87;
opposition to May-Johnson bill,
117–19; and Quebec Agreement,
abandonment of, 145 and n., 147;
on Truman's committee on expanded
bomb production, 304; urges atomic
league, 241; on Vandenberg, 356; on
"Z Committee," 314, 315, 320
Acheson-Lilienthal Report, 152,
158–61; Baruch's transformation of,
151, 161–5, 167, 367; leaking of, 159
Africa, 49–50, 56–7
African Metals Corporation (Afrimet),
102
Agreed Declaration, Anglo-American,
65, 66, 71–4, 81
"Agreement and Declaration of Trust,"
see Hyde Park aide-mémoire
air-atomic strategy, 6, 196, 224, 247; air
force proponents of, 195–6, 211–14,
271, 308–12; Bikini tests and, 225;
and Broiler, 227; Finletter Report
and, 244; navy opposition to, 249,
253, 308–12; "new navy" proponents
and, 203–4; offensive, *see* atomic
blitz; preemptive strike; in Pincher,
220–21; public knowledge of, 285–7;
see also specific war plans

air force, U.S.: and air-atomic strategy,
195–6, 211–14, 271, 286, 287, 291,
308–12, 324, *see also specific plans;*
authorship of NSC-30, 268;
Charioteer nuclear war plan, 284,
387; Eighth Air Force given nuclear
clearance, 226; Fleetwood war plan,
271–2; made independent of army
(1947), 236; navy opposition to
strategy of, 249, 253, 308–12; 1948
increase in atomic-capable bombers,
241; paper on "doctrine of atomic air
warfare," 270; and proposed use of
bomb in Korea, 332n.; Trojan plan,
286, 291–3; *see also* Army Air
Forces; Strategic Air Command
Air Staff, *see* Army Air Forces
Alamogordo test, 18, 44, 108, 114, 224
Allen, James S., 366
Alsop, Joseph, 318
Alsos, *see* Operation Alsos
American Newspaper Publishers
Association, 255
Anderson, Clinton, 29
Anderson, Sir John, 62–4
Anderson, Orville, 319
Armed Forces Special Weapons Project,
198, 242, 243, 263n., 391
Army, U.S.: General Staff strategic
study, 279, 280; and Louis Johnson,
308; and 1946 tests, 224; 1947 view
of Russian atomic prospects, 230,
233; postwar planners of, and atomic
bomb, 204–5
Army Air Forces (AAF), 208, 220; Air
Staff, 198–9, 200–202, 210; and
Bikini test, 224–5; emergence of new
strategic doctrine, 211–13; Harmon

VINTAGE HISTORY—WORLD

VINTAGE HISTORY—AMERICAN